Struggling Giants

GLOBALIZATION AND COMMUNITY

Susan E. Clarke, Series Editor
Dennis R. Judd, Founding Editor

(continued on page 335)

STRUGGLING GIANTS

CITY-REGION GOVERNANCE IN LONDON,
NEW YORK, PARIS, AND TOKYO

PAUL KANTOR, CHRISTIAN LEFÈVRE, ASATO SAITO,
H. V. SAVITCH, AND ANDY THORNLEY

Globalization and Community, Volume 20

University of Minnesota Press
Minneapolis
London

Published by the University of Minnesota Press
111 Third Avenue South, Suite 290
Minneapolis, MN 55401-2520
http://www.upress.umn.edu

Library of Congress Cataloging-in-Publication Data

Kantor, Paul.
  Struggling giants : city-region governance in London, New York, Paris, and Tokyo /
Paul Kantor, Christian Lefèvre, Asato Saito, H. V. Savitch, and Andy Thornley.
     (Globalization and community series ; v. 20)
  Includes bibliographical references and index.
  ISBN 978-0-8166-7742-9 (hc : alk. paper) — ISBN 978-0-8166-7743-6 (pb : alk. paper)
  1. Metropolitan government.   2. Globalization.   I. Lefèvre, Christian, author.
II. Saito, Asato, author.   III. Savitch, H. V., author.   IV. Thornley, Andy, author.
V. Title.   VI. Series: Globalization and community; v. 20.
  JS78.K36 2011
  320.8—dc23   2011040356

19   18   17   16   15   14   13   12   10   9   8   7   6   5   4   3   2   1

Contents

Part IV. The Tokyo City-Region

Part V. Pathways of Change

Abbreviations

CBD	central business district
CCIP	Chamber of Commerce of Paris
CGPME	Confédération Générale des Petites et Moyennes Entreprises
CNDP	Comprehensive National Development Plan (Japan)
CRIF	Conseil Régional d'Île de France
CRS	Capital Region Summit (Tokyo)
CSA	combined statistical area
DCA	Department of Cultural Affairs (New York)
DGE	Dotation Globale d'Équipement
DGF	Dotation Globale de Fonctionnement
DSUCS	Dotation de Solidarité Urbaine et de Cohésion Sociale
ECPI	Établissement Public de Coopération Intercommunale
EDF	Electricité de France
EEDA	East England Development Agency
EIP	environmental impact statement
EIU	Economist Intelligence Unit
EPA	Établissements Publics d'Aménagement
ESDC	Empire State Development Corporation (New York State)
FIRE	finance, insurance, and real estate
FSRIF	Fonds de Solidarité d'Île de France
FUR	functional urban region
GCR	global city-region
GDF	Gaz de France
GDP	gross domestic product
GLA	Greater London Authority
GLC	Greater London Council
GaWC	Globalization and World City Research Network
GFCI	Global Financial Centres Index
GMP	gross municipal product

IDF	Île de France
LDA	London Development Agency
LDP	Liberal Democratic Party (Tokyo)
LPAC	London Planning Advisory Committee
MLIT	Ministry of Land, Infrastructure, and Transport (Tokyo)
METI	Ministry of Economy, Trade, and Industry (Tokyo)
MoH	Ministry of Health (Tokyo)
MPO	metropolitan planning organization
MTA	Metropolitan Transportation Authority (New York)
NJT	New Jersey Transit
NYMTC	New York Metropolitan Transportation Council
NYCSA	New York consolidated statistical area
OIN	Opérations d'Intérêt National (Projects of National Interest)
PANYNJ	Port Authority of New York and New Jersey
PBC	public benefit corporation
PRWORA	Personal Responsibility and Work Opportunities Act
RATP	Régie Autonome des Transports Parisiens
RER	Réseau Express Régional
RPA	Regional Plan Association (New York)
SDRIF	Schéma Directeur de la Région Île de France
SDS	spatial development strategy
SEEDA	South East England Development Agency
SERPLAN	Standing Conference on South East Regional Planning
SME	small and medium-size enterprise
SNCF	Société Nationale des Chemins de Fer
SRDE	Schéma Régional de Développement Economique
STIF	Syndicat des Transports d'Île de France
TARP	Troubled Asset Relief Program
TCCI	Tokyo Chamber of Commerce and Industry
TMR	Tokyo Metropolitan Region
TMG	Tokyo Metropolitan Government
TNC	Trans National Corporation
UASI	Urban Areas Security Initiative

Preface

STRUGGLING GIANTS IS THE WORK of a multinational research team from Japan, France, the United Kingdom, and the United States. As such, it represents an effort to pool diverse expertise in order to answer fundamental questions about an urban phenomenon that is remaking the world—the global city-region.

In March 2007 the five authors met in Paris to exchange ideas about emerging social, economic, and governmental trends in the world's four great global financial centers. We had not collaborated with each other before. Our meeting was planned out of recognition that world cities and their regions are such big and decidedly complex objects of study that their thorough examination is out of individual reach. The initial encounter in Paris underscored this reality. Even though each participant brought invaluable expertise from previous research about world cities, the exchange in Paris provided compelling support for launching a team approach to investigating their changing governance. Our days of discussion also led to several other conclusions that were to guide our research during the nearly four subsequent years leading to the completion of this book.

For one, we all came to the realization that global cities were not urban enclaves that could be understood apart from their surrounding suburban and regional hinterlands. Although the media and even some serious academicians often referred to "global cities" as agglomerations anchored by central business districts, our discourse about social developments in London, New York, Paris, and Tokyo revealed less distinct boundaries. Regionalization of world cities had clearly taken place. This conclusion suggested a range of unanswered questions. In what specific ways were these city-regions changing? What consequences do these changes have for their governments and politics? These were intriguing questions that compelled further study.

For another, all of us acknowledged that most of our questions about political change in global city-regions would necessitate systematic comparative research. Our conversations and research reports highlighted many interesting common social and political trends in the four city-regions. Each of these seemingly global trends begged further study. Yet, as we examined such things as social polarization, emerging political agendas, social policy developments, changing business–government relations, and other shifting patterns of development, it also became clear that global city-regions (GCRs) were often following different political pathways. Although the London, New York, Paris, and Tokyo regions were grappling with many similar problems emerging from the globalization process, their responses to these common challenges were by no means always the same. We concluded that understanding where GCRs were heading in their governmental development would be impossible without intensive comparative analysis over an extensive period of time.

An important finding of the group was the way such research could best be conducted: We saw that deciphering the past, present, and future trajectories of GCRs required a sustained collaborative effort. Thus was born the research team that produced this book. We decided to dub ourselves the PATOLONY group (standing for Paris, Tokyo, London, and New York). The PATOLONY group met at least twice a year in most of our respective cities to bring together shared expertise. In between these meetings the authors continually exchanged papers, data, reports, and ideas in the course of preparing research reports, moving from subject to subject while developing an increasingly detailed profile of change in each case city-region. Each team member participated in all phases of preparing *Struggling Giants*. This included each of us taking a role in the actual writing and editing of every book chapter.

Our team approach probably had some disadvantages, such as extra time for coordinating work and fashioning compromises on how to conceptualize certain areas of inquiry or how to study particular issues. Yet we believe the benefits of our group approach far outweighed the disadvantages. Our extensive collaboration enabled us to reach far, investigate deeply, and otherwise apply multinational expertise to better describe urban governance and globalization. We were able to mount a broad-ranging inquiry touching on many dimensions of the struggle by local, regional, and national governments to respond to globalizing forces and render them manageable. In this way chapters on particular city-regions could be sensitive to each national context yet remain focused on the big questions facing all GCRs. Hopefully, this effort provides the reader with a valuable window on how world developments and the power of place simultaneously shape city-region governance.

April 2011

Acknowledgments

WE ARE DEEPLY INDEBTED to those who played special roles in supporting and assisting the research and preparation of *Struggling Giants.*

Paul Kantor is grateful to Fordham University for financial support and for travel assistance to PATOLONY meetings. Among many individuals providing research advice, special thanks go to Mr. Thomas J. Savage, former chief operating officer of the Metropolitan Transportation Authority, State of New York, and Professor Bruce Berg, Fordham University. Ms. Andria Battista and Mr. Jong Eun Lee furnished valuable manuscript assistance.

Christian Lefèvre would like to thank the Caisse des Dépôts (Institut CDC pour la Recherche) and the Institut d'Aménagement et d'Urbanisme de la Région Île de France (IAU-IDF) for funding works on the Paris region. He would also like to thank his colleagues at LATTS and at the French Institute of Urban Affairs (IFU) for their scientific and personal support.

Hank Savitch would like to express his gratitude to the colleagues and graduate students at the School of Urban and Public Affairs, University of Louisville. His special appreciation goes to the Brown and Williamson Fund for allowing him to travel to different research sites and the University of Louisville's office of the vice president for research for its internal research grants.

Asato Saito would like to express gratitude for the financial support given by the National University of Singapore (Academic Research Grant: R-1120–000–331–12), which enabled him to attend PATOLONY meetings. He also appreciates the administrative service by Ms. Lee Bee Ling in the Department of Japanese Studies, NUS.

Andy Thornley wishes to thank the London School of Economics for their financial assistance to attend and to host some of our PATOLONY meetings.

All of the authors are grateful to Pieter Martin, Kristian Tvedten, and Susan Clarke, Series Editor, the Globalization and Community series for the University of Minnesota Press, for their interest and support in making *Struggling Giants* a reality. Of course, only the authors assume responsibility for what is said in this volume.

Introduction: Governable Giants?

SOME 30 YEARS AGO, AT THE dawn of the global era, many people assumed free markets and advanced technology would render geographic boundaries obsolete. Some saw little future need for traditional densely packed cities (Webber 1967). Globalization, propelled by decentralization of industry, growing suburbanization, new towns, and edge cities, seemed to be displacing center cities and/or severely diminishing their political importance (Garreau 1988; Gordon and Richardson 1997; Kotkin 2000, 2002).

History has a way of challenging grand expectations. Instead of reducing the appeal of cities, globalization and freer markets have enhanced many of them. During the last 30 years, advances in technology have produced contradictory tendencies—the spread of activities out of cities into their surrounding regions while also making the core of world cities more important. Rather than the predicted death of big cities and metropolitan areas, a new urban hierarchy has emerged. A select number of metropolitan areas, or as we call them global city-regions (GCRs), have achieved such world-class status. GCRs have become virtual command posts in the networks of twenty-first-century capitalism (Sassen 1991). London, New York, Paris, and Tokyo head this network. They are the subject of this book. Their governability is our focus.

The View from the Top: The Biggest and Best

When these city-regions[1] are viewed from the top, all four appear as masters of the urban universe. They survive and thrive in similar ways: mainly by virtuosity in performing roles as centers of international finance, producer services, corporate planning, and related high-value activities necessary for a vast, worldwide, and otherwise highly decentralized economy to function. Cultural and political prominence of international proportion accompanies economic power. While many other urban centers have shrunk in size, economic importance, or power, London, New York, Paris, and Tokyo remain giants of the world metropolis. Capitals of capitalism, their global reach ensures what happens in them will have repercussions for business, governments, and people everywhere else in the world.[2] Even in the more recent uncertain world economy, these four metropolises continue to lead the pack not only in business but in respect to many other things. In October 2008 the American journal *Foreign Policy*, in collaboration with a host of experts, published a ranking of global cities based on a long list of social, political, and economic criteria. These criteria included their volume of business activities, human capital resources, cultural assets, political status, and other achievements. Finding New York, London, Tokyo, and Paris ranked at the very top, the editors noted, "The world's biggest, most interconnected cities help set global agendas, weather transnational dangers, and serve as the hubs of global integration. They are the engines of growth for their countries and the gateways to the resources of their regions" (2008, 1).

The View from the Bottom: Governable Giants?

Views from the top tell us about the importance of global cities in the world order. Power, rank, and global reach seem to go hand in hand. Yet when these giants are viewed from the bottom, a rather different picture emerges. They are colossal metropolitan areas with citizens, businesses, and governments contending with the daily realities of life and struggling to use governmental power to deal with wrenching social and economic changes. From this perspective, living at the top is not just a matter of being biggest and best in the race for global importance. GCRs face constant challenges. They must continually change in order to grow, prosper, or even to stay in place. London, New York, Tokyo, and Paris are leading world city-regions because they have successfully undergone massive economic, social, and political changes over the course of many years.

This bottom-up view also suggests why even these top-rank global cities are never really masters in the world economy. They compete intensely with each other as well as with more junior players in the world marketplace. As a result, they are in a constant struggle to maintain their economic position. For instance, during the early 1990s, New York was at the center of a financial boom. A surge in stock markets, waves of corporate mergers, budding new digital technology, and a strong dollar enhanced New York's attraction as a center of international business at a time when a financial crisis hit East Asia and emerging markets in Russia and Latin America collapsed. Only a few years earlier, Tokyo had appeared to be supplanting New York by attracting greater numbers of international banks, headquarters of transnational firms, and the largest population of any city in the world (Slater 2004). In the nearly two decades since then, Tokyo has become mired in a slow economic recovery from years of deflationary trends and experiencing increasing competition from Hong Kong and Singapore. In the 1990s London became absorbed with competition from Paris and Frankfurt. A financial meltdown arising from finance, housing, and real estate bubbles started in 2008, severely testing prosperity in London and New York. At the same time, economic centers in China and Southeast Asia assumed new status and perhaps rivalry for top positions in world financial flows. Time will tell if the top four world cities remain in place in ten or twenty years hence.

The Question of Governability

Looking from the bottom-up highlights why the governability of our city-regions is an important question. Although economists sometimes treat cities as simple and undifferentiated competitive territorial units, this is pure fiction undertaken to facilitate their economic analysis. The reality is quite different on the ground. As entire industries are replaced in these surging urban centers, the job mix is altered for generations ahead. Some businesses sprout while others fade, and the incomes of vast numbers of people change. Growing populations must somehow be accommodated with jobs, affordable housing, and a decent living environment. Changing property values, together with new commercial and residential development, impose new environmental stresses and cause some people to relocate to different neighborhoods or even different cities or suburbs. Achieving global city status calls for continuous public reinvestment in transportation, education, and environmental regulation. So much is changing so fast and is in need of policy remedies. Commuters want better train service, business seeks people with new skills, and quality-of-life concerns grow when more people share crowded common spaces. Concerns about the environment loom everywhere. Moreover, immigration to world-class cities is giving them a new face. Yet these new populations often join or compete with older groups, some seeking help to compete for a piece of the wealth and status they hope to find. The social challenges faced by those who live or work in GCRs are vast, varied, and constantly changing.

These matters almost invariably become political issues for GCR governance. Can they really manage these issues? To do so, they must remain governable in the face of powerful new forces of change that they cannot stop but may try to control. How governable they are in practice is far from obvious.

The question of governability arises directly from uncertainty about the relative influence of global and localized (including national) forces in GCR development. By governability, we are referring to a capacity to undertake collective action in order to address common problems.[3] Exactly how much local government matters in managing stresses caused by international changes is not easy to discern. It may be that GCRs are mostly pushed along in similar ways by forces of the international marketplace, in effect, marginalizing whatever local governments try to do. If the role of governmental intervention is marginal or is receding, then it is difficult to escape the conclusion that their governability is becoming doubtful. They may change, but the changes are driven by winds that public sector decision makers cannot hope to influence. Whether governmental activity in GCRs actually shapes much of what happens is crucial to the ability of citizens in city-regions to choose their own destiny.

Urban Theory and GCRs

Theoretical debate over globalization and urban politics centers very much on the question of governability. This is because there is not much agreement about how economic and political cross-pressures get played out in GCRs. To understand why, we begin by considering the phenomenon of the GCR and how it has generated new issues about urban governance. For decades, many social scientists recognized that a vast postwar restructuring of the entire urban system was under way throughout the industrial West (Bell 1973; Chase-Dunn 1989; Kantor 1995; Reich 1992; Sassen 2006). Studies charted the decline of the older industrial system formed during the 19th century. This system was based heavily on manufacturing through mass-production techniques done in large factories; corporations and their factories were usually organized hierarchically and located in major central cities (Chandler 1977; Pred 1977). During this era, large metropolitan areas possessed compelling advantages of agglomeration, making them highly efficient for many businesses seeking to concentrate production in giant factories and then ship goods to far-flung consumer markets at home and abroad.

This system crumbled considerably during the decades following World War II as business in Europe, North America, and some parts of Asia turned increasingly to services during a process of deindustrialization. In this process, much traditional manufacturing relocated to lower-cost areas in the Asian rim and many parts of the developing world. At the same time, technological breakthroughs in communication, transportation, corporate management, the development of lightweight materials, and other innovations enabled corporate business to decentralize and relocate production activities to multiple locations in order to reap cost advantages. These and other changes in the character of capitalist production spurred a vast reorganization of the entire economy, giving rise to transnational corporations and increasing globalization of economic relationships. Suburban development boomed as people and jobs dispersed. Cities, suburbs, and rural areas everywhere were affected by this.

As suggested earlier, this great transformation by no means made big cities and other urban agglomerations obsolete. This process of change has given rise to a need for strategic command centers—that is, global cities—that play a powerful role in managing, financing, and planning far-flung corporate activities that are becoming highly internationalized. In effect, as increasing business mobility has triggered the economic dispersal of economic activities, this process of economic decentralization actually unleashed an ongoing tendency for centralization of certain strategic activities associated with corporate headquarters and finance in global city centers. These centers are "strategic sites for the global economy," according to Sassen (1998, xxvi). They consolidate advanced producer and financial services in dense urban complexes highly interconnected with each other around the world (Friedmann 1995). As such, they constitute a major restratification of the urban economic system, forming an important core surrounded by a much larger periphery. Most other urban places in the periphery exist in subordination to them in the sense that they are highly dependent on decisions made in these strategic central locations. In recent decades, abundant evidence suggests these central locations are no longer confined to traditional downtowns and historic business districts. As we will explain in more detail, many world city functions have spun outward around the older central cores, creating complex networks of interdependence between city, suburb, and region. As the world city becomes more of a world city-region, this development also becomes more politically complex.

Although globalization may favor GCRs as powerful economic centers, this form of urbanization has precipitated new threats to their governability. Three consequences of economic globalization are particularly important because they may outstrip the capabilities of the fragmented governmental systems found in GCRs: (1) new stresses arising from social polarization; (2) growing competition for investment and trade, which favor growth over equity considerations; and (3) new intergovernmental conflicts and burdens. Global and local influences both need to be considered in determining how these emerging stresses affect governability.

SOCIAL POLARIZATION AND GOVERNABILITY

First, global city development unleashes new forms of sociospatial polarization (Abu-Lughod 1999; Fainstein 2001; Soja 1989, 1991). These include increasing social polarization by income, competition for space, and labor market dislocations. One reason for this is that GCR labor markets tend to be highly bifurcated between high-wage corporate jobs and more mundane and routinized low-wage jobs in the formal and informal economies of GCRs. There is fear that this is precipitating a shrinking middle class, expansion of poorer population groups, and increased efforts by well-off residents to insulate themselves socially and even physically from the rest. It is possible that a "dual city" is developing (Mollenkopf and Castells 1992; Davis 1994). As the economies of global cities thrive and grow, many of the people who live there become impoverished while others are enriched as job, income, and housing opportunities change. Some critics warn that global city development breeds new forms of spatial and social segregation. Better-off residents and workers seek ways of avoiding contact with the poor, who are excluded from the fruits of the city. This is provided by enclosed downtown malls, skywalks connecting buildings, privatized office atriums, as well as class-segregated leisure centers (such as private sports clubs) and exclusive entertainment enclaves. Segregation may be further enforced by discriminatory police practices to keep the poor from invading these premises (Davis 1998; Judd and Fainstein 1999; Zukin 1995).

Actual realization of these polarizing threats is complex and uncertain, however. Those who have studied the supposed emergence of a dual city are often equivocal about this characterization of global city social development. Cities vary in the ways they adapt to globalizing pressures, and some of the deep social and spatial divisions have not always materialized as critics have predicted (Swanstrom et al. 2006; Mollenkopf and Castells 1992; White 1998).

Most importantly, social polarization has political causes, not just economic ones. For one, social stresses caused by the impact of economic globalization may not be uniform across various GCRs and nations due to political intervention. Differences in the public regulation of immigration, the promotion of job mixes, housing opportunities, and the provision of social safety nets can limit social polarization. Land use and housing policies may inhibit the social isolation of the poor. Indeed, in the literature on globalization and city-region development, there has been increasing recognition of the significance of state power and authority in mediating the course of international modern capitalism. While early theories of globalization focused on the impact and dynamics of new forms of international economic restructuring in urban development, today few students of globalization discount the importance of nation-state political influences in shaping outcomes in trade, finance, social development, labor markets, and urbanization, to name just a few (Abu-Lughod 1999, 400–417; N. Brenner 2001, 2004; Fujita 2003; Hill and Kim 2000a, 200; Sassen 2001, 351; Sassen 2006).

How much local or regional governmental influences matter for social polarization is difficult to say, however. But it will surely depend on particular political contexts. For example, the willingness of citizens to support public social safety nets, and particular systems of intergovernmental financing for them, vary from nation to nation. The distribution of fiscal and governmental responsibilities within nation-states for implementing programs of social regulation often differs from country to country and sometimes even among states and provinces. Consequently, the ability of GCR governments to manage such stresses by charting their own policy directions is likely to be easier in some places than in others. If this is so, then increasing social polarization need not invariably undermine GCR governability. But where government can make a difference in managing social polarization is difficult to say.

PUBLIC POLICY AND GOVERNABILITY

Second, global economic pressures may strongly influence governmental policy activities in guiding GCR development. This issue has long been at the center of debate about the nature of globalization. Many fear that the race for global competitiveness encourages—perhaps even forces—government to emphasize progrowth programs of public policy to the neglect of considerations of social equity or environmental health. To the extent that this is true, it surely is a major obstacle to governability. If distant economic forces are driving what local governments are doing, public officials are unable to respond to what their citizens wish in shaping community building in GCRs.

This tendency is thought to derive from the different ways global economic pressures may affect public decision making. Some theorists argue that government tends to displace many public sector activities as cities fall under the sway of the global marketplace. In this context, it is said that business claims for a larger role in public activities of interest to them grow more easily. For example, programs of deregulation and privatization may replace direct governmental control over things like land use planning, transportation, finance, and other areas of public policy. Even parks and other public spaces have fallen under the management of private sector organizations in many cities as their governments have encountered fiscal stress. Progrowth policies also occur through enlarging private sector responsibilities for social action (in effect, leaving social welfare more to charity), particularly as governments seek to shed burdens in response to business demands for lower taxes.

Others suggest that global competition shapes development policies. In this view, the formal distribution of decisional authority between private and public sectors matters less than the pressures on public officials to promote economic competitiveness. As global cities are forced to compete against each other in intensive races to stay in the game, their governments may have little choice but to use public power and resources to attract new investment and highly skilled workers and to ensure a state-of-the-art infrastructure that supports key global city economic activities. It can include massive expansion of advanced infrastructure for communications and transport, as well as programs to boost tourism, downtown real estate development, and other activities. This may often result in programs whose benefits bypass many residents and workers (Abu-Lughod 1999; Dear 2000; Graham and Marvin 2001; Sites 2003).

For example, the economic intensification of specialized city functions in producer services and international finance often tilts public spending toward the support of these industries rather than other job sectors, especially small business and labor. National governments are prone to use GCRs both symbolically to enhance their image as a great power and tangibly to advance their political interests. By the same token, if global city development tends to encourage focus on short-term economic growth, longer-term considerations about environmental justice or social equity may be neglected by public officials and citizens who struggle to just keep up with what the competition is doing.

Nevertheless, there are political forces to consider that can diminish the impact of global economic pressures shaping local policy making.[4] Global economic pressures are unlikely to dictate governmental policy if only because there are different ways of promoting economic competitiveness and managing economic change. Although GCRs compete in similar global markets, there is little reason to assume they must all compete by offering similar advantages of economy, lifestyle, housing, and environment. In particular, the notion that the race for global competitiveness fosters only one model for GCR development and that it invariably discourages state intervention seems problematic.

To date, it is unclear that governments in advanced economies are actually settling on a single set of strategies that emphasize regional competitiveness. Although there has been growing interest in some countries in favor of neoliberal strategies to encourage regional economic development, other studies suggest this is not the case everywhere (Harding 2007; Hill, Park, and Saito 2011; Jouve and Lefèvre 2002; Salet, Thornley, and Kruekels 2003; Savitch and Kantor 2002; Savitch and Vogel 1996; Sellers 2002). For example, Peter Newman and Andy Thornley (2005) explored the balance between the pressures of economic globalization and local politics in the strategic planning of world cities to find mixed results. H. V. Savitch and Paul Kantor's (2002) study of North American and Western European cities found that some of them have greater political discretion and policy choices than others. They argue this is because cities vary in their bargaining power in the international marketplace.

How much politics matters in containing progrowth policy bias in GCRs remains a question, however. Critics of economic globalization theories have yet to be very precise about the actual reach of state authorities for asserting public power in shaping the urban development of these strategic regions. In particular, why certain kinds of state intervention matter more in some places than in others remains unclear. For example, differences in urban economic development have sometimes been attributed to the variable cultural, social, and governmental traditions between the East and the West (Fujita 2000; Hill and Kim 2000a, 2000b). Others have emphasized how history and path dependency in national economic development appear to be important in encouraging divergence in governmental regulatory activities (Abu-Lughod 1999; Crouch et al. 2001; Pierson 2000; Sassen 2001b). Still others see emerging economic interests at work in changing the political regulation of urban change in order to cope with new global economic developments (N. Brenner 2001; Smith 2000). These are sweeping interpretations. They provide broad theories of culture, historical path dependency, and political adaptation to afford interesting big-picture interpretations of global and local changes. Yet they leave much to explore. Lack of many detailed comparative case studies of GCR politics makes it particularly difficult to understand how and when governmental forces may favor particular strategies for public action. What we know is that they are invariably cross-pressured to take into account global as well as local influences. But does this end up producing enough policy bias to compromise their governability? In what specific areas of policy or governance?

INTERGOVERNMENTAL STRESSES AND GOVERNABILITY

Finally, global influences can challenge governability by precipitating a need for intergovernmental changes that are beyond the capacity of politically fragmented GCR political systems. Like virtually all GCRs, the London, New York, Paris, and Tokyo metropolitan areas have complex governmental systems in which political authority is quite dispersed or poorly organized. For the most part, they are creatures of another age. They were surely never designed to grapple with the transition into the global metropolises they are today. Yet global economic changes are now generating two kinds of intergovernmental conflicts that challenge the capacity of these divided and multitiered systems to pull together in order to solve public problems. One is intergovernmental conflict over delinking of GCRs from national economies. The other is conflict over the regionalization of GCR systems.

Delinking and Intergovernmental Rivalry

Economic delinking occurs when the power of GCRs assumes such large proportions that they become more independent from national economic and political influences.[5] Some theorists believe world city-regions are becoming so immensely important in national economies that they are redefining the meaning of a national economic order (Barnes and Ledebur 1998; Scott 2001; Scott and Storper 1998; Storper 1997; Veltz 1996). Sassen (1998, 195–218) contends that leading global centers are already relatively independent from the fortunes of the particular national economies within which they are otherwise embedded. Spotty evidence of delinking of the economic fortunes of some global city economies from national economies exists, although there is little agreement on the meaning of the term (Lever 1997; Fainstein 2001; Hill and Kim 2000a; Sassen 2006; Savitch and Kantor 2002, 2003). For example, movements of global capital and labor, as well as changes in real estate values, often follow patterns in command-post economies that differ from what is happening elsewhere in other city-regions.

To the extent that delinking is happening, however, it is likely to precipitate new conflicts and rivalry in the power relations of GCRs with respect to higher-level governments. Governments at local, regional, and national levels clearly have a stake in taking advantage of such global trends for their own purposes. Growing concentration of economic power may enable some GCRs to more easily assert claims on higher-level governments. This can lead to "autonomization," a form of delinking that weakens national authority by increasing the independence with which GCR governments decide major issues. If this happens, nation-states may well resist the political implications of concentrating greater economic power in one or a few urban regions. National governments are unlikely to tolerate excessive political delinking or autonomization of particular growth centers having national importance for the functioning of nation-state economic systems. In order to preserve their own self-governance, cities and suburbs may start to pull together politically in order to defend their region's autonomy in the face of expanding national oversight and intrusion. But this task is itself likely to occasion political conflicts within regions as different local governments compete to promote their regions' growing economic power for their own purposes.

Theoretical ideas about political GCR delinking or autonomization must remain highly speculative. Exactly how such economic and political cross-pressures get played out in particular circumstances can enhance or diminish governability. Growing concentration of economic power on this scale may encourage GCR governments to pull together in order to defend their new autonomy. But it could also lead to new political divisions in a fragmented governmental context lacking either consensus or organization about promoting joint regional interests. This intriguing matter has rarely been studied, in large part because there is so little modern-day precedent for such a shift of economic power. Nevertheless, delinking has occurred in some historical politico-economic systems (Sassen 2006, 1–140).

Regionalization and Rivalry

GCR governability also is threatened by the regionalization of global city functions. Although some strategically placed cities like Los Angeles have become more densely populated, most world cities have spread beyond their original cores, as suggested earlier. These cities can now be said to function within a larger territorial scale (Savitch and Vogel 1996). This makes the regional territorial governance more important. But is political regionalization possible?

Closer examination of the economic and political dimensions of this question suggests why it remains difficult to answer. Pressures of regional economic development are indeed powerful in GCRs. This is because regional networks and local territorial assets are increasingly crucial for their businesses' economic competitiveness (Saxenian 1994) throughout the industrial world. As Scott (1996) put it, the global economy is being driven by "regional motors." Regional economic linkages and "untraded interdependencies" play a huge role in sustaining business innovation, competitiveness, and economic growth (Scott and Storper 1992, 1998, 2003).[6] Michael Storper speaks of "a new borderland where specificities and flows are both operating in varying measure" (1997, 300), highlighting the fact that it is often unclear where the regionalization begins and ends. Indeed, regional production networks (Amin and Thrift 1992; Hirst and Thompson 1996) can take many forms. They include tightly and informally organized industrial districts of small and medium manufacturing enterprises in north central Italy and networks of engineers, scientists, and universities in Silicon Valley in California and at Cambridge in the United Kingdom (Kantor 2008).

While we are still unsure about the extent to which global "cities" have effectively become city-regions, their regional interdependencies are nonetheless present and widely recognized (Sassen 1991, 2006). N. Brenner (2004a and b) asserts that growing global pressures toward regionalization are moving governments in Western Europe and elsewhere to change the distribution of governmental authority and responsibilities. He argues that nations are in the process of creating "new state spaces," reorganizing and reconstituting themselves in order to help stimulate greater national and regional economic competitiveness.

How governments actually respond to the challenge of regional economic development is ambiguous because of political considerations. Regional theorists acknowledge the role of government in enabling economic regionalization to work well (for instance, Jonas and Ward 2007; Newman and Hull 2009). In fact, there has been increasing recognition of the importance of their active management.[7] But this kind of governance is not easily done in GCR political systems. GCRs are located within governmental networks that were never intended to manage the regional problems associated with strategic centers of international capitalism. Their fragmented local governmental systems are widely believed to lack much capacity to pull together for many joint purposes (Benjamin and Nathan 2001; Jouve and Lefèvre 2002; Newman 2000; Salet, Thornley, and Kreukels 2003). Scott sees "growing realization that some sort of administrative and institutional coordination across the spatial organization of the city as a whole is a necessary condition for achieving efficiency, workability and local competitive advantage" (Scott 2008, 557). However, he also notes that there is often a "deep resistance to wider metropolitan political integration" (560).

Political response to growing regional economic integration is unlikely to be driven only by economic "imperatives" for several reasons. Regions do not govern themselves, and it is rare for GCRs to have a single unified government to manage and promote them. Indeed, the leading global cities in this study are situated in politically fragmented governmental systems where unified planning and implementation are very difficult to achieve. There is scant evidence of how much governance actually matters for regional economies to perform effectively (Macleod 2001; Savitch and Vogel 2009). Many public functions may be provided by private sector businesses and organizations, perhaps even on an informal basis. Most importantly, there are huge political stakes in governmental regionalization. It may be opposed and defeated by purely local interests seeking to preserve their political independence. GCRs may need to compete as regional economies, but their local governments may not make this a priority. Do local public officials perceive an important role in managing economic relationships beyond their own borders? Will this interest outweigh other more parochial concerns about defending local political autonomy? If regional political cooperation is becoming more important, it is necessary to see how this is being accomplished and over what issues.[8]

All of this suggests political regionalization is likely to be quite variable. Increasing need to attend to global city issues on a regional scale creates an incentive for fragmented political systems to find ways of pulling together, but public officials and citizens must play a sustained mediating role in bringing this about. It makes multilevel governance more important. Leaders, whether private or public, must be mobilized and coalitions need to be built to support big governmental changes. This may be easier to do in some political systems than in others. For instance, GCRs with large numbers of governments and decision makers may find it more difficult to forge programs of change in more centralized political orders. Systems where business leaders play a prominent role may discover it is easier to get around public officials seeking to block these kinds of proposals.

Further, political regionalization is likely to be variable because it can happen without relying only on lateral intergovernmental cooperation. For example, higher-level governments can intervene in local problem solving to influence or even dominate critical regional decisions. There are many governmental alternatives for addressing growing regional economic interdependence. As a result, the governability of GCRs does not have to weaken or converge along a single path. Rather, it is likely to be strongly influenced by local, regional, and national preferences. GCR governments can seek different intergovernmental solutions.

In essence, big changes in international capitalism are under way that impact on GCR governability. How this engages political forces that also count is not obvious. On the one hand, global economic developments are clearly transforming urban regions everywhere and unleashing new stresses in GCRs. The emergence of common social polarizing issues, pressures to favor progrowth policy agendas, and economic delinkage and regionalization all present local governments with new problems to manage. On the other hand, these changes are unlikely to be in one direction. How these new issues are addressed is also a matter of politics in particular places, not only about global economic influences. How much and when politics matters remains uncertain and ambiguous because local governance is invariably a cross-pressured phenomenon.

GCRs and State Mediation: A Contextual Approach

Our view is that the question of governability is best examined from a perspective that focuses on the mediating role governments play in coping with urban change. Although this approach may not allow us to definitively resolve all the uncertainty about GCR governability, it works in that direction. This is achieved by considering policy responses and intergovernmental changes within particular political contexts, rather than assuming city-regions must conform to one or another model of policy change due to compelling global influences. In addition, by comparing the mediating activities of government in a comparable group of city-regions over a period of decades, it is possible to describe the sustained interplay of global and local forces in a systematic way.

Focusing on several similar leading world city-regions makes it possible to track and compare the urban impact of many common economic forces in each of these city-regions. This bottom-up perspective brings into view the big picture arising from global developments as they engage local governmental organization and interests. The approach avoids falling into the methodological trap of assuming that globalizing and localizing influences are mutually exclusive. Globalization and localization do not represent win–lose alternatives from the perspective of local governance; sometimes political choices can favor policy and governmental directions encouraged by international economic developments and pressures. Viewing the political dynamics within particular city-regions provides a window on why particular forms of governmental intervention are taken, however.

In addition, by comparing GCRs in detail over time it is possible to identify precise areas of governmental activities where state mediation matters more or less. That is, we are able to follow Sassen's (2006) own call to identify and evaluate particular areas in which "thick environments of the national" engage "standardizing global systems" to influence particular policies at particular times and in specific places (Sassen 2006, 227). Therefore, we explore the production of public policies not by looking only for general trends but also by identifying specific areas of convergence and divergence between them and intergovernmental relations.

This enables us to undertake a more nuanced assessment of governability than broad theories about GCRs allow. With respect to public policy, our focus is on examining whether GCR policy agendas and governmental responses are in fact leaning in any one direction. Are progrowth and neoliberal public policies prevailing in the capitals of capitalism? If not, what policy variation is evident? In regard to intergovernmental relations, the focus is on probing whether common forms of governance are emerging in GCRs. To what extent are delinking tendencies evident as the economic power of GCRs grows? Are there signs of regionalization of GCR governance? If not, what competing changes in intergovernmental politics are happening and why? By answering these questions, it is possible to better understand how and when governance matters in the development of these strategic urban enclaves.

One of our main conclusions is that the governmental systems of London, New York, Paris, and Tokyo are indeed constrained by globalizing economic influences, but it is not as some anticipate. The following chapters explain that powerful globalizing tendencies mark the trajectory of city-region governance, but that convergence in policy and intergovernmental politics is hardly the whole story. Big differences in policy pathways and in intergovernmental change also prevail. In fact, political divergence among our four case city-regions is not exceptional, but common.

Although we cannot explain all of these variations, we find that important differences in city-region governance do matter. In large part, this is because multilevel governance often can be sustained even in the face of powerful internationalization pressures, making possible different directions in GCR policy agendas and politics. Variations in the ways political systems are organized, mobilize power, and manage different forms of governmental fragmentation are big factors in governability. Overall, however, London, New York, Paris, and Tokyo all show considerable political capability for mediating urban change for public purposes, albeit in different ways and to different degrees in particular areas of activity.

This finding about the importance of the local helps explain why progrowth, antiegalitarian, or weak environmental agendas are not inevitable in GCRs. Some of these policy responses win support more easily in some political contexts than in others, but the particular context matters a great deal. The variable role of national governments, regional bodies, local bureaucracies and agencies, political parties, and other institutions that compose GCR government profoundly affect sustained support for particular policy agendas. It makes it all the more important to identify how the dynamics of particular GCR political systems make them liable to serve some interests more or less than others, a task we undertake throughout this book.

Further, the dynamics of particular regional political systems ensure that no single model of intergovernmental change pervades GCRs. In particular, economic pressures that may favor delinking and regionalization are virtually always strongly mediated by governmental and political actors seeking their own objectives. Thus, changing patterns of policy and governance are quite dependent on particular local–national circumstances.

Our findings have implications for understanding how multilevel governance can add up to regional governability. If local governance matters, how do such fragmented political orders manage to achieve this? All four GCR political systems suffer serious flaws and biases as agents of mediation in a globalizing world. Yet they also can pull together in many ways to assert public direction. How is this possible?

Reformers differ over how multiple governments ought to function in order to achieve effective city-region governability. Some believe that greater centralization of governmental power and authority is crucial for this (Caro 1974; Orfield 1997; Rusk 1999), while others advocate more decentralized possibilities (Bruegmann 2005; Ostrum, Bish, and Ostrum 1988; Schneider 1989; Tiebout 1962). Our study concludes that there are different pathways to governability; neither centralization nor decentralized politics is always necessary for this. Fragmented government is not invariably a virtue or a vice. In virtually all local political contexts, considerable governability also can arise by means of incremental adjustments among multiple governments, as well as by creating governmental reforms. Political modernization need not always be deliberate and well-planned to achieve governability. In fact, incremental adjustment among multitier and fragmented governments tends to prevail in all the city-regions in this study.

To highlight our central argument, we recapitulate in Figure I.1 the essential variables explained earlier to show how change works in GCRs. The figure displays the causal and systematic pattern of relationships among the major independent, mediating, and dependent variables.

Basically, we explain that the independent variables of globalization, economic competition, and suburbanization strongly influence the political actions of GCRs. However, these independent variables are modified by mediating variables consisting of the nation-state, thick environments, and historic path dependencies. The results can be seen in independent variables whose primary effects touch governability of city-regions—its institutions and processes of cooperation—as well as secondary effects on public policies related to economic development, environment, social welfare, and quality of life.

As we will show, the making of GCRs is a complex affair involving numerous structural factors, but it is also very much made by human beings who engage in elaborate politics at multiple levels. The governability of GCRs is neither foreordained by global flows nor left entirely in local, regional, or even national hands in the London, New York, Paris, and Tokyo regions.

UNDERSTANDING CHANGE IN GLOBAL CITY REGIONS (GCRs)

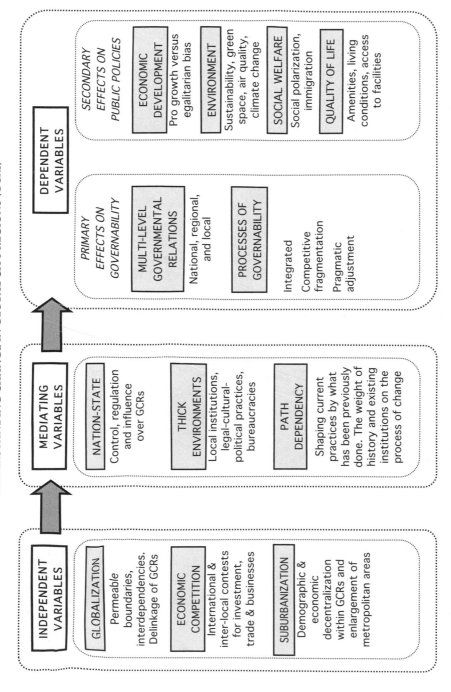

Figure I.1. Understanding Change in Global City Regions (GCRs).

Applying Territorial Scales to New York, London, Paris, and Tokyo

The city-region is the major unit for this analysis. For our purposes, the latter means the central city and the peripheral area surrounding it whose key economic, social, and political relationships are reasonably integrated and interdependent. It comprises three segments or areas. Within this region, the municipal area is distinguished as a legal/political jurisdiction incorporating the central city. Where a formal metropolitan government has been formed, the central city will encompass the entire territory under its umbrella. In effect, a legally formed metropolitan government is considered here as the municipal area. This is the case with New York, London, and Tokyo, each of which either has been consolidated into a single municipality (New York City) or has adopted an additional metropolitan tier with lower-tier municipal authorities conducting different functions (London and Tokyo). Where no formal metropolitan government is in place, the municipal area encompasses the smaller incorporated city. This is the case with Paris.

The following maps display each of our four city-regions in terms of the larger regions around them and their municipal areas. Note that the five boroughs of New York City are designated as the municipal area and can be seen within the region or combined statistical area (CSA). New York's CSA contains thirty whole counties. Greater London can be seen within its larger South East region. The city of Paris can also be viewed with its region of the Île de France (IDF). Paris's IDF holds eight departments. Last, Tokyo is presented along with its surrounding region, which is formed as prefectures.

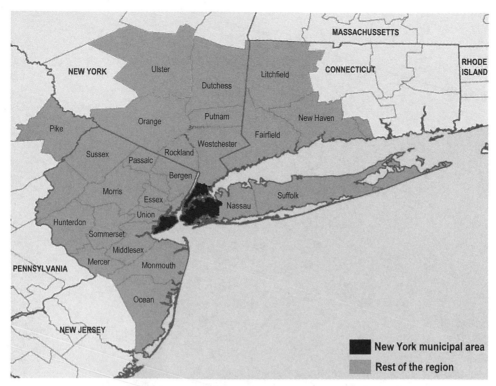

Map I.1. New York Municipal Area within the Region (Partial Views of the Combined Statistical Area)

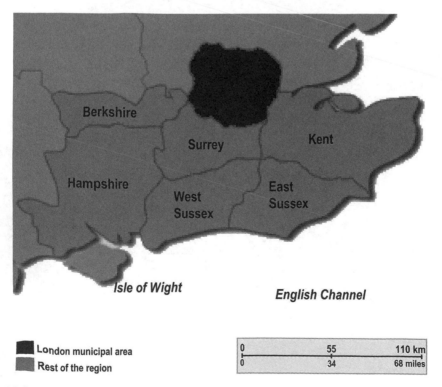

Map I.2. London Municipal Area within the Region (South East Region)

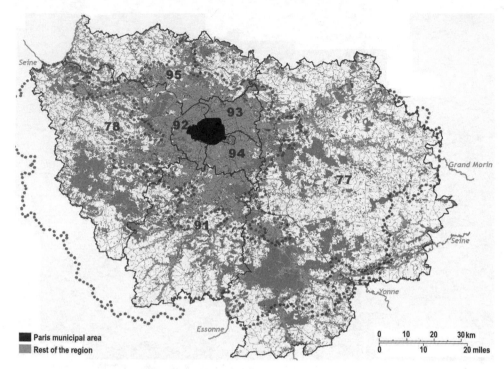

Map I.3. Paris Municipal Area within the Region (Île de France)

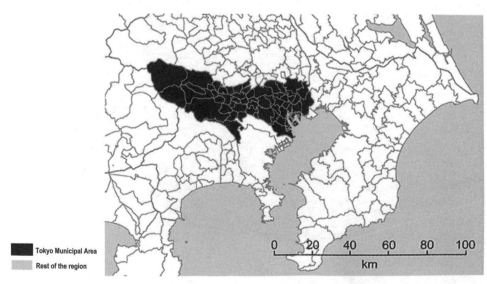

Map I.4. Tokyo Municipal Area within the Region (Prefectures)

1. *Four Global City-Regions*
A Profile

THIS CHAPTER PROVIDES a profile of the four world city-regions, examining what they have in common as places for people and business, as well as how they are changing. Paris, Tokyo, London, and New York are hardly ordinary urban places.[1] They are city-suburban agglomerations that happen to be command posts in a worldwide capitalist system. But what is distinctive about these places beyond the fact that they are at the top of the world urban hierarchy? Do they share common trajectories of social and economic change? Or are these city-regions really undergoing very different pathways of development despite their shared global status? The answers to these questions will place the analysis of their politics in context, telling us how much or how little we are comparing similar urban phenomena in later chapters.

Accordingly, the following sections examine (1) basic demographic patterns, (2) the economic profile of our city-regions, (3) patterns of social stress, and (4) quality-of-life assessments. Although the comparisons are as accurate as possible, we are limited by the availability of comparable data. Nevertheless, it is possible to produce a broad statistical picture of New York, London, Paris, and Tokyo as cities and as regions. The evidence suggests there is much that they have in common—enough to be able to speak of them as a single kind of urban place, a global city-region (GCR). Moreover, we find they are experiencing many similar problems as they grapple with urban change, specifically:

- All are wealthy growth centers attracting population and becoming increasingly socially diverse.
- All are global economic command centers that increasingly rely on advanced tertiary production sectors and are becoming regionally integrated in economic terms.
- All are experiencing many similar forms of social stress, from income disparities to sociospatial segregation.
- All share many similar quality-of-life problems and struggle to overcome quite common kinds of disadvantages as places to live.

At the same time, however, these patterns of socioeconomic convergence are limited. Each of the four city-regions is developing in different ways, displaying important variations in population, in economic change, in social stress, and in quality of life, in particular:

- They vary in their scale, pace, and form of population growth.
- They compete in the international marketplace with different economic assets and liabilities, even though they have relatively similar economies.
- They manage forms of social stress that differ in scale and severity due to particular historical, social, and governmental influences.
- They constitute fairly different places to live and work because each possesses many different lifestyle advantages and disadvantages.

Demographic Patterns: Growth and Change

Let us first turn to basic demographic characteristics. Are the four city-regions growing as major population centers? Are the city and regional patterns of population change similar? The level of population change will impinge on many policy issues, such as the need for house building, provision of local services, educational facilities, transport congestion, and the like. Tables 1.1 and 1.2 show population and rates of change for each of our city-regions over the last quarter century.

TABLE 1.1. POPULATION IN NEW YORK, TOKYO, LONDON, AND PARIS

City-region	Population	Year
New York	21,918,000	2006
Tokyo	33,472,000	2005
London	21,357,000	2006
Paris	11,532,000	2006

Sources: London: NOMIS; Paris: CRCI 2009; Tokyo: 2005 Population Census of Japan conducted by Ministry of Internal Affairs and Communication (MIAC).

TABLE 1.2. PERCENTAGE CHANGE IN POPULATION

City-region	25 years	Average annual increase	Recent period
New York	14.9% (1980–2006)	0.57%	0.4% (2000–2006)
London	11.5% (1981–2006)	0.46%	0.7% (1996–2006)
Paris	14.1% (1982–2006)	0.59%	0.7% (1999–2006)
Tokyo	16.6% (1980–2005)	0.57%	0.27% (1995–2005)

Sources: London: NOMIS; Paris: Insee; New York: US Decennial Census and American Community Survey 2006; Tokyo: 2005 Population Census of Japan conducted by MIAC.

Even allowing for the variation in boundary definition, our four city-regions vary considerably in population size. Tokyo is the largest with over 33 million and holds 26 percent of Japan's population; New York and London closely follow and respectively hold 7 percent and 23 percent of their nation's populations; the Paris region holds about half the number of residents as its sister city-regions, though it accounts for nearly 19 percent of France's population. We can understand that these regions are quite large and hold sizeable populations. If the Tokyo region were a country, it would be the thirty-fifth largest in the world; New York would be the fiftieth largest, followed closely by London as the fifty-first largest with Paris further down the line as the seventy-fourth-largest nation.

Looking at the city-region as a whole, all four grew significantly over the twenty-five years. The New York and Paris regions had similar population increases of around 14 percent, while the London region was lower with 11 percent and the Tokyo region the highest with over 16 percent. When looking at the annual rate of population increase over the period, we see that New York, Tokyo, and Paris had a very similar rate of increase while London was significantly lower. However, the picture is rather different when looking at the rate of change over more recent years. Then we see the fastest growth in London and Paris while Tokyo has slowed down significantly. Demographers are predicting that the Tokyo region and metropolitan area will start to actually suffer a population fall from 2015, reflecting the national decline in population.

We now take a more fine-grained view of our city-regions to describe the distribution of population changes, focusing on differences between the urban core (i.e., the central business district [CBD]), municipal or metropolitan area, and the rest of the city-region. Table 1.3 shows the internal demographic distributions within each city-region.

When we examine different parts of the city-regions, we detect further variations. The proportion of the regional population currently living within municipal boundaries of New York City, Greater London, and Tokyo varies between 35 percent and 38 percent. However, Paris stands out with a much higher proportion (56 percent) living within the municipality. This is so because we consider the municipality the so-called first ring of the city-region, thus encompassing the city of Paris (what we call the urban core) and the adjacent densest municipalities. Another pattern to notice is that New York, London, and Tokyo have a very small proportion of people living in their central business districts, at about 1 percent or less. By contrast, Paris again contains a significant proportion of its regional population within its CBD (19 percent).

Although the regional growth rate in London over the twenty-five years is similar to that of New York, the rate in the metropolitan area (Greater London Authority [GLA]) has been slower. In the central area, there was even a decline in population during the first part of our period. An important feature of the London pattern has been the way the growth rate picked up very significantly from around the mid-1990s for the GLA and the central area. This more recent rate of growth for the GLA is similar to that of

TABLE 1.3. CITY-REGION POPULATION DISTRIBUTION AND RATES OF CHANGE IN PERCENTAGES

	Population distribution				*Change over 25 years*				*Change in recent years*			
	New York	London	Paris	Tokyo	New York	London	Paris	Tokyo	New York	London	Paris	Tokyo
Urban core (CBD)	0.7	1.1	19	1.0	12.8	22.7	0.0	0.0	4.7	13.8	2.0	21.5
Municipal area	37	35	56	38	16.1	10.4	6.5	6.6	2.5	2.6	5.1	4.2
Rest of city-region	63	65	44	62	14.2	14.4	25.6	19.8	2.4	3.1	4.7	−2.1

Sources: London: NOMIS; Paris: Insee- IAU- CRCI; Tokyo: 2005 Population Census of Japan conducted by MIAC.

New York City. Regional variation is more noticeable in our other two cities. In both Paris and Tokyo, over the twenty-five-year period, there has been no growth at all in the urban core, small growth in the broader metropolitan area, and major growth in the outer region. In both cities, however, the growth rates in the outer part of the region are most significant in the first part of the period. In recent years, there has been a slight increase in population in the city of Paris. In Tokyo, there has been a more dramatic shift. As in London, an important change can be detected in the mid-1990s with a significant increase in population in the central area, which was losing population in the early part of the period, and a decline in the growth rates in the outer part of the region. Toward the end of the period, this part of the region was actually losing population.

So what are the major similarities and differences among our four cities regarding population change? Over the long period, all city-regions grew significantly, with the rate for the London region being somewhat slower. When looking at more recent years, however, we see that the London and Paris regions are growing fastest while the Tokyo region has been slowing down significantly. All cities have seen a growth of population in these recent years in their central areas, although the rate of growth has varied considerably with the largest percentage increases in Tokyo, where land prices dropped dramatically during the economic crisis of the 1990s, and the smallest in Paris. In looking at the variation in growth within the regions over the twenty-five years, our cities seem to fall into two types. New York and London have a relatively even growth pattern across their regions, while Paris and Tokyo have a fairly static central population with most growth in the outer parts of the region.

The GCR Economies: Evolving Capitals of Capitalism

The four GCRs are generally considered to be among the dominant command posts of capitalism. What does this mean from a local and regional economic perspective? Does this suggest they are alike in their mix of economic activities and that they manage similar economic changes? Or are there important differences among them that provide each with distinct niches in the world economic system?

Globalization is a process that entails both decentralization and centralization of production. On the one hand, the different stages in the production of most goods and services—design, production, assembly, and so on—do not all have to be located in one place. For example, manufacturing can take place anywhere in the world where the costs are lowest. Improved telecommunications and cheaper travel can ensure that the stages remain linked. On the other hand, the centralization of certain functions is quite necessary in order to manage far-flung economic activities. Central decision making related to management, finance, advertising, and other white-collar functions tend to be located in central cities, particularly global cities that can act as command centers of the global economy. The leading players in such centers, top financial firms and major transnational corporations, enjoy the benefits of networking and face-to-face contact. They also require high-level support services from specialist business advisers. These factors mean that only a few city-regions can become the host to these central aspects of the global economy. A second economic sector that grows with the ease of global communication is tourism. This sector can potentially be tapped by a wider range of cities, but it is often an important part of the economies of major cities having economic and cultural importance, a high-quality built environment, and the wherewithal to provide the necessary facilities for international tourism.

As discussed in the introduction, globalization theorists usually emphasize signs of convergence in world city development during recent decades. From this perspective, cities strongly linked into the changes in the global economy are expected to increase in economic prosperity and also attract more international corporations and banks. More global trading and connectivity is expected. As manufacturing tends to move away from GCRs, these activities are replaced by growth in international corporations, international finance, and supporting specialized business services. As the workers in these global companies move into the city, they will bring with them high incomes and lifestyles—world cities will therefore also experience a growth in high-level services in retailing, entertainment, leisure, and eating establishments. There will also be a demand for high-quality housing (Bell 1973). Thus, from a globalization perspective, there are several avenues of economic convergence that seem particular to GCRs.

In this section, we will explore the degree to which our GCRs have experienced such changes and whether there is much variation among them. After exploring these aspects of our four cities, we will then look at how the structure of economic activity and employment has changed over the period. Our interest is in the broader region and so we describe the extent to which economic change in the city and the region follows the same patterns, particularly whether there have been increased linkages between the city and region or other signs of greater regional integration.

The evidence suggests that all four city-regions share similar features as command post economies. But they also display differences that enable them to compete by offering significant comparative advantages as urban places.

GLOBAL CONNECTIONS

At the core of any great city is its capacity to attract capital, recruit business, and generate additional revenues. By these criteria, London, New York, Paris, and Tokyo stand at the top of the hierarchy. Yet what world economic leadership actually means, and how each city ranks, are matters of considerable debate because there are different ways of measuring world economic prowess. One approach puts emphasis on the way cities have linkages with other cities across the world (e.g., Castells 1989; Sassen 1991, 1994). The Globalization and World City Research Network (GaWC) research has tried to measure this networking by identifying "connectivity" scores. These scores are based on the networking by high-level service firms, such as law and accounting, which it is assumed can be used as a proxy for general global networking. The more a city is connected to such international business, the higher its global standing. Table 1.4 shows the results of this research for our cities and it indicates that London, New York, Paris, and Tokyo are in rank order among the five most globally connected cities in the world.[2]

Since there are a number of ways to measure these activities, we cast a wide lens on local economies and rely on multiple financial indicators. Two indicators, the *Fortune Global* 500 and the *Financial Times* 500, describe and rank each of our cities (not the regions, however) with respect to the location of major corporate headquarters included in their respective groups of 500 and also rank the total amount of revenues generated by these corporations in each location. The MasterCard Worldwide Centers of Commerce Index provides a much broader picture. It employs forty-three indicators and seventy-four subindicators that include such things as measures of financial flow, ease of doing business, and other attributes to measure the competitiveness of core functional commercial traits of each city.

Table 1.5 reports these indicators for the four cities. Most importantly, it shows that all four are within the top four or five cities with respect to numbers and revenues of corporate headquarters—just as suggested by the global connectivity data.

The broader MasterCard index is also suggestive of the world leadership of these cities, although it places Paris as seventh in commercial competitiveness. The Table also confirms the ambiguity of general city economic rankings. *Fortune Global* and the *Financial Times* report that Paris and Tokyo lead London and New York in corporate locations and revenues. By contrast, London and New York are ahead of Tokyo and Paris in overall commercial competitiveness.

What all this suggests is how much the four cities are world economic powerhouses

---

TABLE 1.4. GLOBAL NETWORK SERVICE CONNECTIVITY IN 2000

City-region	Total connectivity	Rank out of 315 cities
London	63,354	1
New York	61,859	2
Paris	44,296	4
Tokyo	43,763	5

Source: Globalization and World City Research Network. Accessed April 22, 2008, from http://www .lboro.ac.uk/gawc/datasets/da12.html. Another way of looking at global economic leadership is by measuring critical economic activities indicative of leading GCRs. This includes the location of headquarters of transnational companies and international banks as well as the concentration and flow of finance both within city-regions and between them and the rest of the world. The latter is particularly important. After all, finance reflects the existence and the movement of assets. Follow the money and we may very well be able to trace both the sources and the tendencies of financial power.

by any measure, but that each lines up somewhat differently depending on what particular attributes are considered. Although London has recently replaced New York as the world's leading global and financial city with respect to connectedness and overall commercial qualities, London's ranking diminishes when it comes to more direct measures. Here we see that Tokyo surges ahead with almost twice the number of corporate headquarters as its counterpart cities.

The ambiguity of any single world city rank order suggests that important differences materialize as particular areas of economic activity are considered. This is illustrated by tourism. All of the four cities are major world tourist destinations, but their competitiveness in tourism has more than one side to it. Table 1.6 displays figures for tourism (Judd and Fainstein 1999). Shown are numbers of tourists from foreign countries. Note that London is the top tourist destination with respect to the number of tourists it attracts from abroad, and Paris is ahead of New York and well ahead of Tokyo.

TABLE 1.5. GLOBAL HEADQUARTERS, MARKET SHARE, AND COMMERCIAL COMPETITIVENESS

City-region	FG 500 headquarters (2007)	FG 500 rank (2007)	FT 500 (% market, cap 2007)	FG 500 global revenues (US$)	FG 500 global revenues rank (2007)	Market flows ranking (MasterCard Index)
London	22	3	6.1%	$1,085,187	4	1
New York	22	3	7.2%	$1,174,439	3	2
Paris	26	2	4.6%	$1,240,919	2	7
Tokyo	50	1	n/a	$1,725,362	1	5

Source: *Fortune Magazine*, July 23, 2007. *Fortune Global* (FG) 500 ranks the world's top 500 corporations by revenue. The FG 500 rank identifies the top 10 cities by number of FG 500 corporations. The FG 500 global revenues measures the total amount of revenues generated by FG 500 corporations by city. The FG 500 global revenues rank identifies the top 10 cities by total dollar amount of revenues generated by FG 500 corporations. *Financial Times* (FT) 500 ranks cities by total market capitalization of FT 500 corporations located within.

TABLE 1.6. INTERNATIONAL TOURISM

Region	International tourists, 2006 (millions)
New York	7.0
Tokyo	4.8
London	15.2
Paris	9.6

Sources: Visit Britain; NYC Statistics; Paris Convection and Visitors Bureau; Tokyo Metropolitan Government 2007.

In sum, there is something to be gained in ranking our cities, since so many indicators point in similar directions. Yet the conclusion is not always clear because fortunes shift over time.

PRODUCTION, WEALTH, AND INVESTMENT

The medieval cities of the Hanseatic League used their international economic power to accumulate great wealth; our four GCRs have benefited similarly. How much have their leading positions in the global marketplace led to greater riches? All of them have enormous productive capacity and, in varying degrees, they enjoy a surfeit of resources. Indeed, it is difficult to imagine that their respective nations could be the same without these great cities. Table 1.7 gives us a broad picture of the extent of this wealth. It shows the gross municipal product (GMP) of each city-region as well as their proportionate economic contributions to their respective nations.

In just five years, New York's GMP climbed from $800 billion to more than $1 trillion, amounting to more than a 41 percent increase. The current GMP production in these cities is extraordinary, with London and Paris producing 25 percent of their national total, while Tokyo generates 18 percent. New York is lower at 9 percent, but this proportion is understandable, considering the size of the American economy at $9.8 trillion for the year in question.

To further examine wealth in our four cities, we turn to some basic indicators on the value of traded and fixed assets. The data include the capital owned by major trading firms, telling us something about existing corporate wealth and the value of stocks traded, indicating monetary flow.

Figures 1.1 and 1.2 depict this assortment of wealth. Figure 1.1 shows bar graphs for each city indicating the capitalization of firms in each stock exchange and Figure 1.2 shows the values traded as of 2008.

On the first two criteria, New York holds a top position, followed by London, Paris, and Tokyo, all of which hold fairly similar values. By this measure, New York is indeed the capital of capitalism because so much global wealth trading is funneled into its trading floors—indeed, the value of shares traded is several times greater than all of its competitor cities. Nevertheless, London's increasing competitiveness, particularly

TABLE 1.7. METRO GROSS MUNICIPAL PRODUCT (GMP), 2006

	Billions of US dollars	Per capita US dollars	Proportion of national GDP
London	$452	$21,164	20.10%
New York	$1,133	$51,693	9.10%
Paris	$460	$40,740	21.50%
Tokyo	$1,191	$35,582	26.10%

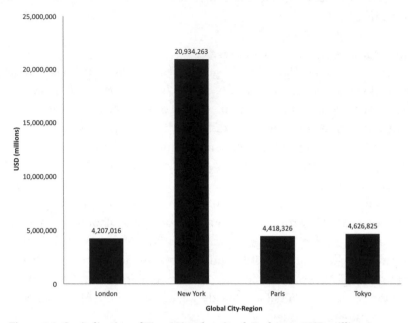

Figure 1.1. Capitalization of Firms Listed on Stock Exchange (USD millions)

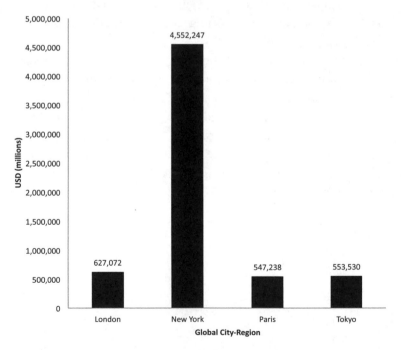

Figure 1.2. Value of Shares Traded (USD millions)

following the "big bang" of 1986, which deregulated the stock market and curbed government controls, has eroded New York's trading advantages during more recent years. Paris and Tokyo also have claimed larger roles.

EMPLOYMENT AND INDUSTRIAL SECTOR CHANGE

As leading-edge global economies, the four city-regions are undergoing major economic transformation. Their increasing wealth derives not only from their global connectivity but also because these metropolitan areas are modernizing from within, replacing older job sectors with more new rapidly expanding economic activities. This has profound effects on every part of the city and its suburbs. City and suburban areas that are favored by expanding new-economy investment witness prosperity and rising property values. Their commercial sectors experience multiple spin-offs in the form of profitable restaurants, retail establishments, and professional services. By contrast, disinvested locations shrink when work disappears. Properties inaccessible to employment lose value and are more likely to cater to transitional residents or remain vacant. Buildings that are closed down or shops that are boarded up convey a forbidding quality about an area (Abu-Lughod 1999; Sites 2003).

The scope of such changes in our city-regions is evident in the pattern of employment change over the last twenty-five years. Tables 1.8 and 1.9 present a broad picture and also suggest how this has varied across the individual city-regions.

As we can see, the employment totals within each municipal area and region are

TABLE 1.8. MUNICIPAL EMPLOYMENT (MILLIONS)

1980 employment	1995 employment	2000 employment
3.07 (1981)	3.9 (1995)	4.5
3.3	3.2 (1997)	3.4
1.8 (1982)	1.7 (1990)	1.6 (1998)
5.8 (1982)	9.0 (1996)	8.6

Sources: Savitch 1988; Miyamoto 1993; Drennan 1985.

TABLE 1.9. CITY-REGION EMPLOYMENT (MILLIONS)

City-region	1995 employment	2000 employment	2002 employment	2004 employment	2006 employment
London	9.2	10.1	10.3	10.3	10.5
New York	8.0 (1997)	8.5	8.5	8.6	8.9
Paris	5.0 (1997)	5.0 (1998)	—	5.3	5.5
Tokyo	17.2 (1996)	16.7	—	14.8	18.3

Source: London: ONS; Tokyo: Labor Force Survey by MIAC; definition is the population in employment.

impressive. In the municipal (or metropolitan) area of London, employment increased from 4.2 million jobs in 1980 to 4.6 million in 2006, a 9.5 percent increase. However, this encompassed a considerable employment decline in the early 1990s. Tokyo also rose by a substantial amount, going from 5.8 million jobs in 1982 to 8.6 million in 2004, a 38 percent rise. The gains in New York City were more modest; jobs went from 3.3 million in 1980 to 3.6 million in 2006, an increase of 9 percent. Paris was the sole municipality to have lost employment, going from 1.8 million jobs in 1982 to 1.6 million by 2005, a reduction of 11 percent. In making this assessment, we should recognize that the territorial size of our cities differs. Thus, Paris contains the smallest land area and its absolute numbers reflect that. Also, much of its corporate employment is located just outside the city in La Défense and this is not added to the municipal total.

The patterns in the four regions were more modest but also more consistently upward. For London, the percentage changes in employment in the city-region have shown a steady increase and have been slightly higher and less volatile than the changes in the metropolitan area. For example, between 1995 and 2006 the population in employment increased by 14 percent (UK Office for National Statistics 2008) to reach over 10 million. In New York, this increased by 11 percent and in Paris by 10 percent. As we see from the table, Tokyo once again dwarfs our other cities with an employment base of 18 million, but it has a slower rate of growth at 6 percent.

Looking within each of our city-regions, transformative evolution of major industrial sectors is evident over the past quarter century. Generally speaking, postindustrial societies are characterized by deemphasizing secondary industry (manufacture, mining) and concentrating on tertiary sectors (including high technology, finance, management, and professional services; Bell 1973).

Figures 1.3 and 1.4, respectively, show us how London, New York, Paris, and Tokyo have restructured. So that we might better compare city-regions, each city is represented by a separate bar. Where a bar is missing for a given year, data are not available. The tables show results at the municipal and regional levels for four leading industrial sectors: manufacture, services, construction, and a grouped category of finance, insurance, and real estate (FIRE).

Beginning with the municipal level, note the declines in manufacturing for all of our cities. The municipalities of London, New York, Paris, and Tokyo lost at least half their proportions of manufacture over approximately 25 years. Even the Tokyo region, long known for its manufacturing prowess, declined. In all four city-regions, manufacture shrinkage began in the 1970s or 1980s and has continued since then. In its place, we see a fairly uniform rise of services. While services rose in all our municipalities, the most dramatic increases occurred in Tokyo and Paris. The changes in the FIRE sector are uneven, with some municipalities showing gains and others remaining more or less the same. Again, at the municipal level FIRE did very well in London, no doubt spurred by the big bang. Paris and New York were next and Tokyo is well behind. Tokyo's low proportion may well reflect its lagging property markets

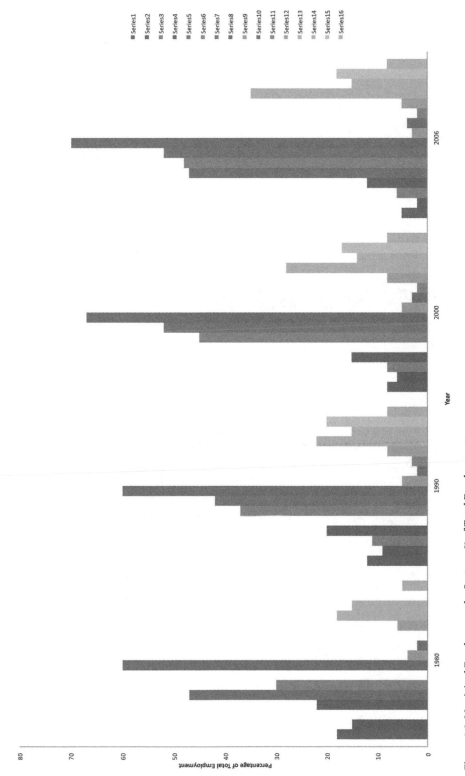

Figure 1.3. Municipal Employment by Sectors, % of Total Employment

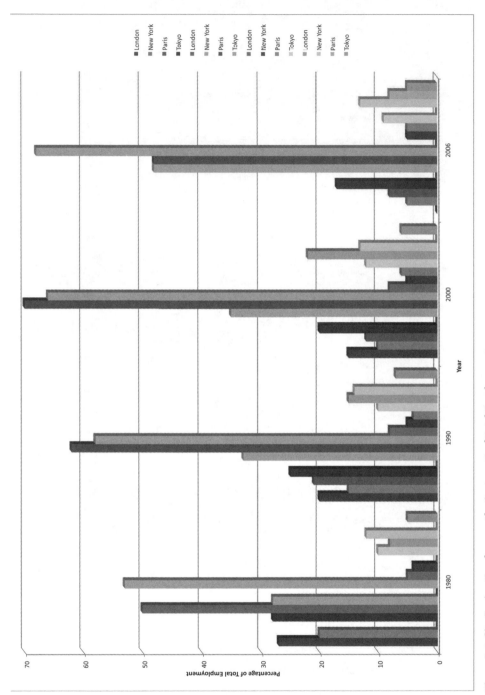

Figure 1.4. City Region Employment by Sectors, % of Total Employment

as well as its earlier banking crises, which lasted for more than a decade. The last sector concerns construction. By and large, this sector holds the smallest proportion of employment. Within the bounds of our four cities, there were few steep rises or declines.

Turning to the region, the results reflect increasing decentralization with suburban economic activities becoming more important over time. Insofar as manufacturing is concerned, all the regions incurred declines. However, Tokyo appears to have done best, with Paris occupying a second position. Again, the story is one of increasing services across all regions. For most of the years, the Tokyo region is ahead of its sister cities, though Paris does quite well and its proportion of services was higher than Tokyo's in 2000. FIRE occupies a relatively small portion of the regional economy in all our cities. Here again, New York and London show the highest proportion for the years 2000 and 2006. Judging from these results, it appears that central city activity in financial and property markets carries into the region. The notion that urban cores generate jobs well beyond their boundaries warrants further attention and the implications of this are taken up in subsequent chapters.

In sum, all four world city-regions have been experiencing relatively similar dominant economic trends. All of them have been forging dense connections to the global marketplace and undergoing rapid modernization within. Although there are differences in degree, they share a common direction, shedding older manufacturing activities in favor of services in the central cores, as well as regionally in suburban locations.

The Social Fallout of Urban Growth and Prosperity

The growth and prosperity associated with world city-regions also produces social fallout. As noted in the introduction, many globalization theorists do not expect social tensions to abate in cities and regions that are major players in the world economy, even though these urban areas are becoming wealthier. Rather, leading GCRs may experience even greater tensions because their economic transformation easily precipitates social conflicts and divisions (Lipset 1981; Sassen 1991). One source of conflict arises from changes in the population mix as a result of immigration of new groups from abroad seeking work and residence in world city-regions, making these regions cosmopolitan but also increasing social differences. Other sources of conflict spring from increasing divisions based on income. Some critics warn that this process encourages the formation of a "dual city" in which social polarization and territorial segregation among income groups increases because of changing occupational and neighborhood mixes (Mollenkopf and Castells 1992; Sassen 1991). Surveying both forms of social division later on in this chapter, we find that social divisions have accompanied growth in our city-regions, but the city-regions vary considerably in the degree and scope of this pattern.

IMMIGRATION AND EMERGING SOCIAL DIVISIONS

We begin our inquiry with foreign immigration into cities and urban regions. Our own city-regions are very much a part of this transnational phenomenon, and the data show the extent to which that experience is common. Table 1.10 shows the proportion of foreign-born residents for both municipality and region.

Examining the percentage of the foreign-born population, a significant increase in foreign-born residents is evident over the last twenty years in three of our four cities, especially in New York and London. In New York City, the percentage jumped from 24 percent to 36 percent, while London's pace nearly doubled to reach 30 percent. By the turn of the century, Paris had only half as many foreign-born residents as New York and London, though its level of 18 percent is significant. By comparison, Tokyo's foreign population is quite small. The small numbers of immigrants that do exist in Tokyo are concentrated in certain areas where immigrants can find work: the entertainment district in the center, international business districts, and certain manufacturing districts in the broader region. The Tokyo region is the location for about a third of immigrants to Japan, and although the numbers are small, the national immigration increased 2.5 times between 1980 and 2006.

Globalization is also changing the composition of immigration into our city-regions. There is now a wider range in the origins of the migrants and more high-level, educated people moving into the supposed command centers of the global economy. At the same time, each of the city-regions is sustaining traditional immigration, often from regions connected with each country's imperial past.

TABLE 1.10. FOREIGN-BORN POPULATION AS A PERCENTAGE OF
TOTAL POPULATION: MUNICIPALITY AND REGION

City-region	Subunit	Period		
New York		1980	1990	2000
	New York City	23.6%	28.4%	35.9%
	New York Region	15.4%	18.7%	26.4%
London		1986		2006
	Greater London	17.6%	—	30.5%
	Southeast Region	—	—	—
Paris		1982	1990	1999
	City of Paris	18.4%	18.5%	18.2%
	Île de France	13.3%	14.0%	14.7%

Sources: New York Region: US Census Bureau; New York City: New York City Department of City Planning; London: NOMIS; Paris: Insee; data is not available for Tokyo.

The largest groups of immigrants to New York are Caribbean and Latino. The former are concentrated in Manhattan and the rest of New York City, while the latter settle in more suburban locations. Other groups are South and Eastern Europeans, East Asians, and in recent years, Indian, Pakistani, and Chinese. In London, the origins of the immigrants have widened enormously over the twenty-year period. In 1986, approximately 76 percent of immigrants came from countries with colonial links, but this dropped to 59 percent by 2006 (Gordon et al. 2007). In 1991, net international migration into the GLA was 32,000 and this had increased to 70,000 by 2007. The numbers moving into the rest of the city-region in 1991 were much smaller at 14,000 but this had also increased significantly to 61,000 by 2007 (UK Office for National Statistics 2008).

As we have already noted, the flow of immigration has been particularly high in the last 10 years. This has included increases in two categories not based on colonial history. The first group is job seekers from the EU and accession countries, particularly Poland, with 5,000 to 10,000 people entering per year. However, this number has fallen since the economic crisis in 2008 and many of these migrants have returned. In recent years, about half the immigrants have come from other developed countries. The second group results from the international upsurge in asylum seeking. The traditional immigrant arriving in the last ten years has been above average in level and range of qualifications, and this has contributed to a more cosmopolitan, young, and well-educated population within the metropolitan area (Gordon et al. 2007).

Immigration to Paris has traditionally been from two main areas: southern European countries, especially Portugal, and the Maghreb. Between 1990 and 1999, we see a decline in the first group but a continued increase in the second. Although smaller in numbers, there was a faster increase in immigration from black Africa, Turkey, and more recently, East Asia. In Tokyo, the small number of immigrants has come mainly from Korea and China. The first group is the largest ethnic group in the country and in the city-region and has been entering for a while, but those from China have been increasing recently.

The degree to which our cities can be said to be cosmopolitan varies somewhat from New York and London at one end, Tokyo at the other end, and Paris in between. The more cosmopolitan urban centers changed most during recent years as migrants from nontraditional world regions sought residence there. New York, London, and Paris have seen the most significant influx of immigration in recent decades, while Tokyo has not. Regional and colonial links remain dominant. London and Paris have drawn many immigrants from Eastern Europe as well as South Asia (London) and the Maghreb (Paris). New York absorbed large numbers of immigrants from Latin American and the Caribbean, while Tokyo has settled smaller numbers from Korea and China.

INCOME AND POVERTY

Whether globalization has been accompanied by social polarization and territorial segregation has been fiercely debated (Moulaert et al. 2005, 32). We first assess this relative to levels of income and poverty in the cities. Although our city-regions have generated tremendous wealth, the income and poverty data indicate that this has not always benefited the resident populations. In the last twenty years or so, our four cities have performed differently in terms of personal wealth. According to Table 1.11, in New York, the median income per household has constantly declined since 1989—in the region from $59,518 in 1989 to $56,120 in 2005, and in New York City from $46,971 to $43,434 (SOCDS 2006). In Tokyo, the trend has been the same since the mid-1990s, with a significant drop in the average income per capita from 1997 to 2003 in the municipality of Tokyo, though there has been a slight improvement in recent years. At the regional level, the median income per household in the Tokyo metropolitan region was 2.08 million yen in 1983, but this increased to 3.29 in 1993 and then declined to 2.99 in 2003 (Toyoda 2007).[3] The upper-income group (top 20 percent) and lower-income group (bottom 20 percent) showed a similar trend, but the former showed a bigger increase and smaller decline compared to the latter. Tokyo Metropolitan Government (TMG) data reveal a similar trend. The share of households with a low annual income (below 5 million yen) decreased between 1986 and 1996 but increased after that and exceeded the 1986 level in 2005. The trend is similar across the different income groups as the income level peaked in the early 1990s. Even the higher-income group (annual income between 10 million and 20 million yen) followed this pattern, indicating there may be a difference between Tokyo and the metropolitan region.

By contrast, the populations of London and Paris generally have experienced rising average incomes. The GLA area has shown a significant increase in the average income of its population since 1997, going from £17,574 per household in 1997 to £24,654 in 2004 (ONS). There has also been an increase in the southeast but this has not been so rapid. As for the Paris region, Île de France has experienced a rather

TABLE 1.11. AVERAGE INCOME PER HOUSEHOLD, MUNICIPALITY, AND REGIONS FOR VARIOUS YEARS

New York region	New York City	Tokyo region	GLA	Île de France	Paris
59,518 (1989)	46,971 (1989)	2.08M (1997)	17,574 (1997)	15,461 (1984)	15,493 (1984)
56,120 (2005)	43,434 (2005)	2.99M (2003)	24,654 (2004)	18,457 (2002)	21,113 (2002)

Note: All numbers in national currency: New York in US dollars, London in pounds, Paris in euros, and Tokyo in yen.

Sources: Paris: DGI; London: ONS; Tokyo: Family Income and Expenditure Survey by MIAC

constant progression of the average income of its population since the early 1980s, going from €15,461 in 1984 to €18,457 in 2002 (DGI), and the municipality of Paris has followed the same pattern with an average income going from €15,493 in 1984 to €21,113 in 2002.

Regarding poverty, here again the situations vary greatly. In New York, the poverty rate has been more or less constant during the last twenty years, going from 19.3 percent in 1989 to 19.1 percent in 2005 in the municipality and from 12 percent to 12.6 percent in the region (SOCDS). The Tokyo metropolis shows a very different picture, at least in terms of numbers. A very small proportion of its population lives below the poverty level if we take social aid as a proxy for poverty rate. However, there has been a significant increase in recent years of people receiving social aid of 71 percent in the Tokyo municipality between 1997 and 2004; this rose still higher (by 84 percent) in the rest of the region (Social Indicators by Prefecture, Japan Statistical Yearbook).

In the Paris region, the data available on poverty rate for 2000 shows that 8.6 percent of the population live at half the median income level. If we use social housing as a proxy, we note increases of 11 to 12 percent in requests for social housing between the years 1992 and 2006 in both the city and the region (City of Paris and IAURIF). The usual measure of poverty used in Britain is households with disposable incomes below 60 percent of the median national figure. In presenting the data, it is usual to remove housing costs because these vary between tenures and geographical areas. On this basis in 2007/8, 24 percent of working-age people in metropolitan London were in poverty compared with a national figure of 21 percent. This overall figure masks some serious problems among particular age groups and in specific parts of London (Mayor of London 2002, 2009). The biggest issue is the number of children living in poor households; London has the highest incidence in the United Kingdom. For this group, the London figure was 27 percent, compared to the national figure of 19 percent. This represents a considerable improvement on the high point of 44 percent in the mid-1990s.

One of the major factors contributing to London's poverty has been the low employment rate for certain people. Although the London economy has been buoyant over the period, large numbers of Londoners have not benefited from this. Income levels in manual work have not increased at the rate of other jobs; the openness of the London economy has meant that there has been competition in the labor market from people moving into the city. The London economy also suffered a slump in the early 1990s that particularly affected the poor population, leading to the high poverty figures of the mid-1990s.

Poverty is also concentrated in ethnic minority populations. London has a major concentration of such groups. For example, in London in 1998, 55 percent of black children and 73 percent of Bangladeshi and Pakistani children lived in poor households. Over the period, child poverty was highly concentrated in inner London. Although this improved slightly, the situation became worse in the outer parts of the metropolis. Generally, London's poverty has been a metropolitan problem, while the rest of the city-region has been more affluent with poverty figures below the national average. Nevertheless, there are poverty pockets within the broader region, mostly on the fringes of the region, such as in the towns on the south coast and Thames estuary.

Put briefly, we do not find one trajectory of income changes in our city-regions. Prosperity in two of the four city-regions (London and New York) has not trickled down to generate rising overall incomes, supporting some of the fears of those who believe GCR development breeds social polarization. By contrast, however, two of the world city-regions have not experienced such an extreme form of social polarization, suggesting it is not invariably inherent in the globalization process itself. Still, we find that New York, London, and Paris contain populations that suffer from high levels of poverty, and this does not seem to have improved over the period. Tokyo stands out as the exception, although in recent years there has been an increase in people needing social aid. This mixed picture suggests there are complex forces—not just global influences—at work to produce income patterns.

SOCIAL DISPARITIES: VARIABLE GAPS

Social disparities have to do with how groups fare relative to one another. The four GCRs have shown different patterns in the last fifteen to twenty years. Among them, the New York region shows the widest gaps. Between 1989 and 1999, there was an increase in the percentage of low-income households in both the region and the municipality. This amounted to an increase of 17.4 percent to 19.6 percent in the region and from 24.3 percent to 27.1 percent in New York City (SOCDS 2006). Over a more recent period, between 2000 and 2005, low-income households in New York City rose from 17.6 percent to 18.6 percent (American Community Survey 2008). Moreover, the relative shares of household income are also deeply disparate. By the year 2006, the lowest quintile living in New York City received just 2.3 percent of the household income, while in the rest of the region the lowest quintile did little better with 2.8 percent of the household income. At the same time, the highest quintile received 52.8 percent of the household income and the top 5 percent of households received 24.7 percent of the income (American Community Survey 2006).

The situation in the London region has been less severe, but with a growing gap nonetheless. Hamnett (2003) shows that London experienced an increased income differential between 1979 and 1993 as more people were included in the upper income echelons. He points out that the main change has been in the increased number of professionals in the workforce, with large numbers finding employment in the financial district. This trend can be seen in the numbers. Between 1996 and 2006, the percentage of households earning less than £150 per week actually decreased from 21 percent to 14 percent, while the percentage of those earning more than £750 has almost doubled, from 21 percent to 37 percent (ONS).

The patterns in Tokyo and Paris are more stable or show a modest narrowing of social inequalities. In Tokyo, there were no significant changes in the distribution of incomes between 1979 and 1999. Elsewhere, the poorest sector of the population shrunk a bit (from 3.5 percent to 2.9 percent) and the richest sector of the population grew slightly (from 23.1 percent to 24.5 percent; National Survey of Family Income and Expenditures). Similarly, in the Paris region between 1990 and 2000, the lowest income quintile decreased slightly (0.1 percent) while the highest quintile increased its per capita income by 17 percent (DGI).

In sum, London, Paris, and Tokyo achieved a considerable stabilization of relative poverty and enlarged their pool of higher-income households. By contrast, New York not only inched up in its poverty, but those at the very pinnacle of the social structure also absorbed more income.

SPATIAL POLARIZATION: CONTRASTING PATTERNS

There is a significant sociospatial segregation in all our cities, with the possible exception of Tokyo. Nevertheless, we cannot say that this has been exacerbated during the last twenty-five years because the spatial pattern of income distribution varies considerably.

Traditionally, Tokyo's built-up area was divided into two: Yamanote (upper-town) in the west and Shitamachi (downtown) in the east. The former has been an exclusive residential area for the elite, while the latter functioned as a mixed-use area for the others. This basic urban structure still holds today. The former is a location for white-collar office workers, while the latter has a concentration of blue-collar workers engaged in manual labor and clerical work. Thus, they have different levels of wealth. At the regional scale, the poverty measured by household income, unemployment, and welfare support is mainly concentrated in two clusters. One is the part of Shitamachi mentioned previously and its extension to neighboring areas in Saitama and Chiba prefectures. The other is part of Kawasaki and Yokohama in Kanagawa prefecture. Both had strong concentrations of the manufacturing industry and suffered from the relocation of major plants after the 1980s. By contrast, Yamanote and some of the suburban commuter towns show a concentration of higher-income groups.

Public concern with social polarization in Japan has grown since the mid-1990s after uninterrupted postwar economic growth since the 1950s came to end. In terms of geography at the regional level, the variance in household income grew between 1983 and 2003 throughout the region, but the area within 10 kilometers from central Tokyo showed the highest degree of polarization. In fact, in 1983 data, some suburban commuter towns in the 20- to 30-kilometer-range showed equally strong concentrations of higher-income groups, but they stayed at this level, while the city center area attracted more high-income groups, particularly between 1993 and 2003. The 2003 data revealed that the share of middle-income groups is lowest in the city center within an area of 10 kilometers (Toyoda 2007).

In the municipality of Paris, much of the wealth is concentrated at the very center and in western sections. Poverty is lodged in its suburbs, particularly north of the city.

The suburb of Seine-Saint-Denis has the highest unemployment rate and the lowest average income in the region of Île de France. In terms of income, the situation has deteriorated over the years—in 2002 this department had a per capita income of 71 percent of the regional average, down from 86 percent in 1984 (DGI).

London has a more complex pattern: some central areas are very rich, but inner suburbs contain the poorest neighborhoods while the suburbs further out on the fringe of the metropolitan area are generally middle-income or higher. This pattern has been stable over the last decade or so (ONS). To be sure, the inner part of London contains wealthy areas, such as Westminster, Camden, Canary Wharf, Kensington, and Chelsea, but it also has deprived neighborhoods, such as Hackney, Tower Hamlets, parts of Islington, and Newham. A prominent feature of London's inner area is how it contains such social extremes in close proximity.

By contrast, New York City is generally poorer than its suburbs (the exceptions are to be found in lower and mid-Manhattan and parts of Queens). The municipality's average income was 77 percent of the suburban average income in 2005, a fairly constant proportion over the years (SOCDS 2006). This is corroborated by other indicators, such as the unemployment and poverty rates. For example, in New York, the Bronx shows signs of social difficulties with the highest unemployment rate in New York City, a poverty rate of 29 percent in 2005, and a per capita income less than half the regional average (American Community Survey 2005).

To conclude, it is difficult to substantiate fears regarding increases in social polarization in our GCRs as they are developing in recent decades. It is true that increases in wealth of the city-regions have not usually diminished poverty or always increased resident incomes, but there are no signs of increasing socioeconomic division overall. The four GCRs show considerable variation in both the state of their social structure and their twenty-five-year social trends. Nevertheless, one common phenomenon does emerge: traditional patterns of social polarization and the spatial concentrations of rich and poor have not markedly changed. In Paris and London, the contrast between the east (poor) and the west (rich) has remained, and in New York, the disparities between the city and its suburbs are largely intact. By international standards, Tokyo remains a relatively socially unsegregated metropolitan area.

Quality of Life: Where Is It Better and Why?

Are some GCRs better places to live than others? Or do they suffer or enjoy similar fates because of the kind of places they are? The answers have important political and economic implications. Urban quality of life affects local politics, influencing which issues get on the governmental agenda. It also affects profoundly the satisfaction of citizens with their governments. At the same time, livability is also an asset in global economic competition. Workers, investors, and businesses are more inclined to go to communities where they can enjoy the good life.

MEASURING QUALITY

Quality is a subjective notion, however. New York often appeals as an exciting place to live. The glamour of Manhattan with its aura of fashion, entertainment, and energetic business climate exists side by side with incredible ethnic and racial diversity in its neighborhoods. Paris is a center of culture, cuisine, art, and refinement mixed with commercial verve. London affords one of the most sophisticated urban environments on earth, freely blending the ancient and modern in a truly international setting. Tokyo excels as an important interface of East and West, expressed in its dramatic building skylines, plethora of commercial districts, and refined Japanese cultural traditions that permeate nearly everything.

Which of these settings provides the best quality of living? This is ambiguous. There is little agreement about what quality of life is or how to assess it (Hasan 2008). As we will describe, it is possible to rate our urban communities by using objective measures, such as cost of housing, educational spending, and the like, and by surveying what people say about their localities. But it is impossible to accept these data as definitive. People disagree about what particular aspects of community living are most important for the "good life." People in the same community differ in their access to valued resources and their relative worth. For example, a college student, a factory worker, and an executive business traveler will have very different ideas about the livability of a locality. Further, quality-of-life rankings are heavily influenced by cost factors, but cost of living easily changes. For example, New York is favored in 2009 in part because of the dollar's low foreign exchange value while price increases have made London very expensive. In 2000, Tokyo was the most expensive place in the world (Mercer 2000), but today it is not because of recent deflation.

Finally, statements about the quality of life in world cities can hardly take into account many variations *within* the region, a factor that assumes greater and greater importance as cities are compelled to compete as entire city-regions. In big sprawling GCRs, there are large intraregional differences in such things as crime, green space, educational spending, housing opportunities, and even water and air pollution. For instance, in the New York region violent crime rates per 1,000 population range from more than 1,010 in poor, decaying Newark, New Jersey, to 638 in New York City to as little as 70.7 in wealthy Wayne, New Jersey. City–suburban differences in wealth, government spending, health, and other resources tend to be especially prominent in the region (US Census 2006).

Despite these obstacles, we survey multiple kinds of evidence about many characteristics that matter to most people as contributing to living quality in the four cities (we are unable to provide comparable data on the regions). Although imperfect, this review includes comprehensive quality-of-life rankings and public sector asset audits, as well as what people who live in Paris, New York, Tokyo, and London have to say. By examining these different dimensions of livability, it is possible to provide a comparative perspective on life atop the urban hierarchy.

COMPARING QUALITY OF LIVING: GENERAL RANKINGS

We begin by considering composite indicators of the overall desirability of living conditions in the four cities.[4] Among the most general are the annual surveys by Mercer Human Resource Consulting and the Economist Intelligence Unit (EIU). Both carry out regular assessments of cost of living and quality of living in cities all over the world.[5]

Mercer's 2007 Quality of Living and Cost of Living surveys compare our four global cities to fifty other urban places in Table 1.12 (Mercer Human Resource Consulting 2007a, 2007b). What stands out is that all our cities have more in common than they have differences in quality of life. The table shows that all of them are very expensive places to live in comparison with most other major cities in the world and they have a lower quality of life than average. London ranks second out of fifty cities in cost of living, while Tokyo, Paris, and New York rank fourth, thirteenth, and fifteenth, respectively. As for quality of living, none of our four cities stacks up as highly desirable compared with most other major urban centers surveyed in the West. Paris ranks thirty-third out of fifty cities. Tokyo, London, and New York rank thirty-fifth, thirty-ninth, and forty-eighth, in that order. Data provided by the EIU for the same period generally reinforces this picture (EIU 2005, 2007b). Although the EIU employs some different indicators and comes up with slightly different rankings, it tends to confirm Mercer's pattern of relative higher cost and lower living quality. Where are the "best" places to live? According to Mercer, the two top spots are in Switzerland—Zurich and Geneva—followed by Vancouver, Canada; Vienna, Austria; Auckland, New Zealand; and Dusseldorf, Germany. The EIU placed Vancouver as the most livable city in the world, followed by Melbourne, Geneva, and Vienna, sharing second place (EIU 2007a).

This essentially adverse pattern of high cost and lower living quality suggests that residing in global cities has significant human discomforts. Why? In part, it is because economic powerhouse status brings higher costs and some diminished living qualities that otherwise are not commonly found in less powerful economic places. As big

TABLE 1.12. 2007 MERCER COST AND QUALITY-OF-LIFE INDEX RANKINGS

City-region	Cost-of-living survey index	Rank	Quality-of-living survey index	Rank
London	126.3	2	101.2	39
New York	100.0	15	100.0	48
Paris	101.4	13	102.7	33
Tokyo	122.1	4	102.3	35

Note: Rank is out of 50 cities, with New York City as the base city at 100.
Source: Mercer Human Resource Consulting 2007a, 2007b (134.4 to 85.1).

players in the world economy, our four cities are popular and crowded places in large and sprawling metropolitan regions. In this kind of urban environment, land costs are inevitably higher, as are the costs of many other goods, particularly housing. Residents in all of our cities face high housing costs relative to income. The average house price to income ratio in recent years was about 5:0 in Tokyo, 4:4 in London, and 4:1 in New York City. Housing burdens shared by global city residents are higher than the national average. For example, 42 percent of homeowners in New York City spent more than 30 percent of their income on housing compared with only 25 percent in all other US cities. Renters are also hard-pressed in New York City: 48 percent of them paid more than 30 percent of income on housing and 25 percent paid more than 50 percent (Furman Center 2007).

Commuting in world cities is a chronic problem. The plight of the commuter is worst in Tokyo, where nearly 85 percent spend more than 45 minutes daily getting to their jobs. In comparison, 46 percent of New Yorkers do the same. In London and Paris, 43 percent commute more than forty-one minutes. The impact of traffic congestion on quality of life is considerable. The New York City Department of Transportation reports that the annual cost of traffic congestion exceeded $5 billion in lost time and $4.5 billion in lost business revenue (Partnership for New York City 2006).

THE BEST AND THE REST: AN URBAN PECKING ORDER?

How do our four cities stack up against each other? Since all of the surveys differ in their indicators and relative weight values of particular characteristics, it is impossible to come to a conclusion about lifestyle rank by attempting to resolve differences among them. At best, we can collate the various surveys, treating their rankings equally to see where the four cities fall with respect to each other. Table 1.13 displays the collated rank order of cities based on the comprehensive cost and quality-of-living indicators of Mercer and the EIU, followed by the more fragmentary asset reports of the City of London's Global Financial Centers Index (GFCI) and the Partnership (discussed later).

Looking at this big picture, New York leads the group in high rankings with a 19-point score (lower number is better rank). Behind are Paris, Tokyo, and London, in that order, with scores of 20, 24, and 27, respectively. This contrasts with the Mercer overall rankings described earlier, where Paris led New York, London, and Tokyo, in that order.

OTHER PERSPECTIVES ON GLOBAL CITY LIFE

General living-standard ratings provide only one perspective on quality of life, however. These surveys focus on things like housing and food costs, which are easily quantifiable. They do not fully capture, and may even exclude, some lifestyle assets that matter to many people but are more likely to be found in global cities than elsewhere. These include enormous business opportunities in the "capitals of capitalism"; international cultural environments; the stimulating creative and intellectual atmosphere that is part of everyday life; the excitement of being "where it's at" in business, culture, and government; and the almost endless choices in education, leisure activities, entertainment, and human interaction that only world-class cities afford. Indeed, some lifestyle amenities are unique to our four cities. After all, there is only one West End, one Broadway theater district, one Champs-Élysées, and one Sinjuku; they all happen to be in London, New York, Paris, and Tokyo alone.

Ironically, some of the economic success achieved by our global cities actually depends on the material discomforts shared by their residents. For example, part of the reason our four cities attract so many business people is that they are crowded and afford many opportunities for finding people with special skills. Yet crowding is usually associated with higher land values, making them more expensive places to live. Indeed, if our cities are looked at from the perspective of business visitors, their value is different from what general quality-of-life indicators suggest. Business visitors tend to have particular needs, such as good hotels, restaurants, and meeting places. But these facilities thrive and proliferate only in crowded high-income markets. For this reason, one of the same survey organizations that graded each of the four global cities at the lower end of quality of life found them far more valuable "as a potential venue for business travel." A survey by the EIU in 2008 rated Paris, Tokyo, and New York all within the preferred upper 50 percent of 127 surveyed cities; London ranked 72nd (EIU 2008).

Another perspective on the quality of life in our cities views the particular kinds of resources found there that contribute to living standards. General indices of living quality ignore differences in the complex local mix of assets and liabilities found in individual cities. Although comprehensive comparative data are not available, it is possible to look at resource variations among Paris, Tokyo, London, and New York by examining some data provided by the City of London's Global Financial Centers Index in 2007 and by the *Cities of Opportunity* report prepared by PricewaterhouseCoopers for the Partnership for New York City in 2006 (City of London 2007; Partnership for New York City 2006). Although assessing the relative economic competitiveness of the top global cities, both reports also examined certain key assets related to quality of life. The GFCI reported on "people factors," such as lifestyle and educational indicators, and "infrastructure factors" measuring the quality of the working environments. The survey for the Partnership included transportation assets, demographic advantages, lifestyle assets, and safety and security. Although fragmentary, these data in Table 1.14 display some interesting findings about our cities.

Most importantly, no one city dominates in quality-of-life resources in all asset categories. For example, the Partnership data show that New York is highest in transportation resources and demographic diversity. Paris leads in lifestyle assets, including such things as entertainment, recreational space, and hotel beds. Tokyo's safety and security, including such things as hospital beds and personal safety, as well as crime statistics, are greater than in all the others. The GFCI shows London leads the rest in "people" and "infrastructure" resources. All this suggests that general city quality-of-life

	Overall city rank	Mercer quality of life	Mercer cost of living	EIU cost of living	GFCI people	GFCI infrastructure	PNYC transportation	PNYC lifestyle	PNYC safety	PNYC demographic	Total score
New York	4	1	3	2	2	1	2	3	1	19	
Paris	1	2	1	3	4	2	1	2	4	20	
Tokyo	2	3	2	4	3	3	4	1	2	24	
London	3	4	4	1	1	4	3	4	3	27	

Sources: Adapted from Mercer Human Resource Consulting 2007; EIU 2007; City of London 2007; Partnership for New York City 2006.

TABLE 1.14. RANKING OF NEW YORK, PARIS, LONDON, AND TOKYO: QUALITY-OF-LIFE ASSETS

City rank	Transportation	Demographic	Lifestyle	Safety/security	"People"*	Infrastructure*
1	New York (1 of 11)	New York (1 of 11)	Paris (1 of 11)	Tokyo (2 of 11)	London (1 of 10)	London (1 of 10)
2	Paris (2 of 11)	Tokyo (4 of 11)	New York (2 of 11)	Paris (3 of 11)	New York (1 of 10)	New York (2 of 10)
3	Tokyo (3 of 11)	London (5 of 11)	London (3 of 11)	New York (5 of 11)	Paris (below 10)	Tokyo (7 of 10)
4	London (4 of 11)	Paris (9 of 11)	Tokyo (8 of 11)	London (7 of 11)	Tokyo (below 10)	Paris (below 10)

*Indicates data from City of London 2008. "People" factors include 12 human condition indicators, including educational, psychological, and environmental measures. Infrastructure factors include nine indicators of office and work environment. Other data are from Partnership for New York City 2006. The scores are based on the following indicators: Transportation: registered taxis, underground track, airline carriers, passenger flows, and airport cargo. Demographic: population density, working-age population, and racial/ethnic diversity. Lifestyle assets: entertainment, recreational space, and hotel beds. Safety and Security: hospital beds, crime statistics, and personal safety and security.

assessments can be quite misleading because they discount differences in the asset mix found in particular cities. Each of our four cities really provides *different kinds* of urban living environments, not just better or worse ones.

Thus, even though the four cities share much in common as places to live, they also afford distinctive communal settings. It is possible to compare the overall quality of life of one city versus another, but as one looks closely this becomes a little like comparing apples and oranges. Paris, London, New York, and Tokyo offer different choices as places to live, not just better or worse alternatives. This rivals or even overshadows their differences in relative rank. Simple "better" or "worse" comparisons are misleading.

THE PUBLIC SECTOR AND QUALITY OF LIFE

Is quality of life in the city-regions linked to the caliber of public sector performance? The latter plays a key role in regulating housing quality, the purity of the air and water, providing education, ensuring security in the neighborhood and workplace, and providing many other assets that contribute to an environment of civic health and happiness. How do our cities measure up in public environmental quality? Do some cities add more than others? Are the cities that rank high overall in quality of life the same cities enjoying the highest levels of public sector quality?

These questions can be answered by looking at three aspects of public sector quality. One is the civic atmosphere and political system that pervades public life, particularly the extent to which free and democratic values are present. Second, the material resources allocated by governments, such as parks, public schools, transportation infrastructure, and other things must be considered because they add to overall quality of urban living. Finally, what local residents say about problems where they live gives a view "from the bottom" about the quality of government.

When we look at all three kinds of evidence, we again find far more similarities than differences among our cities. Turning first to the quality of civic life, the cities share much in common. By international standards, all four cities are in nations that have highly democratic political systems and rich civic environments. The most comprehensive assessment of this is the EIU's index of democracy (EIU 2006b). This index is based on the view that measures of democracy include not only the state of political freedoms and civil liberties but also four other factors that are believed to be essential to free and fair elections: the electoral process and pluralism, political participation, the functioning of government, and political culture. In its survey of 165 independent states and territories, the EIU's 2006 index places all of our cities in nations that compose the top 27 "Full Democracies." Rank order differences are minor; the United States, Japan, the United Kingdom, and France have positions 17, 20, 23, and 24, respectively (Sweden, Iceland, and the Netherlands hold the top three ranks). As our later chapters suggest, our cities conform to these national profiles. Political corruption is minor in each. Good government is widely expected and demanded. Law and order is the rule, although all four cities suffer from the insecurities of being prime terrorist targets of domestic as well as international groups because of their economic and political importance.

Examining governmental resources in Paris, New York, London, and Tokyo, we find greater differences, but even these differences must be placed in context. All are wealthy cities in regions that lead the world in public sector resources. Although comprehensive evaluation of the public sectors is not possible, surveying available scattered indicators that permit international comparison mainly reinforces this picture of high quality. Three of the four cities—New York, London, and Paris—are in nations that enjoy levels of educational spending on par with Scandinavian countries (the highest spending is in Denmark at 6.82 percent of gross domestic product [GDP]). Although New York City is much less tied to national governmental sources of revenue for local education compared to London or Paris, New York City is above the US average in school spending per capita. Japan spends considerably less per capita than the other three nations, yet this is counterbalanced by high private sector contributions. It manages very high academic achievement levels with less public financial contribution. All four cities have well-developed mass transit systems that add a great deal to quality of living in cities and regions that are relatively congested. With densely settled populations, traffic congestion is common. The average journey to work is above 30 minutes in all four city-regions and many commuters take much longer.

The cities are most different with respect to public transit, public open space, security, and economic regulation. Daily public transit use for commutation ranges from 47 percent in London, 49 percent in Paris, and 56 percent in New York to as high as 75 percent in Tokyo. The private auto share of commutation tends to inversely mirror public transit capacity, ranging from as much as 50 percent in Paris to as little as 6 percent in Tokyo. New York and London have a relative abundance of green space with nearly more than 26 square feet per capita, while Paris has 11.8 and Tokyo has the least—2.9 feet per capita. There are significant differences in crime rates among our cities. Tokyo's crime rate is lowest of all four cities for such things as murder and car theft. By contrast, New York has many homicides compared to all the other cities. London has relatively few murders but has the most thefts. Paris is more or less in the middle in these crime categories.

We see that no city achieves highest ranking in all areas of public activity. For example, Tokyo has the fewest parks but the safest streets. Traffic congestion is worse in London than in New York, but violent crime is rare in London. How do all these patterns of material resources add up? Table 1.15 summarizes and collates the city rankings with respect to basic qualitative measures of public sector life expressed in relative educational spending, crime rates, open space, transportation, and traffic congestion. Although this offers only the crudest synthesis, what emerges is that Tokyo and New York equally share the highest ranking in public environments, followed closely by Paris, and with London last.

TABLE 1.15. SYNTHESIS OF PUBLIC SECTOR QUALITY-OF-LIFE RANKING BY COMPONENT: PARIS, LONDON, NEW YORK, AND TOKYO

Overall city rank	Education spending	Crime: Violent deaths	Crime: Auto theft	Open space	Transpor- tation	Traffic	Total score
Tokyo	4	1	1	4	1	1	12
New York	2	4	2	1	2	2	13
Paris	1	2	2	3	3	3	14
London	3	3	2	2	4	4	18

Note: Scores are based on national educational spending per capita; murder/violent crimes and auto thefts per 1,000; open space per capita; share of commuters taking mass transit; and average commute time for respective cities.

Data sources for public sectors: Census 2000, Japan; Ministry of Environment, Japan; Metropolitan Transport Census, Japan 2000; Office of National Statistics, Labour Force Survey, UK; Greater London Authority, Transport for London 2004 and London Travel Report 2006, UK; Census 2001, UK; Metropolitan Transport Census, France; New York City Department of City Planning 2000, New York; Census 2000, US; Uniform Crime Statistics, FBI 2008.

TABLE 1.16. PUBLIC OPINION IN NEW YORK, PARIS, TOKYO, AND LONDON: THREE GREATEST PUBLIC CONCERNS

City	Cost of living	Cost of housing	Crime	Poverty	Unem- ployment	Traffic	Public health
New York 2006	X	X	X		X		
Paris 2005			X	X		X	
London 2006	X	X					
Tokyo 2007			X	X			X

Sources: Adapted from Greater London Authority 2007; *New York Times*/CBS News surveys; Tokyo Metropolitan Government 2007; Institut d'Aménagement et d'Urbanisme de la Région Île de France 2002, 2003, and 2005 surveys.

It is interesting that this ranking of public sectors differs considerably from the general quality-of-life rankings described earlier. What seems clear from this is that material investment by the public sectors does not drive overall living quality in our global cities. Because our cities all have huge private sectors, differences in public contributions are important but not determinative. For example, private schools help substitute for public ones and stable families can reduce the incidence of street crime. This does not suggest that public investments are unimportant, however. It suggests that our local governments face large obstacles in seeking to change overall living quality because so much is outside their control.

Finally, how citizens perceive their local public sectors is undoubtedly of great importance in evaluating their quality. Unfortunately, we do not have comparable direct evaluations of this in our cities. The best available indirect evidence comes from surveys that ask about the most important public concerns shared by citizens. Since the four different city surveys asked about things that mattered most to citizens in very different ways in each city during 2005, 2006, or 2007, there is only rough comparability of responses. Nevertheless, there are some interesting patterns describing the public concerns or problems that matter to residents. Table 1.16 shows that the three greatest concerns expressed most frequently in the four cities were about matters of economic security, especially the cost of housing and living or about employment difficulties. Economic security issues were considered the most important concerns in New York, London, and Paris; it was also of importance in Tokyo. Crime is also of high concern in three of the four cities, including Tokyo, where crime rates are low.

This pattern falls very much in line with our earlier finding about the general quality of life in the cities. They are attractive but high-cost places where citizens are absorbed in economic challenges. That economic difficulties dominate public concerns even in four of the world's most potent economies suggests relative prosperity alone does not diminish the importance of pocketbook issues. Economic development and its insecurities remain most important to citizens despite their living in communities awash in wealth and growth at the top of the international marketplace. This impression is reinforced by a European Union quality-of-life survey of citizens in 2007. In this survey, 95 percent of Londoners and 85 percent of Parisians disagreed with the statement, "It is easy to find good housing at a reasonable price." Only 50 percent or fewer of the respondents in both cities agreed that "it is easy to find a good job" (European Commission 2007, 6).

CONVERGENCE AND DIVERGENCE IN QUALITY OF LIFE

Convergence strongly marks quality of living in Paris, London, Tokyo, and New York. None is considered among the most livable communities in international rankings. They are prosperous, sprawling, and crowded metropolitan areas embedded in four of the world's most successful democracies. Thus, their governments struggle to manage many of the same quality-of-life burdens, especially high living costs, economic insecurity, and other everyday discomforts, such as traffic congestion and fear of crime. These are ills that come with residing in crowded, busy, and successful urban places.

Our cities also display important differences in their relative quality of life. They are accorded different places in international rankings although they are not distant. The quality of their public sectors varies due to differences in governmental performance in certain areas of public policy. Yet no one city can lay claim to the highest achievement in all or even most of the areas that contribute to having a high quality of life. Some cities can claim a lead in enjoying certain assets, such as low crime rates or excellent transportation systems, but they are lacking in other assets compared to their sister cities. This applies not only to each city's overall living quality but also to the quality of its public environment.

Thus, in the competition for livability, the four cities offer different mixes of amenities and disadvantages, affording *lifestyle choices* that are particular to London, Paris, Tokyo, or New York. Nevertheless, these differences in lifestyle do not add up cumulatively to large differences in *living quality* to make any one of them clearly superior.

The GCR as a Social Phenomenon

Looking at the Paris, Tokyo, London, and New York regions with respect to population, economic development, social stresses, and life quality, they share much in common. As urban command posts in the global system, all attract population into metropolitan areas growing in wealth. Their world-class prowess is sustained by high global connectivity and similar kinds of modernizing changes in their mix of people and businesses. Their success also has precipitated many similar problems, particularly difficulties accommodating social diversity, and persistent income and spatial inequalities among resident populations. Finally, they struggle to sustain a high quality-of-life environment because GCRs share deficiencies that are not common in many other cities and regions in the world.

This profile of socioeconomic convergence compels thinking about them as identifiably singular urban phenomena: They have forged special networks in the global order and are undergoing similar kinds of economic and social transformation. This allows us to compare and examine them in the following chapters in order to learn how these global giants are acting politically in managing their opportunities and social stresses.

At the same time, their patterns of social and economic development differ in important ways. They differ significantly in their pace and scope of economic restructuring, their evolving demographic composition, their changing income distribution, their social polarization, and their differences in quality of life. This makes them rather unique as places to live or work. These variations confer on each GCR many unique qualities as urban centers. It means each GCR competes to prosper not only as a world economic giant but also as an urban community having distinctive social assets and liabilities. How do their governments manage these dual realities? Do they follow similar political agendas and approaches to governance in addressing their problems? To what extent are they able to pursue alternative political pathways as GCRs? The following chapters examine this.

PART I   *The Greater London Region*

2. *Global Pressures and Governmental Innovation*

LONDON HAS BEEN a world city since the Middle Ages. That is to say, it has had links with the rest of the world and these international links have underpinned its economy. However, the nature of this economy has changed. In the early days, it was based on trade; ships were moored along the Thames after journeys to Europe and, later, Asia and America. Through conquest, this world orientation developed into the British Empire, with dominions spread across the globe in, for example, India, Malaysia, Australia, the West Indies, and Canada (e.g., King 1990). This empire brought not only an exchange of goods but also a migration of people in both directions. Although these colonies eventually obtained their independence, the historic linkages, including migration, continued to play an important role in London's global position. Meanwhile, London also developed an important national role as the location of central government and a major manufacturing and service center, partly oriented to the increasing population of the London region.

This dual role as both the international and the national focus of the country means that the London city-region contains a very dominant proportion of the national population and economic activity. The whole country depends upon the economic viability of this region, particularly under the conditions of economic globalization over the last twenty years. How to foster the potential of this economic reality while satisfying the political demands from national politicians, who mostly represent constituencies in the rest of the country, has been a difficult issue not only since the 1980s but throughout history. This has meant that the government of the region has been continually debated and has taken on special forms (Davis 1988; Rhodes 1970; Robson 1948; Travers 2004). As Britain has a highly centralized political system, such debates and reforms have been strongly influenced by the political ideology of central government. In this chapter, we will set out the main issues concerning the governance of the London city-region over the last twenty-five years. As we shall see, this has been a period of considerable institutional change, moving from an ideologically led laissez-faire approach to one of strong political leadership. However, first we will outline the key challenges that the region has had to face over the period.

Issues and Challenges Facing the Region

As we have noted, the London region has been the most prosperous in Britain. This brings with it the pressures of growth and environmental challenges. However, at the same time the picture is not one of universal health. Beneath this overall trend, there are two important issues. First, there has been significant economic turbulence over the period and, even more importantly, the benefits of growth have not spread evenly. There is extreme social polarization; the region contains in its metropolitan core many of the poorest neighborhoods in the whole of Britain. The three challenges of sustaining a strong economy, improving the environment, and ensuring social inclusivity have been the basis of all the London plans that will be discussed in the next chapter.

As Figure 2.1 shows, London's economy during the period has experienced a number of downturns and hence economic challenges. London's employment rate fell constantly during the recession of the 1970s, but this was reversed in the early 1980s on the back of service sector growth. The deregulation of the London financial market in 1986 (known as the big bang) was a significant contributor to subsequent growth. However, another recession occurred in the early 1990s, although this was short-lived. Since then, the globally oriented service sector has led a period of dramatic growth. This was then halted by the financial crisis of 2008. Two challenges result from this picture: the pressure on the region from the overall growth during our period and the impact of economic volatility and restructuring.

GROWTH PRESSURES

Overall, both the London metropolitan area and the Greater South East grew significantly in population and employment in the period since 1980. This created competition for land use and problems of "overheating" in parts of the region. Issues included transport congestion and lack of sufficient space for development, particularly new housing. The problem of coping with this pressure for expansion has been compounded by the desire to retain a good-quality environment and guard against the impact of growth on climate change. In the period after the Second World War, central government designated large parts of the region for environmental protection, for example, the North and South Downs Areas of Outstanding Natural Beauty. In fact, this period could be said to be a high point of regional thinking directed by central government. Abercrombie was commissioned to prepare his Greater London Plan, which included a green belt around the city to prevent sprawl and the transfer of people from the congested city core to a series of new towns throughout the region. Many of these new towns were built, and in 1955 the national government also passed green belt legislation that prevented any new development within a band of about eight miles around metropolitan London. This policy has been strongly enforced ever since and, along with the other environmental protection areas, has limited the land available

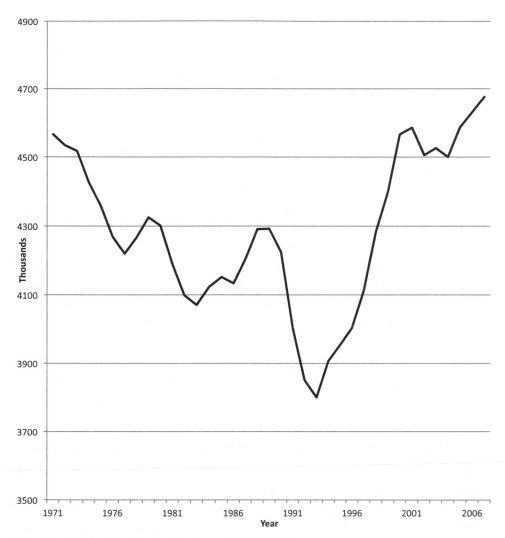

Figure 2.1. Metropolitan London Employment, 1971–2007

for satisfying growth pressures, particularly in the more attractive parts of the region, where private house builders prefer to operate.

However, the patterns of regional change have not been constant over time. As we have noted, in the postwar period there was a decentralization process taking place, whereby population and jobs were moving out of London, especially into the surrounding region. It was felt necessary to reduce the density of housing in London to improve living conditions and also to relocate industry outside of the capital—because of both congestion problems and fears of the vulnerability of concentration that had been brought home during the war. Manufacturing firms preferred greenfield sites, and government policies were to encourage this with incentives to move to other regions of the country and the new towns (during the 1960s, there were even attempts to restrict new office development in London). Thus, throughout the 1960s and 1970s, the metropolitan area of London was rapidly losing population and jobs. By the 1980s, most manufacturing jobs had left this part of the region and the city's historic port functions had moved downstream. From the 1980s onward, any remaining manufacturing jobs also declined—this time as a result of the pressures of globalization. The last two car factories in the region closed in 2002. One of the major challenges for the London region has therefore been to cope with this economic restructuring.

A change in the direction of regional policy took place from the 1980s onward with the encouragement of growth in both London and the South East. At the beginning of the period, a market-oriented ideology prevailed, which encouraged the natural growth potential of the region. From the mid-1990s onward, it was the threat of globalization and competition from other cities that continued the focus on the London region as the nation's best performer. During the 1980s, growth took place in the areas most favored by business and led to considerable growth in areas such as the west of the region around Reading and Heathrow airport. As a result, the challenge of dealing with overheating in certain areas increased while in others, such as the eastern part of the region, neglect was the issue. As we shall see in the next chapter, by the 1990s the difficulties of finding further growth areas in the more desired parts of the region led to policies encouraging more development in the neglected areas of the region and also to increased employment and population densities within the metropolitan area.

There has been a particularly strong surge in the economic growth of London in recent years. This growth has been in services, with the leading sector being "other business services," which include professional services such as law, accountancy, marketing, consulting, and computing. In contrast with popular conception, employment in finance remained fairly static (see Figure 2.2). Other growth sectors were tourism, media, and cultural industries. This structural shift reflected the growing world city role of London; by the 1990s, London was ticking all the boxes listed in the literature that defined a world city (e.g., Friedmann 1986; Sassen 1991, 2001). This economic role also created a policy challenge. It was now widely felt that London was facing competition from other global cities and needed support. It was also realized that although the economy of the city was doing well, the infrastructure to back this up needed urgent attention. Transport provision was suffering from neglect and there was a need to ensure that sufficient housing, skills, and good environments were provided. The economic and population growth meant that the interconnections across the region increased with greater flows of commuters, expansion of airports, and stronger economic linkages across the region (Hall and Pain 2006; Pain 2008). The pattern of sectoral employment change we have described for the metropolitan area of Greater London was replicated in the wider region of the South East. Thus, economic and population growth have been seen as necessary in the face of intercity competition, but this has put pressure on other aspects of the urban and regional system.

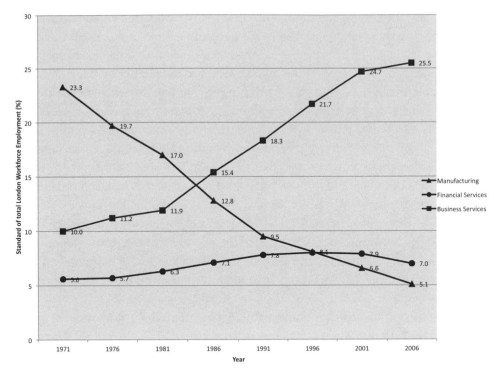

Figure 2.2. London Workforce Employment by Sector

THE FINANCIAL CRISIS OF 2008

The latest economic challenge for London has been the impact of the financial crisis and economic recession since 2008. There are a number of dimensions to this. There is the effect on particular economic sectors, especially finance. There is the impact on house building and other developments as a result of the lack of financial investment. There is the fall in consumer spending. Finally, there is the impact on the city budget. We will look at these in turn.

London as a center of international finance was clearly badly affected by the crisis. There was a fall in jobs in the finance sector (about 6 percent between 2008 and 2009) and a lowering of income levels for highly paid bankers. This meant there was less money around to be spent on top-level leisure and consumer activities. However, the position has proven more robust than first predicted. Many employees in the sector moved jobs as companies reshuffled (e.g., Nomura taking over Lehman's London office). As we have seen, in London there are far more jobs in the business services sector than in finance, and this sector may be more robust as lawyers, accountants, or consultants remain in demand. Many retailers have felt the impact of a drop in consumer spending and some well-known High Street names such as Woolworths have disappeared. However, again the picture is uneven; for example, the major Westfield London shopping mall opened the week of the 2008 crash and has been thriving. Between

2008 and 2009, the retail sector expanded employment by nearly 4 percent, partly because of the weakness of sterling against the euro and an increase in European tourists. However, a fall in tourists from the United States meant that the tourist sector as a whole remained fairly static. The economic sector in the United Kingdom that was most affected by the recession was manufacturing, and so it is cities in the United Kingdom that are dependent on manufacturing (e.g., cars) that have been worst hit. London has a very small proportion of workers in this most vulnerable sector. In turning to construction, we find that many development projects in the region were put on hold—for example, much of the Thames Gateway housing development. House prices fell in London by 15 percent between 2008 and 2009, although still costing 150 percent above the national average. However, some projects that had already secured their finance were able to proceed. The Olympic development continued on schedule, although central government finance had to replace some of the private funding for the athletes' village. Central government has stressed its support of the games and the major Cross Rail project and has pointed to the value of having such projects in a period of economic recession.

The impact of the crisis on municipal budgets in London and in the rest of the United Kingdom took a while to work through the system. Cities do not raise tax from local business and hence are not affected by bankruptcies. Business and income taxes are centrally collected and redistributed by central government to cities, so there is no immediate crisis in the city budget. The lag in the impact of the crisis on the public sector meant that there was continued growth in the numbers working in this sector from 2008 to 2009. However, the change in national government in 2010 led to a major program of public sector cuts, and these are expected to have a major impact on public sector jobs and local government finance from 2011.

Overall, the view of most economic forecasters has been that the London economy would recover after a couple of years (see GLA Economics 2009 for a review; Gordon et al. 2009). According to GLA Economics, London's gross value added was expected to fall by 3.5 percent in 2009 and then remain negative until 2011 when it would rise by 1.5 percent. There is evidence that the construction sector is picking up again. However, it was thought that it would take a few years longer for the unemployment situation to improve. A similar picture was presented for the broader South East region, although the high-tech area around Cambridge was expected to recover faster than elsewhere (Insight East 2009).

SOCIAL INEQUALITY

From the 1980s onward, one of the major concerns over British urban governance, both in academia and in practice, has been to find ways to balance the twin goals of economic competitiveness and social cohesion. In the 1980s, and again in 2011, the country experienced major urban riots led by severe disturbances in London. These demonstrated high levels of social polarization and alienation. This issue is of particular concern in the London region, where polarization is at the highest level in the United Kingdom. Within the metropolitan area, there are communities that are among the most deprived in Britain and some that are among the richest in the world. This social disparity is therefore one of the major issues both within London and, to a lesser extent, across the region. Since the Second World War, there has been inward migration into London, particularly from various parts of the old British Empire (see chapter 1). Such migrants form a substantial proportion of the population in many parts of metropolitan London, and many of these areas are also the poorest.

This huge social polarization tends also to be linked to spatial polarization. This is particularly noticeable when one compares the data on different boroughs within London (e.g., Hackney or Tower Hamlets on the one hand and Richmond or Kensington on the other). This spatial contrast is also evident at the broader regional level, with more poverty in the east. There are also pockets of poverty on the fringes of the region, particularly in seaside towns. By contrast, many of the highly paid workers, for example, in the business services industry, live in villages in the environmentally attractive parts of the region and commute into the city. There is therefore a broad ring of wealthier areas around the outer edge of the metropolitan area spreading out through the green belt into the more environmentally attractive parts of the region. On the other hand, over the last ten years or so there has been an increase in wealthier people wanting to live more centrally and an escalation of the gentrification process in some inner neighborhoods. The pattern of social and spatial polarization has not changed significantly over the period of our study.

The System of Governance in the City-Region

THE NATIONAL SYSTEM: A UNITARY STATE

The British system of government is a unitary state comprising two main levels: central government and local government. In contrast with many countries, these two parts of the system are very separate and do not overlap. For example, they have their own career structures for officers, and politicians rarely move between the levels. It has been described as a dual system or dual polity (Bulpitt 1989; Leemans 1970). Central government sets out the legal framework for local government, formulates policy, and allocates finance. It supervises local governments who act as agents of central government, implementing the policies and ensuring the delivery of services (Stoker 1991).

Since the Second World War, this arrangement has been used to deliver social policies under the welfare state. This built upon the famous Beveridge Report of 1942, which identified the five giant evils of society as squalor, ignorance, want, idleness, and disease. National programs for education, health, employment, old age, and social security were put in place. This was based upon the principle of universal provision modified according to need. This remains the underlying framework, although it has been much modified and eroded, especially because of the increasing costs of the system. The 1980s, under Mrs. Thatcher, witnessed the erosion of many policies and the privatization of some provisions. Another diminution of the system is taking place under the new national government of 2010. However, national government remains the most important actor in the formulation and financing of social policies. For example, until 2000, it was national ministries with their national programs that dealt with the concentrations of urban poverty in cities, including London.

It is also important to understand how this relationship between national and local government works in relation to finance, as this differs from many other countries. Income tax and business tax are collected by national government and grants are made to local authorities on the principle of equalization of need. A complex formula is used to distribute the money, and this is done under specific headings. Local authorities must spend within these headings. These grants make up about 75 percent of the resources for local authorities in providing their services. The other 25 percent is raised by a local property tax. However, central government also controls this latter process and can cap the amount raised and the way it is spent. Because business tax goes to central government, there is no fiscal incentive for local authorities to promote development, although there is of course a political benefit in presiding over a thriving city with good employment prospects. These financial arrangements demonstrate the high degree of central government control. National government can use this control to switch resources between cities and regions and help to overcome the problems of uneven development and concentrations of poverty. These two levels of central and local government are the backbone of the system, but at various times some intermediate level of government has been attempted. These regional arrangements are constantly being reformed but in most cases do not have a great deal of independent power.

THE STRUCTURE OF LOCAL GOVERNMENT IN LONDON

How do these arrangements of government work in the London city-region? The Greater South East contains hundreds of local authorities including, within the metropolitan area, thirty-two London boroughs and the city corporation. There is also a higher-level local authority called a county, and the region is divided into fifteen of these. They have a limited number of responsibilities, principally to do with strategic policy such as transport and the environment. However, over the years these counties have lost importance as some large town local authorities have taken over the county functions for their areas and, in recent years, regional bodies have also made inroads into their functions. This pattern of local authorities has been overlaid with attempts at more strategic governance for both the Greater South East and the metropolitan area of Greater London. Before we look at these initiatives, we need to say a word about the city corporation, which is a kind of local authority but with a special status and power.

The City Corporation runs the area called the City of London. This area, sometimes called the square mile, is a small area that lies at the center of the city and is almost coterminous with the central business district (CBD), the area of finance and business offices. It generally operates as a local authority, like the others at the lower level of the hierarchy. However, it has special features and influence that derive from its past. In medieval times, London was governed in a dual fashion. On the one hand, there were the king, court, and later, Parliament, based in Westminster, and on the other, the City Corporation, a group of businessmen that controlled trade and economic activity through a system of guilds, based in its guildhall headquarters in the city. Despite constant attempts to reform the City Corporation, it retains many of its medieval privileges, such as its own police force and ceremonial mayor of London. The election of members to the City Corporation is still not based upon the votes of residents, as everywhere else, but by business representation. As the City of London is the location for most of the activities that form the basis of London's world city role, it can be seen that the business sector, in the form of the City of London Corporation, still has considerable power today. The relationship between the business sector and the elected government will be a feature running through this chapter and the next.

Throughout the period, there has been a search for a regional level of government but, as we will see, this level has not developed very far and regional government has been a weak, sometimes almost invisible, element. We will find that policy at this scale is largely national government terrain. However, for the metropolitan area at the core of the region there have been extensive policies and much debate and media attention. London dominates the nation and the South East region in both population and economic activity. The arrangements for London government have therefore always been special and do not find an equivalent anywhere else. The Greater London governmental arrangements have been a hybrid between a regional authority and a city council (Travers 2004). After a region-wide discussion, we will explore the government of this metropolitan area.

We need to divide this story of metropolitan government into three parts, each representing very contrasting approaches. At the beginning of the 1980s, London was governed at the metropolitan level by the Greater London Council (GLC), with thirty-two boroughs and the City of London at the lower level. In 1986 the GLC was abolished and until 2000 London had no metropolitan-level government. We need to explore why the GLC was abolished and how the city managed without any strategic-level government during this second period. The third period started in 2000, when an authority for the metropolitan area was reestablished called the Greater London Authority (GLA). What were the pressures that led to this? How did it differ from the GLC? One of the new features of the GLA was a directly elected mayor. The first mayor was Ken Livingstone, who served two terms before being replaced by Boris Johnston in 2008. In the next chapter, we will explore the strategic policies that emanated from these different governmental structures. We will also examine how much difference the change of mayor made to the direction of policy.

IS THERE A REGIONAL LEVEL OF GOVERNMENT?

The governance of the Greater South East region is very disjointed and receives very little public or media attention, except when there is a particularly controversial project in the region. However, many activities in this broader region are essential to London's world city role, such as airports and seaports, centers of research and development, and pleasant homes for the high-income professionals who work in finance and business services. As we have already noted, this broader region is the real functional region, encompassing the journey-to-work patterns of commuters and the full interlocking regional economy. However, there has never been a single political or administrative entity covering this area, and there is never likely to be as it would be too dominant within the national picture (it produces about 40 percent of the country's gross domestic product [GDP]). During the last twenty years, there have been some attempts to coordinate the fragmented situation of hundreds of local authorities to generate a more regional approach. However, these attempts have been weak and the agencies formed have only had an advisory role. It is central government that has the power and responsibility both to make any strategic policy for the whole region and also to make decisions on the key infrastructure projects.

In 1962 the Standing Conference on South East Regional Planning (SERPLAN) was established. The aim of this body was to take a regional perspective, and it comprised representatives from the local authorities in the region. It produced numerous reports and planning ideas for the South East, but it was only an advisory body. Central government produced official regional guidance every five years or so (e.g., in 1994 and in 2001), and this provided the broad-brush policy framework that local authorities had to follow. This guidance included the allocation of housing targets to the various local authorities of the region based upon regional population projections. Since 1994, central government has established regional offices to coordinate the work of the 11 central government ministries with interests at the regional level and act as a focus to liaise with local government.

After the Labour Party's arrival in government in 1997, a greater interest was shown in regional development and regional institutions. Across the country, regional development agencies were set up with responsibility for economic development and regeneration. One of the reasons for this was to integrate better into the EU's regional development framework and grants, and to promote the regions in the context of global economic competition. In England, these agencies have no directly elected element and are answerable to central government. The Greater South East was divided into three parts, each with its own regional development agency. First, there was the London Development Agency (LDA) for the metropolitan area, which was put under the GLA umbrella when this was established in 2000 and thus made answerable to the mayor. The rest of the Greater South East was divided into two agencies—South East England Development Agency (SEEDA) and East England Development Agency (EEDA). Central government appointed the boards of these agencies, which were chaired and led by business representatives. Other board members came from local government, the voluntary sector, and trade unions. The board appointed a chief executive and the agency prepared a regional economic strategy. This was subject to consultation and was formally approved by central government, or the mayor in the case of the LDA. This strategy then provided a framework for the policies of local government and an influence on regional actors and central government (e.g., over funding priorities). The work of these agencies was scrutinized by regional assemblies, two-thirds of which were to be appointed by local government and one-third by other regional interest groups (in the case of the LDA, the scrutiny would be by the directly elected London Assembly).

From 2004, spatial strategic planning, previously conducted at the local authority county level and by central government through regional planning guidance, was abolished and replaced by regional spatial strategies under the regional assemblies. However, this picture was changed again in 2007 with the idea of a single regional strategy (spatial and economic) produced by the RDAs, with scrutiny from a smaller regional leaders forum. This arrangement was due to take effect from 2010, but the arrival of a new national government in that year brought yet further changes. The new government has abolished regional agencies altogether and the new mayor of London is disbanding the LDA. The division of the Greater South East region into three regional development agencies and the constant change and complexity of the administrative arrangements have created a confusion of agencies, making regional policy coordination difficult. It could be argued that, as a result, it has only been central government that has been able to look at the overall regional picture. The development agencies produced considerable documentation on the economic potential and deprivation issues in their areas and policy statements with priorities similar to the earlier central government regional guidance documents (these policies will be discussed in the next chapter). Meanwhile, SERPLAN was abolished in 2001.

Thus, the governance of the Greater South East region can be seen as one conducted by hundreds of local authorities carrying out their statutory local duties, with strategic decisions made by national government. These strategic decisions focused on major infrastructure projects, environmental protection, and the identification of broad locations for population expansion. Central government has made these decisions within a regional strategy that they also prepared but that did not go into much detail. In doing this, they were advised until 2001 by SERPLAN, a consortium of local authorities, and then by the regional development agencies until 2010. However, another major actor needs to be brought into the picture. This is the government of the metropolitan area of London, which sits at the center of the region. This metropolitan area contains seven million people—about half the population of the Greater South East. The metropolitan area is therefore a key element in the regional picture. However, there has not been much interaction between the governance of the outer region that we have been discussing and this metropolitan area at the center. The story of the governance of metropolitan London therefore stands almost in isolation from the broader regional picture. It is to this story we now turn—a story that has many twists and turns and that has been exposed to considerable media and public attention.

THE ABOLITION OF LONDON'S METROPOLITAN GOVERNMENT

The GLC was established in 1965 following considerable discussion and commissions of inquiry. This reform was led by experts of public administration trying to find a solution to the fragmentation of London governance and the geographical expansion of the city population. The government of the time eventually adopted the idea of a two-tier approach, with the metropolitan scale covering all the area within the green belt and the lower tier comprising the thirty-two boroughs and the City of London Corporation. The lower tier was responsible for day-to-day services, including housing and social services, leaving the upper tier with restricted responsibilities of a strategic nature, principally transport and planning. Most of the GLC's early life was spent on protracted road discussions and the slow production of the strategic land-use "Greater London Development Plan" (Hebbert 1998; Travers 2004).

However, from 1981 a more political approach was adopted, under the direction of the GLC Labour Party leader, Ken Livingstone. Central government elections in 1979 had been won by the Conservative Party with its laissez-faire ideology, under the leadership of Mrs. Thatcher. The GLC under Livingstone aimed primarily to provide a challenge to Mrs. Thatcher's approach and adopted a New Left antigovernment rhetoric. Policies included cutting public transport fares, support for minority groups, and advocating alternative economic strategies. These policies were popular with most Londoners; however, they enraged Mrs. Thatcher. One of her well-known slogans for those who doubted her ideology was that "there is no alternative," and yet here at the GLC (and also in some other of the country's metropolitan cities), an alternative was gaining a lot of publicity and support. Her reaction was dramatic. She abolished all metropolitan-level governments, including the GLC. Thus, from 1986 the capital city of the country was left without any overall government.

The removal of this tier of government fit into the political ideology of the period, which stressed minimal intervention and market freedom (Thornley 1993). Some saw this as a welcome move that led to the strengthening of the lower-tier boroughs (Hebbert 1992) or an opportunity for spontaneous innovation through the creation of more action-oriented, and financially efficient, ad hoc bodies. However, the new arrangement lacked a coordinated strategic perspective and this was to prove a problem over the years that followed. The powers of the old GLC were reallocated to central government, the lower tier of the London boroughs, or to some kind of joint body. The London Planning Advisory Committee (LPAC), made up of representatives from the boroughs, prepared strategic planning reports, but it was only an advisory body. This committee presented its ideas to central government, which now prepared the statutory strategic planning guidance for the city. In tune with the noninterventionist ideology of the period, the first guidance in 1989 was only a few pages long and simply set out the main parameters within which the local authorities should operate. Thus, as a result of the ideology of nonintervention and institutional fragmentation, very little strategic planning took place in the years following the abolition of the GLC.

It was during this period of minimal London government that one of London's biggest development opportunities arose. London's docklands had moved downriver as a result of the greater space needs of containerization and larger ships. Throughout the 1970s, attempts were made to organize the development of this vast area involving the GLC, the Port of London Authority, and the local boroughs. This was a difficult job because of the nature of the land, with considerable areas of water and poor land access; the different objectives of the various authorities; and a vociferous opposition from the local community. Not much progress had been made by the time the Thatcher government decided to speed up the development process with the formation of the London Docklands Development Corporation in 1981. This body was run by a board appointed by central government and dominated by business leaders. It had powers of land acquisition and substantial grants from central government for preparing the land for development and took over the role of granting planning permissions from the local boroughs. Its approach was to try to attract developers to the area by subsidizing their land costs and allowing them to develop in the way they wanted without planning constraints.

The London Docklands Development Corporation only attracted small-scale developments until the proposals for Canary Wharf appeared in 1985. The eventual developers, Olympia and York, had a grand scheme with several high-rise office blocks. These global developers saw their development as an alternative to the traditional office location of the City of London, providing the modern space needs for global financial operators. In other words, it was a location for the command-and-control functions of the globalized economy. The first stage of the development was built, but its progress was hindered by lack of appropriate transport links. In line with the Thatcherist ideology of minimal intervention, the government did not want to subsidize the transport provision and looked to the private sector to finance it. They required Olympia and York to provide a substantial contribution to the costs of the underground link that was needed for the next stages of the project. However, a slump in the development market left Olympia and York bankrupt and the underground projects stalled. It was another decade, after an alternative financial package had been organized and the underground built, that the Canary Wharf development was able to move forward again. The traditional location for such world city functions had been the City of London, and the City Corporation saw Canary Wharf as a potential threat. It therefore revised the land use plan for its own area to allow increased densities and reduced the constraints imposed by heritage policies.

GLOBALIZATION AND THE PRESSURES FOR FURTHER GOVERNMENTAL REFORM

It was not long before problems started to arise with this minimalist approach to London's government. Increasing concern was expressed at the lack of overall vision, the inability to coordinate transport and development as in Canary Wharf, and poor city leadership (Newman and Thornley 1997). From the late 1980s onward, pressure was developing for yet another reform to London's government. The establishment of the GLC had been largely a technocratic reform searching for greater administrative efficiency, while its abolition had been a politically motivated action based upon ideology. The institutional changes during the 1990s can be said to have been the first to respond to the pressures of economic globalization and intercity competition. It will also be seen that the private sector played a significant role in pushing these institutional changes forward. These pressures of globalization can also be said to have dominated the policy agenda ever since and, as we will see in the next chapter, the private sector had an important role in the formulation of this agenda.

During the period when London had no overall government, the City Corporation was active in commissioning reports and funding promotional bodies that were concerned with the competitiveness of London. Studies were undertaken on London as a world city and these concluded that London was at a disadvantage in not having a single voice to promote the city (e.g., Llewelyn-Davies 1996). By the early 1990s, central government had also accepted the view that more needed to be done to enhance London's competitive position and counteract its fragmented institutional structure. In 1992 central government set up the London Forum to promote the capital.

However, the business sector had also been mobilizing. Traditionally, business in London had been organized under two main umbrella bodies: the London branch of the Confederation of British Industry, which represented the manufacturing industry but was becoming more broadly based, and the London Chamber of Commerce and Industry, with a tradition of representing retail and small traders. In 1992 a new body was set up called London First, with the aim to "engage the business community in promoting and improving London, using the vision, energy, and skills of business leaders to shape and secure the capital's future" (http://www.london-first.co.uk). It is interesting to note that the principal sponsors of this new body were companies that could be described as linked to the new global economy—for example, British Airways, the Airport Authority, British Telecommunications, the internationally oriented business service and financial firms, and international developers involved in the biggest development projects in the capital (for details, see Thornley et al. 2005). In 1993 the government merged its London Forum into London First. This pattern of private sector leadership combined with central government backing dominated strategic thinking in London over the next five years.

To fill the vacuum in political leadership and overcome fragmentation, central government itself was becoming more and more involved in strategic planning for the city. It wished to keep its control over "the UK's number one asset" (Gummer 1996).

It established a minister for London, a cabinet subcommittee for the capital and a government office for London with representation from the different ministries with interests in London policy and produced new enhanced strategic planning guidance for London. The period can therefore be seen as an interplay between institutional fragmentation and an increase in the perceived need for strategic leadership result-ing in greater central government involvement (Newman and Thornley 1997). How-ever, notwithstanding these efforts by central government, one of the features of this period was the proliferation of more and more organizations with complex interrela-tionships. These lacked any clear channels of accountability and created a confused network that made it difficult to identify who was responsible for decisions. The net effect was that during this period the strategic policy vacuum was filled not by a gov-ernment for London but by central government, heavily influenced by representatives of the business sector and with little local accountability.

So by the time that Blair's Labour Party was elected to national government in 1997, London offered a complex pattern of governance. In response to demands from within the Labour Party and supported by the London newspaper, the *London Evening Stan-dard,* the Labour government proposed a new experiment in British government—a directly elected London-wide mayor. The *Standard*'s regular polling put the issues of coordination and the lack of a democratic voice for Londoners at the top of its readers' concerns. The mayor would run a new metropolitan authority, to be called the GLA, covering the same area as the GLC. There was some discussion among academics that the authority should be larger and represent the true functional urban region. How-ever, politicians were not prepared to consider this as it would have taken too long to put together legally and would not have been possible to put into effect within the first four-year term of the new Labour government.

THE NEW GLA WITH AN ELECTED MAYOR

The new Labour national government of 1997 pledged itself to increase transparency in government, to tackle the issues of the proliferation of unaccountable ad hoc bod-ies, and to devolve governmental power. They also indicated that they would give greater emphasis to issues such as social exclusion and environmental sustainabil-ity. Policy coordination, or "joined-up policy thinking," was also a priority. These con-cerns were translated into the plans for the new London government set out in the Greater London Act of 1999 (Travers 2004). The approach sought greater accountabil-ity and wider social inclusion although, as we shall see, business interests continued to obtain privileged access to the agenda-setting process within the rhetoric of broader participation (Thornley et al. 2005).

In setting up the new arrangements with an elected mayor, the government had to decide on the relative strength between the mayor and the other elected rep-resentatives. They explored the variants that exist across the world and went for a "strong mayor" model. The mayor was given strong executive powers while the other

25 elected representatives who formed the London assembly were allocated only a scrutiny and checking role. It was hoped that the strong mayor would overcome the problem of lack of political leadership in the capital and that the electoral and scrutiny processes would introduce greater transparency and accountability into strategic decision making.

One of the major features of the new model was that it was a streamlined authority. The mayor was to have a few hundred staff, compared to the thousands employed by the GLC. The mayor formulates London-wide strategies, proposes a budget, coordinates all the different partners, and makes appointments to four functional bodies—police, transport, and fire and emergency services plus the London Development Agency (with an economic promotion and urban regeneration function). The mayor also has to produce an annual progress report followed by a State of London debate and face a twice-yearly People's Question Time. The act also specifies that the mayor should prepare eight strategies covering economic development, transport, biodiversity, noise, waste management, air quality, culture, and spatial development. This last strategy, the spatial development strategy (SDS), subsequently called the London Plan, is a strategic land use plan that is required to draw together and coordinate all other strategies. It is also the only one to have statutory, or quasi-legal, status. There are strict procedures that have to be adopted in its formulation, including public involvement through an examination in public, and once adopted it has to be followed by the second-tier boroughs in the production of their own plans and granting of planning permissions. As this particular strategy has a higher status, and incorporates the policies of the other strategies, it will be the focus of our attention when we explore the mayor's policy response in the next chapter.

While the mayor has a strong list of executive powers, it is very important to note that his or her financial autonomy is highly restricted. The GLA's independent resources are limited to a very small amount of local tax income coming from a precept on the boroughs—less than 15 percent of its gross income (Travers 2004). Money can also be raised from congestion charging—this policy will be discussed later. Central government allocates the rest of the finance and in doing so maintains considerable control. The mayor, for example, cannot switch funds between the different functional bodies. This power of central government means that there is considerable tension in the relationship between central government and the mayor. While the mayor is strong within the organization of the GLA and has a high public profile, he or she is weak in relation to central government. The mayor also has to deal with the second-tier authorities, the boroughs, which have considerable powers over day-to-day services. With limited independent finance, powers, and staff, the mayor often has to rely on influence, persuasion, and the support of partners. The powers of the London mayor are very limited when compared with many big city mayors across the world. For example, the mayor lacks the comprehensive powers and large staff of the mayor of Paris or the substantial budget of the mayor of New York.

There is another feature that needs to be noted concerning the new authority—that is, the directly elected process for selecting the mayor. This gives the post considerable visibility and, once elected, the mayor can trade on this mandate—an electorate that is far greater than any national member of Parliament. Candidates can be put forward by political parties or stand as independents. Business interests do not generally get involved in the electoral process, although the media can have an influence. The first election in 2000 proved very controversial and had considerable relevance in understanding the first period of the GLA's life. The election was won by Ken Livingstone, who we have noted was the radical leader of the last GLC administration in the 1980s. The national government put numerous obstacles in Livingstone's way and manipulated the process so that he did not gain the Labour Party nomination. The prime minister, Tony Blair, said that Livingstone as mayor would be a disaster for London. He did not relish the idea of Livingston using the very visible base of the London mayor to challenge his national government in the way he had so successfully challenged Mrs. Thatcher.

However, Livingstone won as an independent, beating the official Labour Party candidate. The main point for our analysis here is that this first elected mayor had no political links with central government and was free to act independently. For example, he mounted a vociferous campaign against the central government plans for privately financing the underground. After a period of some antagonism, Livingstone eventually lost this debate, although he had the support of most academics and citizens. This battle illustrates the tense relationship that existed between the mayor and central government at this time. This was to change as Livingstone proved successful, popular and less radical than feared. By the second election in 2004, he was welcomed back into the Labour Party.

A review of the GLA powers began in 2005, culminating in the Greater London Act of 2007, which gave the mayor some extra powers. This showed that central government did not think that Livingstone had done a bad job, despite their initial concerns, and the granting of extra powers was probably a reward for his rejoining the Labour Party. However, the extra powers were fairly modest. The GLA was given responsibility for the allocation of national funds for London's social and affordable housing (previously in the hands of a national quango, the Housing Corporation). Strategic direction of funding for skills and training was also transferred to the GLA. He was also given more powers vis-à-vis the boroughs. These strengthened his ability to ensure they followed his housing strategy and shifted the balance of power over the planning control of major developments away from the boroughs. There were a number of smaller adjustments, including an increased presence on the boards of the various bodies within the GLA. On the other hand, the scrutiny powers of the assembly were also increased slightly.

We have explored the way that the institutions of government have adapted and changed over the last twenty-five years and noted how the pressure of globalization has been an important factor in shaping the most recent configuration. London has a long history of reforming its city government and there has been a constant tension between the perceived needs of central government, regional or city government, and local neighborhood responsiveness (Pimlott and Rao 2002). The most recent reforms continue to seek some kind of balance between these levels in the new context of globalization. The relative roles of each level have changed and the degree of responsibility and autonomy has been a constant issue of controversy. The approach to dealing with these tensions—the continuing pressures for absorbing growth in the city-region and the changing global economic context—has been one of centrally orchestrated governmental innovation. During the period we have seen a shift, determined by central government, from a hierarchical interlocking system of governmental levels, through a period of minimalist regional and metropolitan government, to a new experiment with an elected mayor and a strategic authority with strong power to exert policy leadership.

How were the challenges of the city-region, identified at the start of this chapter, met in this changing institutional context? To what extent did these institutional changes produce significant changes in the policy response? These issues will be explored in the next chapter.

3. *Strong Metropolitan Leadership*

IN THE LAST CHAPTER, WE SAW how the governance of the London region has developed through different stages. We also saw how considerable attention was given to reforming the governance of the metropolitan area from 2000 but that the broader regional level has lacked a clear governmental framework throughout our period. These features of governance were also reflected in the changing approach to policy formulation. We will see that in the first part of the period, there was little in the way of strategic policy formulation but that there was then a reaction against this in the face of intercity competition and globalization. This reaction was led by the private sector. The creation of the Greater London Authority (GLA) in 2000 provided a governmental structure that allowed for the preparation of a very detailed and comprehensive strategic policy for the metropolitan area in the form of the London Plan.[1] However the broader regional level continued to lack a strong overall policy approach.

Regional Policy for the South East

During the first part of the period, policies for the wider region were formulated by central government in the form of regional policy guidance. The advisory body SERPLAN (Standing Conference on South East Regional Planning), comprising representatives from local governments in the region, submitted its view to government for consideration. After the arrival of the national Labour government in 1997 and the establishment of the Regional Development Agencies, the regional policy function was taken over by these agencies. However, as we have already noted the region was divided into three, and as the agencies were arms of central government, there remained a strong central control over broader regional policy.

Even though the administrative arrangements changed during the period, there was considerable consistency over policy. The major issues in the regional guidance documents were to promote the region in the face of European competition while coping with problems of environmental sustainability and congestion. As we have noted, development overheating of parts of the region has been a strategic concern,

especially as large parts of the countryside are protected by environmental conservation policies. Thus, a constant theme of the strategic guidance has been to restrict development in the west of the region, which has the advantages of good environment,
proximity of Heathrow airport, and motorway access to the rest of the United Kingdom, while trying to encourage investment in the more deprived east.

In the early 1990s, central government set up the Thames Gateway initiative as another way of approaching this problem. The area covered by the initiative stretches
from the edge of the City of London, and the site of the 2012 Olympics, right out to
the end of the Thames estuary, covering both banks of the river. This initiative has no
statutory status and is aimed at raising the profile of the area, trying to attract investment, and coordinating the various agencies involved in developing the area. To this
end, a broad-brush advisory document called the Thames Gateway Planning Framework was produced in 1995. Since then, the governance of the area has involved three
regional development agencies, numerous local authorities, urban development corporations, central government ministries, and the Olympic development agencies.
However, no detailed strategy for the whole area has been produced. The initiative
has attracted criticism for its institutional complexity and fears that resources are not
guaranteed to support the social and physical infrastructure for the sustainable development that local authorities would have to provide. As we will see, this initiative
gained increased visibility from 2003 as the search for new house building land in the
region intensified.

In addition to supervising any regional strategic guidance, central government
makes decisions on major regional infrastructure projects such as major roads, port
development, and airport expansion. Airport development has been one of the most
contentious regional issues. There are a number of airports in the region: Heathrow,
Gatwick, Stansted, City, and Luton. The last two are relatively small, with City airport,
located in London Docklands, restricted to short-haul aircraft and specializing in European business flights while Luton, just to the north of the city, caters for holiday
charter flights. Heathrow is the largest airport in the region and claims to be the world's
number one in terms of international passenger traffic and the third busiest airport in
the world. It is located just inside the GLA boundary in the west of London. However,
the mayor has no control over Heathrow, as international airports are a national matter and also, as it is on green belt land, any expansion can only be agreed by central
government. The second largest airport is at Gatwick in the southern part of the region.
This has good access to London and has expanded rapidly and is now the eighth largest
in the world for international passenger traffic. Over the last twenty years, central government has been concerned about the restrictions on expansion at Heathrow and the
need to ensure airport expansion in the London region to maintain economic competitiveness. It was noted that Paris has more potential for airport expansion, and Amsterdam was expanding into a European hub airport. In 1984 it was decided to develop
Stansted airport, thirty-eight miles to the northeast, as London's third airport and a new

terminal building was completed in 1991. Stansted is now a major airport for European destinations.

However, the need for further expansion of regional airport capacity continued to be a major issue with proposals for expansion at Heathrow, Gatwick, and Stansted (a fifth terminal was opened at Heathrow in 2008). Central government has produced an airport strategy to 2030 with new runways at Heathrow and Stansted around 2015 and, toward the end of the period, at Gatwick (Department for Transport 2006). Airport proposals have been the most controversial development issues in the region, with very vocal opposition from environmentalists and local communities. Heathrow, being the closest to existing built-up areas, has been the most contentious. Proposals for expansion have pit local authorities, the London mayor, local residents, and environmentalists against airport interests and the business lobby. Central government was due to make a decision on the third runway at Heathrow by the end of 2008 but found this difficult—they were minded to accept expansion but there was opposition from central governmental politicians with environmental responsibilities. They sought a way of expanding within strict environmental constraints in order to maintain their environmental credentials. The new national government that came to power in 2010 has now to grapple with this dilemma. Meanwhile, the new mayor of London, Boris Johnson, suggested a new airport on an island in the Thames Gateway, but most people think that this is unrealistic as it would be very costly and would need considerable investment in improved access.

Seaports are another regional infrastructure issue and central government also produced a report on this (Department for Transport 2007). Again, limited facilities are seen as a constraint on economic growth and further capacity is considered to be needed beyond 2020. The strategy is to expand the major regional commercial ports at Felixstowe and Harwich to the north of the region and build a new port in the Thames Gateway. The London Gateway Port will be a deep-sea container port linked to one of the biggest logistics and business parks in Europe. This will be built on a former oil refinery and, because of the isolated and environmentally poor location, has not attracted opposition (planning permission was granted in 2007). The project will be developed by DP World, owned by the government of Dubai, and is expected to provide 14,000 new jobs and a catalyst for further development as part of the Thames Gateway strategy.

London and the South East region have constituted the most prosperous part of the nation for hundreds of years. This has attracted inward migration from the rest of the country and abroad. The dominant pattern has been an increase in migration into the metropolitan area from Europe and other parts of the world and, at the same time, a migration out into the surrounding region of Londoners seeking affordable family homes. In addition, recent population projections show that people are living longer and more single people want to live on their own. All this adds up to heavy demands for land for house building in both the metropolitan area and the region beyond. One of the major policy issues has therefore been how to balance this demand against environmental and sustainability objectives.

A large percentage of the land in the region is protected by central government policies to preserve its environmental quality and the strictly enforced green belt. Under this severe pressure on land for house building, these restrictive policies have been challenged. The main focus has been to question the continued relevance of the green belt. There was an attempt to relax the policy in the 1980s when the house-building lobby, who had the ear of the prime minister, Mrs. Thatcher, attempted to use the ideology of laissez-faire to relax this green belt policy. However, this met a backlash from other Conservative Party supporters who lived in the protected villages that existed in the belt before the advent of the policy. They did not want their pleasant environment and house values disrupted with new development. Another attack on the belt was initiated by the central government treasury about twenty years later because they were worried about the high cost of housing. The commissions set up by government to look at this problem, and other commentators, suggested a rethinking of the belt (Barker 2004, 2006). However, once again, the policy survived with the backing of other departments of central government concerned with environment and planning. The continuation of the green belt constraint has resulted in considerable growth over the last twenty years in the towns just beyond the belt, bringing with it increasing journey-to-work distances, as most people continue to be employed within London.

Thus, one of the ongoing regional issues has been how to find land to cope with the continual demand for housing without relaxing any of the environmental or green belt constraints. In 1998 the government set up an urban task force to explore this problem of development pressure in the south (and the opposite problem of urban decline in the north). This review, chaired by the architect Lord Richard Rogers, advocated the need for an "urban renaissance" involving improved urban living conditions, better housing design, and tax reforms (Urban Task Force 1999). This was taken up by the government with the idea that major urban areas should increase their populations and that in the South East, 60 percent of the new housing demand should take place within urban areas on brownfield sites. This policy, with its implications of higher densities in new development, was later embodied within the mayor's London Plan. However, it still meant that land needed to be found for the other 40 percent of demand on greenfield sites throughout the rest of the region. In 2003 central government produced its sustainable communities policy, which included a strategy on how the demand for housing would be accommodated in the South East (DCLG 2003). The national strategy can be implemented through central government's allocation of housing building targets that local authorities have to include in their local plans—these were made through the regional development agencies after their formation.

Most of the development was envisaged to take place within the Thames Gateway—from housing associated with the Olympic site at the western edge through large developments on the fringes of the city and onward along both banks of the estuary.

These housing developments would be accompanied by expected new nodes of employment. Two of these, the Stratford city retail center and the Ebbsfleet office development, are located on new stations of the recently built Channel Tunnel rail link. The consortium of companies that built the rail link, and will operate the services, was given the land around these stations to develop in order to pay their costs. From 2009, this railway will also take the first national high-speed rail trains and so both locations will be very accessible to the center of London for commuters. The Thames Gateway already includes the two largest out-of-town shopping centers in the region at Bluewater and Lakeside.

The area is clearly experiencing major change although, as already noted, there are concerns about whether the governments will be able to provide the funds necessary for the support infrastructure, such as public transport, roads, schools, and hospitals. The world financial crisis of 2008 also created what is expected to be a short-term drop in house-building activity. Another issue is how the strategy will be coordinated and implemented with the large number of different organizations involved. There are several central government departments, numerous local authorities, and several special regeneration agencies but no single overall body taking a lead in coordinating strategy or development (Haughton et al. 2009, ch. 8). It could also be said that the Thames Gateway has moved from an initiative concerned primarily about regional balance to one that sees its role as supportive of London as a competitive world city, especially when connected to the Cross Rail project and the Channel Tunnel link. The other areas to absorb the housing growth in the region are an expansion of the new town at Milton Keynes, which has been steadily growing since the 1960s; the area around Cambridge and Stansted airport, which has become a research and development node; and the entrance of the Channel Tunnel at Ashford, which will be another station on the new high-speed rail link to London.

Many cities have given increased importance to policies that improve the quality of life in their cities. Improving the attractiveness of a city is seen as essential in a competitive environment. As we saw in chapter 1, such quality-of-life policies can cover a wide range of issues, some of which can benefit all citizens and others of which can be oriented to specific groups. At the regional level of the Greater South East, there have been concerns throughout our period over problems of road congestion and the threats to the most attractive countryside. These concerns have led to transport improvements and the continued enforcement of environmental protection policies. As a consequence of these policies, there are many areas within the region that provide very attractive, and often very exclusive, residential environments. Many of the highly paid personnel working in the world city business functions commute by rail from these communities in the region that can provide the kind of facilities that they desire, such as golf courses and private schools. However, as we will see the most conscious environmental policies have been formulated for the metropolitan area.

Formulating a Policy for a World City

As we saw in the last chapter, there was an increase in concern during the 1980s, particularly expressed by business interests, about London's ability to compete in the conditions of economic globalization. It was thought that the absence of any metropolitan government meant that the city lacked leadership to promote itself. Constant comparisons were being made with Paris, which was seen as possessing such leadership. However, in addition to the need for institutional change it was felt that there was a need for a stronger policy approach. London needed a vision statement as part of a city marketing strategy. We have already seen that there was little strategic policy at the regional level, and between the abolition of the Greater London Council (GLC) in 1986 and the establishment of the GLA in 2000 there was also very little strategic policy for the metropolitan area. Central government, which performed this role during this period, only produced broad and rather vague guidelines. The private sector started to take more interest in strategic policies for the city and in the 1990s there was a stronger partnership between central government and the private sector. However, once the creation of the GLA was announced in 1997 the private sector switched their attention to this level of government and organized themselves very effectively to influence the strategic approach of the GLA. We will now look in more detail at this interaction between public and private sectors and the way this influenced the strategic policy agenda.

Following abolition of the GLC in 1986, business interests had a significant influence on urban policy and the City Corporation took a more active citywide role. Then in 1992, the newly formed business alliance London First identified London's international competitiveness as its central policy issue and produced a series of London-wide strategies, including a transport strategy. In 1995 the *London Pride Prospectus*, a public–private initiative led by London First, set the frame for strategic priorities. In its opening statement, it said that its aim was to ensure London's position as the only world city in Europe. The priorities of the *Prospectus* then had a strong influence on central government thinking, for example, as input into the revised and expanded strategic planning guidance for London. However, the return to metropolitan government from 2000 presented a new environment for the business lobby.

Business organizations generally supported the establishment of the GLA, although they wanted to ensure they had a voice in the new organization. For example, London First argued that "London's prosperity and competitiveness depends on business. For London to remain competitive, business needs access to decision-making, a coherent voice to articulate its needs and the ability to make things happen. The GLA and its agencies must work in close concert with businesses" (quoted in Kleinman 2001, 11). The energy of the business lobby was to be spent on influencing the priorities at the agenda-setting stage of strategy formulation. To ensure a business voice in London policy, business leaders set up the London Development Partnership (LDP) before the GLA was in place, with the aim to "establish a business-led board" that would work to "fill the strategic gap" in economic development thinking for London (LDP 1998a, 2). Their first report, "Preparing for the Mayor and the London Development Agency" (LDP 1998b) was produced at the end of 1998, and a draft economic development strategy was produced in January 2000, just in time to pass on to the new mayor (LDP 2000). The eventual economic development strategy produced by the London Development Agency (LDA), the arm of the GLA responsible for economic development, drew heavily on this work. There was thus continuity in the access of the business lobby to strategic decision making and in the policy priorities. The LDP board, as well as containing representatives of various public bodies, included representatives from the London Confederation of British Industry, London First, the London Chamber of Commerce and Industry, and the Corporation of London. Many of these business representatives were to sit on the LDA board after 2000. The LDP board itself had a great deal of overlap with its predecessor, the London Pride Partnership, and the issues identified for priority treatment—business competitiveness and transport—were also similar.

The London Development Partnership also established a group focusing on attracting inward investment and visitors to London. This included the key promotional organizations the London First Center and the London Tourist Board. The group produced a report in May 2000, called "Promoting the World City: Memorandum for the Mayor and the GLA." The purpose of the report was to ensure that the new London Authority would prioritize working with business to promote London and would focus on improvements to attract more inward investment. They presented the vision that by 2004 London would be "The World City." They said, "When London First was set up in 1992, there was a belief in the business community that London was losing its status as a world class city. Over the last eight years, London has not just regained that status; it has reinforced its position as Europe's business capital and, along with New York and Tokyo, is one of three world cities. With the arrival of the directly elected Mayor and the LDA, the authors believe that London can aspire to be the undisputed World City by 2004" (LTB and LFC 2000, 9). They looked to the mayor to prepare key development sites, to fund an International Convention Center, and to improve transport, air quality, skill levels, and crime prevention.

The desire to influence the new mayor continued, and the London Chamber of Commerce and Industry promoted the idea of a London Business Board to provide a focus for business interests. The London branch of the Confederation of British Industries and London First agreed to join this board and they held many meetings in the lead up to the mayoral election, producing a document called "The Business Manifesto for the Mayor and the GLA" to set out their priorities. This report suggested that competitiveness should be the key focus for the mayor: "The health and global competitiveness of London's economy must be at the heart of the GLA as the prerequisite for achieving all other policy aims. All the GLA's policies must be tested against the aim of promoting a strong, stable, diverse, competitive, sustainable and flexible economy" (London Business Board n.d., 2).

The first mayoral election in 2000 was won by Ken Livingstone who had a radical image from his GLC days. However, he responded positively to the business agenda. His election manifesto stated that he expected to work closely with the business community. He said that as mayor he would "work with the Corporation of London and major City institutions to ensure London remains the financial capital of Europe" and "support jobs and competitiveness in London by working with businesses and business organisations." He said that he would only be able to succeed if he worked "with the active involvement of successful entrepreneurs and business people." Given the mayor's limited powers and budget, it is not surprising that he sought out potential partners with resources to put behind his priorities. The need for such a stance was reinforced by the difficult relationships between the mayor and central government at that time. Having left the Labour Party in order to run for office, Ken Livingstone could not expect to exert much influence over his former colleagues. Influential business leaders might be friendlier.

The London Business Board increased in importance after the establishment of the GLA because the mayor made it clear that he wanted a single coherent view from business. London's business organizations were well resourced and had long experience in engaging with local and national government. They developed contacts with all levels and departments of the GLA, not just with the mayor and his office, and this was something the mayor supported. Business organizations dealt regularly with officers of Transport for London and the London Development Agency, and the mayor appointed several business people to the boards of these two bodies. Indicative of the mayor's close relationship with business were his appointments of the political leader of the City Corporation as his business advisor. This enabled the City Corporation to continue its role in influencing the strategic priorities of the capital. Very soon after his election, the mayor set up bimonthly meetings with the London Business Board. A representative of one business organization said they were in touch with the mayor's office "weekly if not daily." Business groups were also proactive in arranging meetings with the GLA; for example, London First set up a series of breakfast meetings for members on issues concerning the spatial development strategy.

Business access to the agenda-setting process can be seen to have a number of significant characteristics. First, business established an early presence in the process. It was active before the mayor was elected and, through its involvement in the LDP and the London Business Board, was well prepared to instill its priorities into the process. There was continuity in the promotion of London's world city role. The economic development strategy was the first of the mayor's strategies to be drafted, drawing on this earlier work by the business sector, and it therefore influenced the other strategies. The chief executive of the LDA, responsible for the strategy, stated that this was the aim in getting the strategy done quickly. This early involvement of the business lobby meant that it was less necessary for them to engage in the later stages of general consultation or assembly scrutiny. This focused approach meant that business access was established right at the center of power through regular and confidential discussions. Relationships between business and the governance of London show continuity over the years since abolition of the GLC. To the close business links with central government in the 1990s have been added close working with the mayor. The emphasis on London as a world city that emerged in the early 1990s continued into the mayor's economic and spatial development strategies. However, it can be argued that the ambitions of national government for a more open and accessible London government are brought into question by this privileged access of business.

The Priorities of the Mayor and the London Plan

Although Ken Livingstone accepted that he had to work with economic interests, many of his early statements suggested a consensus-seeking and inclusionary approach—sometimes referred to as the "Big Tent."' He had promised in his manifesto to "introduce the most open, accessible and inclusive style of government in the UK." He was not able to stand for election as the official Labour Party candidate as he had not been seen as sufficiently compliant by the prime minister, Tony Blair. His late emergence as an independent candidate meant he couldn't run on the Labour Party manifesto, but had to come up with his own. His team therefore relied heavily on input from outside bodies, particularly Friends of the Earth. The Green Party also said many of Livingstone's ideas were originally theirs. Once in office, he continued this inclusionary approach in making his appointments to the various boards within the GLA. These appointments came from a wide range of interest groups and political parties. By July 2000, the Civic Forum, which Livingstone had said he would consult, had a membership of 325 organizations, including voluntary, church, and minority organizations.

The new form of London government brought new interests into citywide policy making. But there was a clear difference between the open consultative approach and the mayor's regular and confidential relationship with business. The broader consultation was very diffuse and covered many, often conflicting, interest groups that lacked a focused agenda. It was also clear that the mayor did not feel he had to take much notice of the views emanating from the various consultation processes or the assembly. As we will see, the policy implication of this imbalance between the business interest and other views is reflected in the priority given to London's role as a world city. Next, we need to examine the way in which priorities were shaped in the new citywide London Plan.

A draft London Plan was produced in 2002 for consultation and, after the examination in public in 2003, this formed the statutory version in 2004 without undergoing much change. This 2004 plan was then expanded slightly and, after a further examination in public, led to a 2008 version. The mayor was also required by the legislation to prepare a further seven nonstatutory strategies. The GLA staff prepared draft strategies and these had to be presented to the assembly and undergo a period of public consultation. The first draft strategy to be produced, in November 2000, was the economic development strategy prepared by the London Development Agency. As we have noted, this was highly influenced by the reports of the private sector–dominated London Development Partnership. The transport strategy was also produced quickly because this was the mayor's top political priority at that time. The final versions of these two strategies were published in July 2001. Meanwhile, work was continuing on the London Plan, theoretically seen as the coordinating strategy, but as this was a statutory document it had to go through a lengthier procedure including the examination in public. The remaining strategies required by the GLA Act—biodiversity, noise, waste management, air quality, and culture—came out later, reflecting the fact that the mayor gave them less priority at that time. Over the years, the mayor produced many additional strategies not specified in the legislation—including those for children, the elderly, alcohol, drugs, food, and energy.

All these strategies, whether optional or required by the London Act, were incorporated in the statutory document, the London Plan. We therefore concentrate on this document in our policy analysis. The power of this plan varies according to the policy area. Many of the economic aspirations and environmental goals require action by businesses or individuals and thus the plan's role is in changing perceptions and behavior. However, in other areas, particularly transport, the mayor controls the implementation agency and can therefore ensure that the policies are fulfilled (within the financial constraints set by central government). As far as land use and development are concerned, the plan has a significant impact as it has to be followed by the lower-tier boroughs in their own plans and decision making. Let us now turn to some of the key policy priorities contained in the London Plan.

RESPONDING TO ECONOMIC COMPETITION

The plan said that London had two strategic choices. It could rein back its economic and population growth through policies of dispersal, as took place in the decades after the Second World War. This would take the pressure off the overloaded infrastructure but compromise London's development as a world city and, it was said, damage the whole United Kingdom economy. Alternatively, it could accept the processes of economic and population growth, recentralize, and create the adequate infrastructure to cope with the pressure. The growth would then create the improvements in services and transport the city needs. This second option was the one adopted. The role of the plan was therefore to ensure that the mayor could provide the facilities needed for the world city growth strategy and to formulate policies to deal with the pressures that this increase in economic activity and population created. The basic priority of the plan was to ensure that London remained competitive, and it claimed that other major cities, such as New York, Berlin, Paris, and Tokyo, had invested in growth infrastructure on a massive scale (Mayor of London 2002).

However, the growth had to take place in a way that also created social and environmental benefits, and the overall slogan was "to develop London as an exemplary sustainable world city" (Mayor of London 2008a). It was said that this involved three interwoven themes: to ensure strong, diverse, long-term economic growth; to ensure social inclusivity to give all Londoners the opportunity to share in London's economic future; and to make fundamental improvements in London's environment and the use of resources (Mayor of London 2002). Thus, policies followed that covered economic, social, and environmental issues and growth, equity, and sustainability. However, it can be argued that these were not given equal importance. It will be argued that the economic policies dominated, whether because of the pressure from business interests or the mayor's financial restrictions (Gordon 2003). It can also be argued that these economic priorities then had adverse effects on social and environmental conditions.

One of the consequences of the economic world city goal was that the London Plan placed particular attention on the expansion and improvement of the central area, advocated taller buildings, and encouraged the further development of the Canary Wharf project to accommodate global companies. To enable growth to occur within the fixed boundaries of the green belt, a general policy of intensification was adopted, with the identification of Areas of Opportunity for major development—particularly on large brownfield sites. This accorded with central government policy of increasing urban densities and the recommendations of the report they commissioned, led by the architect Richard Rogers (Urban Task Force 1999). (Richard Rogers was also appointed as an advisor to the mayor to promote good-quality urban design in the city.) In particular, the plan needed to find space for an expansion of world city office and service functions. The major areas proposed to accommodate this were around the fringe of the existing financial center and in nearby major developments around King's Cross and London Bridge stations. The plan paid considerable attention to the enhancement of this central area. Central London accommodates national government, international financial business services, and substantial cultural assets and is the location of the United Kingdom's primary tourist destination. However, the plan has been portrayed as giving too much attention to globally oriented activities and producing a central area bias in its spatial strategy (Buck et al. 2002). This was also one of the themes raised by objectors at the examination in public in 2003.

One of the mayor's most controversial policies was to allow an increase in the development of tall buildings. Such developments have been constrained in the past through various heritage and building height limitations and the protection of historic views. Livingstone, supported by the business sector, promoted an increase in tall buildings. Two broader policies can be detected as lying behind the support of tall buildings. One was the desire to promote London as a world city and the need to ensure that the city had a good stock of suitable office accommodation to attract the

global activities. It was expected that international companies favor modern tall buildings—as the London Plan states, tall buildings "can offer a supply of premises suited
to the needs of global firms—especially those in the finance and business services sector" (Mayor of London 2008a, 249). The City Corporation was a strong advocate of the
policy, as they said that the city was full and so the only option was to expand upward. It was proposed that the tall buildings would be clustered in the central activity
zone (covering the city, West End, and South Bank) and the Canary Wharf area. Other
smaller locations would be around central railway nodes and the suburban office center at Croydon. The plan stressed that such buildings should be constructed to the
highest design standards and would stimulate regeneration in the surrounding area.

The second policy that underpinned the tall building approach was that of increasing the population and employment density within the city. This increase needed to be
achieved in a sustainable way and so the intensification of activity through tall buildings around locations with good public transport facilities contributed to this policy.
However, the tall building policy was strongly opposed in some quarters. A battle was
joined between heritage organizations, who wanted to protect the city's historic architecture and skylines, and developers, who wished to take advantage of the new policy.
Many borough councils also challenged the mayor's imposition of the policy.

Another dimension to the provision of world city facilities was the policy to further expand the Canary Wharf development. After its slow start, the area began to expand rapidly once the transport provision was put in place in the 1990s. Major international companies like Lehman Brothers moved there from the city, and Norman
Foster designed a new tower for Citibank. Although the City of London could now expand through taller buildings, there is a limit to how far this area can provide all the
accommodation for the companies that London is seeking to attract through its world
city approach—the London Plan says that the Canary Wharf area can "support a globally competitive business cluster" (88). New projects—Riverside South twin towers
(28 and 34 stories), designed by Richard Rogers, and the North Quay site (towers of
36 and 39 stories) would add to the density of development around Canary Wharf.
Thus, Canary Wharf and the surrounding Isle of Dogs provide plenty of accessible
new office space. The availability of land with development potential also means
that space-intensive activities such as conference and exhibition centers have also
been constructed in the adjacent Royal Docks and contribute to the area's new economic role.

The London Plan also identified tourism and culture as major economic growth
sectors. London should expand its role as a major tourist destination. It sought to ensure that the tourist destinations, which are primarily in the central area, are improved
and retain their international competitiveness and 36,000 more hotel bed spaces are
planned by 2016 (Mayor of London 2004, 140). It was hoped that some of this tourist
activity could be attracted to areas of opportunity that need regeneration outside the
central area. The plan sought to enhance strategic cultural areas and establish cultural

quarters with workshops for the creative industries, which are seen as another growth sector. Although there is an attempt to establish these cultural and tourist activities across the city, they remain heavily concentrated in the central area—all but three of the city's top 20 tourist attractions are in the central area.

The focus on the central area, the promotion of tall buildings, and the continued development of Canary Wharf and Docklands were all clearly oriented to ensuring that London has space for future world city functions. Other policies in the London Plan can be seen to have more diverse aims. These were concerned with increasing the quality of life in the city and had a more direct benefit for citizens. However, at the same time they also create the necessary conditions for a well-functioning world city. This concern for improving the quality of life in London includes the policy areas of transport, housing, and urban regeneration as well as policies more directly aimed at quality of life.

TRANSPORT POLICIES

The transport policies in the London Plan were drawn from the earlier GLA transport strategy and involve improving access to airports, ports, and international rail termini, especially by public transport. Three new express transit lines across London and two new tram systems were proposed by 2016. The mayor had to convince central government of the need for these projects as they decide the spending priorities over such transport infrastructure. This is a clear indication of the lobbying role of the plan, setting out the strategic transport priorities but having to rely on other people to produce the funding.

The most significant piece of infrastructure is called Cross Rail. This will be a new rail line from west to east going underground through the central area. It will link existing rail lines in the west and east and some underground stations. It will have a significant impact on accessibility patterns, particularly for central locations. According to the London Plan, "Cross Rail is critical to support the growth of the financial and business services sector in central London and the Isle of Dogs (Canary Wharf)" (Mayor of London 2008a, 142). In 2008 central government eventually agreed the £16 billion funding package for Cross Rail. They had refused to commit their funding without a significant contribution from the private sector, who they said would benefit. London First had been behind the scheme from the outset and in the eventual funding package, major contributions were obtained from Canary Wharf, the City of London, and British Airways Authority. These bodies would benefit from the better links between the city and Canary Wharf—the two financial quarters—and between them and Heathrow and Stansted airports. Cross Rail will therefore have a very clear role in relation to London's world city functions.

Reducing road congestion was the top policy priority of the mayor in the early years of his tenure. He identified transport, both congestion and poor public transport, as the main concern of London citizens and wanted to ensure that he did something visible by the time of the second mayoral election in 2004. He decided to adopt a policy of charging vehicles for entry to the center of the city. The policy was also intended to provide him with an independent source of income from the fees, which he decided to invest in improved bus provision. Opposition came from some residential communities living on the edge of the boundary, small businesses in the zone, and major retailers, but it is interesting to note that the policy had the support of most of the business organizations, such as London First. Better communication within the central city clearly helps the world city functions that are located there. The policy was very controversial and it was seen as a brave decision by the mayor. Once implemented, it proved to be generally popular, and successful in reducing traffic by about 20 percent. It did not generate the adverse side effects that many predicted and it attracted worldwide interest. The initial charge was £5, later raised to £8—a level that has been generally accepted, which is not surprising given the high costs of public transport. More controversial was the mayor's decision to extend the zone to the west, where there had been a lot of opposition to the original scheme from residents of this wealthy part of the city. In his manifesto for the 2008 election, he announced his plan to charge a higher rate (£25) for larger, ecologically unfriendly cars.

HOUSING AND SOCIAL POLICIES

The housing policy in the plan had two dimensions. One was to increase densities, as already mentioned; the other was to provide more affordable housing. For a long time, the provision of social housing had dwindled and private housing costs had risen. One of the problems of world city status is that the housing market is international and the wealthiest people in the world want to buy a house in London. The high housing costs affect not only the low-paid and unemployed but also workers in many of the essential services of the city, such as police, teachers, nurses, firemen, and transport workers. The city has difficulty in recruiting to these jobs and many of these workers travel great distances from outlying areas or live temporarily in the city during the week, returning home on weekends. This threatens the efficient functioning of the city and its world city position. In the plan, the mayor set out the target for all major housing developments of 50 percent affordable provision. This percentage is partly social housing and partly housing at a level affordable for key workers. This is achieved through agreements with developers when they are seeking planning permission. In the plan, he also set targets that each borough had to achieve in the provision of affordable housing. Some developers objected to this on the grounds of the burden on their profits, and some boroughs were concerned about an increase of lower-income residents, and higher densities, in their more suburban environments. This was probably the most contentious issue in the plan as far as the boroughs were concerned.

The London Plan also attempted to steer development into areas that were suffering from deprivation, particularly in the east. The plan highlighted the existing social and spatial polarization in the city (Hamnett 2003), echoing the world city literature.

The plan therefore advocated the need to focus attention on the poorer parts of the city and to tackle the problem that, although London is the wealthiest region in England, it is also the second highest in terms of unemployment. The plan set out areas with potential for development in terms of new employment and housing. The aim is to ensure that the benefits of such new development can be linked to areas of poverty that require regeneration—for example, through improved physical and job access. However, the detailed regeneration and social policy is a lower-tier borough responsibility.

Thus, although addressing policies to try to overcome such polarization, the plan could be said to operate in two independent ways: on the one hand, pursuing policies to promote the world city functions and, on the other, dealing with polarization. It lacks sufficient consideration of the interconnections between these two strands. For example, Hall has criticized the transport proposals for not paying enough attention to their role in overcoming polarization (Hall 2002). The plan identifies two key zones for concentrated effort: the central activity zone and the east of the city. The central activity zone has the highest land values in the city and is under constant development pressure. Here, the plan seeks to open up more development opportunity and increase the quality of the environment to ensure the city remains competitive by providing enough high-quality locations for world city functions. By contrast, the east, which has always been the poorest part of the city and the least favored for development, relies on more concerted state intervention. The Docklands development saw a major reversal to the east's historic position. However, this development has become an island of global and higher-income development within the general poverty of the east. Any major regeneration of the broader area would require concerted action by many different agencies, notably central government.

In 2008 the mayor produced a revised plan that included changes to take into account London's successful bid to host the 2012 Olympics. However, this did not require any major modifications as the bid was based upon the first plan's regeneration policies for the east of the city. Winning the Olympics meant that this regeneration policy was more firmly embedded in the broader structures of governance and ensured that all the different organizations would work together. In particular, it meant that central government commitment to the financial aspects of the strategy, especially transport infrastructure, could now be guaranteed and the whole program given a faster timetable. The Olympic project has therefore become the most important element of the mayor's regeneration and social policy as it is located in the most deprived part of the city. However, its success in reducing social polarization will depend upon whether the project can benefit the surrounding communities rather than become an isolated new development attracting tourists, elite sports enthusiasts, and shoppers to the adjacent new major shopping mall. It is also likely to trigger a gentrification process in some neighborhoods in this part of the city and fuel the debate over whether gentrification is a positive or negative process in reducing polarization.

ENVIRONMENTAL AND QUALITY-OF-LIFE POLICIES

The 1999 GLA Act required the mayor to produce a number of environmental strategies, many of which were innovative for Britain. They included strategies on biodiversity, noise, waste management, and air quality. Although Livingstone gave environmental issues prominence in his election manifesto, once in office they did not get top
priority. Initially, he was more concerned with economic and, particularly, transport
issues, as these would be the ones that would influence the electorate at the election
in 2004. His view was that the impact of environmental policies was not demonstrable
within a four-year term of office. The implementation of such policies was also outside the control of the mayor and relied on persuading individuals and other organizations to take action. However, the environmental strategies were produced and included many interesting and sometimes path-breaking policies, such as setting high
targets for recycling of household waste, improving air quality, increasing efficiency of
energy and water usage, and producing an innovative urban noise reduction strategy.
In the first London Plan (2004), the mayor states in his introduction that the plan "is
designed to ensure that Londoners benefit from sustainable improvements to their
quality of life" (xii).

As soon as the London Plan was adopted in 2004, work began on a revised version
that was adopted in 2008 (Mayor of London 2008a). This second plan included one
major new direction: policies to tackle climate change over the next twenty years. This
involved new policies for London and also put pressure on individuals and central government to do more. This demonstrated a shift in emphasis by the mayor, who was
now taking environmental issues more seriously. The aim was to make London a world
leader in responding to the challenge of climate change. He set the target of stabilizing
London's CO_2 emissions in 2025 at 60 percent below the 1990 level, which means reducing emissions by 4 percent per year. Included in the plan were the reduction of household emissions by greater energy efficiency and offering grants for insulation, decentralizing energy generation (target of 25 percent local systems by 2025), and methods of
reducing transport emissions. There was also more emphasis on the threat of flooding.

However, in addition to these policies oriented to all citizens, there were more specific ones that linked quality of life to enhancing London's global competitiveness.
There were two dimensions to this. One was the development of culture as an economic activity, often oriented to boosting the tourist industry. We have noted the production of a cultural strategy, the creation of particular cultural quarters, and the support for creative industries. The mayor was promoting these aspects of the city and
helping to create the conditions in which such activities could thrive. Tourism, culture, and ethnic diversity were all seen as essential strengths in London's economy.
However, as with many of the mayor's policies, this is dependent on other actors to
make things happen. Finance for major attractions, such as the museums, is not in the
hands of the mayor and much of the popular culture, such as in the vibrant street markets, is based on small-scale private actions.

The second dimension was the improvement of quality of life, oriented to the international business sector and ensuring London does better in the various quality-of-life indices we summarized in chapter 1. One of the major aims of all the London Plans has been to ensure a supply of high-quality office accommodation. However, there has also been a focus on mixed-use development and the need to ensure high-quality residential environments within the city. In the latest economic development strategy (Mayor of London 2009), the new mayor, Boris Johnson, reproduces a table of indices comparing London with its European competitors and notes that it is not doing well on quality of life. He particularly points out the poor environmental quality of the city's neighborhoods that "contribute to the perception of London as a less attractive place than some of its competitors." His policies involve upgrading these areas, improving run-down parks, and planting 10,000 trees across the city. In his economic recovery plan of 2008, he again noted the poor Mercer quality-of-life score but pointed out that this does not cover London's "urban buzz," which attracts so many young people. We will now turn to a wider discussion of the impact of this new mayor.

The 2008 Mayoral Election and the Arrival of Boris Johnson

Ken Livingstone easily won the second mayoral election in 2004 but lost in 2008. Although he lost, he was still very popular with certain sections of the electorate, especially residents of inner London and the city's significant minority populations. There were a number of factors that led to his demise. The Labour Party nationally was very unpopular; some people just felt that it would be interesting to have a change after eight years with Ken, and there was a backlash from suburban residents. There was also a history of antagonism between Livingstone and the city's daily newspaper, the *London Standard*. The newspaper conducted a very vociferous and personal campaign against him. As a result, the Conservative Party candidate Boris Johnson won, even though he was widely regarded as rather a laughable and superficial figure. This image was based on numerous gaffes in the past, including slights on the black community. However, this image of being a clown seemed to have an appeal to the electorate and also meant he tended to be immune for making mistakes, as this was almost part of his image. He expressed a feeling of enthusiasm while Livingstone came over as rather tired. The election showed the importance of image and the media—Boris Johnson certainly did not have a clear and alternative policy manifesto.

A NEW MAYOR WITH A NEW STYLE

The new mayor brought significant changes in management approach. Livingstone's whole career was steeped in local government and so he was an expert in the mechanics of how such organizations worked and was able to get involved at a detailed level whenever he wished. His period of office was characterized by a very clear and single-minded policy approach, which stemmed from him personally and was put into effect through his mayor's office—a tightly organized group that had worked with him before and shared his political aims. Johnson had no experience whatsoever of local government—his main working life had been spent in journalism. He was therefore very dependent upon his senior appointments. As soon as he was elected, he set about changing the senior staff—in the US tradition of replacing the bureaucracy to match political leaning. He appointed a number of people as deputies and advisors, with responsibilities for different policy areas. In this way, he himself did not have to know about the details and could act as a kind of board chairman and public relations figure. However, his lack of experience was also evident in his choice of new senior appointments, as many resigned for one reason or another within months of taking up office.

In terms of significance for urban policy, it is interesting that Boris Johnson's election demonstrated a divide between inner and outer London and between wealthier and poorer sections of the community. We have already noted that the suburban areas of London disliked the affordable housing policy and felt that too much of Livingstone's attention was oriented to the inner and central parts of the city. In his election campaign, Boris picked up on this sentiment and said he would work more closely with the boroughs, particularly the outer suburban boroughs and give them more autonomy. In office, he set up a city charter and an outer London commission to improve relations between the GLA and the boroughs, and promised to reduce the policy constraints on the boroughs. He is in the process of replacing the London Plan with a less detailed version that will provide a looser framework for the boroughs' own plans.

However, there have been complaints that Johnson's polycentric management approach lacks a clear unifying mayoral voice. He has been more inclined to ad hoc policy statements than coordinated policy, and many of these statements conflict with each other. For example, he has introduced a new cycle hire scheme based upon Paris, while at the same time he is seeking to speed up car flows with reorganized traffic lights and road changes. One of his first pronouncements was to implement his manifesto pledge to phase out the unpopular bendy-bus (single-decker double-length vehicles) and reintroduce a new version of the famous Routemaster bus—even though this will be very costly and mean less money for other transport improvements that he is also promising. He is reviewing the western extension of the congestion charge zone and has cancelled Livingstone's idea to impose the higher congestion charge on environmentally unfriendly large cars. However, he says he supports policies to deal with climate change. He also said he would not continue with Livingstone's approach to ensuring affordable housing in new developments, but at the same time he wants London as a whole to provide enough affordable housing—how he will do this is not yet clear. These affordable housing targets had been particularly opposed by the suburban boroughs. With most of these new policy statements, there is clearly a strong element of populism at work, with an eye to his middle-class suburban electors.

Johnson's overall transport priorities involve continued improvement to underground and buses and the building of Cross Rail. However, as we have already noted, the inclusion of transport projects in the plan is important as a vehicle to lobby for central government funding and he has scrapped the ideas of a new tram route from central government to the Peckham in the South East and the extension of the Dockland light railway eastward to Beckton. Whereas the main beneficiaries of Cross Rail will be the central area, Canary Wharf, and business and airport interests, these two cancelled schemes were important ones for upgrading the poorer parts of London. The cancellation of these projects, together with the lighter control over the boroughs, could be interpreted as a shift of spatial priorities away from these poorer communities and toward the outer middle-class boroughs.

In 2009 Johnson published his draft proposals for new versions of the London Plan, transport strategy, and economic strategy. These went to public consultation and an examination in public and were adopted in 2011. As required by the legislation, these proposals seek to balance the economic growth, environmental sustainability, and social equality of London. The general approach of the London Plan, which looks forward to 2031, is similar to the previous ones. The city is expected to continue to grow in population and employment, and a major aim is to retain its world city status. Alleviating climate change also remains a central focus. The major development projects of Cross Rail and the Olympics are fully supported, although there are no firm proposals for the remaining fifteen or so years of the plan period. The main difference is that the plan is less detailed and will be used less forcibly. At the end of the day, the London Plan gains its strength from being a statutory document that can be used to control the boroughs, a lobbying document to influence central government, and a means of trying to influence the behavior of private interests and the public. As we have seen, Boris is loath to impose his powers on the boroughs and may not use his powers to enforce as many major planning applications or lobby central government for the funding of so many transport projects. Taking these issues alongside his ad hoc management style, a weaker strategic framework is likely under his watch. How this light-touch approach will fare in the face of the economic downturn will be the crucial issue over the coming years.

Finally, what has been the policy response to the 2008 financial crisis? As we have seen in the London region, there is a fragmented institutional landscape at the level of the broader region but a very focused and highly visible political entity for the Greater London area. So it is not surprising that the mayor of London took the lead in responding to the economic crisis. He was very vocal in supporting the finance sector and, against the public mood and central government rhetoric, he supported the bankers' high salaries and bonuses. At the same time he produced an economic recovery plan (2008b) that took a broader approach. This plan contained numerous piecemeal measures, many of which were already contained in other polices. There were fifty-seven different actions, covering aid to small business; more aggressive city marketing;

improving Londoners' skills; help with household budgets; schemes to mitigate impact of decline in housing; market and infrastructure projects, such as new convention centers; transport; and the Olympics.

Conclusions

What have been the strategic policy priorities in the London region over the last
30 years, and have globalization and competition influenced the agenda? As far as strategic policies for the Greater South East are concerned, it could be said that through
the dominant role of central government, and their regional development agencies,
major projects and strategies have supported economic growth and competitiveness.
At the same time, very strong environmental protection policies have been maintained. Policies have also been formulated to try to deal with the social imbalances
between the west and east, but these have been largely limited to trying to influence
the locational decisions of the private sector. Over the period since the 1980s, little
has changed with regard to this imbalance. However, in recent years there are signs of
some movement. The west has become progressively more congested, limiting further
development, while the new rail links and the Olympic Games in the east are opening
up opportunities for private sector investment there.

Turning to the metropolitan core of the region, we can see that economic competitiveness has also been a priority there. This has been particularly the case since the establishment of the new government for Greater London in 2000. The idea that London
needed to be more aggressive in promoting itself as a world city was first identified
by the private sector in the 1990s. The establishment of an elected mayor was a direct
response to this perceived need for more leadership and vision. It can also be seen
that environmental issues have been given more attention. The new Greater London
government in 2000 was required to produce new strategies on issues such as biodiversity and noise, and from 2008 climate change was given serious policy attention. In
recent years, the quality of life in the city has also gained prominence, often linked to
the goal of improving competitiveness. Meanwhile, social issues are mainly dealt with
by national social programs and local implementation. However, throughout the period there have been attempts to redress the spatial imbalance between rich and poor
across metropolitan London. Nevertheless, there are few signs that such spatial polarization has diminished over the thirty years.

A second question is whether the increasing role of London as a thriving world city
has led to adjustments in the way the city-region is governed. Have there been changes
in intergovernmental relations? A key tension in the government of London has been
the relationship between the central, metropolitan (or municipal), and local tiers of
authority. At the level of the broader city-region, these tensions have not been so evident. This is because central government takes a dominant role in regional strategic
policy and has only exerted its power in a limited way. Regional strategies have always

been fairly broad documents covering major transport strategy, environmental protection, and locations for major housing expansion. Occasional conflict arose when local authorities did not want to accept further housing, but as the British system is one of hierarchical government, central government's view usually prevailed. Specific development projects such as airport expansions have created significant conflict between central government and local authorities and communities. In these situations, central government again has the power to enforce its decisions, but public opinion can have an influence. In recent years, a regional tier of government in the form of regional development agencies was inserted into the institutional landscape. However, these agencies did not have a lot of power, were still arms of central government, and were abolished in 2010.

The intergovernmental tensions become more complex when looking at the metropolitan area. This is because the sheer size of Greater London, with a population of around seven million, makes it difficult to govern. Various attempts have been made to find an appropriate metropolitan level of government. During our period of study, three approaches have been tried. At the start of the period, the GLC was in place and this produced detailed policies for the metropolitan area. The system of government was straightforward at this time—a hierarchy whereby the borough policies had to conform to the GLC development plan and this had to conform to national policies. The GLC plan had to be submitted to central government for approval. However, this system fell apart when the national and GLC levels were controlled by ideologically opposed political parties that used their positions to influence public opinion. Central government abolished the GLC in 1986.

The second period, which then lasted over a decade, was one in which there was no metropolitan-level government. This obviously eliminated the conflicts created by having an intermediate tier; however, it raised its own problems. In strategic policy, vacuum change took place through individual development projects, most noticeably in London docklands. However, the lack of strategic coordination meant that problems arose, such as the lack of advanced transport provision for Canary Wharf and competition between the Dockland Development Corporation and the City of London, resulting in the danger of overprovision of office supply. The lack of overall strategic leadership and vision was seen as a major problem by the early 1990s. There were fears that globalization was creating a competitive environment in which London was losing out. The private sector took a leading role in pressing for change.

So by 2000, a new metropolitan government was in place in the form of the GLA. This time, there was greater leadership in the form of an elected mayor and a more selective and strategic approach to policy. However, the intergovernmental tensions returned with even greater force given the visibility of the mayor. This was very evident in the early days of the administration, in which Livingstone was in constant battle with central government. During his eight years in office, this interaction improved, but the mayor still had to expend considerable energy in lobbying government for resources. Meanwhile, he did not expend the same energy on his relationship with the boroughs, relying on his legal powers, and paid the price in the 2008 election. The new mayor is seeking a better relationship with the boroughs, and is likely to succeed as he is taking a weaker stance regarding his strategic role. During this more recent stage, the central government relinquished many of its strategic policy functions to the metropolitan level; it is retaining its overall power through legal and fiscal controls, however.

How far can it be said that government has regionalized over the period? The answer to this question is not simple. It is clear that at the broader city-region scale, there has been little move to an overall framework of government—there remains a confusion of regional agencies operating under the arm of central government. However, at the metropolitan (municipal) scale of the Greater London area, the period shows a strong move toward a more coordinated form of government, from a period of institutional liberalism after the abolition of the GLC in 1986 to a highly visible GLA with strong leadership and coordination powers. Nevertheless, the GLA is still constrained by its lack of financial independence and there remains a lot of political tension between local, strategic, and central governments.

How have these governmental changes dealt with the pressures of globalization? Throughout the period, major infrastructure developments such as international airports and ports have been in the hands of the national government and, although there has often been public opposition, the strength of the central government has led to the avoidance of many potential political blockages. At the metropolitan level, the pressures of globalization were identified in the 1990s by the private sector, which pressed for greater policy involvement to address London's competitiveness. The new system, involving a directly elected mayor, was the direct response and Livingstone provided the leadership and vision that many saw as necessary in the era of globalization. The emphasis on London as a world city pervades all policies. However, tensions remain between the pressures of economic globalization and local politics based on citizen needs (Newman and Thornley 2005). Globally oriented private sector interests can be seen to have influenced the priorities of the strategic agenda, but the dangers of continued social polarization remain a threat. The mayors, with their strategic policies, can be seen as lying at the center of these tensions, attempting to forge a viable way forward.

So is it possible to identify a dominant system of governance in London during the period? Is there some model that can convey its essence? The answer is probably "no," as the period can be characterized as one in which there has been a continuing search for reforms and solutions to the difficulties of governing a city-region that dominates the national economy and contains a city of seven million at its core. In the city-region beyond the metropolitan core, the model has been of national government dominance of strategic policy. However, within the core there have been three approaches during the period. The pre-1986 model of a formal hierarchical structure of the three governmental levels of local, metropolitan, and national was abandoned.

For a while, a liberal approach was taken, with ad hoc arrangements taking the place of any formal metropolitan government. However, this was not seen to be up to the job of developing London's competitiveness. The GLA, with a directly elected mayor, was established in the hope that it would prove flexible enough to provide the necessary leadership and vision while also satisfying demands for democratic legitimacy and social and environmental policies.

At a very general level, one could say that the prevailing model is one in which the central government is strongly involved in city-regional governance through pulling all the strings, providing the policy framework, and maintaining powers of overall control. Within this structure of a powerful unitary state, various reforms and experiments have been explored at the regional and metropolitan scale in a search for an approach that can respond to the pressures of globalization and competition while also ensuring public legitimacy.

PART II   *The New York Tri-State Region*

4. *Fragmented Metropolis, Decentralist Impulses*

THE NEW YORK REGION REPRESENTS A radically fragmented and decentralized means of grappling with global city-region development. How this political order is organized—and disorganized—to compete as a capital of capitalism while managing the social consequences is the subject of this chapter.

Although the New York tri-state region has been called "one of the great unnatural wonders of the world" (Wood 1961, 1), its growth into the premier economic center of the United States was hardly an accident. New York has a long history of political craftsmen seizing natural advantages to create regional wealth and power. During the first decades of the 19th century, city and state political leaders dramatically extended the city's and region's commercial reach by building the Erie Canal in 1825 to connect New York City to the Great Lakes. This innovative public works project enabled New York City merchants to scoop up the trade of the western states and funnel it to their wharfs, warehouses, and shipping companies for foreign destinations. It catapulted New York City to a preeminent economic position unequaled by any other American city (Kantor 1995).

Just before the turn of the century, New York political elites again crafted a means of managing its burgeoning growth. In 1898 regional governmental consolidation by the state created the five-borough city of today's greater New York. By establishing a highly unified regional governmental powerhouse, governmental consolidation reached outward to allow New York City to capture wealth and business spilling over the city's traditional borders. Throughout the twentieth century, New York City solidified its position as North America's leading world city of commerce. While it achieved global sway, it became surrounded by a vast, sprawling, and politically fragmented metropolitan area that now rivals it in power, wealth, and people. Today the tri-state area is a giant metropolis having a world city at its center. Making this region work well despite its political division and economic complexity remains a familiar challenge. This chapter examines the main features of metropolitan governance and the emerging problems in this globalizing region. The following chapter probes how this system has responded to the changing regional agenda during the past several decades.

Above all else, the New York region embodies the American predilection for decentralized government. Almost a half-century ago, Robert Wood (1961) published his classic work on the New York region emblazoned with the title *1400 Governments*. Today the same region looked at by Wood has more than 1,600 governments, amounting to one locality for every 11,700 residents. Since Wood wrote, the region has grown substantially. Presently, the New York combined statistical area (NYCSA) contains 2,088 local jurisdictions, located in thirty contiguous counties, and crosses four states.[1] Thirteen of these counties are in New York (the five counties or boroughs of New York City and seven suburban counties), another thirteen are in New Jersey, three are in Connecticut, and one is in Pennsylvania. This combined statistical area (CSA) is one of the largest urban concentrations in the world; it comprises a population of over 21 million people, it extends nearly 15,000 square miles, and holds nearly 12 million jobs. Such is the power of path dependency that an already fragmented system has proliferated even further. For the now enlarged CSA, this amounts to one locality for every 6,400 residents. If the region were a separate county, it would be the fiftieth most populous in the world.

Map 4.1 displays the New York CSA, showing the region's counties broken down as the central business district (CBD), core counties, the nearby suburbs, and the distant suburbs. The island of Manhattan is treated here as the CBD, while the remaining four boroughs (Brooklyn, the Bronx, Queens, and Staten Island) are considered in our terminology to form the urban core. These five boroughs legally define New York City, also referred to in this text as "the city."[2] The nearby suburbs consist of eight counties in New York, New Jersey, and Connecticut (Fairfield, Westchester, Nassau, Bergen, Essex, Hudson, Passaic, and Union). In the same fashion, the distant suburbs compose seventeen counties in those same states (New Haven, Litchfield, Suffolk, Putnam, Rockland, Dutchess, Orange, Ulster, Pike, Sussex, Morris, Hunterdon, Somerset, Middlesex, Mercer, Monmouth, and Ocean).

Given the size of the CSA, its enormous diversity should come as no surprise. Much of New York City and many of the nearby suburbs developed in the nineteenth century and up through the early decades of the twentieth century.[3] The distant suburbs were settled mostly in the years after World War II and up through the present time. These areas have experienced explosive growth in recent years and are overwhelmingly white and middle class.

Within these thirty counties, the sheer number of local governments operates as a sponge for private sector interests. In different ways, these interests attach themselves to municipalities, townships, and special districts. Business influences land use, shapes taxes, affects infrastructure, and holds sway on most aspects of local politics—from financing candidates for office to setting local agenda. It might be said that most local governments are "corporate regimes," used to create a favorable climate for investment and economic growth (Stone 1989; Stone and Sanders 1987).

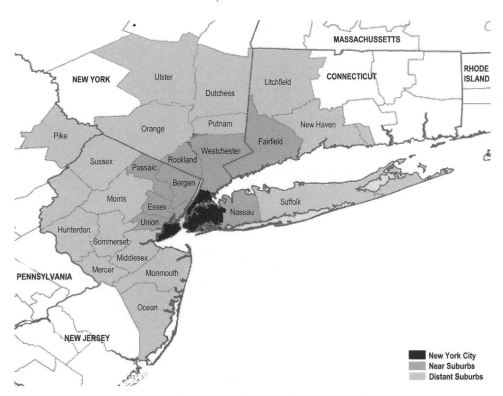

Map 4.1. New York's CSA: New York City, Near Suburbs and Distant Suburbs

Controversial as this may be, there are upsides to this structure. It has led to an extraordinarily vibrant regional society filled with energy, innovation, and pragmatism. Initiatives often well up from the localities themselves, where business, interest groups, and citizen organizations are likely to be setting priorities. The downsides are also considerable. The economy is highly erratic and characterized by sharp upswings as well as dramatic downswings. The social order is also fraught with glaring disparities, and the overall geography of the New York region is unevenly developed. We should add to these problems a system of fractionated governance that lacks coordination and often falls into the hands of small but powerful local governments. It might be said that the aggressive vitality of the system generates many of its own problems. It struggles with divided governance to address common challenges. Establishing agreement about how to attend to problems of regional scope is perhaps the greatest political obstacle in this system. Yet it is this flawed system that also enables New York to maintain a world-class status in the global order. It also obtains this success while producing important social costs.

The following pages begin to explore how this is possible by describing how regional challenges have been changing within the context of a highly decentralized and fragmented world city-region in a nation with a similarly divided federal system of government. We begin by examining the regional issues and then describe the characteristics of the region's highly pluralist system of governance, especially by examining the CSA from the perspective of its relationship to New York City.

Regional Issues and Challenges

ECONOMIC ISSUES: THE FITS, STARTS, AND COLLAPSES OF GROWTH

Despite continued decentralization, Manhattan still constitutes the region's economic core. This mere twenty-two square miles of hard granite island is the region's most densely populated terrain, its object of public attention, its cultural capital, its corporate headquarters, and perhaps most importantly, its economic engine. As the economy has decentralized, Manhattan has relinquished its monopoly, but it still holds the lion's share of land values, business profits, and income. By the beginning of the current century, Manhattan's gross domestic product amounted to over $400 billion, whose proportion made up over 38 percent of the much larger region (Hill and Lendel 2005).

The Manhattan economic engine is propelled by what are now called global industries, consisting of finance and insurance; professional, scientific, or technical services; information; management; and real estate. Wages within these sectors are particularly high, and business profits have soared (Monthly Labor Review. October, 2006). The increments of money flowing from global sectors have created enormous multiplier effects, giving rise to hotels, restaurants, recreation centers, and an array of personal services.

Over earlier decades, economic performance has been patchy. New York City did experience a growth spurt in the last decade, albeit in different proportions. In the city's urban core, some neighborhoods thrive while others are stagnant and very poor. Brooklyn has a lively downtown and boasts gentrified neighborhoods such as Park Slope, while other neighborhoods are in a ragged condition. Staten Island is a white, middle-class suburb filled with workers from the city's 400,000 civil service workers, while the Bronx is largely black and Hispanic and is smothered by welfare and unemployment.

Outside New York City, nearby suburban counties like Westchester, Bergen, and Fairfield are mostly posh, upper-class, and heavily white. These are typically modern suburbs, characterized by private housing, shopping malls, and low, sleek corporate headquarters. Here is where power is broken down into smaller parts. The counties themselves deal mostly with routine issues of allocation (roads, welfare). Real power lies in real estate, land use, and development policy. These prerogatives are mostly held by townships, incorporated municipalities, and in some instances by special districts. These localities jealously protect themselves from outside intrusion by controlling zoning, lot size, and building codes that favor single family housing.

Elsewhere in the nearby suburbs are older communities lying in Essex, Hudson, Passaic, and Union counties. These localities too exercise power of a sort, but since middle-class investors have abandoned many of them, they have little leverage in the use of that power. Some of the cities within these counties are desperately poor and degraded (Newark); others continue to struggle and have seen some rays of light (Yonkers, Jersey City); and some others are still lively, diverse, urban communities with meaningful political discretion (Montclair, Hoboken).

Employment is always a useful measure of investor interest and local prosperity. Job increases often bring with them higher local revenues, enhanced land values, and greater multiplier effects for local business. Likewise, job losses often entail fiscal crises, depressed land values, and business bankruptcies.

By this criterion, the Manhattan CBD is preeminent. Today, it holds over 2.7 million jobs, accounting for 23 percent of the region's employment. We should also recognize that while its percentage of the CSA and rate of growth softened over the last two full decades, the absolute numbers in job growth were significant and came to more than 300,000 new jobs. This growth alone equals the total employment of a medium-sized city. Elsewhere in the region, the job growth in core counties actually exceeded performance in the nearby suburbs, telling us that the rest of New York City had begun to recover from the decline of the 1970s. The other big story centers on job growth in the distant suburbs, whose 48 percent spurt outpaced every county group. Like so many regions in the rest of the world, New York has experienced a rapid industrial decentralization. Nevertheless, as we look at the distribution of employment in different parts of the region, the proportions are not terribly askew. Approximately 37 percent of this total is located in CBD and core counties, while the nearby and distant counties share a little more than 31 percent.

Even more important are the structural changes taking place within industrial sectors of the regional economy. What was once a city and a region heavily reliant on manufacture has now transformed into a corporate and service-centered economy. During the 1970s, the region began to shed its manufacturing industry and this accelerated during the last two decades. Basically, transformation in the region and its geographic subdivisions meant a stark decline in manufacturing, a moderate rise in finance, insurance, and real estate (FIRE), a very steep rise in services, and relatively flat performance in wholesale industries.

Rather than a moderate decentralization to another part of the CSA, manufacturing simply took off for further reaches. By the year 2000, blue-collar jobs had dropped from a previously depleted total of just 18 percent of regional employment to a paltry 8 percent. Within CBD, core, and suburban counties, similar jobs followed suit and they too more than halved their manufacturing capacity. At least some of the replacement could be found in finance, insurance, and real estate. Between 1980 and 2000, most counties saw an increase in FIRE sectors. The only exceptions were in the core counties, where FIRE stagnated.

The biggest and most consistent boosts were in the service sector. Here every geographic group jumped by 10 percentage points or more. By the dawn of the new century, services consumed more than a third of all economic activity within the region and within each of its geographic subdivisions. Clearly, the region had become heavily

white-collar, with its population relying on a buoyed corporate and financial apparatus to promote a huge workforce. Known as knowledge workers, many, though not
all, plied service skills from complicated information technology to health care and
personal services like hair styling. A portion of service workers were less skilled and
staffed cleaning or security services for large office buildings as well as doing housekeeping for an affluent elite.

Culture and Economic Development

New York misses no opportunity in promoting culture as a tool for economic growth.
While suburban and exurban cultural centers provide local residents with an array of
the arts, much of the region's cultural life is situated in the downstate area, closer to the
municipal bounds of the city. The strongest linkages between culture and economic
development occur within New York City. Within these municipal bounds, culture has
acquired a unique division of labor, where different types of creative industries form
highly interdependent clusters. At the very center of the CBD core is the clothing and
fashion industry. Here bevies of designers, color coordinators, and fabric specialists
scurry between high-rise buildings to gain a competitive edge against Paris and Milan.
The CBD core also contains the Broadway theater district, whose worldwide renown is
unparalleled. The theater district is complemented by off Broadway theaters and play-
houses in other parts of Manhattan.

Elsewhere in Manhattan, the Soho and Chelsea neighborhoods hold the largest
stock in the nation of art galleries and artist studios. The division of cultural labor continues into the Greenpoint and Williamsburg sections of Brooklyn, where factory studios actually apply the arts to profit-making enterprise. The converted factories and
old garages of these neighborhoods are ideal for artistic craftsmen who build niche
kitchen appliances and decorative lighting fixtures. Still further away from the CBD
core, in sections of Queens called Astoria and Long Island City, larger studios are busy
with commercial photographers, television producers, and independent film makers.

The geographic clustering of New York's cultural industries has very tangible economic ramifications. Through the turn of the new millennium, New York's cultural
workforce comprised over 300,000 people, amounting to more than 8 percent of its
total workforce. The region is home to over one-third of the nation's actors; over a
quarter of the country's fashion designers; and approximately 10 percent of all film
editors, set designers, graphic designers, and fine artists (Center for an Urban Future
2005, 3–5).

The economic magnitude of culture should not be underestimated. By the year
2000, it had contributed over $15 billion to the region's economy and generated addi-
tional billions of tourist dollars. Culture not only counts toward the regional GDP but
contributes significant tax revenues to local government—New York City alone collected over $250 million in taxes from the arts and related activities (New York Founda-
tion for the Arts n.d., 10).

Culture is supported by a vast infrastructure of schools, institutes, foundations, nonprofit organizations, profitable businesses, and the city's Department of Cultural Affairs (DCA). In addition to federal, state, and private funding, the DCA has spent over $300 million in inflation-adjusted dollars to support the arts (New York Foundation for the Arts n.d., 11). Through the DCA, the city continues to donate hundreds of millions of dollars for the improvement of cultural facilities.

Finally, culture has enormous direct effects on New York's quality of life and ability to recruit entrepreneurs and investors and enhance the region's creative class. As the region's affluent population changes, so too do its tastes and spending disposition. Increased opportunities for discreet spending not only serve as a lure for this population but snowball into more jobs, a greater sense of liveliness, and a more dynamic city-region. Few cities in the world can equal the innovative capacity of New York's cultural life. Yet for all the talk about the purity of the arts, New York's reputation as the cultural capital of the world is intimately connected to its reputation as the economic capital of the world.

Jobs, People, and Boom–Bust Change

In examining the regional economy, how do job numbers fit population size? Where did the jobs go relative to demographic trends and how does the region break down by proportion of jobs to people? Table 4.1 displays employment relative to population for the region as a whole as well as within various county groupings.

The table shows that for each person in the CSA there was little more than one-half of a job for the most recent year. As we move down the table to the CBD, we see that the job proportion increases significantly to 1.80 jobs for each person. At the same time, core county jobs drop to a little more than a quarter of a job per person, and in nearby and distant suburbs this ratio picks up again to little more than half of a job for each person.

For the most part, economic restructuring in the region has been robust, but as mentioned the process is erratic with periods of wild booms followed by serious busts. A national recession in the early 1980s hit New York as it was transitioning and had

TABLE 4.1. EMPLOYMENT TO POPULATION RATIO FOR THE CSA: 1980–2000

	1980	1990	2000
Total CSA	0.51	0.56	0.56
CBD	1.73	1.79	1.80
Core counties	0.24	0.26	0.26
Near suburbs	0.53	0.59	0.59
Distant suburbs	0.44	0.53	0.55

Source: US Bureau of the Census.

some effect on the region's recovery. The subsequent stock market collapse of 1987 affected the city and the unemployment rate reached 11 percent by the early 1990s. From the mid-1990s onward, Manhattan and the region enjoyed a prolonged period of growth, only to be upset by the 9/11 attack, which set off another period of contraction. The recovery from 9/11 was relatively rapid, as the mid-Manhattan CBD took up the lost office space and firms poured into surrounding areas in New Jersey and Connecticut.

That same recovery was helped along by a boom in housing, by rampant mortgage lending, and by the conversion loans into portable financial packages that were sold to investors around the world. While these practices were risky (if not irresponsible), they propelled the circulation of capital and reaped enormous profits for Wall Street firms. As the financial sector prospered, so too did the real estate business, the hotel business, and a host of smaller industries. The city with its region saw itself as a fortress for an army of white-collar workers who made the global economy possible, the only question being whether it would be London or New York that led the charge.

All this came to an abrupt and shocking halt in the autumn of 2008, as financial houses discovered their practices could not be sustained. New York's economic boom was now set in reverse. The stock market quickly tumbled and some of Wall Street's most prominent firms fell into bankruptcy. In serial fashion, the crisis reverberated through all levels of the economy, precipitating job losses, retreating property values, falling public revenues, and large-scale retractions of public projects. As of this writing, the bottom has yet to be reached and we will not know its effects on the region for years to come. Undoubtedly, the region's institutions and policies are being mobilized and will play a role in economic recovery. Whether or not these efforts are effective remains to be seen (see discussion later in this chapter).

In some ways, the geography of economic growth is contradictory. That is, both centrifugal and centripetal forces have been at work in the New York region. It can be said that while jobs are decentralizing, they are in some respects also centralizing. Undoubtedly, back-office functions, retail shopping malls, and medium- to low-level services have gone to the suburbs. But corporate headquarters, high finance, and advanced-level services gravitate to the CBD. Put another way, capital and spending have a tendency to spread out, but capital accumulation and management remain very much concentrated.

One important indicator of this can be found in what census takers call residential adjustment. Residential adjustment measures the amount of income that originates in one place and is spent in another. Figure 4.1 profiles the region in a bar graph. A bar below the base indicates an outflow of income, while anything above the line shows an income inflow. Income flows are shown for the CSA, CBD, core counties, and nearby and distant suburbs.

Between 1980 and 2000, the flow of dollars from the CSA to areas outside the region increased from little more than one billion to over eight billion, and this does

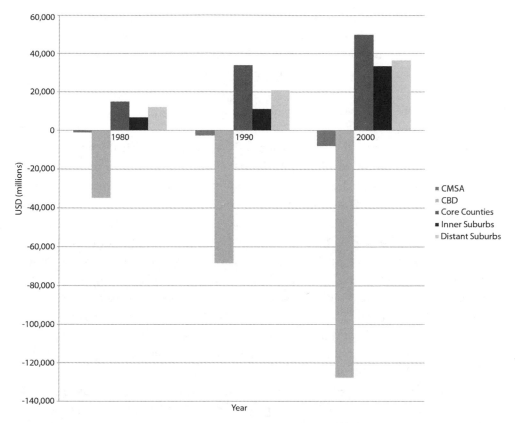

Figure 4.1. Residential Adjustment in New York Region's CBD, Core, and Near and Distant Suburbs, 1980–2000

show its continuing role as a job creator. The major story lies within the region itself. The CBD continues to accumulate capital and pays a signification portion of salaries and wages to workers who live outside of it. In the last twenty years, that amount went from $34.7 billion to $127.6 billion. At the same time, other parts of the region increased their generative capacity for income, but nothing like the amounts originating in Manhattan.

Put in somewhat different terms, by the year 2000, nearly half the income of those living in core counties was earned in Manhattan. For nearby suburbs, the proportion of Manhattan-earned income was 16 percent, and in distant counties, that proportion was nearly 19 percent.

Transportation Challenges

The regional economy consists of a complex interdependent network of capital and labor markets. Accordingly, transportation plays an extremely important role in keeping the region vital. New York's nearby and distant suburbs show that no more than 4 percent of the labor force works at home and in most counties that proportion is just 2 or 3 percent. Indeed, the highest proportion of residents (5 or 6 percent) who do work at home can be found in Manhattan rather than outlying counties (New York Metropolitan Transportation Council 2003). This suggests that reasons other than distance from central places account for home work stations.

Today the numbers of commuters remain high and the last decade has seen an increase in the numbers traveling throughout all parts of the region who keep the economy humming (see Table 4.2).

Automobiles, buses, railroads, and subway (metro) systems create the fluidity so necessary for regional markets. Despite the persistence of huge traffic snarls during peak hours, billions of dollars have gone into improving the region's transportation infrastructure, so vital for moving goods and people. This is no easy task because New York City is surrounded by waterways of various sorts. There are nineteen crossings into New York City accommodating over 2.5 million people. The heaviest traffic occurs at East River, Hudson River, and Harlem River bridges. East River access routes serve commuters from Brooklyn, Queens, and the middle-class suburbs of Long Island; Hudson River access points serve a large clientele from the mixed-income suburbs of New Jersey; Harlem River access routes mostly serve commuters entering the city from the affluent suburbs of Westchester County. For the most part, the frequency of crossing has been steady with no visible declines and, in fact, significant increases projected into the next decade.

The sheer volume of people moving to and fro within the region suggests why transportation is so important for the region's agenda. Without the carrying capacity of highways, bridges, tunnels, and mass transit, the region would be paralyzed. Obstacles to mobility threaten the generative power of the CBD and the powerful satellite economies scattered in the rest of the region.

SOCIAL POLARIZATION AND THE REGION: INCOME AND IMMIGRATION
Income: Concentrations of Wealth and Poverty

The most striking feature of this region is its geographic concentrations of wealth and poverty. The disparities of social class tend to be cumulative and couched in different parts of the region's geography. That is, counties with the highest income tend to

TABLE 4.2. COMMUTATION INTO PARTS OF NEW YORK CITY		
	Workers	*Percentage change*
	1990	2000	1990–2000
CBD	1,435,258	1,458,790	1.64
Core counties	585,905	610,686	4.23
New York City	2,021,163	2,069,476	2.39

Source: US Bureau of the Census.

be white and nonimmigrant and hold large corporate enterprises, particularly global industries. Those counties with lower incomes have more immigrants and are largely bereft of corporate enterprise. Furthermore, geosocial distinctions coincide with large stretches of terrain—spatial segregation, class, and place remain the most salient characteristics of the region. After all, we are talking about a metro region that has one of the highest indices of racial dissimilarity in the country. With an index of 84.3, the New York metropolitan area is only exceeded in its spatial segregation by Gary, Detroit, and Milwaukee (US Bureau of the Census 2000).

Table 4.3 displays per capita income by county within this region. The table takes the most recent year of available data and displays them for New York City (the Manhattan CBD and four core counties) as well as nearby and distant suburbs.

We see that Manhattan leads the region with a yearly per capita income average of $56,310. At the other end of the scale, the Bronx falls to a per capita income of just $16,496. We also note there may be great differences between suburbs, depending on whether their municipalities hold sleek corporate centers or run-down, abandoned factories. The gaps are equally conspicuous among the nearby suburbs of the city. Here Westchester County (with corporate-centered White Plains) holds the highest income with each resident earning over $46,021 annually. At the same time, per capita income in Essex County (with poverty-ridden Newark) is just $30,078.

Moving out to the distant suburbs, the differences are less severe because many of these counties do not contain worn inner cities. Nevertheless, a few do stand out as particularly affluent. Morris and Somerset counties in New Jersey fit the mold of wealthy bedroom counties and enjoy per capita incomes of more than $44,000 annually, while more rural Ocean and Ulster counties show incomes in the range of $26,000.

As far as regional income is concerned, we can say that as of the year 2006 the top 5 percent of households accounted for close to 25 percent of the regional income. When household income is divided into quintiles, we see that the highest quintile received nearly 53 percent of the total regional income, while those in the lowest quintile received less than 3 percent of the total regional income. As income ratios go, the top quintile received 19 times the income as households in the lowest quintile (US Bureau of the Census 2006).

Another way to examine these differences is by showing the proportion of income disparities over time. Figure 4.2 portrays this for the period of 1980 up through 2006. Shown in the figure are the proportions of per capita income for nearby and distant suburbs relative to New York City and the four counties of New York City (urban core) relative to Manhattan (CBD).

Observe that in 1980, nearby and distant suburbanites had 126.8 and 110.3 percent of the income of city residents. For every $1.27 earned by a nearby suburbanite or $1.10 earned by a distant suburbanite, the city resident earned just 73 cents or 90 cents, respectively. The disparity continued to widen during the intervening years,

TABLE 4.3. PER CAPITA INCOME AND POPULATION IN NEW YORK CITY AND NEAR AND DISTANT SUBURBS: 2006

Counties	Per capita income ($)	Population
New York (Manhattan)	56,310	1,613,257
The Bronx	16,496	1,369,859
Queens	23,841	2,263,858
Kings (Brooklyn)	21,631	2,520,835
Richmond (Staten Island)	29,228	478,501
New York City (PCI average and population total)	*29,501*	*8,246,310*
Westchester	46,021	949,091
Nassau	39,329	1,313,526
Bergen	40,958	894,299
Essex	30,078	779,203
Hudson	28,300	600,129
Passaic	24,622	492,301
Union	32,448	524,992
Fairfield	47,195	894,724
Near suburbs (PCI average and population total)	*36,119*	*6,448,265*
Litchfield	34,140	188,165
New Haven	29,927	843,571
Hunterdon	46,530	129,111
Mercer	34,086	364,567
Middlesex	31,539	785,479
Monmouth	38,706	641,721
Morris	44,961	487,123
Ocean	28,657	561,394
Somerset	46,020	320,213
Sussex	34,083	151,174
Dutchess	29,371	292,322
Orange	26,780	374,066
Putnam	34,378	99,405
Rockland	33,606	295,682
Suffolk	34,177	1,457,115
Ulster	26,982	181,755
Distant suburbs (PCI average and population total)	*34,621*	*7,172,863*

Source: American Community Survey 2005–7 estimates.

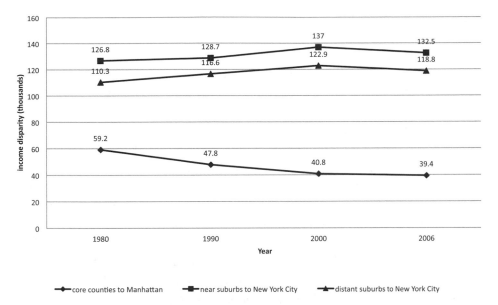

Figure 4.2. Income Disparities within the New York Region: 1980–2006

and by 2006, nearby and distant suburbanites had reached 132.5 and 118.8 percent of the city's income.

By the same token, Manhattan far outpaced the rest of the city (and the region) during the last quarter-century. The spread has also widened. In 1980 the four core counties earned just 59.2 percent of the average Manhattanite's income. By 2006 the gap widened to just 39.4 percent of the income earned by the average resident of Manhattan. Clearly, geographic disparities are coupled to class disparities and the gaps have continued.

Last, we should recognize that counties are sizeable, ranging from twenty-plus square miles in the urban core to more than 600 square miles in the outer suburban counties. Social disparities within each county can also be enormous and sometimes even larger than the differences between counties. One of the wealthiest and smallest counties in the region, Manhattan, also holds the sharpest disparities. The most recent data show the highest quintile in Manhattan received nearly forty times as much income as the bottom quintile. In the wealthy suburb of Fairfield, the highest quintile received more than twenty-two times the income as the lowest quintile. In any given county, twenty-fold differences between the highest and lowest quintiles are not uncommon. These disparities have persisted over the last twenty-five years and tell us that as the region prospered, the good times have not been shared across social classes (Beveridge 2003).

Immigration: Growth and Diversity
As described in chapter 1, the proportion of foreign-born residents in the region has also increased over the last two decades. The great bulk of these have settled in New

York City and to a lesser extent in some of the nearby suburbs. In 1980, 23.6 percent of the city's population was foreign-born and two decades later that proportion had increased to 35.8 percent.

Elsewhere in the nearby suburbs, the proportion of foreign-born residents was smaller, though still growing and still substantial. These nearby suburbs increased their proportion from 13.5 percent in 1980 to 22.9 percent by the turn of the century. The greatest absorption occurred in the least well-off areas, with heavily urbanized Hudson County holding 38.5 percent foreign-born. Once we move to the distant suburbs, the numbers and proportions grow smaller. Even in these counties, which have always been considered old-style, white American, the weight of new immigrants is felt. Twenty or more years ago, just 7.6 percent of those living in the distant suburbs were foreign-born. By the year 2000, that proportion had risen to 12.1 percent.

Most immigrants entering the region have arrived from the Caribbean, Central America, or parts of Latin America. In recent years, immigrants from India, Pakistan, and China have also settled in the region. Patterns of geographic settlement also interact with social and economic disparities, leading to very distinct neighborhood profiles. Immigrants cluster in the South Bronx (Dominicans); central Brooklyn (Caribbean islands); western Queens (Asians); and Hoboken, Jersey City, and Union City in Hudson County (Hispanics).

Immigrant labor is an important component of New York's global economy. Some serve as skilled construction laborers while others are small business entrepreneurs or work in restaurant trades. A good many are also nonskilled workers who commute to Manhattan's corporate offices and labor at night shifts to clean and maintain buildings. Still others take a reverse commute, traveling from working-class neighborhoods in the city to work as domestics in wealthy suburbs.

All told, patterns of immigrant settlement reinforce the territorial segregation of social classes. What public or subsidized housing does exist is relegated to New York's boroughs or poorer municipalities in other parts of the region. Even school systems cater to populations based on territory and social class, so that wealthier families either send their children to private schools or avail themselves of local schools that serve exclusive communities. In effect, globalization, in fragmenting the social geography of income and immigration, has deepened and regionalized issues of haves versus have-nots in the tri-state area.

The System of Governance: Federalism and Governance and the Tri-State Region

Unlike the London, Paris, or Tokyo city-regions, the New York tri-state area is part of a federal system of government. This system provides an exceptionally fragmented and decentralized governmental environment for world city-region development.

By constitutional provision, the federal or national government shares many powers with the state governments, creating many areas of overlapping governmental activity. The state governments exercise ultimate control over all lower-level governments because in constitutional law they are essentially creatures of the state. Although this gives state authorities prerogatives over all policy issues, in practice states delegate considerable policy authority to local governments (counties, towns, municipalities, etc.). The effect is that localities exercise major influence over some of the most vital policy areas, such as land use, police, education, housing, and roads. Nevertheless, their influence is part of a complex and layered system of extensive shared authority that makes multilevel governance inevitable in most policy areas that are important to the functioning of a world city-region.

One way to appreciate this massive diffusion of power is to follow the money, tracing the general pattern of local revenues from federal, state, and own sources. Raising and spending funds provide an important clue about where authority and discretion truly lie.

Figure 4.3 portrays this flow as it pertains to localities in the NYCSA. Revenue sources and amounts are designated for a typical year (2002).

The revenue totals for all governments amount to over $99 billion. This includes New York City's nearly $55.5 billion, which accounts for more than half of all local

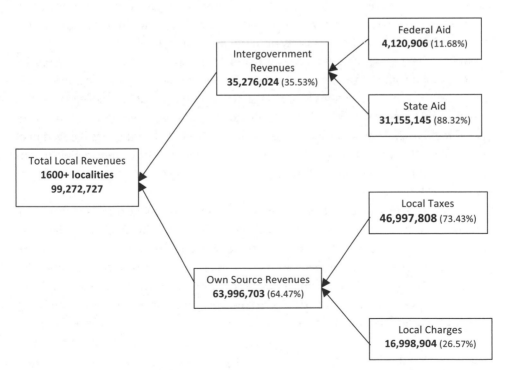

Figure 4.3. Revenue Flows 2002: New York's Consolidated Statistical Area (in Thousands of Dollars)

revenues in the region. Revenues from intergovernmental sources account for a relatively small portion of local funds (35.5 percent) and most of this comes from state
rather than federal sources. This means localities derive most of their revenues from
their own sources, namely taxes and miscellaneous charges. As a rule, the heaviest
local taxes are levied on property and retail sales (at the local level, only New York City
levies an income tax).

The political consequences of this system are profound. Because localities are so
dependent on their own source revenues, they fiercely compete for private investment. The fiscal system motivates localities to internalize benefits and slough off social liabilities onto weaker jurisdictions if they can. It is both a cause and refraction of
the fragmentation we see in the NYSCA. With the exception of a single bi-state agency
for transportation, the region is devoid of an overarching authority that can pull together its numerous centers of power. The region's political fragmentation *extends
downward, outward, and upward* to players at multiple governmental levels. Let us examine this closely to see the several faces of this highly pluralist system.

DOWNWARD: LOCAL GOVERNMENTS

Local government actors are strongly oriented toward their respective communities of
cities, towns, villages, and other jurisdictions. Localities with money, assets, and political clout do better than those that are short on resources. These communities strongly
value local control and usually evince little interest in intergovernmental cooperation
except on technical issues of low political salience involving few other localities. Voters
generally see few ties to New York City or to the region as a whole.

Indeed, increasing patterns of commutation between home and job within particular suburban counties reinforce this view. A survey of residents in the region showed
that only 22 percent of residents living in the nearby suburbs have a chief earner in the
household who works in New York City. When suburbanites were asked if they ever
visited relatives in New York City, only one-third answered affirmatively. Barely half of
suburbanites indicated that they would travel to New York City to attend a play or concert. Moreover, the percentage of suburbanites expressing an attachment to New York
City has declined (Glaberson 1992).

Nevertheless, its huge size and economic importance give Gotham a solar-type
presence in a regional system comprising many smaller satellite localities. New York
City's gigantic population of voters, importance in state politics, and role as the region's dominant economic engine cannot be ignored by other local communities. Indeed, suburban governments usually must accommodate some of its claims no matter how inward-looking they try to be. The New York State government ultimately has
legal control over this giant metropolis, and rival sources of regional power are found in
functional regional agencies, like a bi-state port authority or in specialized state agencies that deal with economic development. Yet states tend to act cautiously. This is because politicians are often products of the jurisdictions that elect them. Governors and

state legislators are ultimately chosen by citizens who are anxious to preserve rather than consolidate local power.

PANYNJ
These are public corporations that are usually appointed by the state governors, but they function with considerable financial and political independence to build and operate transportation infrastructure projects, such as ports, toll highways, bridges, tunnels, as well as some other services, including other economic development projects and recreational areas. As such, they function as a distinct governmental face in the region. But only one such PBC of much consequence operates in two states, the Port Authority of New York and New Jersey (PANYNJ), while others operate within a single state portion of the tri-state region.[4]

The PANYNJ has considerable power and resources for managing transportation infrastructure of the two states within twenty-five miles of the Statue of Liberty, the historic center of New York port. The PANYNJ is responsible for all highway links between New York and New Jersey, including bridges and tunnels; it operates all three of the region's major airports (and is planning a fourth) and seaport facilities; and it runs a commuter railroad between New York and New Jersey. The PANYNJ is sometimes considered the region's official economic development agency.

Historically, the authority has played a commanding role in regional development in part because of its access to revenues. It derives revenues from its various projects that, except for the commuter railroad, have usually earned surpluses that have been used to launch still other projects. For example, the PANYNJ built and owned the World Trade Center in lower Manhattan, a veritable cash cow until it leased it to a private developer just prior to 9/11. Although the PANYNJ has sometimes attempted to assert a leadership role in developing the region's economy, in recent years this has waned as a result of opposition to some of its activities by the governors of the two states and flat project revenues since the 1990s. Moreover, there are institutional impediments to its regional leadership. Most important, it does not represent any of the constituent governments in the region and lacks a platform for encouraging political cooperation.

Other PBCs
PBCs operating within each of the states vary considerably in their activities and their territorial reach. They include small independent authorities that run housing complexes, sports arenas, and other particular services within or across other local governmental jurisdictions, as well as much larger PBCs whose activities invariably have considerable regional implications. Among the latter are three powerful institutions: the New York Metropolitan Transportation Authority (MTA), New Jersey Transit (NJT), and the New York State Empire State Development Corporation (ESDC). The MTA owns

and operates New York City's public mass transit, including subways and buses, and also the commuter rail system, which runs from the city to the east and north to Long Island and across the Connecticut border. In addition, it operates through a subsidiary seven toll bridges and tunnels. The MTA is part of the New York regional development machine. In addition to transit operations, it is a big land owner. In 2006 it negotiated a deal with the city to sell its railyards by the Hudson River to a private developer as part of a city plan to spur West Side revitalization. It did the same thing a few years before in a Columbus Circle redevelopment project. Across the Hudson River, NJT, an agency organized not just in the region but statewide, operates the largest commuter rail system in the United States. ESDC is a powerful agency that is authorized to build and participate in urban development projects all over New York State. It is empowered to borrow on its own account to finance many of its projects and is authorized to override virtually all local governmental restrictions, such as zoning and building regulations, in order to get its job done.

Informal Regional Partnerships and Groups

These are few and weak. In the private sector, there has been some interest in promoting regional planning through the Regional Planning Association (RPA), organized in 1929. This private nonprofit group is the region's only consistent advocate for regional cooperation. Although it receives some funding from restricted state and local government, the RPA has no earmarked public funding and no elected officials or representatives from the region's various governments. It relies heavily on corporate support and in recent years its major activity has been environmental and infrastructure research. The RPA alone has been the source of published regional plans for transportation, housing, and economic development as well as for housing (but see the following discussion of transportation planning). At best, however, these plans can do little more than provide some regional perspective for governments that are free to disregard them.

Business associations, including chambers of commerce and business–government roundtables run by corporate executives, abound in the cities and counties of the region. But these private associations are not organized on a regional basis and are usually absorbed in the goings-on of the locality. Even New York City's leading business group, the Partnership for New York City, is not highly focused on the region. It tends to be more of a promoter of New York City business, especially the city's big corporate sector, than a booster of the regional economy. This is partly due to the kind of perspectives reflected by the organization's business base. For example, a recent survey of top New York City corporate executives reported to the Partnership their views on how to enhance the competitiveness of New York's financial sector. From these executives' perspective, the most important issues affecting New York's leadership as a global financial center were overwhelmingly national issues that affect other financial hubs as well, such as the legal environment, regulatory burdens, and access to highly skilled workers from abroad. Regional issues were hardly mentioned. Further, most of those surveyed believed that New York's economic interests were largely aligned with those of other governments and businesses in the broader tri-state area (McKenzie 2007).

Political Parties

The major parties sometimes provide a platform for cooperation among officials within the region. The two major national political parties, the Democrats and the Republicans, dominate control of governments throughout the region, although many suburban local governments are officially nonpartisan. New York City and its suburbs increasingly have become more Democratic in party registration and government control. Since 1974, Democrats have controlled the assembly because of this. Yet shared partisanship across the governments of the region provides a weak foundation for horizontal political cooperation. The suburban electorate tends to be richer and whiter and often supports a different political agenda from that of New York City voters, especially on matters like highways, taxes, and transit. In order to retain power, Democrats need to attract suburban voters, forcing them to resist being too responsive to New York City demands. This makes Democrats in the New York City region increasingly dependent on a heterogeneous political base that is not of one mind on regional issues. For example, in 1999 many Democrats in the state assembly supported repeal of a commuter tax on suburban residents to maintain loyalty of voters outside of New York City. New York City's declining percentage of the state population (it has fallen from 50 percent to 40 percent since 1980) suggests common agendas will not easily find party support in the near future (Stonecash and Widestrom 2006, 54–57).

Although party control of the various governments in the region and at the state levels can be a source of cohesion on managing some issues, the disorganized character of the parties precludes much party discipline. The two major parties lack a well-organized base. In a political system where media campaigns and candidate-dominated financing is the norm, state, county, and local party leaders lack much leverage in the policy-making process. Partisan voting has declined for some important offices, particularly for the mayoralty in New York City. Nevertheless, pressures of partisanship usually play a role in organizing local–state government alliances when state governors or legislatures intervene on local and regional matters.

UPWARD: THE FEDERAL AND STATE GOVERNMENTS

Federal Government and Urban Policy

Regional politics is profoundly shaped by lack of a national urban policy. Although many federal urban programs in housing, community development, social services, and other policies were founded during the period from the 1930s to the 1970s, this attempt to build a piecemeal national urban policy did not last.[5] The three decades have been one of almost continuous withdrawal of the federal government from addressing social inequality through national urban programs (Savitch and Kantor 2002,

267–312). Direct federal aid to cities per capita fell from 17.5 percent of city own source revenues in 1977 to 5.4 percent in 2000 (Wallin 2005). It has since remained relatively flat (US Office of Management and Budget 2009). Programs for new public housing virtually ended, while subsidized housing assistance shrunk. The federal Department of Housing and Urban Development was emasculated during the 1980s and 1990s and has not since recovered. Welfare reform in 1996 cut the public assistance rolls while providing little special relief to cities with high concentrations of poor. Since the 1980s, no single new urban assistance program was enacted save for the 1993 Empowerment Zone program of the Clinton administration. This program, based on the British concept of urban enterprise zones, was primarily for economic development, however. Its funneling of cash assistance to poor areas was miniscule because it spread funding widely, and much of it was in the form of tax incentives for private sector business.

The George W. Bush years continued an essentially conservative social agenda that was averse to evening out urban social inequalities, but still accepting (and sometimes expanding in health policy) the contours of a relatively decentralized American welfare state. The Department of Housing and Urban Development, cut down in size during the Clinton years, remained under constant attack. The ideal of harnessing faith-based initiatives favoring religious organizations, churches, and other voluntary associations bringing assistance to inner-city populations grew into an approach of minor policy significance. But otherwise, Bush's urban initiatives remained largely symbolic, reflecting the low priority given to poor urban areas outside the Republican electoral base.

This disinterest in urban social policy essentially reflected the national political coalitions favoring conservative Republican representation in Congress and the presidency. The ascendancy of this coalition accompanied the decline of political power on the part of central cities during the past half-century. Together, they led to the marginalization of issues of urban social inequality even while welfare state building in the form of federal tax and entitlement programs continued. The flight from federal urban social policy was not caused by deeply rooted antipathy toward big government itself. Rather, it is because cities lost their place at the policy table, leaving them vulnerable and dependent on electoral changes in partisan politics and broad ideological shifts in political sentiment. This marginalization of urban policy has not yet been reversed by the Obama administration, even though the president has called for changes that favor metropolitan-wide planning and greater attention to the plight of cities (Kantor forthcoming; Obama 2008). The economic crisis starting in 2008 led Obama to undertake massive federal intervention in the economy—with powerful consequences for New York City and its region, as we shall see—but the recession and the election of a divided federal government in 2010 have all but ended any major new urban initiatives.

The Regional Faces of Federal Policies

Even without a national urban policy, the federal (national) government is in a potentially powerful position to encourage or sometimes to even impose regionwide policies on matters of national importance, such as social policy, environmental, transportation, and health planning issues. Federal funding in all of these areas of public policy provides federal officials with a source of financial leverage. In tandem with the states, federal policy makers set important parameters for how the tri-state region is governed. Yet lack of any formal national urban policy and significant decentralist tendencies in the organization of many federal programs often leave governments in the New York region to cope with urban change without the degree of intergovernmental support and oversight found in London, Paris, or Tokyo.

A brief examination of some key national programs in social welfare and environmental policy illustrate how social equity remains highly contingent on local and state impulses. Overall, the US welfare state programs essential to the poor are characterized by considerable interstate and even intrastate variation in administration and levels of assistance.

A look at two big programs shows how. The major national income maintenance program serving the poor is the Personal Responsibility and Work Opportunities Act (PRWORA). The main medical care program serving this group is the Medicaid program, officially a state program subsidized by federal monies. Unlike many federal income assistance and health care programs serving the nonpoor, however, both PRWORA and Medicaid require substantial state governmental funding. In New York State (but not in New Jersey or Connecticut), counties are required to finance one-half of the state's share of the programs for the poor. Since so many poor are concentrated in New York City and some of the inner suburban counties, this burden falls disproportionately on localities within the region. Further, since state governments are responsible for administration, benefit levels for these programs also vary among states and sometimes even among jurisdictions within states (General Accounting Office 1998).

Since the 1996 welfare reform made the benefits temporary and terminated traditional income relief in favor of work-oriented objectives, state and local governments have had increasing latitude in choosing how to make the program work. The latter includes issues involving the severity with which regulations are enforced and the populations of recipients being denied or given benefits or required to engage in work or training (Blank and Haskins 2001; Hacker 2002). It remains unclear how much the decentralist features of welfare and medical care for the poor precipitate interstate rivalry to avoid becoming welfare magnets, although officials are known to be absorbed in the problem (Peterson and Rom 1990). In the tri-state region, however, it is mitigated by the fact that all three states are among the more generous benefit providers compared with many other states. Other major federal programs to aid the poor frequently also leave state and local governments as key decision makers. For example, federal housing policies are highly contingent on state and local government participation. As federal policies have moved away from public housing construction in favor of rent and construction subsidy efforts, the discretionary local and state roles probably have increased (Turner, Popkin, and Rawlings 2009).

In environmental policy, federal policy also sets important parameters on governments within the city-region, but devolutionary practices enable the states and even local governments to play key—and often dominant—roles in shaping environmental quality of life. During the 1960s and 1970s, Congress established the Environmental Protection Agency and enacted strict water and air quality standards that have measurably improved air and water quality throughout the United States. Yet federal regulatory activities make room for substantial decentralized policy making (Davies and Mazurek 1998; Hamilton and Stream 2008). This is because implementation of almost all environmental regulations depends on state and even local cooperation in order to meet legislated standards (Rabe 2000). For example, cities must build waste treatment plants to enable water quality improvements. Federal mandates for environmental impact statements (EIPs) for all projects involving the national government create access at the local level for groups, courts, and governmental agencies seeking to influence these projects. Since the 1990s, when amendments to federal environmental laws moved away from command and control implementation to negotiation, the role of the states has almost certainly grown in importance (Vig and Kraft 2000).

Probably the most important limitation on federal power in environmental and even social policy is the reality that land use development and the protection of green space is largely under the control of the states, which in turn often relegate their regulatory power to their local governments, as is the case in the tri-state region. Outside of coastal areas and federal lands, the national government has very limited involvement in programs to regulate urban sprawl, promote new town development, or create green belts, as national governments do in the London, Paris, and Tokyo city-regions. American federalism and the absence of a national urban policy have placed the New York global city-region (GCR) in a position of considerable independence in managing its most scarce resource, land.

Federal officials have sometimes used their considerable resources to assert regionwide policy changes in metropolitan areas like New York. Generally, however, this has obtained mixed results due to state and local opposition and due to divided support at the national governmental level. In recent decades, national officials have rarely acted as major players, seeking to overcome many barriers to regional cooperation in order to realize their own objectives. For one thing, congressional and senatorial representation is organized within state political boundaries; consequently, members of Congress are inclined to take a district- or statewide view of their responsibilities. There are few electoral rewards for regional political engagement. Finally, federal interest in encouraging regional approaches to issues of air quality, highway planning, mass transit, and other matters has diminished along with shrinking funding for many federal urban programs.

One area where federal authorities have recently advocated a regional perspective has been in transportation planning, but it is illustrative of the national government's limited success as a regional actor. Since congressional reforms in the 1990s, the federal government has required more metropolitanwide transport planning by means of metropolitan planning organizations (MPOs), which also won power over spending some federal transport funding. Yet this has hardly regionalized transportation decision making very much (Katz and Puentes 2005). State government transportation departments continue to dominate MPO transportation planning almost everywhere in the United States, including in the New York region. Nationally, MPOs have direct control over less than 7 percent of federal transport funding (Puentes and Bailey 2005, 150). For example, the New York Metropolitan Transportation Council (NYMTC) is the major MPO in the region, but its reach is actually quite limited. The only voting members are representatives of five near–New York metro area counties and state and city planning and transportation officials; officials from the federal government, New Jersey, and the major transportation PBCs in the region play merely advisory roles. A self-described collaborative forum, the NYMTC is no master planner. A separate North Jersey Transportation Planning Authority is the MPO for northern New Jersey (http://www.nymtc.org/about,cfm?img=B).

Despite the often fragmented presence of the federal government, events sometimes can catalyze intergovernmental cooperation and create a semblance of a regional agenda on a particular issue, however. 9/11 was one such event, though here again the cooperation and attention to region is limited to concerns over security. Terrorism not only struck the World Trade Center in lower Manhattan, but subsequent plots were uncovered against tunnels leading into New Jersey and the site of a major insurance company located in Newark, New Jersey. New York has received $124 million in antiterrorist funding through the Urban Areas Security Initiative (UASI). The funding is premised on combating terrorism on a regional basis and UASI has focused attention on establishing joint security operations, particularly as they pertain to mass transit, ports, bridges, and tunnels. UASI funding is now used for inspecting cargo, checking vehicles that operate between New York and New Jersey, and patrolling the area's waterways. New York City's Antiterrorism Bureau, which numbers over 1,000 police operatives, works regularly with federal agencies. Further, the federal government allocated nearly $20 billion to assist in the city's recovery—a boost that has enabled the city to initiate some new programs, although much of this money has not been spent.

THE STATE GOVERNMENTS

The state governments provide a degree of centralized power over their respective parts of the region that is somewhat akin to that found in European nation-states in national–local governmental relations. The biggest difference is that in Europe one national government holds this ascendant position, while in the New York City region three states do. Consequently, the state governors, legislatures, and their agencies un-doubtedly are the biggest power brokers in the region.

Despite home rule traditions in the tri-state area, all three state governments rou-tinely mandate obligations on local governments, often without providing funding. Although these mandates, together with state fiscal assistance programs to local gov-ernments, can stimulate some de facto regional policy cohesion within each state, devolutionary practices also limit the reach of state power in critical areas of public policy. This is particularly the case in land use planning and housing. New York, New Jersey, and Connecticut all follow the dominant American practice of relegating most control over land use to the lowest levels of incorporated local government. As dis-cussed in the next chapter, this powerfully shapes how the New York GCR manages issues of development, social provision, environmental protection, and quality of life.

Even in social policy, where state government programs work in tandem with fed-eral programs to dominate income, employment, housing, and other services to in-dividuals, decentralist arrangements create considerable local variation in services and access to benefits. For example, assistance to homeless families and individuals is highly dependent on local provision of shelter and other assistance. The federal gov-ernment has little or no policy for coping with homelessness, although it has provided some funds to states and local governments in recent decades. For their part, the three states in the New York region have tended to shift most of the responsibility for the homeless to their local governments and the private sector. Even though New York State is exceptional in constitutionally guaranteeing shelter as a result of court suits, this responsibility and most of the cost has been delegated to local governments. This has led to severe inequalities. As a result of court mandates, New York City spending on homeless programs soared from $10 million to more than $500 million in the early 1990s (Berg 2007, 80). In contrast, homeless assistance in many suburban communi-ties is often a minor part of local budgets.

Notwithstanding some long-standing decentralist traditions in governance, all three state governments regularly intervene to address issues that spill beyond the borders of particular local governments. There is virtually no significant regional issue that does not eventually ascend upward to intimately involve the three states' pow-erful executives and even their legislative assemblies. Because the respective state governors appoint nearly all of the PBC governing boards, these institutions tend to be highly responsive to gubernatorial political ambitions. State legislators in New York play a big role in monitoring and approving the projects, funding, and perfor-mance of the PBCs by means of special committees. For example, in New York the ESDC usually acts as a development arm of the state in response to these overseers. Big ESDC projects require approval by a Public Authorities Control Board, where rep-resentatives of the governor and the leaders of the two legislative houses sit. Fur-ther, even though they are officially independent, some PBCs actually are highly de-pendent on legislative appropriations to carry out their projects or must seek state governmental approval to borrow in the bond market in order to finance their activities. Ultimately, however, all PBCs are creatures of the states; their existence and political independence depend on the will of the state governments.

Although state governments have legal supremacy, the enormous size, economic power, and importance of New York City create political rivalry and interdependency between city and state policy makers. Rivalry springs from the fact that downstate New York City represents population groups, businesses, and partisan interests that differ dramatically from upstate New York. Interdependence arises from two-sided entanglement of state and city. New York City is the major source of revenues for New York State; about one-third of New Jersey's economy is dependent upon Wall Street alone, even more in the northern part of the state (McGeehan 2008). Thus, New York State's power and oversight over New York City is often highly tempered by the reality of shared fate and shared economic interests. For its part, New York City political leaders are careful to manage state–city relations in order to maximize political support in Albany, the state capital. Home rule provisions and state fiscal aid programs that rely on relatively fixed distributive formulas limit the degree to which New York City must seek program-by-program approval from Albany. Yet New York governors and legislators remain continual arbitrators of what New Yorkers can and cannot do in managing even its own affairs, not to mention its relations with other governments in the region.

Conclusion: Fragmented Metropolis, Decentralist Impulses

The New York tri-state region incorporates a highly fragmented political system with strong decentralist impulses. Political power and authority are divided in outward, upward, and downward directions to make regional governance a highly pluralistic and competitive endeavor. Suburban growth has increased the numbers of incorporated governments in the region. Proliferation of PBCs that manage local and state interests in the region are adding to the complexity of regional governmental networks. Lack of a national urban policy and strong traditions of local government autonomy in critical policy areas create a governmental environment with little central direction.

This fragmented system nevertheless manages major social and economic changes happening in the GCR. As a world city-region, New York City and its suburban periphery have shed older manufacturing industries in favor of services, particularly in so-called global industries that include finance and producer services. In this process of conversion, the Manhattan CBD and scattered suburban satellite economies have been able to prosper together, particularly since the resurgence of the core CBD since the 1990s. At least up until the great recession that started in 2008, job growth marked the region as a whole, with New York City as the prime economic engine having global links. Population growth in the region as a whole and in New York City has been substantial during recent decades. Both city and suburb are internationalizing quickly as they draw immigrants from abroad in large numbers.

The tri-state region's prosperity is not equally distributed, however. Income and job access disparities are a major problem. Although core city and suburban income differences are prominent and widening, significant disparities are also found among suburban areas, especially between older nearby suburbs and the outer ring of suburban communities. The centrifugal and centripetal forces at work in the metropolitan area are creating a complex network of capital and labor markets that are intertwined. These changes are producing traffic bottlenecks and put increasing demands on the regional transportation infrastructure. At the same time, quality of life and environmental amenities are becoming more critical as a result of new pressures by higher-level governments and by voters.

The major dilemma for regional governance is how such a politically fragmented and decentralized governmental system mediates issues of social and economic change arising from GCR development. What kind of regional political agenda has emerged during recent decades? How does such a divided urban political order respond? To this we now turn.

5. *Managed Pluralism*

ON THE SURFACE, THE NEW YORK tri-state region presents a picture of weak and fragmented government struggling to manage a globalizing public agenda. When probed more deeply, however, a profile of greater collective action emerges. For all its divisions, this pluralist political system displays surprising capacity to mount some coherent, if limited, regional governmental responses to the new forces of global change. Conflict and competition, as well as cohesion and collaboration, characterize governmental relations. This process of mediation has produced uneven and sporadic attention to the major political problems facing the metropolitan area, however.

The politically fragmented character of the region means that there is little formal regional planning. Lacking a regional governmental overseer, issues are usually managed piecemeal and the various players rarely respond to admonitions to take metropolitan-wide perspectives more seriously. New York City's political and economic importance for the region sometimes forces state and suburban policy makers to recognize its central economic importance and grant some of its claims. Nevertheless, the city lacks the political power and authority to impose its will, and it faces rivals at the state and local level whose own formidable power often enables them to block or dilute the city's political agenda or to enhance their own.

The only consistent power brokers that regularly can be counted on to take regional perspectives into policy making are the state governments. Governors and legislatures of the respective states often interpose themselves when issues spill over the borders of local governments, in disputes among the various public authorities or among the states themselves. The use of state governmental power, therefore, is crucial for resolving competing governmental interests and mobilizing political cooperation. Such top-down planning that overrides local governmental choices almost invariably happens in cases that occur within a single state's borders, however. Apart from the state governments, only the bi-state Port Authority of New York and New Jersey (PANYNJ) ever claims a regional reach in its policy making and planning, and its success is almost invariably dependent on finding supporters elsewhere in the region or states. In effect, much of what happens across the region springs from the interplay of governments seeking to advance their own interests and priorities, leaving the social and economic outcomes as de facto regional policy.

Nevertheless, this city-region has sometimes promoted a regional agenda since the 1980s and even has achieved a degree of political coordination without much deliberate regional planning. How? By means of competition and bargaining among governments to build common agendas that also function to promote their particular policy interests. In the tri-state region's highly fragmented marketplace of governments, the individual players have little choice but to act in ways that internalize benefits and limit costs in addressing matters of regional consequence. Although this flawed system of regional politics often produces delay and even stalemate on particular issues, the process of bargaining and alliance building is sometimes capable of pulling together to realize policy objectives of regional scope.

Changing Regional Policy Agendas and Managed Pluralism

Common agendas for the region rise and fall in response to changes in the alignment and composition of governmental coalitions that mobilize and demobilize over time. As globalization of the regional economy unleashed new stresses and public problems since the 1980s, the political actors have sought to influence ways of mediating these issues. Most often, the regional political system has remained quite resilient in the face of new challenges to governance, reinforcing established patterns of governmental fragmentation and rivalry. Yet it also displays capacity for intergovernmental cooperation when important governmental interests successfully align, making it possible for new policies of regional scope to emerge. Successful regional intervention has occurred in only limited policy areas, however. Social or redistributive policies have largely been avoided. Governments in the region have shied away from contentious issues regarding social polarities (racial and class segregation, income disparities). As we shall see, trying to resolve social polarities led to immense dissension but little action, especially among well-off and well-ensconced townships. In contrast, policies to enhance economic development have fared better. In particular, regional action has centered on transportation to foster economic development and environmental policies to improve quality of life in the region.

FRAGMENTATION AND RIVALRY: LAND USE, HOUSING, AND LOCAL ECONOMIC DEVELOPMENT

Land use and housing directly touch peoples' personal lives and are invariably seen as subject to bottom-up policies. Local governments are responsible for raising most of their own revenues. Consequently, they are compelled to compete in order to attract taxpayers, jobs, and profitable businesses. Localities also avoid shouldering burdens that drive up taxes or that might make the community less desirable as a place to live or work. This includes low-income housing projects, apartments for large families, racial minorities, environmental hazards, and other things that are likely to drive down property values or might make the locality less attractive to residents or investors.

Consequently, local economic development and housing issues in the region have not changed in major ways since the 1980s. Local governments, big or small, actively promote their own community's economic welfare by maximizing internal benefits and show little interest in cooperating across political boundaries if this compromises their development options (Benjamin and Nathan 2001).

New York City stands radically apart from the rest of the region because of the unique character and size of its population and economy. With its huge polyglot population, gateway role in immigration, and its liberal political traditions, New York City's political agenda is rarely shared by any of its rivals in state or region. The city's high taxes, high energy costs, and extensive regulatory practices contribute to making it one of the nation's most expensive business environments in the United States (ESDC 2007, 9). Further, its economy is massively linked to the international marketplace to a degree that no other locality in the region can claim. As described in chapter 1, New York City is a world financial command post. International corporations that dominate the Manhattan central business district (CBD) essentially form dense pillars to world markets, particularly in finance and corporate producer services. This type of internationalized outward-looking economy reinforces differences with other communities in the region that maintain more regional and national networks of business activity. New York's role as a global hub also helps to maintain on a massive scale ancillary business sectors in medicine, advertising, marketing, media, entertainment, and culture that essentially have no counterpart elsewhere in the tri-state area, even though suburban satellite economies sometimes are linked with and partially replicate particular New York City job sectors.

BOOSTING ARTS, CULTURE, AND AMENITIES: WHY LOCAL INTERESTS DOMINATE

There is growing consciousness of the commercial importance of art, entertainment, and cultural amenities among governmental leaders in the tri-state area. New York City is the cultural and artistic center of the region, and perhaps of the entire United States. New York metro (mainly the city) holds an enormous competitive advantage over any other American metropolitan area because of its huge concentration of jobs in arts, culture, and other fields of creative production (Currid 2007). This concentration is even greater than in finance, law, media, and management. For example, in 2001 over 150,000 jobs were generated in arts and culture, growing by 52 percent from 1992 to 2001. Between 1998 and 2001, the city's creative workers grew by 13.1 percent while its overall job base grew by 6.5 percent. In 2004 cultural visitors accounted for 9.1 billion of the city economy while the film industry contributed $5 billion and 100,000 jobs (Center for the Urban Future 2005). The presence of this vast symbolic economy is an important part of local and regional politics.

Local governmental responses to enhance the so-called high culture (including such things as museums, the arts, legitimate theater, etc.) differ considerably from those connected to popular culture (sport, mass media, and entertainment, etc.). Nevertheless, there is little regional political cooperation among governments in either policy venue, and there is even very little in the way of a coherent culture policy within New York City.

With respect to high culture, the possibilities for any kind of a regional policy are defeated by the fact that these activities are overwhelmingly concentrated in New York City. City officials have little reason to regionalize the advantages they already have. Even within the region's cultural center, however, the city government has yet to develop a policy strategy for boosting its art and culture sectors. For many years, New York City has offered tax credits and refunds on film project spending if the film is produced in Gotham. The Department of Cultural Affairs is the nation's biggest cultural funding agency, with a 2006 year capital budget allocating $803 million in subsidies (and spending for construction/restoration) over four years to thirty-four cultural institutions, from museums, theaters, and performing arts centers (Department of Cultural Affairs 2008; Pogrebin 2007). Most of this money has gone to major institutions, rather than to smaller community arts. In addition, some smaller programs, such as for artists-in-residence, also fill out the city's culture policies.

Although leading politicos and arts groups routinely acknowledge the importance of boosting New York City's cultural development, there is little agreement about how this can be stimulated through public policy. Artistic creativity and cultural innovation are little-understood processes of bringing talent and people together in synergetic ways to be creative or innovative. Although New York City's cultural environment provides critical advantages of agglomeration making this process possible, it is difficult to target any part of it in order to increase it or make it more efficient, sustainable, or productive (e.g., much cultural innovation probably takes place in cafés and bars). At the same time, there are big political barriers to the more obvious policies that could have a positive impact on culture-building. Culture advocates often lament that artistic creativity is hurt by the city's lack of cheap rents and loss of affordable spaces due to commercial redevelopment (Currid 2007). But addressing this dilemma would involve huge costs to the city and would have to overcome competing demands of other interests for development opportunities. At best, strategic thinking about investing in art and culture is something that occasionally gets attended to in the course promoting commercial development. For instance, during the 1990s the revitalization of the Times Square entertainment district included concessions requiring developers to help preserve a number of historic theaters and provide some below-market-rate residential units for actors (Reichl 1999).

With respect to popular culture, the policy responses also have been highly localized. Unlike the case of high culture, however, virtually all cities, counties, and towns spread over the three states of the region are able to compete in this game. Accordingly, governments throughout the metropolitan counties engage in a variety of policies for place marketing through advertising campaigns to attract tourist dollars and to invest in programs to enhance visitor amenities. While New York City officials see this as a means of sustaining their competitive edge, nearby places hope these efforts will help transform them into more important destinations for leisure, entertainment, or sport. Aside from joint media campaigns among some counties and localities to highlight parts of the region for visitors, such as Long Island, the Jersey Shore, or the Hudson River Valley, boosting tourism is intensely localized. For example, aggressive place-marketing campaigns launched by New York City touting it as the "Big Apple" is typical of this posture. New York State's ambiguous "I Love New York" promotion to lure visitors beyond New York City to upstate counties did little to boost the region.

New York City and other localities in the tri-state area have heavily subsidized building or upgrading professional sports stadia, popular performance spaces, convention centers, and entire tourist districts in order to compete for visitors. These kinds of programs have proliferated since the 1980s in almost every urban center in New York, New Jersey, and southern Connecticut, effectively locking in public and private money in huge numbers of brick-and-mortar projects (Berg 2007; Kantor 1995). As discussed earlier, these projects almost always combine local and state governmental agencies with private developers and investors. Nevertheless, the programs have remained highly localized politically, with state agencies employing their power and largess in response to demands by local officials and interests competing to upgrade their commercial attractiveness. For example, in the last decade Newark, New Jersey, received major state assistance in building a new performing arts center as part of its downtown revitalization strategy. The rivalry and pull of New York sports teams playing in the New Jersey Meadowlands arenas helped spark New York City's rebuilding of two of its own major stadiums in 2008–2009. Competition to attract the visitor class is a matter of almost continuous economic warfare in the tri-state metropolis.

City–State Rivalry in Urban Development: The Case of the Olympic Bid
Not surprisingly, New York City's economic leaders often are at loggerheads with other actors in the state government whose priorities differ—frequently for purely local, not regional, reasons. For example, New York City's bid to attract the 2012 Olympics was upended by state policy makers in 2005. The city's bid for the Olympics was highly dependent upon its success in building a new stadium on Manhattan's West Side. This project was expected not only to enhance New York's ability to compete with other international city bids but also to form part of Mayor Bloomberg's high-priority plan to expand and modernize the city's main convention and trade show venue, the Javits Center. Mayor Bloomberg carefully built a broad coalition of supporters for the new stadium and struck a deal with the New York Jets football team, who agreed to pay for the stadium itself while leaving the city and state to pay for the platform over the West Side railyards on which the stadium would sit. The plan was vigorously opposed

by many civic organizations, including the Regional Plan Association and community groups from neighborhoods around the stadium site, as well as certain members of the business community led by the owner of a competing sports and exhibition center. Most of these groups were critical of the environmental impact of the stadium and doubted the stadium's economic advantages.

The stalemate was ultimately resolved by the New York State Public Authorities Control Board. It refused to approve the $300 million state contribution to the stadium as well as the New York Metropolitan Transportation Authority's (MTA) ability to sell property rights it held on the West Side that the Jets needed at lower than market rates. Parochial interests dominated the decision. Among the three voting members of the board—the governor, speaker of the New York State Assembly (a lower Manhattan Democrat), and the state majority leader (an upstate Republican)—only the governor was supportive of the stadium as a means of boosting the city and state economy. The assembly speaker saw the stadium as a threat to commercial development in lower Manhattan, however; the upstate Republican Senate leader had other grounds for antipathy to the downstate project.

NEW YORK CITY AND THE MANHATTAN VISION

New York City's economic development strategy generally has little focus on the regional economy. Rather, for decades virtually every mayoral administration has pursued strategies that privilege the city's important corporate business sector in the Manhattan CBD. This strategy involves constant searching for ways of expanding available space in and around the CBD while granting only token efforts to encourage businesses to shift many activities to locations in the outer boroughs. Consequently, during the past three decades, New York City mayors, whether Republican or Democratic, have pursued essentially similar policies that are intended to capitalize on Manhattan's special assets for attracting or retaining a dense concentration of jobs in the corporate headquarters, producer services, finance, and related sectors. Although the city has sometimes given attention to the economy of the outer boroughs, Manhattan's primacy is an article of faith among all public officials (Savitch and Kantor 2002).

This strategic vision has led one administration after another to use tax subsidies and business incentive programs to lure corporate investment. The city has several agencies that package tax, finance, service, and other business incentives to lure or retain important individual businesses. Further, the city and state governments also have legislated to provide them across the board to certain qualifying businesses. While New York City imposes high taxes and onerous regulations with one hand, it routinely exempts and makes individual concessions to business investors with the other hand.

The city's Manhattan strategy also promotes the use of public money and zoning reform to open up new areas for commercial development. In recent decades, the city's top priority has been to expand the underused west side of midtown Manhattan for commercial development. At the same time, the city's traditional financial center in lower Manhattan has become the target of mixed-use redevelopment as more businesses have abandoned this location for uptown or suburban locations. There also have been efforts to find areas outside of Manhattan for further business expansion, but these are usually uphill struggles against big money already invested in the traditional CBD. For example, in 2001 a report by a so-called Group of thirty-five business and government leaders proposed preparing for future office growth by mobilizing and rezoning land to create three new CBDs in downtown Brooklyn, Long Island City (Queens), and the far west side of Manhattan, along with five new ancillary business districts in Harlem, Jamaica and Flushing (Queens), the Bronx, and Staten Island (Group of 35 2001). This proposal never became harnessed by key players and became even more marginalized after 9/11 altered the city's economic agenda.

HELPING THE REST: SOCIAL POLICY IN NEW YORK CITY

Although New York City has seldom tried to steer much development to its poorer outer boroughs, it has vigorously used social policy to address the social fallout of Manhattan-centered growth. New York City's liberal political traditions and highly accessible interest group–driven political system measurably counterbalances some of the business primacy in economic affairs. The result is remarkably extensive city programs to provide social safety nets for lower income groups in housing, aid to homeless populations, hospitals and medical care services, income assistance, higher education, and mass transportation. These commitments are maintained despite the fact that New York State requires the city to shoulder or contribute large amounts to these redistributive programs compared to virtually all other American cities.

For example, New York City not only maintains the largest public housing sector in the nation but also has undertaken unusually bold housing initiatives by local government standards during the last three decades. During the 1980s it took into public ownership and then recycled thousands of abandoned private housing units left by landlords fleeing the lower end of the housing market. New York City spent far more resources for the development and rehabilitation of affordable housing than any other American city, investing over $4 billion from 1986 to 1997 in a massive capital budget program (Schwartz 1999). Under Mayor Michael Bloomberg, the city also launched big housing initiatives in 2002 that were expanded in 2005 to build or preserve 165,000 apartments or houses for low- and moderate-income families. The capital budget programs totaled more than $7.5 billion and constituted an explicit effort to soften the blows of gentrification and depletion in the city's housing stock as its economy boomed (Fernandez 2009; New York City Department of Housing Preservation and Development 2009). As noted in the previous chapter, the city also has maintained one of the largest and most costly homeless programs in the nation.

Although under Mayor Giuliani some of these social commitments in housing, homeless services, and other social services were diminished, even his relatively conservative Republican approach to government left most social programs intact (Schill 1999). Since Giuliani, the city government relies more on the private sector to put a social face on redevelopment, particularly by cross-subsidy programs requiring below-market-rate housing in most new developments and by greater use of public–private partnerships. Nevertheless, since the 1980s New York has remained a decidedly liberal town in social policy compared to most large American cities (Savitch and Kantor 2002, 101–49).

Even though these achievements in social policy are unusual from the perspective of typical American cities, they are limited efforts with large gaps by any other standard. As described in previous chapters, social inequality in New York City remains a chronic problem. For example, even the Bloomberg administration's big housing capital investment programs could not stem the hemorrhaging of lower-rent housing units in the city as waves of gentrification and rent deregulation swept New York City during the last decade. Indeed, the number of apartments considered affordable to low-income households fell nearly 17 percent between 2002 and 2008 (Fernandez 2009). As numerous studies have demonstrated, the city's social welfare efforts pale before the enormous attention and resources it devotes to promoting its business and economic base (see, for example, Abu-Lughod 1999; Sites 2003). This becomes particularly apparent on issues that occasion clear trade-offs between growth and environmental justice in poor neighborhoods. Racial and low-income neighborhoods frequently suffer disproportionate public health risk effects due to the unequal concentration of toxic and hazardous waste facilities in poorer areas by New York City and state officials (Sze 2007). Whether these effects are mainly matters of discriminatory politics or are an artifact of economic development is a matter of debate, however (Berg 2007, 142).

BEYOND NEW YORK CITY: THE STATE, THE SUBURBS,
AND THE POLITICS OF INTERDEPENDENCE

No matter how much New York City leaders seek to promote internal benefits in economic development, the hand of state policy makers and regional interests is almost ubiquitous. This is because almost any significant economic project attempted by the city also is dependent upon joint financing, participation, or legal approval by state government officials, be they governors, legislators, or public benefit corporation (PBC) boards. Since this often forces city officials to compromise or even abandon what they are doing, it frequently has the effect of regionalizing local development decisions to the state level. For example, a host of state government players made it possible in 2005 for New York City to move ahead with the largest development in the city outside of Manhattan in twenty-five years, the Atlantic Yards project located just outside of downtown Brooklyn. A private developer unveiled a development plan for this area that included office towers, apartments, commercial space, and acres of parkland, as well as a new stadium for the New York Nets basketball team. Even though this project was to be mostly privately financed, the developer and city required sale of some land owned by the MTA, as well as state and city contributions for site preparation. Further, the ESDC's financial backing and power to override normal land use review processes was critical to allowing the developer to proceed. Finally, the same State Public Authorities Board (SPAB) that played a pivotal role in the Jets stadium was necessary in Atlantic Yards. Although the Atlantic Yards project eventually won the support of the key economic development players in city and state, it also drew much opposition from community groups and some New York City officials, who managed to win major concessions from the developer related to project design and execution. After several years of negotiation, the SPAB approved the project over continued neighborhood opposition in 2006 (Berg 2007, 9).

New York City's relations with its suburbs are dominated by interdependence and rivalry. The city depends on a huge suburban commuter workforce—the largest in the nation (Regional Plan Association 2004). In 2006 more than 90 percent of the region's labor force commuted to their place of work. This included nearly 586,000 commuting into the urban core and more than 1.4 million entering the CBD (New York Metropolitan Transportation Council 2003). This enables the city and the region to successfully compete against other cities for white-collar workers. The New York region offers its white-collar workers attractive suburban housing and neighborhood environments, all within easy commuting distance to the Manhattan CBD. City officials have carefully managed this interdependence. That many of these suburban enclaves are exclusive and often segregated by race and income probably works to the city's competitive advantage in attracting executive families; no mayor in recent decades has made any notable effort to open up the suburbs through calling for regional housing reforms. For decades, New York City has turned to its own devices in order to help retain residential property owners. It has maintained a policy of taxing homeowners lightly while shifting a disproportionate burden of taxes on commercial properties.

New York City's rivalry with its suburbs stems from the fact that the city constantly struggles with competitive trends favoring dispersal of economic activities and the growing political power of the suburban electorate in state politics. For example, New Jersey's role in the regional economy has grown after years of being the junior partner. Newark airport has passed LaGuardia in traffic volume while Port Elizabeth and Port Newark dominate the marine terminal business (Salmore 1998, 230). New Jersey's ability to compete with New York City in sports and entertainment increased since the 1970s as the Meadowlands sports and entertainment complex has cut into New York's traditional dominance. As noted later, attempts to get state and local governments in the tri-state area to limit the use of business incentive programs in the competition to lure jobs within the region have failed. Suburban political pressure was instrumental in the state legislature's repeal of the commuter tax that helped support city services.

New York City's rivalry with suburban claims in state politics in New York State is inevitable since so many state agencies lump city and suburban together in critical programs. For instance, in 2005 the MTA capital plan for 2005–2009 provided for dramatic expansion of the MTA network after years of mostly funding maintenance, providing a big boost for strategic projects for New York City. But the state Capital Program Review Board represents state, city, and suburban officials, effectively regionalizing MTA spending decisions. It approved the capital plan only after months of bargaining, and the officials made a deal to increase the number of projects to be funded outside of New York City (Stonecash and Pally 2006).

SUBURBAN GOVERNMENTS AND EXCLUSIONARY POLITICS

Local governments in the suburbs have steadily pursued very parochial economic development agendas in order to maximize internal benefits as places of business or residence. The larger cities and towns, such as White Plains in Westchester County or Stamford in southern Connecticut, usually seek business growth in order to reduce residential property tax burdens; many other suburban communities choose to compete more as bedroom enclaves for workers who travel to jobs within the county or to New York City (Jones 2010). In either case, however, these suburban local governments usually pursue essentially similar exclusionary policies. Except for some older suburbs with fewer options and substantial lower-income populations, suburban bedroom communities almost invariably utilize their power to regulate land use and building development to keep out or at least limit multifamily and subsidized housing (Benjamin and Nathan 2001). The result is that this policy has left disproportionate numbers of lower-income and minority families residing in the region's major cities, such as New York City and Newark, New Jersey, and in older inner-ring suburbs.

Efforts to open up the suburbs to more families and excluded groups were undertaken through court litigation in New Jersey during the 1970s and 1980s. Landmark "Mount Laurel" cases mandated a greater legal obligation on the part of local governments to shoulder a fairer share of regional housing needs. Effective implementation of the court decrees never materialized, however. The court judgments proved difficult to enforce and then were amended by the New Jersey state legislature to limit their impact on suburban zoning and housing practices (Haar 1996). Similarly, attempts to build subsidized housing in the New York suburbs through the ESDC's predecessor, the Urban Development Corporation, resulted in powerful backlashes among Westchester County voters during the 1960s and 1970s. The total failure of this effort taught successive governors and housing departments to stay away from proposals to open up the suburbs via housing policy (Benjamin and Nathan 2001; Danielson 1976).

Immigration to locations throughout the region during the last decade or so has been gradually forcing local governments to address problems of larger numbers of day laborers coming to work and sometimes settling in suburban communities (Fassenden 2006). Yet the presence of these individuals and families has not precipitated anything close to a regional response; local governments have resisted accommodation of these groups (Baxendall and Ewen 2008). With their tight control over land use, suburban local governments easily resist challenges by courts and higher-level governments to open up to include more affordable housing for minorities and lower-income families. Suburban and county officials—Democrat and Republican—actively campaign to oppose below-market-rate housing and wriggle out of deals to oppose affordable housing plans (Schwieger 2010). For example, in 2009 Westchester County officials settled a lawsuit brought by antidiscrimination advocates that attested the county had willfully misused federal housing funds to obstruct fair housing and foster housing segregation during 2000–2006. In a settlement brokered by federal housing officials and the federal court, the county agreed to spend more than $51 million over seven years to develop at least 750 units of low- and moderate-income housing throughout the county by 2016 (Brenner 2009). Although this plan would provide only a tiny amount of new affordable housing, in 2010 a court monitor rejected it, finding county officials were not actually putting any genuine plan into effect. County officials failed to designate who or even which government agency was responsible for implementing the housing plan, to identify any housing sites, or to make any specific marketing efforts for the housing. Westchester officials emphasized they lacked much authority with respect to land use and zoning's housing, but were trying to "be practical" (Roberts 2010).

MEDIATING BOTTOM-UP POLICY MAKING: WEAK REGIONAL MANAGERS

The PANYNJ and ESDC have sometimes played a role in trying to regulate economic competition among local governments and promote regional economic goals. Yet neither of these agencies has been able to significantly change the essentially bottom-up nature of regional development by spreading a regional agenda.

In the case of the PANYNJ, during the 1980s and early 1990s the governors of New York and New Jersey put pressure on the port authority to adopt a broader regional economic development agenda. The long recession of the 1970s followed by New York's fiscal crisis weakened the whole regional economy and awakened many politicians to the desirability of reviving the economy through better regional collaboration. After the appointment of Peter C. Goldmark Jr. as executive director, the PANYNJ ventured into regional economic programming. Goldmark organized a Committee on the Future that developed an economic plan for the region in 1979. In response to gubernatorial threats, Goldmark and later directors adopted a bevy of regional development programs in response to deals struck by the bi-state governors. They included such projects as a teleport in Staten Island, office buildings, a resource recovery plant, industrial parks, and a development bank to repair public works. The port authority also became an advocate of regional economic planning, setting up a study of economic competition, and it issued plans providing regional marketing and investment strategies. Finally, the port authority helped organize forums on regional cooperation that led to a 1991 pact among New York City and the governors of the three states to cease pirating business from each other (Berg and Kantor 1996).

PANYNJ's efforts to provide regional economic leadership faded quickly, however, and the policy changes did not significantly increase regional cooperation on matters of economic development. The regional economic development programs never became a very large part of the authority's portfolio of activities. The individual projects often flagged and imposed operating losses on the PANYNJ's books. The new development programs never found stable political support within the region. Further, because they usually met with resistance within the agency, it usually took prodding and threats by the governors to move them ahead. During the 1990s, the PANYNJ placed less and less emphasis on regional development programs and the failure of several of the projects made the authority wary of new ventures of this kind. With flat revenues during the economic doldrums of the 1990s, PANYNJ all but abandoned its economic development planning role and refocused on transportation programs, as described later in this chapter.

Similarly, the authority's appeals for regional cooperation were insufficient to overcome the economic rivalry among governments in the tri-state region. In a 1991 pact signed by executives of the three states and New York, the four governments vowed not to use negative advertising against one another and to avoid business incentive programs designed to attract companies within the region. They also agreed to increase cooperation in marketing, develop a regional development strategy, and create a committee of policy makers to plan regional initiatives. Although there was some diminution of negative advertising, within less than a year the pact broke down as all three states launched new programs to lure jobs from each other, undermining any semblance of support for the pact (Berg and Kantor 1996). Job wars between New York City and New Jersey accounted for the largest breeches in the pact (Salamore and Salamore 1993).

The ESDC has the potential to be a regional economic development planner. As the state's main economic development arm with a special regional office in the downstate area, ESDC is the logical choice for pulling governments together for common goals in promoting jobs and business. It is well financed, has extensive powers to build anywhere in the state, and can override local restrictions to get its job done. Nevertheless, ESDC has not asserted itself as a regional planner. Like the PANYNJ, it does not represent regional groups and is considered an arm of the governor and state legislature. Its constituency in Albany is far from solid. The agency has a checkered history, having become insolvent during the 1970s due to poor investments and questionable methods of financing some projects.

During recent decades, ESDC has tended to see its role as a builder of one-off projects and it looks very much to the private sector for ways to boost the state economy. Rather than seeking to centralize its activities in urban and regional development, ESDC tends to create subsidiaries to deal with its larger projects, like redeveloping the World Trade Center site and expanding the New York City Javits convention center. Since the 1990s, ESDC programs have leveraged less and less private sector money. Its development is often patronage-driven, in part because of pressures on the agency to spread its investments all over the state and region. Lack of confidence in the agency has caused the state legislature to place many state economic development programs with regional consequences outside of ESDC control entirely (ESDC 2007).

EXCLUSIONARY POLITICS AND SOCIAL POLARIZATION

The decentralized competition for development and the exclusionary housing practices are major causes of the region's increasing social polarization and housing woes. As noted earlier, income disparities throughout the region have been increasing despite the economic rebound of the regional economy as a whole. For example, in Westchester County the highest-earning fifth of households made 20 times as much as the bottom fifth (Roberts 2007). To some extent, this gap is a natural outgrowth of the region's heavy reliance on local taxes and intergovernmental tax competition. It undoubtedly has been exacerbated by the restructuring of the regional economy by global forces. People with means move to places that offer better services paid for by higher taxes, stratifying income and privilege by geography. As global economic restructuring has precipitated changes in the social profile of the region, housing inequalities have also increased. A recent study by the Regional Plan Association showed that both suburban and urban areas in the New York region lacked sufficient affordable housing for lower- and even middle-income residents. They found that housing affordability, choice, and quality were severely limited in all parts of the region for lower-income households and that the gap is intensifying over time. Even moderate-income families were found to face high costs, long commutes, and inferior housing quality compared with other metro regions in the United States (Regional Plan Association 2004).

The chronic social polarization of the global city-region (GCR) is only weakly checked by its fragmented and pluralistic governmental system. Although significant efforts to contain social inequalities in housing sometimes have been made by New York City, regional mediation has been feeble. Suburban governments are motivated to leave social ills concentrated in inner-city and older suburban areas. The shrinking of federal urban programs in a federal system tolerates large inequalities in social services, housing, and job opportunities. Thus, this political order provides little structure for encouraging regional action by other governments to help those at the bottom.

Overcoming Fragmentation: Economic Recovery, Transportation, and the Environment

Greater intergovernmental collaboration can be detected in three issue areas: economic recovery, transportation, and to a lesser extent, environmental policy. Significantly, these issue areas are more distant from the bottom-up politics of local economic development, where powerful traditions of local autonomy prevail and the large number of organized interests discourage change. When top-down politics emerges, the pluralist features of the GCR are more permissive of collective action by governments, if only because coalition building is easier, especially when dominant interests are fewer and they converge around single objectives. The regional coalitions in these policy areas are far less stable than is the case with local development and housing, however. Agendas can therefore rise, fall, and change directions substantially when constellations of powerful interests realign to support new policy directions.

ECONOMIC RECOVERY POLITICS AND THE GLOBAL FINANCIAL CRISIS

Some policy agendas are so deeply rooted in the region's highly fragmented and decentralized politics that any change toward collective responsibility is difficult to achieve. Yet there are exceptions. Some issues fall by default to governments that are large or specialized enough to manage them. An example of this is an economic crisis that redounds upon and threatens the entire system. Issues of this type and magnitude are often subject to top-down policies. Most other issues are very much on the minds of particular actors and tied to powerful local coalitions who exercise a privileged right to draw the rules. Issues of this sort revolve around land use and housing. These are subject to bottom-up policies.

Economic recovery is too big a challenge for most local governments and usually falls to the individual states of New York, New Jersey, or Connecticut; the city of New York; or some of the PBCs like the PANYNJ or the ESDC. During New York City's fiscal crisis of the 1970s and 1980s, policies for recovery were initiated by the state. Because the crisis arose from the city's expenditures and inability to pay debts, the governor placed it in de facto receivership, where appointed boards exercised control over the revenues, expenditures, and labor contracts. After strenuous lobbying, loan guarantees were eventually furnished by the federal government; as it turned out, the aid was carefully funneled to the city via the state or appointed boards.

The economic crises of the late 1970s and early 1980s were largely based on falling demand and severe unemployment. The PBCs went into action trying to stimulate production through land development and housing. At the same time, New York City adhered to a tight fiscal regimen, reducing corporate taxes in the hopes of stimulating private investment. The low-tax strategy sharply changed the city's generous public services, effectively abandoning its low-cost hospitals, free higher education, and generous welfare payments.

The economic crises starting in 2008 arrived in a different form. They immediately resulted in bankruptcies and a drought in the availability of capital. As a result, the municipal area lost over 114,000 payroll jobs and tens of thousands of workers saw their hours reduced. Within the region, unemployment reached 10.3 percent (Fiscal Policy Institute 2009). Ironically, while it was the financial sector that led the collapse, most of the lost jobs were outside the CBD core (in part due to unprecedented federal aid primarily aimed at rescuing Wall Street).

The social consequences for the city-region have been quite serious. Far away from Wall Street, in the Bronx, Brooklyn, and small blue-collar cities of New Jersey, unemployment exceeds 13.3 percent. While white unemployment hovered at about 7 percent, blacks and Hispanics were hit with more than twice that rate of joblessness. Within the region, over 10, 000 bankruptcies were filed in 2009 and more than 40,000 homes were lost to foreclosure (Fiscal Policy Institute 2009). Behind these raw figures lies a human tragedy of ruined lives, distraught families, and abandoned neighborhoods.

Nevertheless, some ways were found to mitigate the effects of this calamity. The crisis was large enough to precipitate federal aid through a program to promote fiscal liquidity, called the Troubled Asset Relief Program, or TARP. TARP came with a price tag of well over $700 billion nationwide, but most of it was targeted at the CBD core and at saving Wall Street banks. Another part of the federal rescue launched by President Obama in 2008, the Recovery Act, was designed to stimulate employment. This entailed hundreds of millions of dollars for emergency repairs, homeless services, neighborhood improvement, health promotion, educational enhancement, and the like. A favorable outcome of this federal largess entails increased regional coordination among top-down actors—the three states, New York City, and the PBCs. How much the region is able to pull together in a sustained way remains to be seen, however.

Still another component of the recent fiscal crises has been the local response. These policies have pulled in an entirely different direction by cutting rather than increasing expenditures. In the wake of plummeting tax revenues, localities invoked a series of reverse Keynesian measures. Many of the smaller cities have cut expenditures, laid off municipal workers, and curtailed services (libraries, sports facilities, social or home support). As the biggest player in the region, New York City led the spree by reducing its budget by over $1.5 billion in layoffs and curtailed services. While localities are trying to fend off further reductions, it is still too early to fully assess the politico-economic consequences of the crisis set off in 2007–2008.

As of this writing, one matter is certain. New York City fared better than most major jurisdictions in the United States and better than most in the industrial world. By the end of 2009, the proportion of jobs lost was in the low single digits and by 2010 recovery began to set in. In 2010 the city's economy grew by a modest 1.2 percent and by the end of the year, city hall proclaimed that more than 74,000 private sector jobs had been created (Goldman 2010; Joint Economic Committee 2010). Unemployment in the city also began to recede and by 2010 stood at 8.3 percent, well below the national rate. House prices were also more stable in New York City than in other parts of the country. In the aftermath of the crisis, house prices fell modestly between 4 and 5 percent, but since then have held their value. This decline should be understood in the context of surging house prices over the last decade. Between the years 2000 and 2010, house prices in the New York metropolitan increased a net 74 percent (Standard and Poor's 2010).

We should understand that much of the gain throughout the region is carried by New York City and particularly within Manhattan. Within that small stretch of land, commercial rents reached new highs and the average weekly salary jumped by nearly 12 percent during 2010. Just two years after the crisis, high-priced restaurants and up-scale boutiques reported significant increases in clientele. Much the same trend occurred for the sale of luxury condominiums (*Economist* 2010, 38). These trends continue into 2012.

In spite of this, the picture is not entirely rosy. As one moves away from the CBD core and neighborhoods proximate to them, the hardships of the most severe recession in recent decades become more evident. Unemployment in poorer parts of the regions is in excess of 13 percent and housing declines still remain at 15 to 20 percent. Poverty rates are also at 15.8 percent and have not receded. Moreover, little is being done about the worst of these conditions (Joint Economic Committee 2010).

With this larger context understood, we can still conclude that in the wake of a severe crisis, the New York consolidated statistical area (NYCSA) has shown itself to be quite resilient. Much of this resiliency can be attributed to the very nature of this leading GCR. For one, the recovery of this globalized economic sector has nurtured the rest of the region. Jobs and multiple spinoffs of globalized business activities took off again in 2010, sustaining other industries like real estate, hotels, and entertainment. Second, the sheer accumulation of capital has exerted a powerful force. New York is one of the leading world sources of venture capital and much of that has gone into the creation of new business within the region. All this has contributed to economic diversity—both in New York City and in the rest of the region. Wall Street may still be the catapult for the region's economy, but health, high tech, education, retailing, and tourism also propel this very complex economy. Last, to borrow a metaphor from physics to describe the GCR, things in motion tend to stay in motion: New York has used its connections throughout the world to reinvest in itself. Reinvestment has its own agglomerative effect, producing a national and international presence that is hard to duplicate.

TRANSPORTATION POLITICS: CONTAINING FRAGMENTED GOVERNANCE

The New York region has been managing the impact of global restructuring with a transportation system changed very little during the last sixty years or so. New York City's subway, bridge, and tunnel systems are essentially creatures of the first half of the twentieth century, while its interstate highway networks have been virtually unchanged since the 1960s. During the Depression and postwar decades, New York's regional transportation was decisively shaped by the hands of two powerful planners, Robert Moses and Austin Tobin. Tobin was chairman of the PANYNJ for twenty-nine years until leaving in 1971, while Moses simultaneously was boss of a number of public authorities and government agencies at various times for decades. Both managed to centralize power within their respective domains and realized an enormous number of projects that transformed the New York region, resulting in the transportation system of today. Both utilized their power bases in the public authorities that could plan, finance, and build public works projects. They were adept in maintaining the support of elected officials whom they spared from voter resentment and anger as their highway, mass transit, urban renewal, airport, and other intrusions sometimes displaced homes and even entire neighborhoods. Although the power of public works czars like Moses and Tobin can be exaggerated—both suffered fallings-out with elected officials who eventually cast them aside—they presided over a remarkable convergence of politics in the region's otherwise fragmented political order. They managed to achieve a vast transformation of the entire region with very broad-based support that lasted for years (Caro 1974; Doig 2001).

By the 1980s, however, powerful construction bosses like Tobin and Moses were almost a distant memory. Bold agendas to keep modernizing the region's transportation networks were nowhere to be seen. The region's characteristic political fragmentation reasserted itself, precipitating modest policy agendas. Nevertheless, limited convergence among regional actors on some transportation issues did emerge. These issues were mostly geared to coping with an economically troubled city region and preserving its aging infrastructure. Lacking powerful leaders and beset with relatively stagnant revenues, the major transportation agencies, the MTA and PANYNJ, were able to muster limited regional cooperation.

The MTA was most successful in pursuing its regional agenda. Unlike the port authority, the MTA has always required significant state and regional cooperation in order to function at all. The political structure of the MTA devolves some power to governments in the region. Although the MTA board of seventeen members is appointed by the governor with advice and consent of the senate in New York State, eleven of the appointments are made on the recommendation of local officials. Four are nominated by the mayor of New York City, one each is nominated by the county executives in Westchester, Nassau, and Suffolk counties, and one is nominated by the executives of four other New York state counties. These seventeen members have only fourteen votes, however, because the suburban county representatives have only a quarter vote each. Political cooperation among state, city, and suburban interests is necessary because all these governments provide subsidies for capital and operating expenses of the MTA authorities. Since fares are never able to cover expenses by a wide margin, the huge transit system has a voracious need for money to meet operating expenses and for capital improvements. This means the MTA also depends on considerable state-level cooperation and its political patrons in Albany.

During the fiscal crisis of the 1970s, the weak condition of the city and state economies led to cutbacks and fare hikes that failed to keep up with the transit system's capital needs. After years of deferred maintenance and declining ridership, in 1980 the state legislature declared a transportation emergency. MTA capitalized on the crisis to put together an ambitious capital program. MTA director Richard Ravitch won backing in Albany for changes that enabled the MTA to undertake a huge rolling capital program for more than ten years and to continue further maintenance projects into the 1990s. Ravitch managed to reduce MTA's dependence on annual legislative funding and bonding that crippled long-range planning in the past. Legislation passed in 1981 provided MTA with a number of new revenue streams that did not depend on annual authorization. A Capital Plan Review Board composed of representatives of the two houses, New York City, and the suburbs was set up to monitor MTA programs and approve future revenue requests.

Although this did not free MTA from financial deficits, the political engineering permitted MTA to undertake an unprecedented regional reinvestment program without creating serious conflicts among key interests (Berg and Kantor 1996). Such a huge public works program could easily have pitted city against suburb. Instead, the entire chain of MTA governance and oversight, from the MTA board to the state review board, was organized to give proportionate weight to New York City, suburban, and upstate claims. Conflicts over the capital plan during the 1980s were limited by an agreement among participants not to contest the division of capital monies. Instead, they agreed to divide new capital monies in a ratio of 77 percent for New York City Transit and 23 percent for the commuter railroads that serve the suburbs.

The PANYNJ also veered away from an ambitious role in remaking the region's transit system during the 1980s and 1990s, but it generally failed to achieve as much intergovernmental cooperation as the MTA. Although the PANYNJ undertook some large airport reconstruction and expansion programs, the 1990s were dominated by unstable executive leadership, chronic conflicts between New York and New Jersey commissioners and the governors, as well as attacks by New York City political leaders. Port Authority capital improvement programs are invariably distributed unevenly within the bi-state region as particular project needs arise at the authority's seaport, airport, and transit facilities. By the mid-1990s, it lost the ability to maintain gubernatorial support by responding to the pet projects of the two governors and maintaining enough attention to projects in both states (Doig 2001).

New York City mayors often criticize the authority for favoring New Jersey and for depriving the city of tax revenues from Authority-owned facilities like the World Trade Center and the two New York airports. This criticism escalated after 1996 among city as well as state officials. New York City officials cited studies suggesting that port authority spending favored New Jersey by a large margin and that port authority profits were dragged down by heavy subsidies to the PATH commuter train operations to New Jersey. After the election of Republican governors George Pataki and Christine Whitman in New Jersey, the criticisms and bi-state rivalry grew. Both governors appointed intensely partisan codirectors and commissioners to the authority. The executive director appointed by Pataki cut more than 1,000 jobs at the authority and eliminated several programs. The port authority became so deeply divided and the feuds between the two governors assumed such proportions that major authority decisions were unable to transpire for weeks and even months as the governors settled their differences

(Smothers 2000, 2000a). During this period new initiatives fell by the wayside. By 2001 the port authority director announced that the institution would go back to its traditional core mission in order to foster greater bi-state unity. One other result of this conflict was the port authority's divesting itself of the World Trade Center as part of a package deal to spread benefits between the states more in favor of New York interests (Smothers 2000).

The New Convergence of Interests: Supporting Regional Megaprojects
The region's transportation agenda began a tidal shift in the late 1990s that produced a major policy change by 2007. Unlike prior years when economic growth in the suburbs far exceeded that in the region's core, the rebirth of the Manhattan CBD spilled onto the political agenda. After the mid-1990s various interests began to call attention to the need to sustain the competitive economic position of the region and its Manhattan-centered engine. As mentioned earlier, the rise in immigration and job growth created a new center of gravity in Manhattan. Transit assumed increasing importance in continuing this trend. In 1996 the Regional Plan Association with the backing of key groups, including the New York City Partnership, issued a major study entitled *Region at Risk*. This report painted a bleak scenario of regional decline and decay in crumbling urban centers unless massive investments were made in the New York–New Jersey–Connecticut transit networks. Its major recommendation was to spend money connecting many underused rail segments and vastly improving access to the CBDs of the area, especially Manhattan.

Although the Regional Plan Association's scenario of impending decay was dismissed by many, during following years one interest after another began to fall into line advocating various expansion plans for the region's airports, mass transit, and even some highway improvements. The big transit agencies, the PANYNJ, New Jersey Transit, and the MTA, also initiated studies that proposed major mass transit expansion projects for a system that had not been changed much in more than sixty years (MTA 1998). Although the MTA lost an attempt to obtain voter approval in 2000 for a big capital plan, it won approval from Albany and the state voters in 2005 for a bond issue after more upstate highway projects were added (Regional Plan Association n.d.; Stonecash and Paley 2006).

At the same time, New York City and other public officials began to unleash proposals to further intensify redevelopment and expansion of the CBD. During the Bloomberg administration, a highly activist development commissioner, the ESDC, and even the MTA promoted large numbers of new projects to accelerate the rebuilding of lower Manhattan after 9/11, spur the commercial development of the West Side, and promote other underutilized areas in and around the CBD. In a city with a transit system that had not had significant changes in decades, but was experiencing a continuous increase in the region's share of population and employment, the transit system was running out of capacity (Regional Plan Association n.d.). Since the MTA region generates 75 percent of the wages earned in New York State and a similarly high percentage of tax revenues (Regional Plan Association 2004, 24), New York governor Pataki joined with Mayor Bloomberg in seeking finance for a variety of transit expansion proposals emanating from the PANYNJ, MTA, and other agencies.

By 2007 funding or construction had begun for a long list of transportation megaprojects focusing on improving commuter access to and within the Manhattan CBD. They include an East Side Access, connecting in Manhattan to the Long Island Railroad; building a Second Avenue subway along Manhattan's East Side; extending a West Side subway; two new transit hubs in lower Manhattan; a direct rail line from lower Manhattan to Kennedy airport; reconstructing New Jersey PATH services; acquiring land for a fourth airport north of New York City; a new railway station; a new rail tunnel under the Hudson River to New Jersey; and other projects, including the PANYNJ's building of Freedom Tower in the former World Trade Center site in lower Manhattan. Despite the national recession starting in 2008 and governmental spending cuts since then, this massive program of public investment has more or less stayed on course. Only in 2010 did a defection from the megaproject coalition happen. The newly elected conservative Republican New Jersey governor abandoned his support for the rail tunnel project on grounds of saving taxpayers. But this event just led other players in the transportation game to pursue alternative ways of continuing the project, including a plan to extend a New York City subway line from Manhattan into New Jersey (Bagli and Confessore 2010).

This megaproject agenda constitutes the largest public works program in a generation. It is only partially rooted in the compelling need to secure the region's economic competitiveness by modernizing its transit system, however. In the past the region's highly fragmented regional political system was often incapable of pulling together even in the face of severe economic crises, as in the 1970s when city bankruptcy, civil unrest, and economic decline combined to threaten regional prosperity. The robust political convergence of recent years has been facilitated by a number of circumstances, making consensus building on big public works easier. One is the availability of greater state and federal aid for public works, especially after 9/11, and then following the election of President Obama in 2008. Although Democratic New York City had to contend with Republican administrations in Albany and Washington except in recent years, transportation funding has been regarded as less partisan than other grant areas, and the flow of federal monies is easier for projects that appear to benefit state, region, as well as city. In addition, the increase in federal aid after 9/11 helped begin some projects that could be expanded.

Perhaps most important for encouraging cooperation, the programs are heavily Manhattan-centered, yet are expected to spin off many benefits throughout the region. By and large, almost all of the transit expansion projects are dedicated to improving access to the core CBD from suburban rail locations or from the airports. This means that virtually all of the construction upheaval is or will be concentrated in New York City neighborhoods and business districts but will result in many benefits to people and commuters in the suburbs who wish to access the central core. Interestingly, transit proposals in the periphery are few because of a long history of suburban opposition to such proposals. For example, in recent years a proposal to add a third rail track for the Long Island Railroad to ease intrasuburban commuting was shelved by the MTA after intense opposition by suburban politicians and voters (Christopher Jones interview November 27, 2007). There is little doubt that if the transit barriers to regional economic growth had not been so anchored in Manhattan, political coalitions seeking expansion in the periphery would be far more conflict-ridden with suburb pitted against suburb.

ENVIRONMENTAL POLICY, QUALITY OF LIFE, AND THE REGION: RIVALRY AND COLLABORATION

Obstacles to Cooperation

Environmental and quality-of-life matters spread across jurisdictions in the region, but its fragmented governmental structure makes it difficult for any one government to assert leadership. By and large, environmental policy is strongly influenced by state and federal mandates to which individual local governments respond. For example, New York City has resisted the US Environmental Protection Agency (EPA) efforts to get the city to place tolls on its East River bridges in order to meet national clean air standards. City and suburbs negotiate routinely with federal and state environmental agencies over how to accommodate air, water, and waste regulations; local regulatory responses, such as placing sewage treatment plants and dealing with brownfield cleanup, have important distributive impacts on groups within the various communities (Sze 2007). Yet as the region has enlarged and become more interdependent, these issues have increasingly drawn local governments directly into the regulatory order. Environmental policies invariably spill across the borders of particular governmental jurisdictions. This creates contention and rivalry, especially because environmental regulations have important consequences for local economic development.

Localities in the region generally seek to promote their development while shifting the environmental costs on to other jurisdictions if they can. These intergovernmental conflicts present big obstacles to regional approaches and discourage bottom-up leadership. For instance, in 2007 Mayor Michael Bloomberg launched a bold plan (entitled PLANYC) to promote greater regional efficiency in energy and ease traffic congestion. This wide-ranging plan that covered a long list of innovative policy changes for transit, energy, conservation, and open space regulation became Bloomberg's major attempt to mobilize governments in the tri-state region behind a single program to address climate change. It included a controversial congestion pricing proposal for autos entering the Manhattan CBD in an effort to discourage auto commutation and encourage use of mass transit.

Yet this kind of proposal can succeed only if other governmental players in the region support it. New York City cannot mandate energy savings regulations throughout the region. Even the success of congestion pricing depends not only on the approval of state officials (it is a tax requiring state approval) but also on the cooperation of hundreds of local governments throughout the region. The latter usually control local parking access near commuter train stations. These communities usually restrict access to local residents and fee holders. In 2008 the state legislature rejected the congestion pricing plan, dealing its centerpiece a major blow. Suburban representatives opposed creating the new tax levy for congestion pricing, arguing it penalized commuters without giving the suburbs anything in return (Confessore 2008). In addition to dropping congestion pricing, the mayor also was forced to abandon pursuing other parts of the plan for reducing energy use due to opposition by building owners in New York City (Navarro 2009). Although PLANYC represents a bold stroke for regional environmental leadership by Mayor Bloomberg, by 2012 little joint public action in the metropolitan area actually has resulted.

Given these obstacles, New York City political leaders pay most of their attention to promoting environmental and quality-of-life improvements within the five boroughs, rather than seeking many regional innovations. During and after the fiscal crisis of the 1970s, the city's quality of life became a major issue in New York City. As the postwar flight of families and businesses to suburban locations continued during these years, years of austerity budgets and deferred maintenance left the city's parks, transit facilities, and even streets and sanitation in poor condition. Graffiti-covered subway cars, broken park benches, dirty streets, and littered access roads greeted visitors to the city and were chronic sources of complaint by residents. Yet during most of the Koch years in the 1980s, addressing the city's fiscal woes by closing public facilities and stretching public services dominated the public agenda.

After the city's economy and revenue streams became more upbeat during the 1990s, however, every New York City mayor gave much greater attention to improving the city's environmental quality. Efforts were undertaken to rely more on the private sector to work in partnership with the city government to upgrade routine neighborhood services and to manage or even undertake restoration of city parks. Business improvement districts were chartered by the city to permit commercial property owners to enhance housekeeping services in business areas. The funding and management of some major parks, including historic Central Park, were turned over to volunteer organizations. Following the election of Mayor Rudolph Giuliani in 1993, the city witnessed high-profile campaigns dedicated to improving the public spaces in the city and changing law enforcement practices to crack down on public order offenses. Giuliani's "broken windows"–style law enforcement led to the arrest of unprecedented numbers of people for misdemeanor offenses, such as jumping subway turnstiles and defacing public buildings. Police also cracked down on the notorious squeegee men who intimidated drivers waiting at intersections; police also often removed vagrants sleeping in public spaces like subways and park benches. Although some of these changes in law enforcement practice have been criticized for unfairly targeting the poor or having little effect on the problems, they proved popular with large segments of the electorate (Jacobson 2001; Vitale 2008).

OVERCOMING RIVALRY FOR ENVIRONMENTAL ACTION

Overcoming intergovernmental rivalry for regional collective action on quality of life and the environment does happen, however (Hamilton and Stream 2008). In fact, since the 1980s policy has been marked by some convergence among regional players compared to most other policy areas. To some extent, this policy direction was stimulated by national policy changes. Beginning in the late 1960s, state and federal intervention to greatly increase environmental standards and preserve public open space dramatically increased. Public support for enhancing quality of life on environmental issues has also steadily expanded in the region. New governmental mandates to upgrade the environment and the proliferation of quality-of-life advocacy groups have worked in tandem to encourage regional action. Cooperation has been spotty and limited, mostly focusing on preserving public open space when this does not cost dearly in developmental opportunities. Limited objectives and careful coalition building make possible environmental policy cooperation in the region. The most notable cases of this include the New York City Watershed, Long Island Pine Barrens, and Sterling Forest.

New York City as Regional Leader: The New York City Watershed

New York City's effort to protect its watershed constitutes one of the city's rare successful attempts to assert regional leadership and power in environmental policy. The city's vast water supply comes from areas in the 31 county regions and beyond, including an important watershed system that reaches 200 miles north of New York City in the Catskill-Delaware watershed. Here 61 percent of the land that comprises 1,969 square miles is privately owned; it includes 60 towns and 500 farms, yet it also provides 90 percent of the city's water. Further, the variety of water and land uses in the area affects downstream residents in and around New York City. In 1989 the federal government passed legislation that changed water quality standards. In order to comply, New York City was faced with the need to begin filtering water from its sources at an estimated cost of over $8 billion to build filtration plants. The staggering cost moved the city to explore other options at lower cost to ensure quality drinking water.

During the 1990s, New York City proposed a solution that focused on watershed protection and management as an alternative to building filtration systems. In response, the EPA waived the filtration requirement in 1993 to allow the city time to explore this nonregulatory alternative. The main contest was with towns and farmers in the upstate watershed areas who saw restrictions on farming and urban development as blows to their economies and businesses. Yet New York City could only protect its watershed by limiting development, runoff from agricultural lands, and discharges from treatment systems in the upstate areas (US Agency for International Development n.d.).

The city negotiated a watershed protection program that eventually won the support of state policy makers as well as most representatives of the watershed communities. A memorandum of agreement was signed in 1997 by New York City, communities of the Catskill-Delaware watershed, the EPA, New York State, and some environmental organizations. It sets parameters for protection and compensation for upstate areas in exchange for a waiver from the EPA that avoids filtration requirements. The watershed protection program is composed of a variety of resource management devices, but at its heart is land acquisition by New York City and payments to those for restrictions on development rights (National Academy of Science 1999). The city government spent more than $250 million to acquire strategic watershed areas and fund programs of compensation from willing sellers for full market price. The city's program is also supported by grants from the federal and state governments for conservation easements. Despite the city's success so far, the results of the program have been under periodic review by the federal government, which could still mandate filtration if it proves insufficient.

Pulling Together: Regional Coalition Building for the
Long Island Pine Barrens and Sterling Forest

Two other important cases of regional environmental policy making also emerged during recent decades. One involved the Pine Barrens in Suffolk County, a vast area (100,000 acres) of mostly undeveloped land on Long Island that is still mostly in private hands. Besides being an important nature preserve, it is also the sole aquifer for drinking water for people living in suburban Nassau and Suffolk counties. During the 1980s, the state government began to tighten up its protection of groundwater areas and sought the cooperation of three towns where the Pine Barrens are located to help plan greater protections and restrictions on development. Eventually, local, county, and state government agencies worked out a development plan, but this became the object of a lawsuit by conservationists who believed that the prevailing policies and governmental oversight of development impacts was unsatisfactory. In legal cases that led up to the state's highest court, each side experienced victories and defeats without leading to the establishment of any effective mechanism to ensure that local government land use powers would be employed in ways to ensure regional needs.

Protection of the Pine Barrens and local development prerogatives were preserved in a deal brokered by a coalition of courts, towns, developers, environmental groups, and state and county officials. Property owners gained clear rules so they could proceed with limited development and local authority over land use was left intact; at the same time, environmentalists gained an important victory. Alignment of key interests at the local, regional, and state levels assured this result (Benjamin and Nathan 2001).

The region's governments also pulled together during a three-decade struggle to preserve a 20,000-acre green belt in the New York–New Jersey Hudson Highlands, Sterling Forest.[1] This dense cluster of beautiful hills and forest 40 miles west of New York City in Orange County is filled with wildlife and functions as an important watershed for residents in adjacent Passaic County in New Jersey. In the hands of a single owner, the Sterling Forest Corporation (SFC), until it was bought as a state park, Sterling Forest was a prime target for housing and commercial development because of its proximity to New York and other cities in the region.

Efforts by the SFC to develop the area were repeatedly opposed by groups seeking to safeguard the green belt from encroaching suburban sprawl. The big difficulty environmental advocates faced was that no single government in the region had power to oversee or regulate its development and no governmental funds were available to purchase Sterling Forest as a public park. Although New Jersey residents depended on Sterling Forest for clean water, the area was almost entirely located in New York State, beyond legal reach. Despite Sterling Forest's importance as a green belt, New York State officials in Albany had other priorities or lacked the funds to contribute to land purchases. Further, federal government agencies were uncommitted to its preservation. In effect, a well-financed and profit-motivated business corporation eager to sell or develop what it already owned faced a fragmented and scattered coalition of governments and activists lacking organization or funding sources.

Nevertheless, in 1996 more than 90 percent of Sterling Forest was spared from development by means of purchase by a consortium of contributors that included the federal government, New York State, and the state of New Jersey as well as a number of private foundations, environmental groups, and private individuals. Additional purchases were made by this group during the following ten years, creating the first regional park in the New York area since 1940 (Collins 2006).

This outcome was a product of years of bipartisan coalition building at the local, state, and federal levels. Environmental groups initially succeeded by knocking down the Sterling Forest Corporation's development plans at the local government level. With these successes, this bi-state and bipartisan coalition expanded its members and agenda to seek public purchase of most or all of Sterling Forest. New governmental networks were forged at the federal and state levels. The big breakthrough came when New Jersey's outgoing Democratic governor and incoming Republican governor supported state legislation to set aside money to help fund purchase of Sterling Forest provided that equal or greater contributions were forthcoming from New York and federal government officials. Jersey officials saw park purchase as the only way of protecting part of the state's valuable watershed areas in New York. Bipartisan cooperation by congressional representatives from New Jersey and New York also was initiated to seek federal funding. Eventually, virtually every major governmental player in the region, including the top Democratic and Republican officials in New York and New Jersey, supported governmental purchase in 1997 (Trust for Public Land 2008).

Such instances of regional cooperation on environmental policy reflect some capacity of the tri-state region's pluralist system to collectively respond to globalization. As the region's economy and its population have expanded, increased development and intensification of land use have precipitated environmental conflicts and stresses. The region was able to pull together around some common policies despite the threats to local development prerogatives in part because the players were able to minimize or avoid adverse impacts on local economies. For example, New York City's resourcefulness in buying land and compensating upstate communities was crucial for its success in protecting its watershed. Sterling Forest was largely undeveloped by a single owner who was politically weak. The Pine Barrens deal made provision for regulated development of valuable parts. Further, deal making was watched and monitored by state and federal officials who stood ready to intervene if and when local solutions were to fail. In the Pine Barrens and New York City watersheds it is doubtful if the various parties would have given up what they did for regional environmental objectives were it not that higher-level governments and courts would have imposed solutions of their own. Regional convergence has greater possibilities on environmental issues than on many other issue areas.

Managed Pluralism, Regionalism, and Inequality

The tri-state region's governmental response to global forces has been uneven with respect to governance as well as policy. Politically fragmented downward, outward, and upward, the metropolitan area lacks a master planner with a political base for asserting a very holistic view of the region. Private organizations, such as the Regional Plan Association, provide merely a shell of collaboration for officials, business interests, and others. Organized business leadership is a weak and fragmented presence in the region as a whole. The state governments, especially in New York, routinely intrude in local and regional political rivalries. Their presence has grown over time, providing increasing management of the decentralist tendencies in the region. The latter forces of fragmentation are very powerful, however. State policy makers are often divided among themselves in policy making, making it difficult to devise or impose solutions. Widespread intergovernmental economic rivalry generates incentives for state and local governments to maximize internal benefits, producing very limited cooperation in planning land use, business development, or in housing policies.

Nevertheless, this highly pluralist system does provide some governmental capacity to sustain common regional objectives. A degree of regionalization has been obtained by means of a process in which state, city, and suburban governments struggle and compete in a process of competition, bargaining, and coalition building. This has enabled the region to support some sustained policies of regional scope. Somewhat perversely, intergovernmental economic competition has led to very stable de facto regional policies in housing, employment, and local development that privilege local control and social exclusion. Though not a product of cooperation, these policies are by-products of governance. As regional issues become more distant from issues of local development, housing, and social inequality, political consensus and compromise are sometimes easier. Coalition building and coordination among key players sometimes have happened to find solutions to common problems, although they are limited and sporadic. Regional collaboration has emerged to address threats to the region's transportation infrastructure and environmental quality during recent decades.

Managed pluralism displays clear political biases. Overall, it has greater capacity to pull together for regional solutions on issues of economic competitiveness than on matters of social inequality. Cross-governmental action for the purpose of enhancing local and regional economic growth and, less often, for safeguarding open space finds support in such a divided political system. By segregating control over the region's economic infrastructure in the hands of special authorities and state policy makers, the possibilities for regional agenda building are eased on transportation issues. Environmental improvements that attract broad coalitions and few opponents also sometimes see life, especially when prodded by higher level governments alarmed by local failure to protect public spaces. Yet matters that pertain to social and housing equality are usually relegated to the catch-as-catch-can rivalry among local governments. Consequently, those seeking to address problems of social disadvantage find their influence is systematically weakened or entirely undermined by the fragmented governance of managed pluralism.

Despite its flaws, this fragmented politics probably has contributed to the New York region's increasing global competitiveness since the 1980s. It fosters governmental support for growth and private sector dominance. Yet managed pluralism also obstructs the capacity of the governments to deal with the social fallout of the region's upward economic trajectory. As the tri-state metropolis becomes more socially polarized, regional coalition building for the purpose of ameliorating this condition rarely emerges because it is so easily discouraged. Yet in the long run, regional economic competitiveness is unlikely to be sustained if social divisions continue to grow and territorial segregation by class, race, and income remain embedded by government.

PART III   *Paris–Île de France*

6. *A Fragmented and Conflicting Territory*

THE HISTORY OF PARIS LOOKS IN some significant ways very much like the history of London. To understand current problems and dilemmas of this French metropolis, it is important to keep in mind two major aspects of its politics. Paris is the capital of France and has been the capital of the French colonial empire for a very long time. These two elements play a large role in the conception Parisians have of their city and of its future. They profoundly affect how the global city-region (GCR) is organized to mediate globalizing changes.

As a national capital, Paris has always been treated differently by the French state (i.e., the central or national government), for better or worse. While the state has always been watchful, notably because Paris has very often been the site of revolts, the national government has also used its monuments to celebrate and glorify the French state (Arch of Triumph, Eiffel Tower, the Arch of La Défense, the new National French Library, or the Operas). As the capital of the French colonial empire, Paris has played a powerful role at the international level. This has considerably structured the feelings the political and economic elites have of its status—that is, a de facto and a de jure world city. As an example, the mayors of Paris have always chaired the International Association of French-Speaking Cities, whose membership of about 150 cities goes well beyond the French-speaking countries (e.g., Cairo, Sofia, and Tbilissi are members). For many, Paris does not compete with the world because it has no need to compete; the world has always come to Paris. In a certain way, Paris has conquered the world. In the globalization era, this arrogance and self-confidence may be an obstacle to the continuation of such an international status.

But Paris is also a metropolis and it is this metropolis that will be dealt with in this chapter under the appellation of Paris–Île de France. More than 11 million people live in this city-region today but only about 2 million live in its core—that is, the very city of Paris. Outside the city of Paris, there is the so-called first ring, which comprises about one third of the regional population. Classically, Paris and the first ring represent the densest part of the city-region. It is in this densest part that one finds the regional central business district (CBD), which is composed of most of the central and western districts of the city of Paris and the La Défense district located further west in the Hauts de Seine *département*. The second ring, which is the fastest growing area, is also the largest part of the region and its "green lung."

The Paris–Île de France region is by far the largest urban area of France and its only world city. Paris–Île de France indeed outstrips any other French second-city contender (Lille, Lyon, or Marseille) in terms of size, economic power, social and cultural dynamism, and political leadership (see Table 6.1). With its 11 million inhabitants, it represents five to six times the population of any French second urban area and almost one-fifth of the national population. As shown in Table 6.2, in the Paris–Île de France region, there is a concentration of a large part of the assets and resources of the French territory.

It contains 29 percent of the national gross domestic product (GDP), 38 percent of all firms' headquarters, 22 percent of national employment, more than 30 percent of scientists and researchers, and 50 percent of the national total of superior jobs (*emplois supérieurs*). Although this national domination is also true for London and Tokyo, the gap between the first and second French cities has no match in either Japan or the United Kingdom, where other big urban areas can be found, such as Birmingham, Manchester, Osaka, or Nagoya. This feature of the urban French system is extremely important and has to be remembered if one wants to understand the evolution of national policies in terms of territorial balance and the political obstacles that Paris–Île de France has faced, and is still facing, in maintaining its world city status.

TABLE 6.1. EVOLUTION OF THE POPULATION OF PARIS–ÎLE DE FRANCE: 1980–2008

	1982	1990	1999	2004	2008
Paris	2,176	2,152	2,125	2,164	2,181
First ring	3,903	3,987	4,039	4,170	—
Second ring	3,991	4,518	4,787	4,958	—
Île de France	10,071	10,650	10,952	11,291	11,694

Source: INSEE, CRCI.

TABLE 6.2. ÎLE DE FRANCE WITH RESPECT TO THE NATIONAL TERRITORY IN 2006

	2006
% Population	18.3
% GDP	29
% Researchers/scientists	34.6
% Labor force	22

As in the case of New York, the governance system of Île de France is very much fragmented, as we shall see. With the decentralization process initiated in the early 1980s, this metropolitan area has lost a leading institution, the state, and today no political entity is able to pilot this world city. Indeed, both decentralization trends and globalization processes have produced a more and more conflicting governance system. As a consequence, the metropolitan area has difficulties in addressing problems and issues it has to face because it is unable to produce any significant collective action of a strategic nature.

This chapter is composed of two parts. The first section focuses on the evolution of the major issues faced by the Paris metropolitan area over the last three decades. A second section is a presentation of the main characteristics of the governance system of Île de France. An analysis of the various responses given to the issues is presented in the next chapter.

Challenges and Issues

TOWARD A PARADIGM SHIFT? PARIS AND THE "FRENCH DESERT"

Until 2000, the state attitude regarding the development of Paris and its metropolitan area was shaped by a paradigm best captured in the expression "Paris and the French desert," derived from the title of a famous book written by a high-positioned civil servant, J. F. Gravier. The book was about national and regional planning (*aménagement du territoire*) in France, and was first published in 1947. According to this paradigm, the development of Paris had to be controlled in order to better balance growth at the national level, very much in the "Keynesian State spatial policies" sense identified by N. Brenner (2004). In order to do so, Paris had to be "punished" and growth had to be "transferred" from Paris to regional metropolises (Lille, Lyon, Marseille, Bordeaux, etc.). National plans were the instruments of such a policy, with specific mechanisms such as the agreement procedure,[1] transfers of public central government organizations in the "Province," and fiscal incentives given to firms to settle outside Île de France. This agenda was clear in the national five-year plans of the 1960s, 1970s, and 1980s, which very much contributed to the development of some of the major urban areas outside Île de France. The result of this Malthusian attitude toward Paris–Île de France was not very successful since the metropolitan area continued to grow, as we have seen in chapter 1. The gap between Paris and the rest of France did not diminish much.

This does not mean that the capital city and the capital region were abandoned by the state. On the contrary, and in a somewhat paradoxical way, the central government at the same time developed the Paris metropolitan area through various policies and projects: the building of an extensive and efficient public transport network at the regional level; urban projects of an international scale such as La Défense, which has become the largest business park and center of Europe; or what were to be called the *grands chantiers du Président* (the great works of the President)—that is, the embellishment of the capital city through new museums, facilities, and symbolic architectural buildings (a second opera, the enlargement of the Louvre, the *Arche de La Défense*, etc.). However, all these developments were conceived because Paris was the largest city in France, with specific problems due to its size, as well as because it was the capital of the country, not because it was a global city or a world city-region.

Whether the "Paris and the French desert" paradigm still prevails today is a matter of debate. On one hand, the first decade of the twenty-first century has brought some significant changes regarding this agenda. The state has gradually changed its attitude regarding the development of Paris, acknowledging today the necessity to conceive of the growth of the capital in a global perspective (Lefèvre 2003, 2009), as we will see in chapter 7 with the Grand Paris project. On the other hand, the central government still pursues some Keynesian spatial policies, such as in research and development, to the detriment of Île de France. We will discuss this further in the next chapter.

THE EVOLUTION OF ISSUES IN LATER DECADES

From the late 1980s until the early 1990s, at least four major issues were considered important. In the economy, unemployment and the industrial crisis were high on the agenda, and the housing shortage and marginalization of some neighborhoods were big problems in the social domain.

With an unemployment rate of more than 9 percent in the early 1990s, France had been hard hit by the industrial crisis. Île de France was no exception, and the capital region suffered with an unemployment rate of 9.4 percent in this period. Because it was still an industrial area with about 18 percent of total jobs in that sector at that time, the industrial crisis had devastating effects. As a result, maintaining a strong industrial basis in the economy was considered a major economic objective to keep the diversity of economic activities. The shift toward what is now called the knowledge economy was not envisaged at that time.

The impact of the crisis on the social situation was obvious, notably in some specific areas that had already begun to show signs of degradation, such as in the north and northeast of the region (the Seine-Saint-Denis *département*, for instance, which had a 14 percent unemployment rate during that period, and the income of which had declined from 86.4 percent of the regional average in 1984 to 75.8 percent in the mid-1990s). Social marginalization of these areas was starting to become a big issue and this was very much reflected in the 1994 Master Plan (*Schéma Directeur de la Région Île de France* [SDRIF]). The housing shortage was also big on the agenda because of increasing housing costs. The solution to this problem, which required the new development of about 50,000 housing units to be built annually, created a fierce debate between the interests who wanted to open up new lands to urbanization and residents and emerging environmentalist groups who placed protection of natural spaces first.

All these issues were somehow spatially embedded in the still vivid east–west imbalance of the region, with the wealthy social groups and advanced economic activities located in the west and the lower classes and more traditional economic sectors in the east and northeast (IAURIF 2001). In spite of some public policies aiming at the reduction of this imbalance, the economic and social gap between the west and the east of the region was still strong.

The last ten to fifteen years have shown significant changes in the issues that the Île de France region must address. While some remain on the agenda and are still important, new ones have emerged. Unemployment and housing problems still persist, as does spatial evidence of east–west disparity. Indeed, although the 1994 Regional Master Plan, the SDRIF, mentioned the need to build about 50,000 housing units per year, the 2008 proposed new SDRIF, approved by the regional council, increased this figure to 60,000, thus showing that the problem had not been dealt with. With regard to the employment issue, there was a concern about the attractiveness of the metropolis with a significant loss of jobs in the central city, while the region as a whole experienced a very slight increase. If the trend remains positive, it is nevertheless half as positive (11.6 percent increase between 1993 and 2005) as in the rest of France (22 percent increase between 1993 and 2005) while it was the reverse in the previous decades (Davezies 2008). However, in the last decades the most important issue very high on the political agenda has been the increasing social gap between the various parts of the region, a trend that has been presented as the sign of a "three-speed city" (Donzelot 2004). The marginalization of some areas of Île de France, which had already been denounced in the mid-1990s, has been reinforced in recent years.

As an illustration of this situation, the Seine-Saint-Denis *département* has gradually declined, showing in 2007 a 10.3 percent unemployment rate against an average of 8.5 percent in the region (a similar difference to that of ten years ago). The average household income, which already represented only 75.8 percent of the regional average, declined even further in 2002 to 70.7 percent, indicating that the economic growth of early 2000 had not been evenly distributed over the region. In November 2005, Île de France, as well as the rest of France, was shaken by suburban riots. Although the riots were general in Île de France, they were nevertheless not evenly distributed and the central city of Paris was not "hit." Whatever the spatial distribution of the riots, they were nevertheless considered a strong sign of a social malaise that was definitely more concentrated in specific areas of the metropolis, and they amplified the feeling that the sociospatial fragmentation of the region was more significant and needed to be seriously addressed.

At the same time, new issues, such as transport and environment, have emerged or have reached such a problematic point that they should be dealt with or at least put on the political agenda. The Paris region has been considered to have the best public transport systems in the world and has benefited from it, notably in comparison with London and New York. However, although the regional subway system and the metro system had been constantly extended and improved in the 1970s and 1980s, in the early 1990s the situation was not that good. The deterioration of transport conditions in Île de France was already denounced in the early 1990s in the national government white paper and considered in the 1994 regional master plan. Today, transport conditions are even worse. Public transport is crowded and presents saturation situations on several regional and metro lines. Traffic conditions have worsened. This situation is largely due to (1) the inadequacy of a transport system based on a radial pattern as compared to mobility patterns, which are becoming oriented toward suburb-to-suburb transport, and (2) a lack of investment in public transport infrastructure (and for many in the road system as well) in the last fifteen years. This diagnosis is shared by most stakeholders today, but the necessary measures, investment, and projects will need so much time to be implemented that the situation will remain critical for the years to come—even provided the governance system can produce the adequate policy making in that problem sector (see the next chapter).

Environmental problems were already present in the 1990s but their focus was different. Today, after the Kyoto Protocol of 1997, the focus has shifted toward the issues of climate change and energy constraints, which are now clearly on the political agenda of Île de France. Although they are partially contested, as we will see later, the importance of addressing them is no longer questioned. At the national governmental level, it would be an exaggeration to state that there is a national environmental policy. Nonetheless, during the last decade the central government enacted several laws and launched a series of piecemeal measures. The first significant act, the LAURE (Law on the Air and the Rational Use of Energy) was approved in 1996, and one of its more important impacts on cities has entailed the inclusion of environmental criteria in urban transport plans. More recently, in 2007, a national public debate on the environment (*Grenelle de l'Environnement*) was launched. Among the most significant results was the doubling of the high-speed train network by 2020, the implementation of an ecotax on cars, a national freeze on airports, a carbon tax, and the development of ecoconstruction. Unfortunately, for political as well as economic reasons (notably the global economic crisis starting in 2008), most of these measures have been either canceled or postponed.

The evolution of the economic and social situation of Île de France over the last decade has gradually structured and strengthened two visions of the future of the metropolis, which emphasize priority-specific issues to be addressed. On the one hand, the priority is to enhance the economic competitiveness of the metropolitan area. This is a very recent evolution, carried through by the major economic players, the state, and some wealthy local governments of the western part of the region. For these players, Paris is competing with other major global cities like London or New York and as such must be supported by public resources. This vision calls for more investment in Île de France, development of competitive policies, and development of the attractiveness of the area through the improvement of infrastructure of international status (better accessibility to the airports, better connection between major development areas and the city center, etc.).

On the other hand, focus is directed toward reducing social and territorial inequalities. In this vision, public resources and public policies must be elaborated and implemented with the aim to alleviate the gap between the wealthy and poor areas of Île de France. This calls for instruments and mechanisms for territorial and social equalization and more public subsidies to the most depressed areas. The economic competitiveness of the metropolis is considered secondary—if considered at all. This vision is supported most by the regional council and most local governments, including the city of Paris.

If these two visions seem presented in an exaggerated way, it is because they are expressed as such by many players. At present, economic competitiveness, once very low on the political agenda of several local governments, is now gaining importance. This is especially the case with the municipality of Paris. However, it is not clear whether this will remain so because of the present global economic recession. So far, the crisis that hits some specific economic sectors (such as the automobile industry) seems to precipitate the urgency of social measures rather than development of competitive policies, but as a whole it does not seem to significantly alter the two visions but, rather, to strengthen both of them.

The Governance System in the Paris–Île de France GCR

THE INSTITUTIONAL FRAMEWORK

France is a unitary state where there is no hierarchy among local governments. It is composed of *régions*, *départements*, and *communes* that occupy the same hierarchical level and, according to the constitution, one tier cannot impose anything on the other. This power remains in the sole hands of the central government. However, the French state is today constitutionally a decentralized state. The decentralization process was launched in 1982 through a vast transfer of responsibilities and resources from the state to the municipalities and *départements*. New regional political authorities were also established in 1982. The basis of French decentralization lies in the absence of hierarchy between local governmental tiers and in the allocation of specific competencies to each of those tiers (e.g., urbanism and housing to municipalities, social affairs to *départements*, skills to the regions), in what is called *bloc de competences*.

The decentralization process is also based on the allocation of resources to all local government levels, which has given local authorities a freedom they never enjoyed before. Indeed, financially and fiscally speaking, France is relatively well decentralized. One of the most recent comparative studies on European countries (Dexia 2008) indicates that France is in the average of the twenty-seven European countries with about 42 percent of infranational government revenues coming from local taxes. There are four major local taxes. The most important one is the business tax (a levy on the turnover of firms), which has increased competition between local authorities to attract firms. This competition has been so acute that the 1999 act on intermunicipal cooperation has transferred this tax to new joint authorities (see later discussion). Other local taxes are levied on property and land. In addition, national governmental transfers amount to about 35 percent of local revenues. The bulk of central government subsidies are derived from two major block grants: the operating block grant (*dotation globale de fonctionnement* [DGF]), which accounts for about 30 percent of local revenues, and the capital block grant (*dotation globale d'equipement* [DGE]), which amounts to about 5 percent of local revenues. The remaining resources come from various indirect taxes (on waste collection, for instance) and fees from local services.

Gradually but surely, several laws called "laws to improve the decentralization process" (*lois d'amélioration de la decentralisation*) have been enacted in the last three decades, the most recent one being in 2004. Each of these laws has improved the decentralization process by specifying and/or enlarging the transfer of responsibilities from the state to local governments. For instance, the 2004 act has transferred the national road system to the *départements*. It has also empowered newly created joint authorities and developed direct democracy (through the provision of local referenda). As we shall see, the Île de France region has been treated differently from other regions. This is because the transfer of responsibilities from the state to the region and local authorities is more difficult due to the central government's intent to keep as much control over the capital region as possible.

The Paris–Île de France metropolis is institutionally composed of one *région*, Île de France, eight *départements*, and 1,281 *communes*, or municipalities. The Île de France *région* was established in 1982 by the first decentralization laws as one of the 22 *régions* created on the main national territory (i.e., the territory located in Europe, without counting overseas regions such as French Guiana). It became a full local government in 1986 with the first regional elections. It is administered by a regional council, the *Conseil Régional d'Île de France* (CRIF), which is chaired by a president elected from among the regional councillors. The electoral system is proportional, which means that usually a coalition of parties is necessary to get the majority of votes and seats. The CRIF is a weak institution. The decentralization laws gave the regions few powers and although they have gained more and more responsibilities since the early 1980s, as we shall see, they remain weak local governments. The CRIF is responsible for professional training, regional planning, public transport, and economic development. It has a budget of about €5 billion (about $7 billion) and a staff of about 2,000 (10,000 if high schools are included).

There are eight *départements* in Île de France, Paris being the most important of them. *Départements* are powerful authorities because they have gained a lot with the decentralization process. They are responsible for social affairs, road transport, and education but do intervene in several other domains such as economic development, professional training, and culture. Like the regions, they have gained more and more powers in the last two decades. On average, their resources and staff are larger than the regional ones if one considers their smaller territory and smaller population. Contrary to the CRIF, *départements* are old institutions (they were established in 1790 during the French Revolution) and are also administrative units of the state. Although many proposals for their abolition have been made, they remain a strong and legitimate tier. In Île de France, some are chaired by very high political figures, such as the *département* of Hauts de Seine which was chaired until 2007 by Nicolas Sarkozy, the current French president.

The Île de France region has 1,281 municipalities or *communes*. Most of these municipalities are very small and only twenty of them contain more than 100,000 people. None reaches 150,000 inhabitants except Paris. Municipalities have benefited a lot from decentralization and are responsible for many policy sectors, such as local planning, public transport, economic development, and housing. Because of their great number, most of them have gotten together to administer services such as public transport and water systems through intermunicipal joint authorities (*Ètablissement Public de Coopération Intercommunale* [EPCI]). There are more than 100 of them in the Île de France area. More recently, new laws have contributed to the emergence of new joint authorities at the intrametropolitan level. Since 1999, due to the new intermunicipal act (*loi chevènement*), many intermunicipal joint authorities of a new type have been set up in the Île de France area. The law has given them more significant powers, such as economic development, planning and spatial development (*aménagement*), and a fiscal resource of their own, the business tax, which before was based in the municipalities, as already mentioned. As of 2010, more than one hundred such joint authorities have been created. The most powerful of them are called *communautés d'agglomération*.

The city of Paris is an important entity. First, Paris is both a municipality and a *département* and as such consolidates the powers and resources of both tiers. Since the decentralization process, it has gained power as both municipality and *département* with a staff of about 40,000 and a budget of about €6 billion (about $9 billion). Combined with the fact that Paris is also by far the most populated municipality (two million people) among the 1,281 other municipalities of Île de France, it is by far the most powerful local authority.

Major Features of the Governance System

Six major features of the governance system of the Paris–Île de France region will be developed in this subsection: (1) the strong presence of the national government or state, (2) the strong fragmentation of local governments increased by decentralization reforms, (3) the power of the Paris municipality, (4) a political system whose conflicts are affected by the rivalry between political parties, (5) the significant fragmentation of the business sector, and (6) the domination of the public sector.

THE STRONG STATE PRESENCE

Although the government is decentralized, France is still a country with a strong state presence, and this is especially significant in the national capital. First and foremost, state presence is felt in crucial policy sectors such as education, health, economic development, social policies, and major infrastructures. Regarding social services, housing, and health, national systems are strongly controlled by the central government through its financial resources, administrative apparatus, and a national setting of criteria and norms. National social security was firmly established after World War II and is administered at the national level. Many policies in health, housing, and support for low-income people are also conducted by the state. A new social program (*revenue social d'insertion*) targeted people over twenty-five who were unemployed and without income. Nonetheless, the welfare system is gradually being eroded because of state reductions and attempts to partially shift the burden to local governments. This shift has been strongly criticized by most local government associations regardless of their partisan makeup. Local governments contend that the state has not provided them with adequate resources to undertake their new obligations.

But the state is also present through its powerful deconcentrated or territorial administration. This administration is headed at the regional and *départemental* level by prefects (one regional prefecture and eight *départemental* prefectures), but in some sectors (education, defense, health) it is directly controlled by territorial branches of ministries. In addition, the state is present through administrative and technical sectoral bodies, such as the regional direction of public works (*direction régionale de l'équipement*) or the many planning and development corporations (*établissements publics d'aménagement* [EPA]). It is also present through its control over powerful public operators such as the RATP (*Régie Autonome des Transports Parisiens*) and SNCF (*Société Nationale des Chemins de Fer*) in public transport, the EDF (*Electricité de France*) and GDF (*Gaz de France*) in energy production and distribution, its control over the airports, and so on. Finally, since 2008, the state is also present with the establishment of a new ministry for "the development of the Capital region." To summarize, in spite of the decentralization process, which is real but conflicting, the state remains a crucial actor in the governance of Île de France, as we shall see in the next chapter.

Indeed, it can be said that the development of the Île de France region has been thought and implemented by the state. It is the state that in the late 1950s decided to build a new business park, La Défense, in the western outskirts of Paris. This business park soon became and still is the largest park in Europe, since the state has constantly insisted on expanding it in spite of enormous conflicts, as we will see in the next chapter. The state also played a pivotal role in planning the early 1960s new towns in order to better balance the urbanization of the region. Five new towns have been built between twenty and forty kilometers from the city of Paris since the late 1960s and some of them are still not fully developed, such as Marne la Vallée in the east, which includes the vast area where EuroDisney is located. Today, almost one million people—that is, about 15 percent of the regional population—live in these new towns. To accommodate the forecast urbanization of the region, it is the state that decided to launch an ambitious regional public transport network, the *Réseau Express Régional* (RER) in the same period. The first line opened in 1969 and today the RER network is about 600 kilometers long. All these developments have been made through regional plans elaborated and implemented by the state, with little consideration for the opinion of local governments. For instance, the 1994 regional plan was approved by the state against the general opposition of local governments, whatever their political affiliation, and as such was imposed upon them. Therefore, as in London, it can be said that the 1960s and 1970s were an important regionalization period under the control of the state. Because of this long history of state control over the destiny of Île de France, one can understand the reluctance of the central government to fully implement the decentralization process and its desire to maintain a strong presence in this territory. The recent return of the state, which we will describe in the next chapter, is to be understood in this historical and political context.

GOVERNMENTAL FRAGMENTATION

With 1,281 municipalities, more than 100 joint authorities, eight *départements*, and one *région*, the Paris metropolis is highly institutionally fragmented. The recent proliferation of joint authorities (EPCI) could have been considered a success in reducing the municipal fragmentation of the metropolis because the municipalities involved in these joint authorities have transferred some of their competencies and resources to them. But these EPCI cover small areas, only grouping a few municipalities, and some of them tend to have their own autonomous policies and strategies. In that context, these joint authorities have been accused of increasing the fragmentation of the Paris region instead of reducing it, a point publicly expressed by the regional prefect of that time, who struggled without success against implementing the 1999 Intermunicipal Act in Île de France. As a consequence, these EPCI add to the existing institutional fragmentation and the *communes* remain strong.

A good illustration of this situation can be found in the north of the region, with the *communauté d'agglomération*, called *Plaine Commune*. *Plaine Commune* was established in 2000. It groups eight municipalities, which altogether represent 350,000 inhabitants and 115,000 jobs. This joint authority is the most powerful of all the existing ones in Île de France with many important responsibilities, not only economic development and planning, which is a legal requirement, but also housing, employment policy, water services, waste treatment, environment, tourism, and local development. *Plaine Commune* has been developing its own policies and recently has published a strategic plan. It is also a strong authority because it benefits from strong leadership and clear political homogeneity; being in the old red belt of Paris, most of the municipalities are controlled by the socialist and communist parties.

This fragmented landscape, which can be found in other world cities such as New York, is all the more important because decentralization reforms, by strengthening the power of some local governments, such as the *départements* and the municipalities, has reinforced this fragmentation. It is indeed here that we can find the pervasive effects of the absence of hierarchy between local governments, because this fragmentation cannot be compensated for by a senior government, the state included. This is so because local governments now have more power and resources than before and use them to develop their own policies, programs, and strategies. The ultimate case is the city of Paris, which has developed a public transport scheme and an urban plan (*Plan Local d'Urbanisme* [PLU]) on its own—that is, with almost no contacts with the adjacent municipalities and *départements*. This is all the more damaging since these plans have had great impact on these very municipalities with, for instance, a shift of traffic congestion or parking pressures on their territories.

In addition, it should be stressed that, although the decentralization laws have allocated specific responsibilities to specific governmental tiers, the real situation is one of interweaving of responsibilities, which has led to a confusion of the respective roles and functions of local governments. This confusion is due to two major reasons. The first one is juridical, in the sense that local governments in France have general competencies and therefore may intervene in almost all domains of public life. Indeed, contrary to the ultra vires model, which can be found in England, for instance, where local authorities have the competencies in domains limited and listed by law, in France, a municipality, a *département*, or a region can intervene in any policy domain. The second one is financial because, in a period when the money is short, a local government must find resources elsewhere, and the first option is to get it from other local governmental tiers, which they do.

For instance, it is fairly common for a municipal public transport infrastructure to be funded jointly by the region, the *département*, and the municipality, although it is not part of the region or *département*'s responsibilities. The same is true regarding many policy sectors, such as social affairs, environment protection, and urban regeneration. Indeed, the allocation of specific competencies to specific governmental tiers (the *bloc de competences* system) established by the decentralization laws has never worked and has been transformed into the reverse, the interweaving of competencies and funding by local players, a classic move from the layer cake to the marble cake.

POLITICAL IMBALANCE

If local power is very much fragmented, it is also politically unbalanced. There is an unequal relation between the regional council (CRIF) and the city of Paris, which is increasing, and this situation plays a crucial function in the (in)stability of the governance system of the metropolitan area. Paris, indeed, is much more powerful than the CRIF. This is so, first, because it has a large administration and staff since it is a *commune* and a *département* at the same time, and as a consequence, its budget exceeds that of the CRIF. The second reason is that Paris is not an ordinary municipality. It is by far the largest one in France and has no contender in Île de France in terms of population, wealth, assets, and aura. Third, the mayor of Paris has always enjoyed a rather stable political majority due to the electoral majority system (whoever is first gets the majority of seats). Although the mayor of Paris has always governed with the support of a coalition, this coalition has always been more stable than at the regional level. This is even more so since the last 2008 municipal elections, when the Socialist Party, which is the party of the mayor, got 75 seats out of the 163 seats in the council of Paris, the Paris assembly.

Contrast this with the CRIF experience in implementing its policies. With few responsibilities, a budget much smaller that the Paris budget, and insufficient staff numbers to even monitor the various policy sectors and programs the *région* is involved in, the CRIF is a weak institution. For instance, in the economic development sector, which represents about one-fourth of the regional budget, the 250 members of the staff are not enough to participate in the various activities that the CRIF funds in that domain. In addition, it is chaired by a politically weak president and board because of the electoral system, which is based on proportional representation and has never been able to produce a clear and stable political majority. Since the first regional elections in 1986, not a single party has been able to hold the majority of seats. Until 2004, the majority coalition, be it from the right or from the left, has always been very composite and highly unstable and has collapsed at some points. Since 2004, the situation has been slightly better with the Socialist Party having only about one-third of the seats (65 out of 209 in 2004 and 61 out of 209 in 2010) but a relatively stable support from some other parties from the left. As a consequence, the president of the CRIF has not enjoyed the kind of stability, margin of maneuver, and political support from which the mayor of Paris has benefited. This is also to be understood in a context of a strong and conflicting party system.

PARTY RIVALRIES, NATIONAL SYMBOLISM

The Paris–Île de France region has always been a highly symbolic place for the rivalry of national political parties. Dispute over the control of this territory started first about the command over the city of Paris itself before the creation of the *région* Île de France in 1982. In 1977, a law established a new political organization of the city with an elected mayor, the first time in all the modern history of France. Jacques Chirac, at that time a young political figure of the Conservative Party, was elected against a leftist coalition principally composed of the socialist and communist parties. He remained mayor until 1995, when he decided to leave the city to run for the national presidency. But he left the keys of the city to his first deputy mayor, Jean Tibéri, who won the municipal elections but with some difficulty, losing five of the twenty municipal districts to the left. After these elections, if Paris had always been considered a conservative fief, the conquest of Paris could then be envisaged and was successfully made in 2001, which saw the victory of Bertrand Delanoë, leader of a coalition gathering the Socialist Party, the Greens and the Communist Party.

Until recently, the battle to conquer the Île de France region—that is, the regional council—was not fierce because the CRIF was a weak authority, as we have mentioned. Also, it was clear that considering the social diversity of this vast area and the proportional representation of the electoral system, a political coalition would be needed. As a result, the CRIF has been constantly unstable, as we have pointed out earlier. However, with the increasing, albeit few, powers given to the regional council by recent decentralization laws (most importantly the control over public transport policy and planning), the conquest of this assembly has become a more acute political stake.

As we shall see in the next chapter, the political divide between the right and the left is more and more ideological and conflicting. At the time of writing, the two most important local authorities, the city of Paris and the region of Île de France, have remained in the hands of the left. However, the Conservative Party has kept control over major strongholds in the western part of the region and is in command at the national level. To summarize, all the ingredients for the pursuit of political conflicts based on political parties are still there.

FRAGMENTATION OF BUSINESS

The fragmentation of the public sector is matched by the fragmentation of business. In Île de France, one finds no fewer than four chambers of commerce, which are mandatory public bodies financed by taxes and fees. In France, as in most countries of the European continent such as Germany, Italy, Spain, or the Netherlands, chambers of commerce are powerful. This power comes from their monopoly of representation of firms and enterprises on their territory (corporatist system), the consequent public funding they get from taxes and fees from their members, and their competencies. As a consequence, they are generally large in size compared to the chambers of commerce of the Anglo model. As a comparison, the chamber of commerce of Paris has about 400,000 members, while the London chamber barely groups about 3,000 firms.

In the Île de France region, the most important of them is the Chamber of Commerce of Paris (CCIP), which covers the four *départements* of the first ring. Chambers of commerce play an important role in the governance of Île de France. There are several reasons for this. First, they hold legal control over important working groups and committees dealing with planning and development, economic, and social issues. Second, they are represented in the Regional Economic and Social Council, which is a consultative body by the CRIF. Third, they administer large public or quasi-public facilities. Chambers of commerce are also rich institutions. In 2009, the CCIP had a budget of about €500 million (about $650 million). They use that budget to manage several professional and training schools (among them well-known business schools), run several large public facilities, and contribute to a number of public–private agencies such as the Paris Development Agency and the Regional Development Agency.

In addition to the CCIs, the private sector is represented by two major business associations, the Medef (*Mouvement des Entreprises de France*) and the CGPME (representing the small and medium-sized enterprises [SMEs]), which are strongly represented in the chambers of commerce. Both have loose structures at the regional level, sometimes at the *département* or group at the municipal level. But their strongest organizations are not defined territorially but by sector. Business associations do not get along with chambers of commerce and the frictions between the CCIP and other business representative bodies are many. As a result, the business sector is not only very fragmented but, as we shall see in chapter 7, very conflicting and unable to speak in a unified voice, contrary to what can be observed in London or even in New York. Therefore, until recently it has been rather absent in the debates over the future of Île de France and the proposed changes in its governance system.

The first source of conflict concerns the monopoly of representation given by the state to the chambers of commerce (CCIs) as part of the French corporatist system. This mode of representation is challenged, first by the business associations (Medef and CGPME), and second by many firms, notably those that are not represented in the CCIs, such as those of the "new economy." Chambers of commerce are accused of representing the traditional sectors of business and acting more as public bodies defending their own interests than representative structures of business. In addition, they are accused of having lost connections with the new economic realities. Indeed, most of them are administered by retired businessmen. As a consequence, they are very much contested and this contestation takes many forms, such as the claim by business unions to take a direct part in discussions over the development of the region and the many position documents issued by these associations to manifest their differences with the CCIs' positions.

The second source of conflict concerns leadership within the CCIs. The major issue relates to the establishment of a regional chamber of commerce (CRCI). As of now, in addition to the four existing chambers, there is a regional chamber of commerce chaired by the Paris chamber (whose area represents the first ring *départements*). However, this CRCI is very small, has a very limited budget, and is strictly controlled by the CCIP. Two conceptions of what a regional chamber should be are in conflict. On the one hand, the CCIP (the Paris chamber) wants to preserve the status quo of a small CRCI dominated by Paris. On the other hand, the other CCIs, which are all in the second ring (peripheral *départements*), want a new CRCI that will act as a federation of chambers of all *départements* and not be dominated by any of them. In that conception, the CCIP would be dismantled and split up into four new CCIs, a conception obviously strongly rejected by the Paris chamber. However, a reform is now under way by the national government. Whether this reform will effectively strengthen the regional level to the detriment of the CCIP remains to be seen in the years to come.

PUBLIC SECTOR DOMINANCE

One explanation of the rather discrete place taken by the business sector in the governance of the city-region is the historical domination of Île de France by the public sector. We will see in the next chapter that the globalization process has not significantly changed this situation. The same can be said of the decentralization movement, which has been jealously captured by local governments. Civil society and the business sector have not benefited much from either process, at least in terms of direct involvement in the decision-making system of the metropolis. At the beginning of the second decade of 2000, political institutions and their public arms are still the central actors in the governance of the metropolitan area and they very much intend to remain so.

Conclusion

In conclusion, the Paris–Île de France region is characterized by a highly fragmented system of governance that is under pressure to address ancient and emerging issues of crucial importance. This does not mean that local governments are not able to work together or that there is no cooperation between them and the state. Indeed, since the early 1980s, several contractual instruments (*contrats de plan*, *contrats de projets*, etc.) have been established to better structure the relations between governmental tiers, the state included. In addition, the French institutional system is flexible enough to have created formal structures (agencies, public corporations, joint authorities) that are de facto used to elaborate and implement public policies, such as in the case of public transport.

However, all these formal arrangements are not sufficient to compensate for the strong fragmentation of the system of governance. Whether this system succeeds depends on its capacity to solve certain conflicts that are strongly connected to the vision of the city-region.

7. *Unregulated Competitive Decentralization*

Paris–Île de France is at a crossroads. On one hand, the metropolis is trapped by its own history, which has led it to believe that it is without rivals and that it is at the top of the world urban hierarchy. On the other hand, old and new problems are plaguing the city-region, such as the deterioration of transport conditions and a general worsening of the quality of living, which pushes households to leave the city and even the city-region (Davezies 2008). In that context, what is striking is the lack of adequate policy responses in the global city-region (GCR). This deficiency is the result of an inappropriate governance system, whose main features have been described in the preceding chapter. Although this system is showing signs of rescaling power and decision making, it seems unlikely that the changes we observe will be sufficient to provide the city-region with the necessary policy responses or, more so, with a vision of its future. This is so because globalization is a source of strong political conflicts among the major players of the city-region and because the governance system is unable to produce the territorial leadership that could overcome these conflicts.

Lack of Adequate Policy Responses

Most of the issues presented in chapter 6 are recognized by the major players in the governance of the city-region. However, as a whole, the conditions have not significantly improved and for some observers (Davezies 2008) they have worsened. This demonstrates the inadequacy of the policy responses at all levels.

The 1994 regional master plan (*Schéma Directeur de la Région Île de France* [SDRIF]), which covered the period from 1995 to 2015, focused on three major strategies: (1) the production of a better environment, including the development of parks, the depollution of water systems, the reduction of noise, and a better treatment of waste; (2) the production of a better urban space—that is, more and better housing, notably social housing; the development of touristic poles; the development of logistics activities; and the growth of the tertiary sector; and (3) the improvement of the infrastructure system—that is, the development of public transport, the road network, airports, better regional access (notably with the high-speed train network), and the telecommunication system. The 1994 SDRIF clearly had a comprehensive approach but the answers given were largely sector focused and insufficient regarding housing, as we saw in chapter 6.

The socioterritorial inequality that plagues Île de France is definitely the issue that is placed high on the political agenda of most local authorities and, until recently, of the state. In 1991, two measures were taken to address this matter from a fiscal and financial standpoint. The state established the FSRIF (*Fonds de Solidarité d'Île de France* [Regional Solidarity Fund]) and the DSUCS (*Dotation de Solidarité Urbaine et de Cohésion Sociale* [Social Cohesion and Urban Solidarity Grant]), two instruments aiming at a better spatial redistribution of wealth between municipalities through a financial transfer from the wealthiest communities to the poorest. Highly symbolic, both instruments have proved not very efficient in achieving their objective, notably because their actual funding, already small, has constantly declined over the years.

On the housing side, the policies have not had any more success. Social housing is still in great demand in the region and its uneven spatial distribution has not been alleviated by the 2000 SRU (*Solidarité et Renouvellement Urbain* [Solidarity and Urban Regeneration]) Act, which required all municipalities to have at least 20 percent of their housing stock in social housing. The east–west social gap in the provision of social housing has not decreased but increased. The Policy for Cities (*Politique de la ville*), a set of measures established as early as the mid-1980s to create social diversity, has failed, notably because of insufficient and inappropriate funding.

The other issue that is also high on the agenda of some local authorities, but apparently less so for the state, is environmental protection, not only of natural spaces of the metropolis but even more so of the planet. In the last decade, the questions of energy constraints (the so-called energy transition) and climate change have been put very high on the agenda of two major players of the region, namely the municipality of Paris and the regional council. The importance given to this issue by the two major local actors may be largely explained by the political weight of environmentalist groups and the Green Party in the executive boards and assemblies of these authorities.

At the regional level, the environmental movement began a climb to power in the early 1990s when it received almost 20 percent of the votes in the 1992 elections. But at that time, it was definitely part of the political opposition. Although its strength had declined in the late 1990s, it received about 13 percent of votes in the 2004 elections and about 17 percent in the last 2010 elections. As such, it is the second party in the new regional coalition, without which the Socialist Party could not rule. As such, it was able to play a significant role in the political orientations regarding the development of Île de France. In Paris, the political entry of the Greens came a bit later than at the regional level.[1] This occurred in 2001, when the socialist mayor, Bertrand Delanoë, was elected, putting an end to twenty-four years of conservative rule. With 14 percent of the seats in the municipal council, the Greens have been able to significantly influence the policies of the city.

In Paris, the Greens launched an anticar policy. They did this by adopting public transport and levying restrictions on automobile use (e.g., restricted parking). This policy has been so rapid and strong that many observers, including some on the left, considered it to be very damaging for the economy because it has made Paris less attractive for firms in a period when the city was losing thousands of jobs. At the regional level, the Greens were able to put forward the idea to make Île de France an ecoregion, meaning that the region should get prepared for the post-oil era and take measures to control climate change. This orientation, which was clearly stated in the document "A Regional Vision for Île de France," was issued in June 2006 as the official position of the regional council in the preparation of the new master plan (SDRIF). However, due to the weakness of the CRIF (Conseil Régional d'Ile de France) and its limited budget, no significant measures have been taken in that matter.

The state has gradually changed its attitude regarding the development of Paris, acknowledging today the necessity to conceive the growth of the capital in a global perspective (Lefèvre 2003, 2009). Contrary to the paradigm "Paris and the French desert" discussed in chapter 6, the prevailing view is that Paris must not be punished any longer for its "natural" development. On the contrary, Île de France must be assisted first because it faces strong competition at the global level, and second because it is in this metropolis that the most severe social problems are to be found. This change of attitude was first introduced within the state by the regional prefect (Préfecture Régionale d'Ile de France [PRIF])—that is, by the local state; this was very much in conflict with the DATAR (*Délégation à l'Aménagement du Territoire et à l'Action Régionale*), the national agency in charge of the regional planning policy.

This new attitude has been translated into a variety of actions and policies, rather than being simply a change in rhetoric. As soon as 2002, the state approved the location of the new European Synchrotron (the "sun project") in the southern outskirts of Paris (Saclay), although Lille had previously been preferred. It also declared the northern part of the region as a beneficiary of Objective 2 European structural funds on the grounds that it was one of the poorest areas of Île de France. In 2004, it launched the policy of "poles of competitiveness." This policy, based on the concentration of tax rebates and subsidies in specific designated areas and on projects presented by public–private partnerships in the knowledge economy sector, is a national policy that aims to enhance the economic competitiveness of some territories. Île de France is such a territory, and the central government designated no fewer than 16 poles of competitiveness in the city-region.

On the other hand, the state has pursued its traditional policy toward a more balanced development at the national level by privileging the provinces in terms of research and development. According to Davezies (2008), the proportion of publicly employed scientists located in the capital region has constantly declined in the last two decades from 49 percent of the national total in 1992 to about 30 percent today, a trend that has not, however, been followed by the private sector.

Although it is difficult to generalize about the policies regarding economic development of Paris–Île de France, the overall direction of change favors greater laissez-faire. This is in strong contrast to the policies of the 1960s and 1970s where the government, particularly the state, was very much in charge. This shift is also to be seen in policies where the state or the public sector had always been very active, such as that of transport. Here, the lack of investment has been the subject of widespread criticism. While some capital investment has been undertaken in public transport (such as an extension of the subway network) or in several segments of freeways, major projects are still needed, including better connections of the airports and the completion of the third ring road. These projects are now matters of chronic conflict among the Île de France GCR players.

This laissez-faire attitude is largely the result of what can be called a cognitive deficiency or deficit of the national and local elite regarding the city-region. As already mentioned, a large number of interests and actors have doubts about the value of globalizing Île de France. From this perspective, a laissez-faire attitude based on older, preexisting analysis and values prevails. A perfect example of this is the prevailing policy response regarding immigration. As in national politics, in the city-region immigration is never addressed as such. It is almost completely absent in the new regional master plan. Immigration is rarely conceived as a positive element and an asset for the economy of the region. This conception is not partisan; it is shared by the Conservative Party and the parties of the left, the major differences addressing how one treats immigrants in social life (in terms of social and political status, for instance). While in cities like London and New York, immigration is often considered a sign of vitality, dynamism, and worldwide attractiveness, nothing of that kind is to be found in Paris–Île de France.

The same cognitive deficit can be seen regarding the matter of quality of life, a new asset in the world competition between territories. Quality of life, interpreted as the cultural vitality of the city, the beauty of its physical forms, and the quality of its amenities and services, has always been considered an attribute of Paris that has worldwide renown. The cultural richness of Île de France, the quality of its transport, and the fact that it was assessed as the first major cultural touristic destination in the world, conveyed the sense that the city-region had no other rivals in the world. This has made national and local authorities less conscious of the fact that urban quality of life could become a significant asset in attracting people and firms, and that, in this context, Paris–Île de France could be challenged by other city-regions.

It is therefore no wonder that, until recently, no specific policies regarding the enhancing of quality of life as an asset in the world competition between metropolises have been made. This does not mean, however, that the quality of life has not been considered in national and local policies for the city-region, nor that interesting actions and measures have not been enacted, but simply that they have not been made as a response to challenges of globalization. Until very recently, explicit policies regarding the quality of life have been implemented, mainly to address the day-to-day problems of the inhabitants.

Thus, the inauguration of the national museum of "primitive arts," one of the world's most important in that domain, by President J. Chirac and Kofi Annan, then secretary-general of the United Nations in 2006, was in total continuity with the Grands Chantiers du Président mentioned in chapter 6. Some of Paris's cultural innovations (Paris-Plage[2] or the White Night) have been copied by many large cities in the world, including Chicago, Madrid, Miami, Rome, and Toronto. These innovations have much more to do with making a beach available to those who cannot go to one on holidays (Paris-Plage) or providing free access to museums and cultural performances (White Night) to Parisians than to position Paris as a world city. The same is true for Vélib,[3] launched in July 2007, and Auto-lib, launched in 2011. Both of these innovations were intended more to solve traffic and pollution problems than to place Paris as an innovative city.

Things have started to change lately as the region's role as the world capital of exhibitions and congresses has been contested by cities like Barcelona. More recently, in October 2009, in various European newspapers, Paris was accused of being *ringarde* (old-fashioned) and abandoned for that reason by young people and tourists to the benefit of cities like Barcelona, Berlin, or London. This has precipitated the decision by the mayor of Paris to appoint a "Mr. Nightlife," a mediator between the neighborhood inhabitants and the entertainment community in order to maintain nightlife as an attractive aspect of the city. By and large, however, there is no policy or regional strategy linking quality of life and global attractiveness, even though some very recent projects (like the City of Fashion and Design in Paris or the European City of Cinema in the northern suburbs) are to be understood in the globalization context.

The weakness or insufficiency of policy responses should also be understood with respect to some specific advantages of the Paris–Île de France region compared with London, New York, and Tokyo GCRs. Contrary to the three other city-regions, Paris–Île de France is the only one that has not dramatically suffered from a deep economic crisis. In the last decades, the region has never been hit by a financial crisis, such as in New York during the 1970s, or by a profound economic recession, such as in London in the 1980s or Tokyo in the 1990s. As a whole, in comparative terms, the last three decades have been rather smooth for the capital region of France. So far, the global economic crisis beginning in 2008 does not seem to contradict this observation. Although it may be too early to draw conclusions, Paris–Île de France has not been hard hit by this economic crisis. True, some sectors such as the automobile industry or construction have suffered much more than others because they have been more directly touched by the breakdown of the world economy. But as a whole, the city-region has been protected by the diversity of its economic base, where the finance sector is less important than in our three other cities, and by its "shock absorbers," such as the importance of the public sector in the economy, a huge consumption market, or its capital status, which gives it international visibility and attractiveness.

The major players have obviously engaged in specific policies to mitigate the effects of the crisis. The state launched a national recovery plan with €1 billion specifically for the Île de France region, an amount split more or less in three equal parts: one-third for public investment in public transport, roads, and higher education; one-third for skills and employment; and one-third for housing aid and solidarity measures. Local authorities have also reacted in spite of their reduced budget. For instance, the regional council has initiated a specific program of about €115 million to support the most fragile small and medium-sized enterprises (SMEs), and the city of Paris has significantly increased its support for housing and for SMEs also.

However, at the time of writing, the issue is rather uncertain. For the optimists, the recession is almost over and the Île de France economy will grow again in the coming months. Yet it is estimated that the rate of unemployment will rise moderately. As of November 2011, the unemployment rate in the region was 8.3 percent, much lower than the national average rate of 9.3 percent. But the figure is increasing compared with two years ago, when unemployment was 6.6 percent. For the pessimists, the crisis is not over yet and the shock absorbers that have indeed been able to absorb the most immediate negative effects of the crisis will not be sufficient. For them, in terms of unemployment, the crisis is ahead of us, although it is also possible the economy may recover very soon. Whatever the scenario, once again, the approach to the crisis is a good reflection of the different visions of the city-region held by major actors and of the continued conflicts these visions entail.

An Inappropriate Governance System

In the last two decades, there have not been any big changes in the governance system of the metropolis, in contrast with London. Ironically, one reason for the establishment of the Greater London Authority (GLA) in 1999 had been that London, unlike its rival Paris, had no institution to speak on its behalf; Paris has had the state and the regional council. Interestingly, when London was reforming its governance system, Paris and Île de France were partially losing their institutional comparative advantage (at least as it was perceived in England) because of the incapacity of the governance system to produce a spokesman for the city-region.

The poor policy response can be largely attributed to the GCR's system of governance, which is best described as one of unregulated competitive decentralization. On one hand, the state, until recently, has not been willing to keep playing its traditional interventionist role. On the other hand, the institutional and political changes and initiatives (decentralization) that have been implemented have not proved successful in creating new mechanisms or instruments to overcome the political and institutional fragmentation and conflicts of the metropolis. The state could have played a strong mediating or regulatory role, but, as we will see, it has chosen to pursue a different role. Two examples illustrate this situation: the city's candidacy for the Olympic Games for 2012 and the first responses to the economic recession commencing in 2008.

By and large, the effort to host the 2012 Olympic Games was the candidacy of the city of Paris. In that venture, the regional level and the *départements* were not very much involved. The political leader was clearly the mayor of Paris and the project was very much concentrated in the territory of the central city. Although it is always difficult to establish the true reasons for the failure of such candidacy, many observers point out that, although the Paris application was technically considered the best, in terms of governance this was not the case and the good cooperation between the city of Paris, the regional council, and the state was more apparent than real. Regarding the economic recession, although it is obviously too soon to draw definite conclusions, it is worth noting the absence of significant cooperation among the players, even though they address the same public and the same issues. On one hand, the state has launched its own plan; on the other hand, the region and the municipality of Paris have separately set up their own responses. These are just two examples of a more general pattern, as we shall see.

A FRAGMENTED AND CONFLICTING PUBLIC SECTOR

The fragmentation of the governance system is largely responsible for the inadequate policies in many sectors. Take the housing sector, for instance. The decentralization laws transferred the power of building permits approval to the municipalities (i.e., to the 1,281 *communes*), but they have not used this new power in coordination with each other. On the contrary, they have competed among themselves to attract new residents. In social housing, the power of mayors has also proved to be damaging for bringing about a more equal distribution of these housing units over the metropolitan area. For instance, the 2000 SRU Act requires any municipality to have at least 20 percent of its housing stock in social housing, as previously noted. The law states that financial sanction will be taken against those municipalities that do not show signs of moving toward this objective. Nevertheless, most of the municipalities have preferred to pay rather than to comply with the law and, because of that, the problem has remained.

What is true for housing is also true for many other policy sectors, such as economic development. Decentralization has indeed given too many responsibilities and too many powers to the *communes* without establishing mechanisms or arrangements for coordination. What is true for the *communes* is also true for the *départements*. The first thing these local authorities did when they received some responsibilities in economic development was to establish new development agencies, so that today no fewer than seven development agencies exist. They do not cooperate but compete with each other since their major task is to attract firms within their own

territorial boundaries. The region, although it has been given some coordinating powers, as we will see later, does not play the role of coordinator; on the contrary, it adds
to the proliferation of bodies. In economic development, once again, the region established its own agency (*Agence Régionale de Développement* [ARD]) in early 2000 but
this agency does not fully cooperate with the other development structures. This lack
of coordination is also to be seen in the international promotion of the metropolitan
area. Here there is no single body to promote Paris and Île de France but several. If
there is an Île de France agency in Brussels, it represents only five *départements* and
Paris and the *départements* of the west (the richest) are not among them and have
their own structures.

The state itself has contributed to the fragmentation of the governance system
by setting up or supporting the creation of many structures and bodies in various
fields. In development and planning, it has maintained the development corporations (*Établissements Public d'Aménagement* [EPA]) it had established in the 1960s and
1970s to conduct and control the urbanization of the region. More recently, it has fully
supported the creation of new ones, such as the EPA Seine-Arche in 2000 to develop
the northwest of Paris; the EPA-Plaine de France in 2002, which is in charge of the development of the northeast; and the EPA Paris-Saclay in 2010 in the framework of the
Grand Paris Project, as we shall see.

This fragmentation would not be so damaging and would not prove such an obstacle to policies or strategies at the metropolitan level if coordination, or at least some
joint regulation, existed. However, as has already been mentioned, such coordination
is lacking; neither the state nor the regional council is willing or able to play such a
role. The state has been unclear about the implementation of decentralization in Île
de France. As we will see, the Île de France regional council until very recently had not
received the same transfer of competencies from the state as those received by other
regions. Because Paris is the capital of France and the largest urban area in almost all
domains, central government has always kept a strong presence in this region. At the
same time, pressures for Île de France to become a normal region, politically similar to the others, have been strong and have come from various actors; these include
local governments, of course, but also some economic actors. In early 2000, business associations indeed thought the regional council was more relevant and more
to be trusted than the central government to implement what they considered necessary policies for a global city (Lefèvre and Romera 2001). Stronger powers for the regional council (CRIF) were sorely needed. As we will see, their expectations have not
been met.

The CRIF has not been able to play a coordinating role either. The regional council
is structurally weak, as we have seen, because of the electoral system but also because
of the ambiguous position of the state regarding decentralization. Decentralization
was not implemented at full strength in Île de France. In two domains at least, the
capital region had not been treated like the rest of France: in planning and in public

transport. The 1994 regional master plan (SDRIF)—which is still in force until the new one is approved—was imposed by the state on local governments, which nevertheless rejected it unanimously. In public transport, the regional transit authority (*Syndicat des Transports d'Île de France* [STIF]) was under the control of the state, which chaired its board and had a casting vote.

Although the last decade has transformed this, the CRIF remains by and large a weak political actor. It is true that the 2004 decentralization act gave the CRIF control over the STIF and the state is no longer a member of its board. This is composed of local governments (region and *départements*) although the central government still controls the two major operators, the national railways (SNCF) and the local transit company (RATP). It is also true that the CRIF is now in charge of the new master plan but in association with the state. It is again true that, gradually but surely, various acts have given more responsibilities to the CRIF in planning and public transport and also a role of coordinator in the domains of professional training and economic development. As a consequence, the CRIF has thus gained strength in legal terms. But this is not sufficient and the regional council remains politically weak.

The CRIF is weak because it does not have the staff or the budget to be able to act as a coordinator. But it is also weak because it lacks leadership. Contrary to the mayors of London, New York, or Tokyo, the president of Île de France is not a political leader and does not have the personal and political resources to act as such. So on the one hand, the CRIF cannot be present or influential enough in the many policy sectors, programs, and projects that need coordination. On the other hand, it is not able to provide guidelines, orientation, or directions that could serve as a basis for coordination. In fact, it is responsible for dispersing scant resources on a broad scale rather than concentrating them on some specific projects. This agency simply does not have clear strategies. This is all the more clear in the recent master plan, which is considered by many as a laundry list (Ascher 2007).

The weakness of the CRIF can be seen in its failure to gather other local governments and private actors around itself. One illustration of such a weakness concerns the Regional Development Agency (ARD). Established by the CRIF in 2001, the ARD was supposed to be a body in charge of economic development strategy at the regional level. In order to do so, the CRIF wanted the *départements* and the chambers of commerce to be part of the ARD board. Two *départements* refused (Hauts de Seine and Yvelines, the richest ones in the western part of the region) on the grounds that they wanted to have their own policies and strategies in economic development. The chambers of commerce agreed to be members of the ARD but on the basis of a weak ARD, claiming that they were the ones in charge of economic development. After about two years of conflict, the CRIF agreed to change the mission of the new body, which has become an agency in charge of the promotion of the region (but not the only one) and which does not play a strategic role at all.

PUBLIC SECTOR RIVALRY AND CONFLICTS

The public sector has proved unable to produce adequate policies not only because it is fragmented and lacks coordination capacity but also because public authorities have been in conflict over major issues, conflicts that globalization seems to have increased.

By and large, conflicts arise from an opposition between those seeking to put economic competitiveness first on the political agenda and those who think social and territorial inequalities should be the priority of any development policy. These conflicts are exacerbated by the decentralization process, which enables some local governments to use their own resources to develop their own policies and strategies. As a general pattern, the opposition is between those who favor economic competitiveness, the state, and some of the western *départements* on one hand, and those who give priority to the reduction of social and territorial inequalities, the regional council, and the remaining *départements*, on the other. Municipalities are much more diverse in their positions, although they tend to follow this general pattern.

The conflict has been most intense regarding the elaboration of the new master plan (SDRIF). The regional council wanted a consensual document and in 2004 launched a very sophisticated procedure for its elaboration. After about two years of debate through many working groups and committees open to all major interests, a draft was approved by the CRIF and sent for appreciation to other public bodies. The verdict was unexpected. The state and two western *départements* (Hauts de Seine and Yvelines) rejected the plan on the grounds that it did not put enough emphasis on economic development and that the question of competitiveness was not seriously addressed, as opposed to the issues of social and spatial solidarity and sustainable development. The state went even further, saying that it would not officially approve the plan, a necessary move for the SDRIF to become law and as such be imposed on other local governments. It explicitly asked the CRIF to submit a new version.

This conflict was pushed even further by the same protagonists challenging the authority of the regional council regarding the transit authority (STIF) and its position on the enlargement of La Défense. Regarding the STIF, which was chaired by the state until 2005, they have charged the regional council to use it as if Paris were simply a normal city. They stressed the lack of international ambition of the STIF policies, notably in its reluctance regarding the building of high-speed direct connections between the city center and the international airports. Concerning La Défense, the state and these *départements* strongly opposed the CRIF rejection to extend this business district (in the draft SDRIF, the CRIF opposed the extension of La Défense on the grounds that the area was already too congested and that the economic development policy should not concentrate on specific areas already very developed but should balance development at the regional level). The state unilaterally decided on this extension by a special decree issued in the summer of 2007 and fully supported by the Hauts de Seine *département*.

This conflict between the CRIF and the *départements* of the west has been rein-forced by the latter's decision to create their own land corporations and their refusal to enter into the regional land body (*Établissement Public Foncier Régional* [EPFR]). In 2004, the CRIF approved the creation of an EPFR whose purpose would be to buy land in order to implement a regional housing policy and fight land speculation. This was accepted by the state and the EPFR was established in September 2006. In 2005, the CRIF proposed that the eight *départements* should join this new organization but three rejected the offer and decided to create their own. Since 2006, Île de France is thus covered by at least five public land corporations: the regional one, the three *département* ones and a state one.

Some conflicts are also developing among the *départements*, and clearly they fol-low a political divide. One illustration is the publication of a declaration launched in June 2008 by the five *départements* of the left, which are located in the north and the east of the metropolitan area. Interestingly, this declaration speaks of Paris–Île de France as "the" metropolis, and among the four elements that the region must con-sider, economic development and competitiveness are not mentioned at all (the four elements are financial solidarity, housing, transport, and environmental protection). This is a clear contrast with the positions of the state and of the western *départements*.

But the conflicts are not only between the wealthy local governments of the west and the CRIF. Conflicts are also significant between the regional council and the mu-nicipality of Paris. In this matter, conflict is definitely linked with the struggle over territorial leadership and is well illustrated by the process of building a metropolitan structure, which will be discussed later in this chapter. It is little to say that the CRIF has not been happy with the decision of the mayor of Paris to launch a metropolitan conference in 2006. From the very beginning, the president of the region has always been clear in stating that "the metropolis is the region." He has very reluctantly agreed to constitute a working group on the *zone dense*, the core of the metropolitan area, in the elaboration process of the master plan, considering that it was a way for Paris to take control over the core of the region.

In such a fragmented and conflicting public sector system, incentives or pressure for coordination and reform could have come from the business sector, notably be-cause some important problems regarding economic development have not been dealt with by the public sector. However, as we have seen in chapter 6, the fragmen-tation and the conflicts in the business sector have prevented it from speaking with a single voice and therefore becoming an influential player at that level. But, as we will see in the next section, another feature of the governance system may also explain this situation.

CONFLICTS BETWEEN THE PUBLIC AND THE PRIVATE SECTORS

The conflicts we have presented previously are not limited to the internal sphere of ei-ther the public or the private sector, the political or the economical milieu. They have evident impact on the relations between business and government, relations that have worsened in the last decades, notably because of the decentralization process.

The objects of conflict between business and government are many. One may recall the quarrels about the regional development agency in early 2000 between the CRIF and the chambers of commerce. The same disagreement is to be seen today between the regional council and business during the elaboration process of the Regional Economic Development Plan (*Schéma Régional de Développement Economique* [SRDE]), the chambers of commerce accusing the regional council of being too interventionist and of not listening to the business needs.

However, the most important conflict continues to be over the issue of economic competitiveness, the private sector largely endorsing the criticisms of the state and of some *départements* regarding the vision that the regional council and the left-wing *départements*, Paris included, have of the future of Île de France. This opposition of the business sector has not been silent but on the contrary has been very public. The business sector as a whole, chambers of commerce and the associations of firms together, expressed their official disagreement with the proposed master plan on the grounds that it put more emphasis on the reduction of social inequalities and environmental protection than on economic development issues. The same conflict has emerged about the extension of La Défense. The Paris chamber of commerce (CCIP) officially supports the project, arguing that "Île de France must strengthen its position in the competition because European cities have to attract the headquarters and the strategic decision centers of international firms. To face this strategic challenge, the capital-region can and must rely on the business district of La Défense" (CCIP 2007).

Contrary to the other metropolitan areas examined in this book, Paris–Île de France is the illustration of a city-region with a lack of good relations between the public and the private sector. This relation deficit has a lot to do with the political culture of France and with the domination of the public sector in the governance of the metropolitan area, domination that many economic players view as an arrogance of government. However, it is unlikely that this behavior will significantly change in the near future, as some recent events demonstrate. For instance, economic players were largely absent from the metropolitan conference initiative and this has not changed with the new joint authority, Paris-Métropole (see later discussion). The Paris chamber of commerce was not invited to the various meetings except to the one on economic development and has not since been considered as a fully-fledged partner. The background and lack of relations are so deep that the mistrust between both sectors is strong and cannot be alleviated in the short term.

However, it would be wrong to say that nothing has changed and that the system is completely blocked. Indeed, some players, notably the state and the city of Paris, have undertaken significant actions aiming at changing the scale of government—that is, at rescaling upward the instruments and policies to address the most significant issues of the city-region.

Rescaling Governance

RESCALING FROM PARIS

The election of a new mayor, Bertrand Delanoë, in 2001 was a political thunderstorm in France, notably because it put an end to the control of the capital by the conservative parties. But this election also brought an important change to the metropolitan area in the sense that for the first time, the city of Paris started to open up to its adjacent area. Indeed, until 2001, Paris saw itself autonomously, enclosed within and protected by its ring road (the *Périphérique*). The very first political decision of the new mayor was to create a deputy mayor in charge of cooperation with other local governments of the metropolitan area. Since then, various actions have been undertaken in order to bridge the gap between Paris and the first ring of municipalities, some of them still controlled by the Communist Party. Agreements have been signed between Paris and some *départements* (Seine-Saint-Denis, Val de Marne) but also between Paris and municipalities. However, this cooperation remains limited to the first ring.

The mayor of Paris decided to launch a metropolitan conference in 2006 recognizing that the city of Paris could no longer remain within the *Périphérique* but also that separate agreements between the French capital and single *départements* or municipalities were limited and insufficient to address the major issues of the core of the metropolitan area. This was a strong political move, first, because he thus showed that he had a political view outside its own jurisdiction and envisaged himself as a political leader over a much larger space than the city of Paris itself and, second, because the metropolitan conference was not at all concerned with the whole of Île de France, but only with the core of the metropolitan area. What is this core? Although everyone has been very careful not to define it with too much precision, it is clear that it refers to the densest part of the metropolitan area, the central zone, which more or less encompasses about 80 municipalities around Paris and which more or less covers the first ring. This scale seemed for the mayor of Paris the relevant territory to address most of the social and economic challenges of its development. As such, it put a lot of pressure on the regional council to acknowledge the specificity of this core, which the CRIF did by establishing a specific working group called *zone dense* in the elaboration process of the master plan, the SDRIF.

Delanoë invited the mayors of the eighty adjacent municipalities, the three executives of the first ring *départements*, and the president of the region to the first meeting of the metropolitan conference, which took place in July 2006. In the next two years, five other meetings were organized. They concerned various policy domains such as transport, housing, and economic development, and the last conference (December 2007) focused on the governance of the core of the agglomeration. In June 2008, right after the municipal elections, which strengthened the mayor of Paris as a political leader (its party, the Socialist Party, has consolidated its power at the municipal level), the metropolitan conference secretariat (which had been in the municipality of Paris) called for a large open political meeting, the *Assises de l'Agglomération*, which for the first time was attended by the most important political leaders from all political horizons, including the new minister for Paris. One major result of this last meeting was the proposed creation of a new joint authority, the Syndicat Paris-Métropole. After much time and controversy, the new syndicate was established in June 2009.

Initially supposed to be concerned with the core area, the new joint authority appears to be much larger. At the time of writing (December 2011), it groups about 200 local authorities and extends further than the densest part of Île de France with the inclusion of the airport areas and some new town development in the northwest and southeast. Its final perimeter will depend on the municipalities and *départements* that agree to participate.

Although it is intended as a non-policy-making structure that should facilitate relationships between members, its future as a metropolitan response to governance problems is very debatable. This joint authority seems to be already trapped in the political and ideological conflicts previously mentioned. It has been established after harsh controversy, notably because the mayor of Paris wanted it to be a consensual structure—that is, to include the *départements* of the west controlled by the Conservative Party. This has meant a weak structure with small resources that is unlikely to play a significant role in the governance of the city-region.

RESCALING FROM THE STATE: THE RETURN OF THE STATE?

We have mentioned earlier that the state has exhibited ambiguous behavior regarding Île de France because it was squeezed between a decentralization process, which meant it should be less present and less active, and the importance of the capital region for the national development, which would require its intervention. It seems nevertheless correct and relevant to speak of the return of the state. This is because the central government had shown signs of abandonment of the capital region in the previous decade and has recently also shown signs of more interest in Île de France.

Signs of abandonment were clear at least in two domains that had remained in the hands of the state: planning and public transport. In planning, the state was largely absent in the elaboration of the new master plan, at least until mid-2007. In public transport, it took it several years to leave the board of the STIF but it did finally. Abandonment was also financial, notably regarding transport, with an ongoing degradation of the transport system largely due to a lack of investment. But the abandonment could also be observed in other policy sectors, and for a longer period, although it is difficult to be certain whether this attitude was specific to Île de France or was more general. Nevertheless, signs that the state is returning to its previous role have become more and more visible and more and more significant. Four elements and events may be put forward to give substance to this return: the establishment of the *Opérations d'Intérêt National* (OIN [Projects of National Interest]), the conflict over the SDRIF, the support given to La Défense, and more significantly, the launching of the debate on Grand Paris (Greater Paris) and its subsequent results.

In 2005 and 2006, the state established three OIN in areas encompassing the three major poles of competitiveness. In these areas, which are quite vast (one covers 50 municipalities and contains 370,000 inhabitants), the state has taken over all planning responsibilities (which by law are local competencies) and has set up its own strategies in cooperation with local authorities. These OIN are to be administered by ad hoc public corporations (*Établissements Publics d'Aménagement*) where the state is involved. The establishment of OIN and, in the same period, the launching of poles of competitiveness were rightly seen as a comeback by the state and as a progrowth and procompetitiveness agenda carried out by the central government. More recently, this move has been confirmed by two significant decisions and actions taken by the new government. In June 2007, the new president, Nicolas Sarkozy, when inaugurating the new Air France terminal in the Roissy airport, made a strong declaration against the new SDRIF that was under debate, asking for a stop to the process on the grounds that the new SDRIF did not give enough concern to the international economic competitiveness of Île de France. In the same vein, as we have mentioned before, in complete opposition to the regional council, the central government approved a specific decree regarding the extension of La Défense in August 2007.

But the state has recently made a stronger move with the launching of the Greater Paris debate. In June 2007, right after his election as president, Nicolas Sarkozy made another speech in which he wondered why "Paris is the only big urban area in France without an urban community"—that is, a joint authority with many powers and its own fiscal resources. This declaration was soon interpreted as the desire of the central government to intervene in the institutional issue of Île de France and was welcomed by those who had always wanted a stronger involvement of the state in the capital region, but at the same time, it was criticized by those (notably the CRIF and the city of Paris) who saw it as a way of putting the decentralization process into question, particularly when the metropolitan conference initiative was showing some signs of success.

The debate over the design for a Greater Paris, as it was soon called, was launched, a debate that the central government wanted very much to put forward and speed up. This is what it did with the creation of a "Minister for the development of the Capital-Region" in March 2008 right after the municipal elections. The new minister was given a very clear and specific mandate: "To enable France to keep its place in the world competition by making its capital a 'world city,' open, dynamic, attractive, producer of wealth and employment, which will be a decisive national asset in the competition of the twenty-first century."

THE GRAND PARIS DEBATE

The return of the state has had a quick initial impact, that of producing ideas and proposals of reform, notably about the institutional organization of the metropolitan area. In 2008 and 2009, almost all major players have issued documents proposing changes aimed at the better governance of the urban area. The creation of a ministry for the capital region was a highly symbolic gesture but, in addition, it carried a threat, that of the enactment of a special law on the governance of the Paris metropolis. To prevent this threat, which was like a Damocles sword on local governments, many proposals have been put on the table.

In 2008, the French senate issued a special report on Greater Paris (Dallier 2008). This document proposed to merge the four *départements* of the first ring, including Paris, and to create an urban community (*communauté urbaine*). This proposal has been very much criticized by almost all actors, arguing that it was politically and technically unfeasible and against the spirit of decentralization. At about the same time, the regional council established a special commission on the future of Île de France. This commission issued a report (CRIF 2008) that put forward "ten proposals for a new metropolitan coherence." Acknowledging the specificities of the core (*zone dense*) and the role of the then metropolitan conference in the development of this part of the metropolis, the CRIF proposed to transform the conference into a joint authority and to strengthen the existing intermunicipal joint authorities (EPCI). In addition, it suggested the establishment of a regional housing authority chaired by the regional council in association with the *départements* and the joint authorities, and the transformation of the transit authority (STIF) into a "mobility authority" (*Syndicat des déplacements d'Île de France* [SDIF]) with new responsibilities in freight, logistics, and urban expressways. These proposals were part of the electoral program of the Socialist Party for the 2010 regional elections.

In the meantime, the state has not been immobile. On the contrary, first, it launched an international consultation (*le Grand Pari*)[4] on the future of Île de France, with 10 teams led by some of the most famous architects in the world. The purpose of the consultation was to come up with visions of what Paris–Île de France should become in 2050 and how to make it happen. In April 2009, the president presented the results of this consultation and endorsed some of the ideas expressed. At the same time, the ministry for the development of the capital region proposed a new public transport scheme (the Big Eight), which was supposed to solve most of the transport problems of Île de France, with a strong focus on the enhancement of its attractiveness. This scheme was publicly approved by the French president.

In order to build such a scheme, a new act, the Greater Paris Act (*Loi sur le Grand Paris*) was approved by the Parliament in June 2010 and it is likely that it will significantly change the governance system of the city-region in favor of the state. First, it decided to build an automatic subway network of about 130 km, which would serve the major centers of the region such as the airports, La Défense, and Saclay. Second, this subway network will be built by a new entity called the *Societé du Grand Paris*, a public company whose shareholders are the state, the region, and the *départements*, but which will be controlled by the state. Third, this public company will be in charge of the development of all the stations and their adjacent areas. Fourth, there will be a new scientific and technological cluster of world importance around Saclay (southwest), and this cluster will be developed and managed by a public development corporation composed of local authorities, the state, the universities, and the private sector.

The Grand Paris Project, as it is expressed in the act, has been seriously criticized on several grounds by a wide range of actors, including local authorities belonging to the central government majority. First, it often is viewed as a declaration of war against decentralization. Indeed, two elements of the project are clearly attacks on decentralization; regarding public transport, the establishment of a *Société du Grand Paris* controlled by the state is an attack against the STIF controlled by the region. What would it mean for the CRIF to be responsible for public transport to the exception of this very important infrastructure? Regarding urban development, the law gives the state (through its control over the *Société du Grand Paris*) the decision-making power in a domain that had been transferred to local authorities by the decentralization laws of the early 1980s. As a consequence, both the CRIF and the city of Paris have refused a seat on the *Société du Grand Paris* board, established in July 2010 and chaired by an important conservative mayor.

Second, the Grand Paris project is also criticized because it largely remains a transport project that is far from addressing the major issues of Île de France. Many architects involved in the *Grand Pari* international consultation have rejected the project presented by the government as a product or a by-product of their proposals, and along with other players they have urged the government to come up with a more comprehensive development project for the city-region.

Finally, the problem of funding remains. The roughly estimated cost of the project ranges from €21 to €35 billion over the next fifteen years. The state will only be able to cover a very small part of this amount and will have to find other sources of funding—that is, in the private sector and essentially in local governments, neither of whom is for the time being willing to participate. Whatever the consequences of all these moves, and notably of the Grand Paris Act, a new political and institutional panorama is emerging. However, interestingly enough, economic actors are largely absent of these reforms. They are neither initiators nor simply active players nor considered potential partners by the political and administrative milieus.

Conclusion

Globalization is part of the context for the governance of Paris–Île de France. However, contrary to the three other GCRs, a progrowth and economic development and competitiveness agenda are not high on the Parisian list of priorities. As we have seen, the issues of social and territorial inequality, as well as the question of the quality of environment, are more important for most of Paris's political and social actors. However, economic competitiveness has not been totally absent in the debate but is very much confined to some specific actors in some specific parts of the metropolis. There is no political consensus in dealing with the impact of globalization on the capital of France, and this is largely due to cognitive differences—that is, differences in the perceptions of political realities. For many players, Île de France is not in the globalization game and therefore the question of territorial competition and economic competitiveness is not an issue. For others, less numerous but perhaps growing, it is urgent for the metropolitan area to realize that it is hit by globalization and must therefore act differently from the way it has in the past. These two approaches and visions are not easily reconcilable; they are the result of different collective values and ideologies carried out by political parties and social groups embedded in the long history of the GCR territory (the red belt of Paris for instance). In addition, these political parties and social groups have in the last twenty-five years used the decentralization process to reinforce their positions.

The Paris metropolis is at a crossroads. One direction the city-region could take is the development of territorial coalitions within the metropolitan level rather than at the whole metropolitan scale. There are many reasons for such a trend to become possible. First, there is a conflict of values between players and it is logical that one wants to find allies sharing the same values in order to enhance them against the others. Second, some actors feel the pressure of global competition strongly and do not want to wait any longer for policies focusing on economic competitiveness to be taken at the metropolitan level. In addition, they think such policies would entail long negotiations and would require necessary trade-offs, notably in the use of resources, and they prefer to act on their own. Third, they think they have enough power and resources, notably because of decentralization, to establish a coalition. Those who believe this are usually from the wealthiest parts of the metropolis and fear they have the most to lose from the status quo and/or a rescaling at the metropolitan level.

It is too soon to assess the reality of this hypothesis. While some local governments, notably those in the western part, may want to act on their own without much concern for the metropolitan area or the region as a whole, signs of such a desire for autonomy are not significant. There are also contrary signs; for instance, the evolution of the metropolitan conference to the *syndicat* Paris-Métropole has shifted the focus from the core area to a much larger perimeter. This seems to indicate a pulling back from an autonomization process of the core.

Another direction would be the development of metropolitan-wide initiatives, such as the metropolitan conference and its successor joint authority, Paris-Métropole. Is such a regionalization of governance likely in Île de France? Considering the fragmented and conflicting governance system, this would be difficult and would require considerable leadership. Such a leader could be the state, however. The first decade of decentralization (1982–1992) has gradually left a vacant place for leadership and this vacancy became more and more significant in the second decade. In Île de France, the fragmentation of the political and institutional system, which had been largely compensated for by the state (Lefèvre 2003, 2009) was quickly transformed into a conflicting one without any actor able to regulate the conflicts, let alone guide the development of the region. None were powerful enough, dominant enough, and legitimate enough to play such a role. The regional council, which could have had some legitimacy because it covers more or less the metropolitan area, was not given enough resources to do so. After about fifteen years of hidden and less hidden disagreements, in the logical absence of a local institutional player able to act as a new leader, the state seems to have come back. However, it is no longer the same state. It does not have the same political and financial resources, does not have the same legitimacy, and does not have the same intellectual capacity to act. If the state was able to govern Paris–Île de France once, it cannot be taken for granted that it will be able to do so again on its return.

In that panorama, the relative absence of the business sector is surprising, but this can be explained. First, in the capital region, the business sector has always had relationships with the state. For big firms or for the chambers of commerce, the state had always been the first recourse, either by direct links with the ministers or even the president or through a direct access to the "local" state (prefects and local state administrations). Through these links, they have been able to convey their messages and their needs. Decentralization has significantly changed this situation but, as we have seen, the context has not been favorable to the building of strong relations between local governments and business. Indeed, after more than twenty-five years of decentralization, the relations between business and local governments have not improved and mistrust and indifference are shared. In addition, the extreme fragmentation of the business sector, its persisting conflicting nature, and its lack of leadership have prevented it from becoming an influential protagonist and a credible strategic partner for local governments. Although there are some signs of change (e.g., Medef's organization of a first public debate on the future of Île de France or the multiplication of conferences on the Grand Paris organized by firms and business organizations), the conditions for building a growth coalition or an urban regime in Paris–Île de France are far from ready.

Globalization and decentralization are two major processes that are strongly influencing the evolution of the governance system of the city-region. For the time being, globalization seems to reinforce an already very unregulated and competitive decentralization process.

PART IV   *The Tokyo City-Region*

8. *New Challenges, Old Governance*

TOKYO TODAY IS ENORMOUS AND COMPLEX. It houses over 8 million people in the densely built-up central part of the city, and over 30 million in the region as a whole. This region covers more than 13,000 square kilometers, stretching from the high-rise office towers in the downtown area, out through the residential suburbs, to more remote rural areas. One way of understanding this complexity is to consider different roles the city plays: it is a national capital, a center of a metropolitan region, and an emerging global city. These are all dimensions of Tokyo's place in contemporary Japanese society, although they are not mutually exclusive. These three roles, however, necessarily bring different sets of social and economic trends, problems, and issues and demand different policy responses. They may overlap and reinforce sometimes, but more often bring contradiction, controversy, and conflict. Political institutions and the system of governance are crucial in dealing with such contradiction and conflict. In the Japanese case, the national government plays a major role in regional policy making and so an important issue of investigation is the interplay between national and metropolitan governance.

In the first part of this chapter, we will briefly review the historical development of Tokyo, showing how its multiple roles have evolved, before moving on to explore the major challenges and issues the region has faced since the 1980s. We then turn to an examination of the system of governance that operates in the region, covering the formal structures, the nature of the developmental state, the degree of interaction between different levels of government, and attempts at regional coordination. Finally, we highlight the debates and changes in this regional system of governance.

The Development of a Multifunctional City-Region

TOKYO AS A NATIONAL CAPITAL

The history of modern Tokyo effectively started with the process of transformation from being the center of the feudal system, when the city was called Edo, into the capital of the newly emerged nation-state. The immediate task for the national government was to turn Tokyo into a respectable national capital and present it to the outside world. They had a few strategic ideas on how to develop the city. One of them was to create a center of a national spatial system. Prior to this nation-building period, called the Meiji Restoration (1868–1912), Japan had had a relatively decentralized spatial structure based on the feudal system. Although Edo was the prime city for administration, the economic center was in Osaka. Each region had relatively autonomous economic and cultural structures. The restoration and the following administration of the Meiji government changed this for a more hierarchical and centralized system. The industrial and business functions of Tokyo were greatly increased as a result and, together with its existing administration and consumption functions, its primacy in the national urban system was accomplished. Centralization further progressed through postwar reconstruction and preparation for the Tokyo Olympics in 1964. Because this was a major event with global exposure, the Japanese government tried to present Tokyo to the outside world as a symbol of a prosperous nation that had recovered from the scars of the war, as well as being able to manage a successful Olympics. This included the construction of car parks around the stadium, multistory intersections of urban main roads, and an overhead motorway (Koshizawa 1991). Thus, as a capital city, Tokyo has received special attention from the national government for more than a one hundred years. It is not just the biggest city in Japan but the symbol of national progress and the gateway to the outside world. This has continued into our period and is also reflected in a centralized and vertically integrated administrative system.

TOKYO AS A GLOBAL CITY

Alongside the national capital, Tokyo's role as a global city has gained much public attention since the 1980s. As the Japanese economy grew and transcended its national borders, Tokyo was increasingly seen as a prime city in Asia for coordinating this transnational economy. The concentration of headquarters of transnational corporations and various financial institutions and business services has made Tokyo a top-tier global city (Machimura 1992; Saito 2003; Sassen 1991, 2001). As chapter 1 described, there are many shared features between Tokyo and the other top world cities, although Tokyo retains some unique characteristics. Major similarities include Tokyo's growth in the finance and advanced service sectors. There are also increasing numbers of foreign workers engaged in manufacturing and service jobs. Some parts of Tokyo have been transformed into ethnic towns with ethnic retail shops and specialized businesses. This started to cause some community conflict with the surrounding Japanese residential neighborhoods (Tajima 2003). On the other hand, differences with other world cities are found in the manufacturing sector. While many cities in North America and Europe have suffered a decline of output and jobs in manufacturing, Tokyo did not. Tokyo's economic supremacy was backed up by a dense network of small and medium-sized highly skilled manufacturing firms that created innovative products

(Sassen 1991). Sassen (1991, 2001) attributes the strength of Tokyo's economy to the fact that Tokyo still sustains a substantial manufacturing base compared to New York, whose major source of wealth is finance and corporate services.

Since the recession in the 1990s, however, Tokyo's status as a global city has been called into question. As the entire Japanese economy contracted, the financial industry was particularly badly hit. Tokyo has been increasingly challenged by other Asian cities that are emerging onto the world stage, such as Shanghai, Hong Kong, and Singapore (Saito and Thornley 2003). Tokyo is now suffering from job losses, a rising number of homeless people, and other associated economic and social problems.

METROPOLITAN TOKYO

Tokyo is not only the national capital and a global city but also a vast metropolis fulfilling the needs of its residents. The main story of the metropolis until the 1980s is one of economic growth, population increase, and spatial expansion. Since it became the national capital, Tokyo has been renowned for its large population. It contained over one million by the late 18th century and is estimated as "one of the largest cities in the world" (Sorensen 2002, 12). Postwar economic growth in the 1950s and 1960s further accelerated the migration from rural provinces. After the oil crisis in the 1970s, the migration scaled down somewhat but still continued.[1] The boom years in the 1980s accelerated the concentration of various social and economic functions in Tokyo. A major problem Tokyo faced then was the unusually heavy concentration of economic, political, and social activity related to its global function and the negative externality they caused. Certainly Paris, London, and New York are important centers of their respective national economies and high-level urban functions are concentrated there. However, the range of activities, their degree of concentration, and their significance within the domestic urban hierarchy are particularly salient in the central core area of Tokyo. While the political center in the United States is Washington, D.C., and the academic/ research centers in the United Kingdom are Oxford and Cambridge, Tokyo is a center for politics, media, contemporary culture, research and technology, and education.

After the collapse of the bubble economy and long recession of the 1990s, there followed a period of relative calm, but urban concentration picked up pace again and changed its nature after the end of the 1990s. The population trend of the Tokyo Metropolitan Region (TMR)[2] in Figure 8.2 shows the long decline was stabilized and has been reversed for the first time in more than thirty years from the late 1990s.

There may be several reasons for this sudden reverse. First, a significant drop and recent stabilization in property prices may have encouraged first-time buyers. Second, there is a change in household formation. More people chose to have a fewer number of children (or not to have them at all). More women chose to work full time after they married. Thus, they do not have to seek space in the suburbs, and they can afford the cost of living in the city center. Third, there is a change in lifestyle. As a result of more flexible working practices in the business service sector, which is concentrated in the

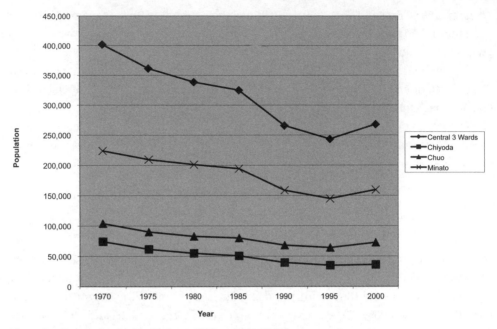

Figure 8.1. Population Living in Central Tokyo, 1970–2000

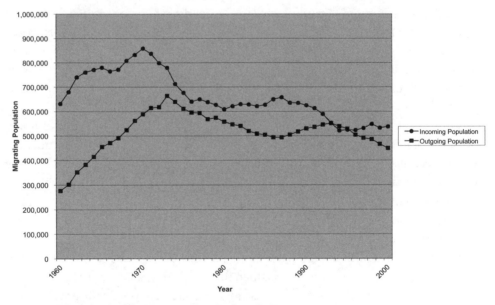

Figure 8.2. Migration in Tokyo Metropolitan Region (TMR), 1960–2000

central part of Tokyo, employees prefer to live close to the workplace. Figure 8.1 shows increased living population in the central three wards of Tokyo between 1995 and 2000. Despite the apparent disadvantage in space, they enjoy the comfort of urban amenities and convenience. Suburban lifestyles have been increasingly superseded by the attractions of urban life (MLIT 2006).

Another significant change in urban structure over the last twenty-five years is the development of business functions in core cities in the surrounding prefectures, such as Tachikawa, Omiya, and Chiba. They have attracted back-office functions and domestic and regional coordinating functions and have increased the employment base in the broader region. As a result, commuting patterns have started to change. In the past, the vast majority of suburban and exurban white-collar residents worked in the offices in central Tokyo, but now more and more people choose to live and work in closer proximity (MLIT 2004). It is not only commuting to work but also shopping patterns that have changed. Out-of-town shopping centers, outlet malls, and roadside shops have mushroomed, creating more self-contained suburban communities.

Major Challenges and Issues Facing the Region

As we discussed in the last section, major urban issues and problems in Tokyo were associated with rapid industrial growth and urbanization. In a way, Tokyo became a victim of its own success. Industrialization and intense urbanization caused various urban problems. The rapid pace of urbanization also created urban sprawl on a huge scale without adequate levels of community facilities and amenities (Matsushita 1971; Miyamoto 1973). Old housing stocks were left untouched on the urban fringe with narrow streets and only a few open spaces, creating a dangerous and inadequate urban environment. Environment became a major national issue in the 1970s. In the Tokyo region, many people suffered from air pollution caused by factories and motor vehicles. The image of a smoke-stack industrial city and overcrowded commuter trains was widely circulated around the world. Although the economic structure of the region has now changed, the legacy of this earlier period continues to create problems. The Tokyo city-region has the highest population of our four cities and is characterized by continuous urban development with a very low open space provision.

However, compared to this industrializing and urbanizing phase, the issues and problems that Tokyo is facing today are very different and, in some sense, the reverse of the previous phase. In the past, it suffered from economic growth, but now the economy has been contracting for more than a decade, and unemployment has become a real issue, particularly among young graduates. Postwar Japan was known as an egalitarian society and social inequality was relatively small between the 1960s and 1980s. However, the gap between rich and poor has widened since the mid-1990s (Sato 2000; Tachibanaki 2009). Globalization continued to integrate the Japanese economy into the rest of the world. However, public perception and the policy response have changed from confidence to pessimism, from outgoing to defensive (Machimura 2003; Saito and Thornley 2003). The number of immigrants coming to Japan keeps rising, though the scale is still minor compared to most other global cities. Nevertheless, Tokyo has started to show serious social problems, such as drugs and crime.

ECONOMY: RESTRUCTURING IN THE LABOR MARKET

By any international or Japanese comparison, Tokyo and its metropolitan region is a very wealthy area. Tokyo's wealth comes from various kinds of service industries, including banking, retail and wholesale, real estate, insurance, and other kinds of services. Manufacturing comes second in total output but is important mainly in the outer edge of the region where industrial clusters are found. Though the 2008 financial crisis hit the manufacturing sectors hard and some plants were forced to close, the biggest economic issue in the region is not the disappearance of the manufacturing sector but the flexibility of the labor market and the instability of jobs.

Though once seen as invincible, lifetime employment started to be superseded by a more flexible working system from the mid-1990s (Dore 2000). Today, only the core workforce in the corporate sector is directly employed, and the rest have to be content with contract work through employment agencies. This kind of flexible labor is not limited to Japan, but what is unique is the gap in working conditions between the core workers and the rest. The latter have to endure lower wages, few opportunities for promotion, and unstable contracts. Graduates are also badly affected, because core workers are protected by law and it is difficult to dismiss them. As a result, young people have to start their working life from a disadvantaged position and are deprived of accumulating skills and experiences (Genda 2005). The term "working poor" has become popular. They are not unemployed, but their wage alone is too low to support themselves, which pushes them into having multiple part-time jobs.[3]

The unemployment rate, though still low by international comparison, has kept rising. In fact, it has doubled in the last twenty years, and the figures for Tokyo are repeatedly higher than the national average. The number of homeless dramatically increased in the late 1990s and stayed high. In 2003, the number was 1.27 times the 1998 level. They occupied public spaces like parks, riversides, and underpasses of some stations. At the same time, the savings rate dropped and the consumption level remained low, which discouraged production and created a deflationary spiral.

SOCIETY: GROWING INEQUALITY

Many researchers have tried to test the world city hypothesis of increasing inequality and polarization on the case of Tokyo. The general consensus is that polarization is not as strong as in other global cities, notably London and New York, but that it does exist and is widening (Sassen 2001; Sonobe 2001; Takei 2007). Over the last 20 years, in Tokyo's 23 wards, the top end of the occupational structure (professional) has increased more than others while the bottom end (manual labor) has decreased (see Table 8.1). This may have been caused by an increase in globalization-related highly skilled workers in finance and producer service on the one hand, and closure/relocation of small manufacturing plants on the other.

Similarly, if we look at household income in the TMR area in Table 8.2, we see how the lower-income groups have become poorer over the last twenty years while the richer groups have improved their relative position.[4] The middle to lower band has suffered a decreasing share of the total income, while the middle to higher band has recorded a rise. The increase in poverty is also clear from the number of households with welfare support. In the TMR area, the figure was less than 67,000 in 1990, but more than doubled to almost 140,000 in 2005. Thus, although weak, the polarization thesis can be applied to Tokyo (Sonobe 2003).

How can these trends be mapped geographically? The increasing polarization is reflected in residential preferences. As we saw in chapter 1, the division between wealthy and poor areas has historical roots, with the former locating in the west. Thus, managers and white-collar professionals tend to live in the western part of Tokyo's twenty-three wards area, although there are also pockets in municipalities on the Tokyo Metropolitan Government (TMG) border in the surrounding prefectures of Kanagawa, Chiba, and Saitama. There has also been a trend, especially since the late 1990s, for more and more of the wealthy population, who tend to work as professionals and managers, to locate in the center core area. Historically, we also noted in chapter 1 that the poor concentrated in the east of Tokyo and this pattern continues with pockets in the northeast part of Tokyo's twenty-three wards, such as Adachi and Katsushika, although other concentrations exist around the borders of the TMG.

This spatial polarization, and the increase in the gap between rich and poor, has policy implications. In the postwar economy, Japanese society was quite wealthy, with a high degree of economic and social equality, comparable to Scandinavian countries (Dore 2000). This, however, started to crumble in the 1990s and accelerated after the Koizumi administration in the first decade of the twenty-first century. The policy debates began to refer to so-called hot spots and cold spots (Hirayama 2006). A hot spot is a place where a positive cycle between the rise of land prices and the increase in wealthy population can be observed, such as the gentrified urban core residential area, and a few exclusive suburbs. A cold spot is the complete reverse, where a negative spiral between property prices and the conditions of the population exists. In the past, land price and population change were closely related to the gross domestic product (GDP) growth rate and were experienced uniformly throughout the region. In more recent years, however, such a correlation is not observed uniformly, and the region has witnessed the emergence of both hot and cold spots at the same time.

As we have noted, most hot spots are located in the center core of Tokyo; more precisely, they are found in a limited part of this area. Old, upper-middle-class residential areas, such as Aoyama and Shirogane, are still popular, but other areas, such as

TABLE 8.1. OCCUPATIONAL STRUCTURE IN TOKYO'S 23 WARDS
(AS A PERCENTAGE)

	1980	1990	1995	2000	Increase (%) 1980–90	Increase (%) 1990–2000
Professionals	10.8	13.7	14.4	15.9	2.9	2.2
Managerial	7.3	6.0	5.9	3.9	–0.7	–2.1
Clerical	22.5	24.3	23.9	23.4	1.8	1.1
Sales	18.0	17.8	17.9	18.2	–0.2	0.4
Service	10.3	9.5	10.3	10.7	–0.8	1.2
Maintenance	1.1	1.1	1.1	1.2	0	0.1
Agriculture/ fishery	0.3	0.2	0.2	0.2	–0.1	0
Transport/ communica- tion	3.7	3.4	3.5	3.3	–0.3	–0.1
Manual labor	25.6	22.6	20.8	20.1	–2.8	–2.5
Other	0.4	1.3	1.8	3.1	0.9	1.8

Source: CENSUS 1980, 1990, 1995; Sonobe 2003, 35.

TABLE 8.2. HOUSEHOLD INCOME STRUCTURE IN TMG AREA (AS A PERCENTAGE)

Band*	1979	1989	1994	1999	Increase (1979–99)
1	3.5	3.1	3.2	2.9	–0.6
2	5.3	4.9	4.9	4.7	–0.8
3	6.4	5.9	6.2	5.8	–0.6
4	7.2	6.9	7.0	6.8	–0.4
5	8.2	7.8	8.1	7.9	–0.3
6	9.2	8.9	9.2	9.2	0
7	10.3	10.4	10.5	10.6	0.3
8	12.0	12.3	12.1	12.4	0.4
9	14.8	14.8	15.1	15.2	0.4
10	23.1	25.0	23.5	24.5	1.4
10/1	6.60	8.06	7.34	8.44	1.84

* The band was artificially created by dividing the population into 10 groups of equal numbers from top to bottom according to the level of household income.
Source: National Survey of Family Income and Expenditure in 1979, 1984, 1994, and 1999 (Ministry of Public Management).

Roppongi, are newly gentrified. Waterfront areas, such as Toyosu and Harumi, are also occupied by newly constructed high-rise condominiums. The number of large-scale and high-rise residential projects has increased rapidly since the turn of the century.[5] They are generally more expensive and targeted to middle-class professionals aged between thirty and forty who have fewer children. On the other hand, cold spots can be found in suburban residential areas located outside TMG (Wakabayashi 2007). They were developed during the bubble period of the late 1980s. Housing here was expensive because the land price was so high. Now, however, many residents are suffering from negative equity and cannot sell their property. All the residential suburbs were previously commuter towns, but now some of them contain a high proportion of the elderly population as a result of demographic change. Some of them live in poverty, and the communities lack supporting infrastructure such as shops and other services within walking distance.[6] Therefore, the distinction between rich and poor has become increasingly apparent in spatial terms. Tokyo and the surrounding region have become highly socially stratified, and a kind of hierarchical order has emerged. This provides a new challenge for urban policy.

ENVIRONMENT: SUSTAINABILITY AND NATURAL DISASTER

As already mentioned, Japan has given top priority to economic growth as it tries to catch up with the West. This has inevitably meant that less attention has been given to environmental concerns, and there have been many occasions in the past when this drive for growth has generated environmental problems, such as pollution and noise. This lack of attention to the quality of the natural and urban environment has affected the structure of cities, particularly in the Tokyo region. As a result, one of the distinctive features, and major challenges, of Tokyo is the extensive sprawl of the built-up area. Past policies to impose a green belt on the city failed in the face of political opposition. As we noted in chapter 1, Tokyo has the lowest amount of open space of our four cities. Tokyo's green space per head is less than one-fifth that of London and New York and less than half that of Paris (MLIT 2006, 40).

As already noted, the level of industrial pollution has become less significant. People in Tokyo enjoy cleaner air and water compared to thirty years ago. Some of the rivers and canals in inner Tokyo, which used to be so polluted that no one dared approach them, are now quite popular for water sports, fishing, and other leisure activities. The waterfront has been gentrified and occupied by condominiums. However, this doesn't mean that the environment has fallen off the urban issue agenda. Global warming and reducing CO_2 emissions have become big national issues since the early 1990s, and Tokyo is often seen as the prime polluter. Although major factories have now relocated to the edge of the metropolitan region and beyond, including overseas, the sheer concentration of such a large population, and the traffic generated, necessarily creates a greenhouse effect. It also causes the heat-island phenomenon, which prevents the central part of Tokyo from cooling down even at night. As a result, during the summer central Tokyo experiences an excessive heat wave and humidity and becomes a very difficult place to live in without air conditioning.

One of the unique aspects of Tokyo among the four cities we compare is its geological condition. Tokyo is close to the earthquake zone, and indeed has been repeatedly hit in its 400-year history. The most recent big disaster was the Great Kanto Earthquake in 1923, which killed more than 99,000 people and affected nearly 700,000 households. Scientists have been warning for years that the next big hit is imminent, but they can't tell exactly when. Thus, national and local governments are obliged to have a disaster prevention strategy and mobilize every possible measure to minimize the potential damage. The danger is exacerbated by Tokyo's built environment; the building structure, density, and road pattern in some residential areas are problematic. First, traditional wooden houses are incrementally replaced by modern architecture, but many of them are still not completely safe from fire. Second, the tradition of strongly protected ownership rights, high land price, and the inheritance system result in a typically fragmented land ownership and small plot size in the old residential areas (Sorensen 2002). These are located in the inner suburbs of the 10- to 15-kilometer radial zone, are densely populated, and often have narrow, winding roads. Critics have pointed out that they are the most dangerous areas in case of earthquake and fire, but improvement is so far slow and patchy.

GLOBALIZATION: COMPETITIVENESS AND IMMIGRATION

It is interesting to make international comparisons with Japan's national wealth, measured by GDP per capita. In 1980, Japan was positioned around 20th after North America, Europe, and some Gulf states. It moved up to the top three in 1995, but dropped back to around twentieth by 2006. In particular, while most other countries recorded growth between 2004 and 2006, Japan actually declined. In 2008, Singapore became the wealthiest country in Asia measured by GDP per capita.

The attitude toward competitiveness may be one of the biggest changes experienced in Tokyo in the last twenty-five years (Saito and Thornley 2003). Until the collapse of the bubble economy in the mid-1990s, globalization can be interpreted as outward expansion: the increase of export output and the expansion of Japanese manufacturing transnational corporations. Trade surplus mounted to a record level, and it was indeed a source of national wealth. It also caused trade friction with the United States and the European Union. Global competition was fierce, but it took place outside Japan. At the same time, the domestic market was protected from import and inward investment (Schaede and Grimes 2003). Even in 2000, direct inward investment only counted for 1.2 percent of GDP. Thus the very term "global competition" did not appear in public policy discourse. Since the late 1990s, however, some of the Japanese transnationals lost their advantage in the global market, caught by new rivals in Korea, Taiwan, and other Asian countries with cheaper production costs. The domestic market was liberalized and has to face tougher competition. It is no longer unusual to see a takeover by a foreign corporation, but some people are worried about the implications of the ruth-less management practice of cost-cutting.

Apart from the descendants of Koreans and Chinese who came before the end of the war, Japan has a very low proportion of ethnic minorities—best estimates show these count for less than 2 percent of the national population. Due to globalization and the shortage of labor in some industries, however, more and more foreigners have come to Japan. The Japanese government has gradually relaxed immigration control but still maintains a kinship-based priority system in which the descendants of Japa-nese are legally allowed to work without any restriction. Second and third generations of Japanese migrants to South America were the first group to come back in the early 1990s. According to the Ministry of Foreign Affairs, the number of foreigners, particu-larly from Asian countries, continued to rise throughout the 1990s despite economic recession, and the total number of foreigners doubled in the past twenty years.

The foreign populations tend to live around the big metropolitan regions of Tokyo, Osaka, and Nagoya. There is an ethnic division of labor; Brazilians and other South Americans tend to work in manufacturing, while Chinese and other Asians tend to work in the retail, service, and leisure (including restaurants and bars) sectors. Conse-quently, their residential locations do not overlap. The former live in the municipalities in the outer region, where big manufacturing plants are located, while the latter reside in the more central part of Tokyo in areas such as Shinjuku (Tajima 2003). Although the number of foreign managers and professionals are increasing, the majority of the ethnic minority population is engaged in lower-paid work and thus has a rather mar-ginal socioeconomic status (Douglass and Roberts 2000). There are cases of commu-nity conflict caused by cultural differences, and their marginal existence forces some of them to commit crimes. The extent of such problems is, however, relatively minor in Japan due to the very small proportion of foreigners within the total population.

The System of Governance: The Developmental State

We have seen how the Tokyo region has to fulfill global, national, and local roles while also facing some major economic, social, and environmental challenges. We now ex-amine the system of governance within which any policy response has to be formu-lated and implemented. In the Japanese case, this system has been shaped over the years by the leadership of national government. It has strong historical and ideological roots and so we start by setting out the philosophical approach of central government, often referred to as developmentalism or the developmental state. Over time, a formal system of government with responsibilities for each level has evolved within this de-velopmental state framework. The second section outlines this formal structure and, as one would expect, the national government can be seen to have a major influence within it. One of the key characteristics of the structure is the weakness of a regional element and so, in the following section, we then explore the rather limited attempts that have been made to overcome this weakness and create some kind of regional co-ordination. The dominance of national government has at times been challenged by local politics and we outline some examples of the way this has happened. Finally, we also outline the major debates and discussions about Japanese governance in recent years. These focus on the limitations of a developmental state approach in a globalized world. As the national government dominates the system of governance, any changes to its approach will have ramifications down through the system and will affect the Tokyo region. We set out the reforms that national government has adopted in recent years and the ideas that are under discussion on decentralization.

DEVELOPMENTALISM AND THE STATE

The ideology that underlies the Japanese governmental system has been called developmentalism. According to this view, economic progress is best achieved when the state leads the nation in promoting economic change. Its characteristics become apparent when contrasted with liberalism, which is the belief that economic growth is best achieved by liberating individuals to pursue their own initiatives. Developmentalism emerged in some late industrializing countries as a reaction against economic liberalism. Developmentalists often considered the laissez-faire creed to be an ideological rationale for Western imperialism (Gao 1997).

Under the developmental state, public ownership, planning, and goal setting are institutional means to achieve national economic development. The state encourages cooperation among businesses, and between business and labor, to speed the adoption of new technology, reduce production costs, and expand the nation's share of global markets (Hatch and Yamamura 1996; Johnson 1982; Schneider 1999). Industrialization is the developmental state's highest priority and industrial policies are the state's primary means for achieving economic goals. The government uses policies to protect domestic industries, develop strategic industries, and adjust the economic structure to changes in the world economy. The developmental state attempts to combine economic policies with competition among private firms through the use of market-conforming methods of economic intervention (Komiya, Okuno, and Suzumura 1984).

The developmental state is often contrasted with the welfare state in the West because government policy is more concerned with economic development than social welfare (Johnson 1982). Because of this emphasis on economic growth, less attention and resources are spent on welfare issues when compared to most European welfare states. Japan set up a social welfare program in the 1920s based upon the European approach. This continued after World War II and was expanded in the 1960s, partly in response to the criticism against its economic-growth-at-all-cost policy of the earlier decade. The welfare program includes a universal medical system, care for the elderly, assistance for the poor, and public housing. However, this system has come under stress with the increase in the proportion of the elderly in the population; by the 1980s, pensioners were consuming around half the social welfare budget. Although this budget was relatively small compared with many other countries, the national state has still been important, with the Liberal Democratic Party and national state bureaucrats playing a leading role. There are, however, two other aspects to welfare provision that partly explain the low expenditure levels. First, many private companies provide welfare support under the concept of lifetime employment. Second, Japan still draws on the older tradition in which the family and local communities play important social welfare roles, as expressed by a high proportion of full-time housewives and retired women fulfilling caring functions. Commentators have noted that, in some respects, the Japanese system is similar to the welfare state but at the same time it has important differences (e.g., Goodman and Peng 1996; Goodman, White, and Kwon 1998). It pursues the welfare state notion of economic and social equity but with a low level of government social spending. The supplement of the corporate and family provision leads many to talk about a particular hybrid approach (e.g., Esping-Andersen 1999) while some see social policy as being mobilized to maximize the productive capacity (Holliday 2000).

National bureaucrats are recruited from among the best and brightest talent and are given the autonomy to take initiatives and make effective decisions. They can counter the claims of interest groups that would undermine economic growth (Evans 1995; Johnson 1982). The political-bureaucratic elite are the leading force in the developmental socioeconomic alliance and political regime. Thus, under developmentalism, the national government has strongly enforced economic and industrial policies through a centralized administration system (Murakami 1992). National plans and strategies have been used not only to give favors to certain industrial sectors but also to justify such centralized and often seemingly nondemocratic and interventionist government actions. The government gained legitimacy by promising that all citizens in Japan would ultimately enjoy the fruit of economic growth and prosperity, and that regional and locational disparities would be minimized. In this sense, regional planning policy in Japan, formulated by the central state, was a crucial policy tool for the national government in achieving this wider goal.

In the developmental state, there is therefore an important relationship between politicians and bureaucrats, who have considerable autonomy. The third dimension of the developmental state is the business sector. The developmental state approach does not necessarily mean direct order and control by state officials. In capitalism, it is beyond doubt that the private business is the main agent to make profit and create wealth. The developmental state, however, utilizes various measures to cooperate with business. Institutions are designed to ensure smooth communication between them—for example, by seconding personnel as well as constant exchange of information. The business community is organized nationally and locally. At the national level, the Confederation of Economic Organizations (*Keidanren*) and the Japan Chamber of Commerce and Industry represent a wide range of sectors and various sizes of businesses. Their role is to represent the business community and to have an influence on public policy. They organize seminars and events, publish reports and recommendations, send representatives to government committees, and lobby ministries and influential political leaders. At the local and regional level, local branches of the chamber of commerce are organized as umbrella bodies and various sector-specific groups are created. Their activities, however, are typically parochial and fragmented. It is often difficult to create a consensus on issues related to economic development and place-making at the regional scale beyond general promotional strategies.

The relationship between central and local government plays an integral part in national economic development. Intergovernmental relations are also crucial for understanding the way in which regions are governed, as they often set the framework for economic development. There have been a number of competing academic interpretations of intergovernmental relations, such as the so-called central control and local subordination thesis (Steiner 1965) and the local initiative thesis (Reed 1986). However, most scholars instead see interdependence between the two levels of government (Muramatsu 1997). While the central control thesis emphasizes vertical order in administrative/legal structures and financial constraints imposed by the central government, the local initiative thesis emphasizes horizontal political processes at the local level. In contrast, the interdependency thesis basically sees the state administrative structure as "centrally controlled decision making . . . with . . . localized service provision" (Jinno 1995, 71; author's translation). Higher-level state officials deploy strategic assets, such as a large database and research findings; devise strategies; make plans; send directives; and oversee implementation. Local officials, who implement policies in accordance with central government guidelines, exercise in turn a high degree of operational freedom within their sphere. In fact, it is often the case that "the central government gives local officials discretionary powers to encourage their initiative, and then monitors the result" (Hill and Fujita 2000, 678).

THE FORMAL GOVERNMENT STRUCTURE

Within this developmental state approach, a formal structure of government has developed. Japan has three tiers of government—national, prefectural, and municipal—and these share the task of tax collection and public service provision. In official government documents, *Tokyo* usually means the TMG, one of the prefectural-level governments. Surrounding the TMG, there are three more prefectures—Kanagawa, Chiba, and Saitama—and these four make up the TMR. This region is the home to more than a quarter of Japan's total population. When talking about a region, it is usual to refer to the functional urban region (FUR) where integrated economic and social activities take place, such as commuting. Looking at Tokyo in this respect, the 40-kilometer radial area from central Tokyo could approximate to the FUR. The TMR is therefore larger than the FUR and includes agricultural, forestry, and fishery activities, which do not have strong economic or social ties to the central part of Tokyo.

The TMG is further divided into municipalities of twenty-three wards and twenty-six cities. The former are located within the 15-kilometer radial ring, a mostly built-up area, while the latter are further away in the western extension of the Tama area. This has become urbanized but is less densely populated, with areas of natural beauty such as large tracts of forest, clear streams, and rivers. The other prefectures in the region—Saitama, Chiba, and Kanagawa—also have cities, towns, and villages. Most of the towns and villages are located in the outer part of prefectures and are less densely populated. They are mainly engaged in agriculture, forestry, and fishery and thus not part of the FUR. Though the average population of a municipality in Japan is bigger than that of other OECD countries, local government structure is quite fragmented. The TMR consists of 269 municipalities and their population size varies from a mere 3,000 to 800,000.

Unlike the New York case, there is no established method of grouping the municipalities into several rings, or dividing them into near suburbs and outer suburbs. Apart from prefectural administrative boundaries, there are no criteria to draw the lines. It is relatively easy to designate the urban core, which is comparable in size to Manhattan. It consists of three central wards of the TMG: Chiyoda, Chuo, and Minato. The immediate surrounding area covering the twenty-three Tokyo wards has a residential population of over eight million. Further out, the ring can be divided into two: the total TMG area and the TMR.

Public administrative duties are shared between prefecture and municipality.[7] They are mutually independent entities and have equal legal status. The scope of their function differs, however, because of their geographical coverage. The prefecture is a regional public entity covering a wide area that includes multiple municipalities within it. The municipality is the basic unit of local government and closely related to people's daily lives. They carry out various daily services, such as resident and family registration; public health and safety, such as refuse collection and sewage disposal; and manage public facilities like primary schools and community libraries. The prefecture is responsible for matters beyond each municipality—for instance, devising a prefecture-wide development strategy, nature conservation, and police and fire services. They also deal with the communication between the municipalities and national government and provide advice and guidance to municipalities. Exceptions to this two-tier system are designated cities, core cities, and special case cities in metropolitan regions. Designated cities should have a population of over 500,000 and are granted special legal status. They are authorized to administer the same level of governmental jurisdiction as prefectures in nineteen policy areas, including social welfare, public health, and urban planning.[8] The TMR has five such designated cities: Saitama, Chiba, Yokohama, Kawasaki, and Sagamihara. They are major commercial and business centers outside the TMG.

Both prefecture and municipal government consist of an executive branch and a legislature. Both the head of the executive branch (mayor or governor) and the members of the legislature (councillors) are publicly elected. They operate on the principle of a separation of power with internal checks and balances. Unlike national government, local government is based on the presidential system and this grants more power to the mayor or governor, and thus their leadership is often crucial in policy making.

Another aspect of the formal structure relates to the way public finance is controlled. Once again, the Japanese system gives considerable power to the national government. The policy to achieve a balanced regional structure was supplemented by the development of a financial transfer system between central and local government. In terms of revenue, a third of the total tax is collected by the local government and the rest is collected by the central government. However, in terms of total public sector expenditure, the local government spends two-thirds. As a result, the local government needs to fill the gap between the amount they collect and the amount they need. This is where the financial transfer system from the central government to the local government plays a crucial part, through grants and subsidies. While the proportion of local tax raised by a local government is around 40 percent of its income on average,[9] the proportion of grants and subsidies is around 30 percent, and the rest is raised from the market by issuing municipal bonds and by borrowing.

The financial transfer system tends to be coupled with the exercise of control and constraints imposed by the central government. There are three kinds of restraint for managing municipal finances. First, the local government has to consult the national government to decide what kind of taxes it can have, other than the statutory one, in its jurisdiction. This includes, for instance, the environmental tax imposed on private operators of waste disposal to manage environmental risk. Second, the level of tax rates is also a matter for consultation and approval. It is difficult for the local government to have top-up rates above the level set by the national government. Third, without national government consent, the local government cannot raise funds through municipal bonds. If the financial balance sheets of the local government are considered to be badly managed, then the central government has the power to take over.[10] Thus, the public finance system enables the central government to monitor and control the level of local public sector spending effectively.

Another purpose of the financial transfer system is to try to ensure fair levels of local welfare in diverse geographical locations. As levels of economic vitality and prosperity vary between cities and regions, there would be huge differences in the levels of public spending without the financial transfer system and, hence, the provision of public benefits. Thus, the transfer system works as a means of balancing quality of life, such as the quality of public health and education services, between localities. This conforms to the developmental state ideology to reduce inequality and strengthen the sense of national unity among the population. Showing that the government has the will to correct the imbalance within its jurisdiction symbolizes its advocacy of sharing the fruit of national economic growth with all of its citizens (Fujiwara 1998). This also contributed to the political support for the ruling Liberal Democratic Party. At the same time, the policy was crucial for government officials in attaining legitimacy. They needed to be seen as impartial and representative of the whole community. The leadership role of the government and its willingness to intervene in market processes was justified on these grounds.

REGIONAL GOVERNANCE

As our focus is on the city-region level, we need to say something specific on the Japanese approach to governance at this level. As one can see, it did not figure greatly in the formal structure outlined previously. As a unitary state, the Japanese government system does not have a regional level of government, and the national government has a significant influence and a major agency in regional policy. Some ministries, such as the Ministry of Land, Infrastructure, and Transport (MLIT) and Ministry of Economy, Trade, and Industry (METI), have regional offices but others have their local offices in the prefectural government (e.g., Ministry of Health [MoH]). This is because the tasks they perform are different. While MLIT has to implement some national projects at the regional scale, such as dams and river improvement, the local offices of the MoH monitor the implementation by the local government, giving advice if necessary, and coordinate various policies at the regional level. The policy itself is prepared at the ministry headquarters in the national government.

The TMR only exists as a statistical unit, and there is no formal institution to govern the region. However, there are informal mechanisms through which regional matters can be discussed within the region. The Capital Region Summit, which now consists of the heads of five cities and four prefectures[11] in the region, was created in 1979. They discuss various issues that the region faces, exchange ideas, and learn from each other but do not have legal status and decision-making power. If they arrive at a common understanding and reach some consensus on certain issues—for instance, measures to tackle air pollution caused by diesel emission—they implement a common policy in their respective administrations. Another major function of the summit is to lobby the national government. A common agenda, such as on regional infrastructure, is put forward to the relevant national ministries for consideration. The summit is held regularly twice a year. Another discussion forum, the Capital Region Forum, was created more recently in 2006. Membership of this forum includes the members of the Capital Region Summit plus the leaders in the local business community, such as the heads of chambers of commerce in Tokyo, Yokohama, Saitama, Kawasaki, and Chiba, and expert advisors in various policy fields, such as urban planning and environment. The forum meets once a year to discuss regional issues. It is basically an extension of the Capital Region Summit, but it can benefit from the realism of the private sector representatives. The issues covered include tourism development, environmental sustainability, and regional infrastructure. Again, the forum does not have real power, but its creation suggests increased attention to regional issues and the need for policy coordination.

POLITICAL DYNAMISM IN THE REGION

We have seen how governance is dominated at all levels by the national government. However, there are some factors that can lead to political pressures arising from the local level. At times, these have the potential to challenge central power. In the Tokyo region, it is the TMG that is most capable of mounting such a challenge. Though the TMR consists of four prefectures of equal legal status, the economic might and socio-political significance of TMG surpasses the others. The TMG has a budget comparable to the national government of Korea or India, and employs more than 17,000 staff. Thus, the TMG sometimes exerts a large political influence over the others in the regional political landscape. In particular, the governor of Tokyo is said to hold a unique position because "capital city Tokyo is beyond normal local government in terms of economic power and political influence. It can be said that the governor is the second only to the prime minister as a political figure representing Japan" (Toki 2003, 135; author's translation). Moreover, the fact that Tokyo is the national capital requires the governor to work closely with the national government. For instance, in the age of global terrorism, policing Tokyo is a huge responsibility, but it is directly under the governor's control. In case of an earthquake, they have to work together to minimize the damage and destruction.

The position of the Tokyo governor also has a symbolic significance in electoral politics. The governorship election is often fought over national or even international political issues rather than regional and local ones and reflects the political sentiment of the majority.[12] The voters sometimes choose someone who is allied to the national administration[13] but often vote for the candidate who is against it—a protest vote warning the ruling party that the voters are not happy with their policies. Also, there have been some occasions when the voters tried to restore a kind of balance when the ruling party had a huge majority in national politics. Thus, inevitably, the policy of TMG often contains an element of tension and opposition to that of the national government. It is said that the politics of Tokyo can be understood not within the local arena alone but in relation to the national government (Mikuriya 1990).

There has been a national change in the attitude of some political leaders at the prefectural or municipal level in the last twenty years. Some are taking a greater leadership role. In the past, their effectiveness was evaluated on the basis of the size of the resources they could gain from the central government. Thus, those who had strong connections to national political leaders and high-level state officials[14] were a popular choice among the voters. The economic downturn and public financial stress in the 1990s, however, reduced the redistributive capacity of the national government and made such practice unsustainable. There were also strong criticisms against the "culture of dependence" to which local interest tended to be subordinated. Also, the grants from the national government often proved to be costly and counterproductive. For instance, the initial construction of infrastructure may be financed by the national government, but the maintenance responsibility is placed on the local government, and this severely affected their budget in the long run.

The reform-minded governors and mayors came into the limelight in the mid-1990s. Though their background and political ideology varied, they had one thing in common. That was to organize political support around a nonpartisan local coalition, claim strong local or regional identity, keep a certain distance from national politics, and try to manage their territory in a more independent manner (e.g., nurturing the local industry, promoting tourism, etc.). In TMR, the then Governor Suzuki of TMG and Governor Tsuchiya of Saitama prefecture were both old-type local leaders in the 1980s. They had served as high-rank state officials before turning to politics, and as governors they utilized such resources for intergovernmental negotiation and deal making. They were replaced in the 1990s by a new brand of governors who did not come from such an established route.[15]

The election of Aoshima, who succeeded Suzuki in 1995 as governor of the TMG, was a clear case of a protest vote. He was an ex-comedian and a playwright but also a popular political commentator. His political mandate was the rejection of alliance between the TMG and the national government under the Liberal Democratic Party (LDP), rampant property development, and exclusion of the local community from decision making. He rejected the idea of project-led urban regeneration and emphasized environment and quality of life. He scrapped the plan for further expansion of the loss-making waterfront project, despite a huge protest from the development industry, local LDP politicians, and some TMG officials. His administration was, however, short-lived because he did not have a clear vision for the TMG or a roadmap for policy implementation beyond the rejection of the status quo.

Governor Ishihara won the election by a huge margin and replaced Aoshima in 1999. He was a long-serving LDP parliamentarian, and ex–transport minister, but because of his radically nationalistic ideology, he has never belonged to the mainstream faction within the LDP. He brought a completely new perspective to Tokyo's politics by arguing that national recovery should start in Tokyo. He understood the strategic importance of Tokyo and tried to utilize it to his political advantage. Such sentiments often remain at the level of political rhetoric because the TMG have to act within the legal and financial framework of the national government. In his case, however, he actually challenged the national government, for example, by imposing a new tax system on the banking sector, by advocating the civilian use of the Yokota Airbase currently managed by the US military, and by arguing for the reform of the tax transfer system. Though he is often criticized for his ultranationalistic views,[16] he is a charismatic and popular leader who shook the status quo in intergovernmental relations between the TMG and the national government.

In many world cities, an alternative focus of power based on local business develops at the city level, and this can influence higher levels of government. This can be through the existence of a strong local organization, such as the Corporation of

London, or a growth coalition between business and local politicians, such as is found in many US cities. This does not tend to happen in Japan under the developmental state approach. Tokyo has a significant concentration of HQs of big business and transnational corporations. Their influence on local and regional issues has been, however, rather limited (Saito 2003). First, this is because Tokyo's economy has been relatively good even during the recession. Local growth coalitions and boosterism, which may be observed in provincial cities where the local economy has suffered badly, cannot be found in Tokyo. Second, Tokyo is too big and its economy is too complex for a single growth coalition to be organized at the city or city-regional scale. Coalitions can be found, however, around specific projects, particular property-based, commercial, or business-oriented megaprojects. Such projects are likely to be carried out by a consortium centered on financial institutions and developers. Prefectural and municipal governments are also involved in negotiation over land use regulation, development contributions, and infrastructure planning. Also, these consortiums are active in lobbying the national government by forming, for instance, a public–private partnership to develop new earthquake-proof construction technology. In fact, Tokyo is known for the rampant and seemingly unrestricted activity of private developers coupled with weak planning regulation and is thus often portrayed as a "corporate playground" (Waley 2007). However, their influence on strategic planning is weak. The Tokyo Chamber of Commerce and Industry (TCCI) often published their own urban policy documents, but they were rather similar to those published by the national ministries and the TMG, such as the general promotion of Tokyo's international economy. It can be said that the business community in the region is well in tune with the general economic development strategy devised by the national and local government, but their role is rather passive in terms of policy making.

Reforming Governance

MODIFYING THE DEVELOPMENTAL STATE: DEVOLVING GOVERNMENT?

The developmental state, though a successful model from the 1950s to 1970s, has been under sustained criticism since the 1980s. The first challenge started in the early 1980s in an attempt to cope with the effect of stagflation caused by the oil crises of 1973 and 1978. The then prime minister, Nakasone Yasuhiro, created the Second Administrative Reform Council. Inspired by the successes of Margaret Thatcher and Ronald Reagan, this council presented a reform package in 1981, which proposed the privatization of government-run corporations and a series of streamlining measures to reform the government bureaucracy. The policy orientation was further developed by the *Maekawa Report*, prepared by Maekawa Haruo, the then president of the Bank of Japan. The report recommended development of policies based on market principles, including thorough deregulation and more liberalization of the Japanese market, and policies taking account of a global perspective. It resembles the economic policy prescribed under the name of "structural adjustment" around the world today.

The reform gained pace and momentum after the collapse of the so-called bubble economy and the long recession that followed in the 1990s. After the recession, the public mood changed from one of great confidence to one of uncertainty and pessimism. The 1990s have been called the "lost decade'" and this illustrates the feeling that Japan had lost its direction and that opportunities were not taken to remedy its basic problems. In 1996, Prime Minister Hashimoto tried to make structural reforms but was soon confronted by opposition from those who had a considerable stake in the existing system and were protected from international competition (e.g., rice farmers and the banking sector). As a result, there was a continuation of the tradition of spending on major public works projects in an attempt to restart economic growth. Meanwhile, local government budgets were severely affected by declining tax revenues and a shift of resources to national pump-priming efforts. In 1998, major security houses and commercial banks went into bankruptcy and, despite the danger of melt-down, the national government did not rescue them. This can be said to signal the possible end to the Japanese corporate system in which the state always safeguarded national industry. It was realized that the old system could not provide the answers and that rather than a new set of policies, a shift in the framework itself, was needed. In this new climate, the closed nature of the old political system associated with the developmental state was seen as a problem.

This was the backdrop against which Koizumi Junichiro became prime minister and initiated a series of structural reform policies in 2001. His campaign slogan for the premiership was to make wholesale changes in the LDP, the party that had dominated postwar politics, for the sake of the nation. He famously remarked that any groups disrupting the reform process were considered to be the opposition, regardless of their political alignment. The government tackled a wide range of issues, but the most fundamental challenge was to reform the government spending program and reduce the amount of public debt. As a result of the prolonged recession in the 1990s and successive Keynesian-style stimulus packages to counter the recession, government debt had mounted to unprecedented and unsustainable levels. A spending cap was introduced and there were drastic cutbacks in public work projects. The government also decided to implement various fiscal decentralization measures, under the principle of "leave to local government what it can do" and "leave to the private sector what it can do." Koizumi's administration clearly aimed to create a smaller government to match limited capacity. There are some commentators who claim that Japan has entered into the "post-developmental" stage (Fujita and Hill 2011). The intergovernmental financial transfer system mentioned previously was reformed, and the role of the local government was strengthened, through receiving more power to raise local tax in exchange for receiving less from the financial transfer system. In other words, each prefecture and municipality was asked to be more financially independent. In this context, national urban and regional policy, particularly its centrally coordinated local equalization aspect, faced a major turning point.

As for the local governments in the TMR, they are relatively wealthy and thus do not have to rely on the transfer so much. In particular, the TMG has received no transfers at all. On the contrary, the reform provided that the tax paid by residents and businesses in Tokyo effectively subsidized other less productive regions. Thus, on the whole, the reform has been popular. Nevertheless, it has created a problem at the national level because regional disparity has become apparent. Critics pointed to the TMG as a major beneficiary of the system, and political tension has risen between local governments in the TMR and peripheral regions. The TMG and other local governments in the region argued that the criticism was not productive because financial autonomy is a necessary element of decentralization even if it causes hardship in local public finance.

The global financial crisis in 2008 and the following recession further accelerated the government debt. In July 2009, the LDP was replaced by the Democratic Party of Japan (DPJ) through the general election, but the new administration seems to be retaining the decentralization policy.

REORGANIZING REGIONAL AND LOCAL GOVERNMENT

Part of the decentralization policy is to reorganize the local government system. The Omnibus Decentralization Act was enacted in 2000 and aimed to transform the governance system from a centralized to decentralized one. It is based on the idea of "subsidiarity," in which daily public services should be provided by the government that is closest to local people. It means, at the same time, that prefecture and central governments should supplement what cannot be fulfilled by local governments alone (e.g., monetary policy, judicial system, national security, etc.). There are several implications of this basic policy change: the merger of municipal governments, a discussion on regional government, and the emergence of fresh local political leaders.

Historically, the number of municipal governments in Japan has been declining for more than a century. Modernization and the need to provide an efficient public service led to mergers.[17] Since the late 1990s, a new wave of consolidation took place mainly in rural regions, which reduced the number of municipalities from 3,232 in 1999 to 1,781 in 2009. This was encouraged by a number of factors, such as increased workload and responsibility, administrative efficiency, aging, and depopulation. Decentralization demands that municipal governments perform a bigger role, but they often lack sufficient resources such as qualified and experienced staff. Thus, a solution is to get together with neighbors and create bigger units. This consolidation also cuts down on costs and increases efficiency. Some of the municipalities are also suffering from an aging and less productive population, particularly in the rural regions. The younger generation has migrated to urban regions and only the elderly are left. Thus, small towns and villages cannot stand alone and are forced to merge with their neighbors. As a result of consolidation, some municipalities are then qualified to at-tain special autonomous status as a designated city, core city,[18] or special case city,[19] which enhances their autonomy by effectively bypassing the prefecture government.

In the TMR, Saitama city and Sagamihara city (in effect April 2010) have become designated cities as a result of consolidation with neighboring cities. It has given them more autonomy and independence. At the same time, the consolidation has started to affect the existing hierarchical structure of prefecture and municipality by transferring some power and responsibility. It could reduce the influence of prefectural govern-ments and, in a way, sideline them. For instance, Kanagawa prefecture has now three designated cities and one core city representing the built-up urban area of Kawasaki, Yokohama, Sagamihara, and Yokosuka. It means, in some policy areas, the prefecture provides public services to less than half of its total population.

There has also been a discussion on creating a regional level of government. Unlike the case of London, there has not yet been a change in the formal structure of local gov-ernment. The Tokyo city-region still has prefecture and municipal governments but no regional level. However, there are some indications of a possible change. Decentral-ization and municipal consolidation are closely linked to the discussion of creating a regional-level government and reorganizing some administrative functions. The fact that the Omnibus Decentralization Act firmly set municipal government as the basic unit for local service forces prefectures to reconsider their role. The consolidation cre-ates more autonomous cities that are directly under the central government. At the same time, the national government aims to restrict its role in a globalized and neolib-eralized world and shift some of its functions to lower tiers of government. Thus, some functions of prefectures are removed and delegated to the municipal level. The crucial question is what the most appropriate geographical scale is for policy coordination beyond the municipal level? The regional scale, instead of the existing prefecture scale, has emerged as an option. Some functions, such as transport and environment, could be better coordinated at the regional level.

There are also economic dimensions to this regional question. First, there is a growing recognition that the local economy is expanding beyond the prefectural bor-der and that existing boundaries have become obsolete. Due to the development of communications and transport infrastructure, the functional economic area covers a wider region. Second, the core cities in respective regions grew rapidly as a regional economic center in the 1990s. Despite the general trend of aging and loss of popula-tion outside the TMR, cities like Sendai, Hiroshima, and Fukuoka have become cen-ters of their respective regions and actually recorded a growth in population and GDP. They attracted population, particularly working-age population, from the surround-ing cities and villages in the same region by providing jobs, education, and other ser-vices, and thus have become more sustainable. Third, smaller prefectures in the rural region may be better off merging with the neighboring prefecture, following the same logic as that for municipal mergers previously described. This discussion implies that, on the one hand, prefectures are too big to make effective public service provision. On the other hand, however, they are too small to coordinate the diverse and complex economy that expands beyond the prefectural border.

Against such a background, the government committee investigating the possible reorganization of local government published a recommendation in 2006. It suggested abolishing existing prefectures and introducing new regional government. The publication contained several plans in terms of how to divide regions, but the final decision was left for further discussion. One plan suggested a region around Tokyo called the Southern Kanto Region, which consisted of the TMG, Kanagawa, Chiba, and Yamanashi prefectures. The Southern Kanto Region was not the same as the TMR because it includes the Saitama prefecture, which belongs to another region. In another plan, the TMG was treated separately and given special independent status, while the surrounding prefectures were grouped together in one region. At the time of writing, the discussion is still at an early stage and it is likely that a decision will take a long time.

Conclusion: Global/Local Tensions

A significant proportion of the problems and challenges that Tokyo is facing today can be seen to result from globalization. Japan is firmly set within the global circuit of production, finance, and services, and this also makes Tokyo a global city. One of the challenges is strongly felt in labor markets and employment. Fierce global competition and the development of East Asian rivals have prompted major corporations to reduce their full-time core employees and introduce a flexible workforce based on short-term contracts. As a result, the priority of the corporate system has shifted from long-term stability to short-term profit and efficiency. This has led to the exclusion of many workers in part-time positions from the mainstream economy and mainstream society. It has transformed Japanese society from a relatively equal and cohesive community to an increasingly divided and fragmented one. Tokyo has become spatially divided in that hot spots and cold spots coexist side by side. Longstanding environmental issues, such as the earthquake threat and lack of open space, have been supplemented by new global ones, such as global warming and international environmental commitments. Tokyo has moved from a confident center of Japanese transnational corporations to a city worried about competition for other Asian cities.

The governance system has also been challenged by globalization and forced a reconsideration of the developmental state approach. The globalized economy pushes national governments into thinking about a different kind of role, focusing on flexibility, responsiveness, and efficiency of administration. Not only has the state had to reconsider its approach, but it has also had to react to a new set of problems and issues. Against such a background, the urban and regional system in Japan, which has traditionally been oriented to balance and coordination and led by a centralized bureaucracy, is regarded as ineffective. It is slow to respond to economic and social changes and restricts the freedom of individual cities and regions. As a result, "decentralization" has become a buzzword. However, unlike the case of London, there has, as yet, been no formal change in government structure. Instead, institutional innovation has occurred in the way the existing intergovernmental system operates, such as through the financial transfer system. There is ongoing discussion about the reorganization of prefectural and municipal government.

It will take time before any reforms are implemented, but it seems clear that the city-region has emerged as an important territorial unit. The position of Tokyo in this new regional system, however, is still not clear and causes some controversy. The region that contains Tokyo would be huge in terms of population, economic might, and potential in the global economy and thus destroy any balance between regions. The national government is unlikely to release Tokyo from its control because of its economic and political role in the nation. There are suggestions that Tokyo, particularly its twenty-three wards area, should be exempt from regional government (TCCI 2008) or even directly governed by the national government. A struggle is taking place between Tokyo's traditional role in the developmental state framework and its potential as a key operator at the global scale. The former role involves playing the leading role in national economic growth plans orchestrated by the central government. In the latter role, more freedom and autonomy could be demanded so that the city can compete more directly with its global city competitors.

As we have seen, there are signs that the Tokyo region is struggling to gain greater freedom of operation. Recent governors have started to challenge the central government and pursue their own agenda. In the next chapter, we will explore the policy responses to the problems of the city-region. In doing so, we will be able to establish the way that this response has changed over time, and the relative involvement of the different actors. The governance of Tokyo at the city-regional scale is underdeveloped and reliant on the national government. We explore the impact that this has had on regional policy coordination.

9. *World City Policies and the Erosion of the Developmental State*

TOKYO'S POLICY RESPONSES TO GLOBAL CHANGE are best understood within the framework of an adapting developmental state. These policies range from urban structure and transport infrastructure to cultural development and tourism. Although some of them have a fairly narrow geographical focus on central Tokyo, they also have implications for the wider region. The processes of governance that lie behind the policy formation and implementation are analyzed in this chapter. Tokyo has its own particular system of governance and political dynamism. The policies are formulated and carried out through close cooperation between multiple agencies at different levels of government within the historical legacy of a developmental state. By looking at this system closely, we show how it actually works in practice.

Some argue that the developmental state has been gradually receding in recent years (Grimes 2001), and that the Ministry of Land, Infrastructure, and Transport (MLIT) may be more willing to work with local government (Ohnishi 2005). We begin with a discussion of the policy shift that favors the center core of Tokyo, as this is the most significant policy change during our period. As the central government plays such a dominant role in urban governance in Japan, such a shift could only happen if the national government accepted it. The analysis starts by outlining the way national government thinking has changed on this issue. We then explore the range of urban policies that accompany this center core focus. The second part of the chapter turns to the other important change during the period—namely, the gradual move toward regional policy cooperation. The implications of these major policy shifts for the intergovernmental power relationship are assessed in concluding the analysis.

Strengthening the Center Core

In response to the new challenges described in the last chapter, the basic policy direction that the Tokyo Metropolitan Government (TMG) and national government have taken so far has focused on strengthening the center core area of Tokyo. This is the area of the central business district (CBD) and the wards immediately surrounding it, which contain the headquarters of transnational corporations, financial institutions, major cultural institutions, media, and upper-middle-class housing. Policies have tried to encourage more of these functions, eliminate obstacles, and purify the area for globally oriented business and high-class consumption. It is regarded as a key location for creating wealth in the globalized economy and thus is given privileged treatment. This has implications for how the wider region is planned, such as through regional infrastructure projects and intergovernmental relations across the region.

The remainder of this section will spell out the individual policies that contribute to this center core development. First, the national framework of land use planning is discussed. Under the ideology of "even development," the postwar national land use system tried to encourage the development of peripheral regions at the expense of big cities through the Comprehensive National Development Plan. The system, however, experienced a major turning point in the late 1990s in the face of the economic downturn. Second, around the turn of the century, Prime Minister Koizumi, who led the neoliberal economic reforms, applied a laissez-faire policy to urban property development. He enforced a series of relaxations to the planning regulations for property development in the CBD and center core. Within this broad framework, a series of policies were pursued: large-scale infrastructure projects, such as airport improvement and access routes; environmental improvements in the quality of life; promoting international tourism and cultural development; and finally, the Olympic bid for 2016 (although this failed).

NATIONAL LAND USE POLICY AND THE OVERCONCENTRATION ON TOKYO

Since the postwar economic growth, one of the major challenges that Tokyo has faced has been how to manage the seemingly uncontrollable sprawl and development pressure. Because of its enormous political and economic gravity, strong centripetal forces were in operation (Cybriwsky 1998; Sorensen 2002). Business functions and employment continued to congregate in the central part of Tokyo. Commuters were pushed further away to the outer suburbs. Though there were minor corrections from time to time, Tokyo's main story between the 1950s and 1980s was uninterrupted economic growth and urban expansion. Tokyo's economic superiority and future growth prospect were taken for granted. How to maintain quality of life, such as affordable housing, open spaces, and clean environment, was a major challenge for the authority (Ishida 1992). Particularly toward the end of the 1980s, land prices increased dramatically and residential neighborhoods in central Tokyo were threatened by office development (Igarashi and Ogawa 1993).

As was discussed in the last chapter, the overconcentration of Tokyo was recognized not just as a local and regional issue but as a national one, because the national government had a strong objective to balance economic development throughout Japan. Each locality has a relative strength in a particular industry, such as agriculture, manufacturing, and commerce, as a result of particular local histories and topographical conditions. Industrialization, however, created an uneven geography in terms of production and level of income, spearheaded by Tokyo and its surrounding region. The Japanese government tried to minimize the regional and local imbalance because it was related to issues of legitimacy of the developmental state and its key agencies of national bureaucrats and the Liberal Democratic Party (LDP; Saito 2011). The main policy tool was the Comprehensive National Development Plan (CNDP), which was a national land use plan authorized by the Comprehensive National Development Plan Act of 1951 and covered all of Japan. The plan represented the spatial dimension of economic growth and welfare provision. Article 1 of the act defined the meaning of national comprehensive development as "[using] the land comprehensively by developing, preserving, and allocating the appropriate industry with the consideration of economic, social, and cultural policies within the limitation of natural resources, as well as increasing social welfare of the population."

The aim of the plan was to use land and natural resources effectively and comprehensively, and so it included plans for industrial location, transportation, and infrastructure development to achieve maximum effective land use. The plan also aimed at creating a balanced regional structure, and one way was to control further expansion and overconcentration of the metropolis, which was suffering from overcrowding and negative externality. The Industrial Location Control Act, established in 1959, intended to constrain the further concentration of industries in the Tokyo Metropolitan Region by restricting the building and expansion of new factories, schools, and universities in the designated built-up area.[1] The plan was also to strike a balance between the economic disparities of different regions (Kawakami 2008; Yamazaki 1998). Policy priority was given first to developing industrial infrastructure (e.g., land, water, transport, and telecommunications) and second to housing, education, and tourist facilities. Core projects, such as the New Industrial City and Technopolis, aimed at creating new growth poles around the areas that suffered from a relative lack of industrial facilities.

After the collapse of the bubble economy and the resultant recession in the 1990s, the policy direction was substantially altered. In 2005, the National Land Development Act was replaced by the National Land Sustainability Act, and the existing planning system was abolished. The new legislation signaled a departure from the old framework by omitting the very word "development" from its purpose (Ohnishi 2005). Instead, it emphasized environmental quality and preservation. The new plan based on the Act is called the National Land Sustainability Plan, and it developed governmental devolution by proposing wide-area regional plans.[2]

Tokyo was long regarded, within the CNDP framework, as being too big, creating national social/economic imbalance and thus the need for decentralization. There was even a plan to relocate Tokyo's national political and administrative functions to another region. Since the 1960s, it was repeatedly suggested that the national capital should be moved from Tokyo (Toki 2003). It was the main remedy against overconcentration and the negative externalities of Tokyo, such as congestion, pollution, and extremely high house prices. In 1990, both houses of Parliament passed a resolution to relocate the three basic state powers of legislation, judiciary, and administration. The plan was approved by Parliament in 1999 but put on hold because of the huge cost and economic downturn. As Tokyo continues to have a risk of earthquake, relocation (or more accurately duplication) of some state functions may be necessary, but the idea of complete relocation is no longer under discussion.

Since the late 1990s, however, amid a decade-long sluggish economic performance and continuing globalization, Tokyo's competitive advantage has been increasingly called into question. There was a consensus that Tokyo's position as the prime global city in Asia was being challenged by other cities, such as Shanghai and Singapore (Saito and Thornley 2003; TMG 2000). Tokyo was regarded as an indispensable national resource in competing in the global economy (Itoh 1998). Current strategic planning thinking is oriented to the new emphasis on city competition. The prevailing view favors urban policies to support Tokyo in this climate by developing the necessary facilities, generating an attractive image, and reinforcing the efficiencies of agglomeration. Compared to the urban policy under the influence of the developmental state, which is rather closed and self-contained, a more open approach is taken in which the attraction of international business and tourism is seen as a key element.

THE SHIFT TO CENTER CORE DEVELOPMENT

The policy for strengthening Tokyo's center core was further aided by national financial policy. One of the underlining issues in the economy after its collapse in the 1990s was the depressed property market and nonperforming loans (Katz 2002). The banking sector was crippled and money flow stagnated. It was not only financial institutions but others in the corporate sector that could not recover from the investments they made in the 1980s in Tokyo's property market. The government was well aware of the need to stimulate the property market. Because of the huge public sector debt, they could not expand the familiar method of public work investment. Instead, they found a new rationale in globalization, city competition, and the benefits of an agglomeration economy for invigorating the market.

Soon after Junichiro Koizumi became prime minister, his government set up a committee within the Cabinet called the Headquarters for the Rejuvenation of Cities, to be chaired by himself. One of the major underlying concerns of the government was a fear that Japanese cities lacked competitiveness. The committee stated that "One of the most important political priorities is to increase the attractiveness and international competitiveness of cities, as they are the source of national vitality in the twenty-first century . . . However, as a result of the prolonged recession in the 1990s, particularly in Tokyo and Osaka where command-and-control functions are concentrated, Japanese cities are under-performing when compared internationally" (HQs of Rejuvenation of Cities 2001).

At the same time, the committee proposed several principles for realizing its goal. First, the government decided to address the issue of competitiveness of cities as a part of structural reform, and utilized the financial and human resources in the private sector in order to create a new demand. Second, they facilitated the construction of the necessary urban infrastructure and conducted a thorough review of various institutions and regulations. Third, they supported urban rejuvenation by the private sector as they thought this would invigorate the currently frozen land market and consequently contribute to the revitalization of the Japanese economy. Fourth, they insisted that urban rejuvenation be organized not only by the government ministries, but through mobilizing various resources and expertise in local government and the business community. A major piece of legislation, the Special Law on Urban Regeneration, was enacted in the following year. It basically aimed to facilitate urban regeneration projects by various means, such as designating the areas for regeneration, relaxing the existing planning regulations, giving private developers the opportunity to propose projects, and providing various incentives to private developers, such as financial aid, tax relief, and a simplified approval process.

The first round of designation created 3,515 hectares of urgent improvement areas throughout major metropolitan areas, including Osaka, Nagoya, Fukuoka, and Sapporo, but with a clear emphasis on the central area of Tokyo, which had 2,370 hectares. The locations included the CBD and major business/commercial districts, such as Marunouchi, Roppongi, Shinjuku, and the Tokyo waterfront subcenter area. 63 percent of private initiatives came from the Tokyo Metropolitan Region, with 28 percent in the TMG area. Moreover, most of the projects proposed in central Tokyo were larger than those outside Tokyo. The dominance of Tokyo is hardly surprising, given the government emphasis and the expectations for commercial return.

It was not only the national government that was keen to upgrade Tokyo. The TMG, under Governor Ishihara, put forward aggressive measures to promote Tokyo at a global level. The TMG also felt threatened by the rapid progress of Asian rivals. As expressed in their 2000 white paper, "it is not an overstatement to say that the future of a city depends upon its degree of attractiveness in inter-city competition. Recently, compared to Asian cities in particular, it is sometimes said that Tokyo is losing its status. It seems to be extremely important to address the urban policy of Tokyo from the viewpoint of increasing its attractiveness as a world city" (Tokyo Metropolitan Government 2000, 5).

Following this concern, the TMG's urban policies were geared toward creating a globally competitive Tokyo, and they identified several key areas for improvement. First, it took a positive attitude to agglomeration, making a U-turn from the previous planning policy of creating several subcenters in order to avoid overconcentration on the CBD (Taira 2001). Instead, it encouraged the accumulation in central Tokyo of global command-and-control functions in business and finance (Iwami 2007). The center core area was singled out as a strategic location in the *Tokyo Megalopolis*

Concept, published in 2001 (TMG 2001a). The concept proposed to upgrade not only the office and working environment but also housing and leisure functions so that global business elite could work, play, and relax in close proximity and convenience.

Second, the waterfront subcenter, a loss-making redevelopment project in the 1990s (Saito 2003), was revived and invigorated. It was first conceived in the late 1980s by the TMG as a teleport, but the idea was soon hijacked by the developers in response to the shortage of office space. The fall in property prices and the stagnation of economy meant that the project faced imminent bankruptcy in the 1990s. A fierce debate arose in the mid-1990s about how to redirect the project. On the one hand, there was a proposal to abandon the project completely and convert it into a nature reserve. On the other hand, others insisted on incremental development (Hiramoto 2000). It has good potential for development because the area has a considerable amount of disused land, such as former factory sites and the reclaimed island, and also good access to central Tokyo via motorways and mass transit.

In previous plans, the waterfront was a subcenter focusing on international business but, having abolished its subcenter policy, the TMG redefined the area for leisure and retail development. It has an attractive location around the waterfront with an artificial beach and houses such facilities as an international exhibition center, huge shopping malls, a TV station, and various kinds of restaurants and bars. It was transformed into an urban leisure center and was an instant success in boosting consumption. Governor Ishihara first proposed to build a casino in the area, based on the expectation that it could attract the elite and rich people from around the world, but he discovered later that it could take years to persuade the national government, which is cautious about gambling development. Thus, he proposed that Tokyo host the Olympics in 2016 and utilize the waterfront as a key location for the main stadium and media center (Ozaki 2007).

CULTURAL DEVELOPMENT AND TOURISM

Some say Tokyo's global city policy is oriented to economic issues and neglects a cultural dimension (Friedmann 1995). The number of tourists visiting Tokyo is also comparatively small. Recently, however, the Japanese government and the TMG have recognized the growing importance of culture for economic development and tourism. They think the Tokyo region has good potential for developing a cultural dimension. First, Tokyo has a rich cultural heritage, particularly in the central part of the city. Many traditional arts, such as Kabuki, Sumo, and ukiyo-e (floating world) originated and developed within the vibrant civic culture that flourished in Edo in the 1700s. Second, until recently Tokyo has suffered from an absence of a clear strategy and direction for cultural development. Contemporary Tokyo was often described as a modern, clean, and efficient city, but a rather boring one without a distinctive cultural character. The downtown is occupied by standardized office blocks and the suburban town centers look exactly the same. It has even been criticized as faceless (TMG 2006, 89). Third,

Tokyo has emerged as a center of contemporary pop culture. This grew as an alternative to the established Western art forms and gained worldwide popularity. Japanese cultural products in fashion, music, computer games, animation, and so on are followed by many younger people worldwide and in Asia particularly. They clearly have a uniquely Japanese character and their popularity has coined the term "Japan Cool" (Ingulsrud and Allen 2010).

The national government and the TMG have started to develop strategic thinking for mobilizing culture for economic development. They have placed tourism and the visitor industry in leisure and entertainment as a leading sector in the twenty-first century, closely tied to cultural industries. The national government established the Japan Tourism Agency in 2008 to devise the national strategy and coordinate projects. The TMG is also keen to promote Tokyo for international tourism (TMG 2001b) and devised the Yokoso (Welcome) Tokyo campaign. The TMG also sent missions to the United States and Europe to promote the city for tourism. This promotion mobilizes both traditional and contemporary culture. For example, the TMG spent $7,000 to help young and up-and-coming artists in 2007. The money was spent funding international workshops and exchange programs (TMG 2008).

The new emphasis on cultural policy has spatial implications. Akihabara, once known as the shopping area of household electric appliances, has been transformed into digital shops for computer games and new media. Moreover, there is a kind of industrial district, an agglomeration of small and medium-sized enterprises (SMEs) for computer software and the digital sector, around Shinjuku station and alongside the Chuo line (Fujita 2003). A small but increasing number of young artists have moved to the Shitamachi district in the east or northeast part of Tokyo to take advantage of low rent and space. They have converted old houses into art studios.

In Tokyo, the cultural promotion policy is not only about the usual cultural products and art forms; it also includes the natural environment and the urban landscape itself. For instance, Tokyo used to be known as a city of canals because boats were the main mode of transport. Once they were polluted by industrial waste, but they are now promoted as cultural heritage. River buses carry tourists to Asakusa district and cruise the Shitamachi (downtown), the center of traditional culture in Tokyo (TMG 2001c). The riverside is also being developed for cafes and green spaces. Roppongi has been a popular dining spot for years, but after the construction of the Roppongi Hills complex and the new national art museum, it has been transformed into a trendy shopping, leisure, and entertainment district.

The TMG thinks that all these resources are potentially very useful but not fully utilized. They can be best coordinated by a big event, such as the Tokyo Film Festivals and the Tokyo Marathon. Tokyo is often described as an ugly city from an aesthetic viewpoint. Critics point to a lack of style in architecture, haphazard development, and motorways cutting across the skyline (Shibata 2008). Tokyo has 400 years of history, and used to be known for its beauty, but it has been destroyed by earthquakes, war, and rapid postwar reconstruction. The TMG is trying to recover this past glory by urban design and beautification (TMG 2006a). The projects include the replacement of overhead electric and telephone wire by underground cable, making the riverside accessible to pedestrians, regulating billboards in terms of color and lighting, and restoring historical landmarks such as the Nihonbashi bridge. Most of these projects are located in the urban-core area. The TMG believes that landscaping the center core area should appeal to visitors and tourists, as well as residents, and it is an important tool for increasing its attractiveness.

SAFETY AND NATURAL HAZARDS

In terms of crime and disorder, Tokyo is one of the safest cities in the world, as noted in chapter 1. For example, with reasonable caution, it is not particularly dangerous for women to walk alone at night in central Tokyo. This is a huge advantage compared to other major metropolises in the world. However, this is offset by the risk of earthquakes. National and local governments have prepared disaster prevention plans. Building regulations have been tightened, building inspections made obligatory, and evacuation drills have become an annual event. Central Tokyo is particularly vulnerable because of its high density and huge daytime working population. A hazard map has been prepared that shows the areas of particular danger in case of fire and tsunami. Because an earthquake is inevitable and there is no way to prevent it, the emphasis has been put on recovery. Public and private corporations are encouraged to prepare business continuity plans to minimize the damage to business and allow a speedy recovery.

A more mundane but increasingly dangerous natural hazard is a sudden and heavy downpour, which can cause urban floods. An unusual amount of rainfall in a short period of time in a limited area will exceed the capacity of rivers, canals, and the drainage system. Railway stations and shops located underground are at high risk of flood. Scientists claim that erratic weather patterns are caused by global warming and the heat-island phenomena. Publicly owned reserve land has been converted into emergency lakes where flood water can be stored temporary. Thus, Tokyo competes as a global city-region with particular physical advantages and disadvantages that are not found in the other four global city-regions (GCRs).

ENVIRONMENTAL SUSTAINABILITY

Tokyo's environmental policy is coordinated under the title of Carbon Minus City (Fujita and Hill 2007; TMG 2006). The policy is based on the understanding that global warming is an imminent challenge to human society and that a policy priority should be placed on sustainability. The TMG has proposed a cut in CO_2 emissions by 25 percent of the 2000 level by 2020 (TMG 2006).[3] The Carbon Minus policy is not the usual environmental policy, which tackles separate environmental issues such as pollution and creating green spaces. Instead, it systematically addresses the issues related to energy consumption and efficiency that cut across a wide range of policy fields like transport, housing, construction, waste disposal, and so forth. It is based on the principle of three Rs: reduce, reuse, and recycle.

Renewable energy is encouraged in offices, factories, and residential buildings. Subsidies and tax incentives are provided to small businesses and households who switch to renewable energy generated by photovoltaic application systems and wind turbines. The zero waste policy is mobilized to tackle the household/industrial waste issue. The national government, local government, business community, and nongovernmental organizations (NGOs) are involved in minimizing the amount of waste and using it as an energy source. For instance, office computers are collected in large retail stores and disassembled and some raw materials are taken for reuse. Other materials are burnt and the energy is used. The final remaining material is transferred to the dumping ground. Consumers are obliged to pay for the collection and recycling of household appliances.

The principle of energy efficiency extends to urban renewal policy, because old housing and offices are major contributors of carbon emission. The urban renewal projects typically create more compact and mixed-use space with offices, residences, retail, and other services, which can reduce the level of energy consumption. The TMG and the national government require these projects to create some green spaces on the ground, rooftop, and building walls. These provide a shield from the strong sunlight, cool down the building, and prevent it from disseminating the heat outside.

OLYMPIC BID FOR 2016

Tokyo made a bid for the 2016 Olympic Games but failed to win the nomination. However, the bid influenced ongoing urban policy a great deal. In fact, the Olympic Games bid was a pet project for Ishihara, intended to advance his urban policy and various projects (Iwami 2007; Ozaki 2007). It was appreciated that big cultural and sports events can help urban policy and projects in many ways, such as improving city image, attracting investment and visitors, installing physical infrastructures, and establishing clear urban identity and solidarity among citizens (Roch 2000). In the case of Tokyo, the Olympics aimed at uplifting Tokyo after its decade-long slow growth and establishing its position on the international stage once again. To this end, the 10-year plan published in 2006 (TMG 2006) expected the Olympics to accomplish the goals mentioned previously. One mechanism was to create a highly efficient regional infrastructure, including three ring roads and modern airports. According to the proposal, the ring roads would make a dramatic difference in the congestion and pollution of Tokyo by improving logistics, and provide a higher quality of life. The Olympics would also have been a showcase for an environmentally friendly city using advanced technology and would have shown the world Japan's commitment to combating global warming. It would have accelerated the internationalization of Haneda airport, which would have shared the gateway function with Narita airport.

It would also have revitalized the struggling waterfront subcenter project in the Bay Area, which, because of the recession and the dramatic fall in property prices, is continuing to be a drain on the TMG budget. The public corporations that develop, manage, and run the project were bankrupted in 2006; it is estimated that it will take more than fifty years to pay back the debt. According to the plan, the main stadium, international media center, and Olympic village would have been constructed within the waterfront area by using the land that TMG owned. Other facilities were also planned nearby and new access roads and bridges would have been constructed. In this way, the waterfront area would have been revived and the remaining vacant land could have been sold at a high premium (Iwami 2007).

It is clear that the Olympics were intended to be a major catalyst to change Tokyo. Tokyo's global city strategy and projects discussed in this section cut across many policy fields. The Olympic bid was intended to create a momentum to coordinate them, including infrastructure, tourism, property development, and environment, into one clear goal of urban promotion. As illustrated in Figure 9.1, major sporting venues would have been constructed within a 10-kilometer radius of central Tokyo in the name of "the most compact Olympic Games ever" (TMG 2006b, 2). Officially, it intended to reduce traffic volume and achieve energy efficiency, but, in reality, it was to justify the investment priority in the urban core.

It usually takes years to build regional infrastructure because it involves complicated negotiations with the national government and neighboring municipalities and prefectures. However, the Olympic bid was a national project and would also have been an international commitment if successful. It would have brought the necessary national resources and set the time frame for implementation. This would have worked as leverage to the global urban promotion strategy. Although Tokyo failed to win the nomination in October 2009, Ishihara has said that he will continue to press for the projects, such as the three ring roads.

From the analysis of the various policy responses, it is evident that there have been three clear and sustained policy directions. First, at both national and metropolitan levels, the previous policy of achieving a balance in the urban structure has been superseded by the new logic of agglomeration and efficiency. Tokyo's potential has been reevaluated in light of the postindustrial and knowledge-based economy. As a result, Tokyo has been retuned from the objective of dispersal and containment to developing as a center of innovation and creation, representative of Japan on the world stage. Second, the geographical focus of policy has been directed to the promotion of Tokyo, particularly to its newly constituted urban core area. This focus has been consistent throughout various policy fields from infrastructure and tourism to the environment. Third, the range of policies in the promotional strategy has been quite limited and in tune with market-oriented, neoliberal ideologies. On one hand, a lot of attention has been paid to increasing the competitiveness of Tokyo by strengthening its comparative advantage through the advanced service sector, global finance, culture, and tourism,

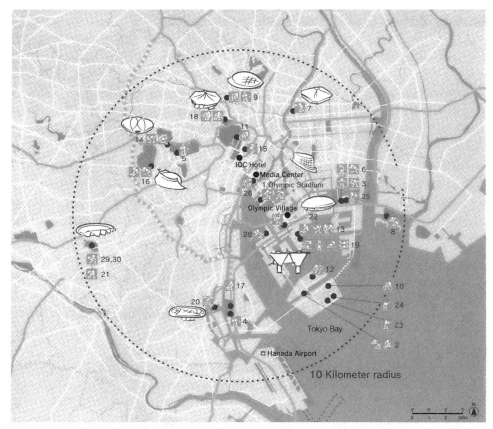

Figure 9.1. Competition Venues and Facilities for Proposed 2016 Tokyo Olympics
Source: TMG 2006b, p. 3.

benefiting the urban middle class. On the other hand, various social problems, ranging from unemployment, polarization, and "cold spots," were left untouched. Policies
for the environment and quality of life, which used to be discussed as part of the general welfare regime, have been increasingly regarded as an effective tool for urban promotion and competitiveness, rather than a matter of social policy.

The Regional Policy Response

The urban promotional policies previously discussed are generally focused on the
center core area of Tokyo. However, the center core is part of an integrated city-region
and cannot stand alone. Various functions of the center core are supported by the
wider region through, for instance, a commuting and production network. Thus, it is
inevitable that the policy changes have some regional implications. Let us now turn to
explore these aspects through the examination of key areas of public intervention: regional planning policy, transport projects, and airport development.

REGIONAL PLANNING POLICY

Between the 1960s and 1990s, regional plans were prepared by the national government through consultation with the local government within the framework of the Comprehensive National Development Plan (CNDP) previously discussed. In the case of the Tokyo Metropolitan Region (TMR), these regional plans took the form of the Capital Region[4] Development Plans and they applied the same principle of balanced development. Instead of one-point convergence on central Tokyo, they advocated the dispersal of employment across different cities. A number of business core cities, science parks, and research and development (R&D) centers were designated around Tokyo, such as Tsukuba science city and Saitama city, which were designed to have self-sufficient economies so that people did not have to rely on jobs and services in central Tokyo. In fact, over the last twenty-five years, such centers have developed to such a degree that recent survey shows increasing commuting between them (MLIT 2006).

The National Land Sustainability Act enacted in 2005 required the preparation of a wider-area regional plan for each region. For the region around Tokyo, the Capital Region-Wide Area Plan was published in August 2009. It listed most of the policies discussed in this chapter, but was written in a rather general manner without showing any priorities. It does not have any map to show locations, nor any numbers and figures. At the same time, the investment strategy and the budget for public infrastructure in the region is to be separately prepared by the national government. Each of them should be complementary, but since the latter has yet to be published, the outcome remains to be seen.

More substantial changes in regional planning were initiated by the TMG. The circular megalopolis concept was proposed by Governor Ishihara of the TMG soon after his election in 1999 as an alternative to the national government idea of relocating the capital functions (Iwami 2006; Taira 2002).[5] The governor's plan aims to show that there is a way of dealing with the congestion problems of Tokyo other than by complete relocation. Instead, he suggested that various capital functions could be shared within the region by dispersing them to multiple locations. It was unusual and unprecedented for the TMG to propose such a plan because it included the area outside its boundary, governed by the other three prefectures.

The urban concept proposed in the circular megalopolis concept does not seem to be a radical departure from the previous regional plan made by the national government. As Figure 9.2 shows, it also encourages core cities outside the twenty-three wards. However, the idea behind this was completely transformed. First, the concept aims to mobilize the regional structure to support the CBD and the central area of the TMG. Unlike the previous strategy, which tried to achieve a more equitable urban development, it implies a more hierarchical idea, with the CBD at the top followed by the surrounding areas in the twenty-three wards and then the rest of the city-region (see Figure 9.3). It embodies the logic of globalization and neoliberalism, whereby the winner-gets-all mentality dominates and competition overrides any social concerns.

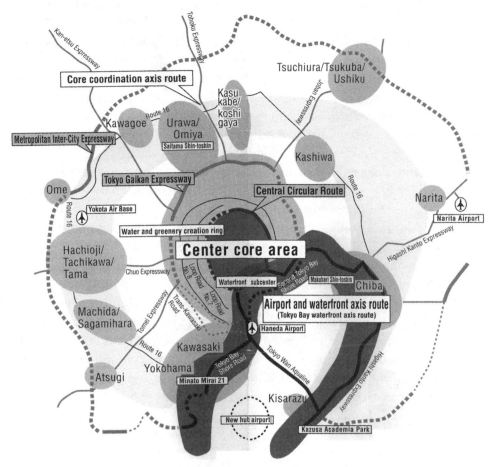

Figure 9.2. Circular Megalopolis Structure
Source: TMG 2001a, p. 25–26.

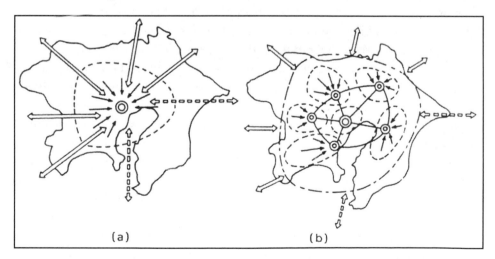

Figure 9.3. Two Models of Urban Structure for the Tokyo City-Region: (a) Single-Point Convergence, (b) Multinodal
Source: Togo 1993, p. 193

The hierarchical pattern is illustrated by Saitama city, which has been designated as one of the regional core cities. It has increased its office space recently, but this is mainly for back-office functions engaging in routine transactions and domestic corporate management. Many TNCs have shifted their domestic operations center from the CBD to such cities and use their central space for global operations or creative functions such as international marketing. In other words, the CBD and the center core have been purified for high value-added activities.

Second, the demographic situation has changed. Japan has already entered into a phase of declining population and, in the long run, Tokyo will also have to face shrinkage. It is completely different from the growth period between the 1960s and 1980s, when a positive-sum game could be played among different cities and areas. Against this background of imminent shrinkage, the idea behind the plan is to develop strict priorities in strategic thinking. As a result, investment decisions have to be based on the principal of "select and concentrate."

Third, the concept has been developed in a different political and ideological environment. The previous strategy was formulated within the framework of a Keynesian welfare regime in which the government was obligated by the constitution to provide a certain level of universal welfare no matter where people lived (Matsushita 1995). In fact, government policy was geared toward minimizing regional differences and achieving a balance. The new strategy tries to maximize the potential of central Tokyo even at the expense of other areas.

REGIONAL INFRASTRUCTURE

There are a few key transport infrastructures that serve the wider region and have regional implications. One of the major weaknesses of Tokyo is its global connectivity. Narita airport, the main international airport, is located on the edge of the region 66 kilometers away from central Tokyo. The airport is served by train and highway but it takes more than one hour to reach the city center of Tokyo. It has a smaller capacity than that of other Asian hub airports in Seoul, Shanghai, Hong Kong, and Singapore. Meanwhile, Haneda airport is located in Tokyo Bay and only thirty minutes from central Tokyo. It used to be an important international airport, but since Narita opened in 1978 it has operated mainly for domestic flights. Thus, various measures have been taken to improve the two airports. On the one hand, a new runway opened in 2002, and this was extended in 2010 to increase its capacity. A new high-speed link was opened in 2010, which connects the airport with central Tokyo in thirty minutes. On the other hand, international flights were reintroduced to Haneda in 2002 with daily connections to Seoul, Beijing, Shanghai, and Hong Kong. Another runway, which operates twenty-four hours, was added in 2010, further increasing its international flights and reintroducing a route to Europe and North America.

At the same time, the seaport also needs improvement. In terms of international freight, the three ports around the region are lagging behind their counterparts in

Asian cities. Their capacity for handling container freight is smaller and more costly because they are governed by different port authorities in Tokyo, Yokohama, and Kawasaki. A remedy is seen in creating a single body to oversee their operation.

Another major infrastructure project is the construction of three ring roads. The inner road is within the TMG boundary, but the outer two cut across other prefectures and thus they are regional projects (see Figure 9.2). The project aims at reducing the volume of traffic, particularly heavy vehicles and freight transport, running through central Tokyo. Radial roads are well established in Tokyo, but not a circular road. As many manufacturing plants are located on the edge of the region, it is necessary to improve transport efficiency. Another aim is to reduce air pollution and road congestion in the central part of Tokyo. The ring road project is widely regarded as an attempt to create an integrated global city-region that serves the center core and enhances competitiveness by easing the congestion and pollution in central Tokyo (Iwami 2007).

Environmental issues have been one of the major discussion points in the capital regional summit (see later discussion) because of their regional nature. The summit successfully implemented a region-wide regulation against diesel-engine vehicles in 2003, which was originally proposed by Governor Ishihara. In recent years, the Capital Region Summit (CRS) has created working groups and subcommittees to tackle such issues as global warming and CO_2 emissions, industrial waste, and a regional recycling system.

THE MOVE TO NEW REGIONAL COOPERATION

The changes in approach to regional planning policy by the national government and the TMG have created a momentum, shaking the established political order and reorganizing regional interests for new purposes. Against the background of increasing demand for decentralization in recent years, regional political leaders also seem to have become more confident in arguing their local and regional interests against the national government. The CRS has been held twice a year since 1979 to discuss matters beyond the borders of individual prefectures. Because of their lack of statutory status, the summits were often regarded as mere talking shops and an organization to lobby the national government. Nevertheless, together with the capital region forum, which started in 2006, they are the only platform where regional political leaders can get together. It is often said that achieving regional cooperation is difficult because of fragmentation, rivalry, and competition among local governments. In recent years, however, there is some indication that a kind of regional cooperation, albeit in a loose form, is emerging around a common understanding of the importance of the region as a strategic site for global competition.

Regional-level plans are prepared by the national government after consultation with the local government, but Ishihara did not consult with anyone when he proposed the circular megalopolis concept. This naturally prompted some concern and suspicion among the neighboring prefectures about whether he was trying to control the regional agenda and upgrade himself as *the* regional leader.[6] The concept was presented as the Tokyo Megalopolis Concept to a CRS meeting but met with a cool reception. After some discussion, the word "Tokyo" was dropped because it implied the dominance of Tokyo in the region. Instead, the Capital Region Megalopolis Concept was published by TMG in 2001 (Taira 2002).[7] The other members of CRS were in an ambivalent position because though they did not like Ishihara's style of politics, it was undeniable that they would benefit from the growth of Tokyo. In the end, they took a pragmatic stance and accepted his idea of promoting the center core of Tokyo for the sake of the whole region. Thus, they adopted a resolution to put to the national government, which stated, "The capital region with its population of 33 million is the greatest metropolitan region in the world. As such, it has been contributing to the development of this country as the political and economic centre . . . To regenerate Japan, what we need to do now is not the capital function relocation, which has already lost its meaning, but the revitalization of the capital region that generates Japan's vitality with its advanced central functional system" (CRS 2002).

On October 12, 2009, Seiji Maehara, the minister of land infrastructure and transport, made an announcement that Haneda airport would be an international hub airport.[8] He said that Inchon in Korea had become a de facto hub airport for Japanese passengers because it connected with so many Japanese regional cities and had international links as well. Thus, the announcement signaled a major change in aviation policy. There was previously quite a strict division of labor between Haneda and Narita airport for domestic and international flight; passengers had to be transported between the two for connecting flights. As discussed earlier in this chapter, Governor Ishihara insisted, as part of his strategy to improve the global attractiveness of Tokyo, that international flights should operate from Haneda. This started in 2001 but only on a very limited scale. This was because of the legacy of Narita development and the nature of the compensation involved.[9] According to the *Asahi Shimbun* on October 15, 2009, Maehara's announcement angered Governor Morita of Chiba prefecture, who felt that Narita's position as Japan's gateway airport would be threatened. He had an emergency meeting with the minister the following day, and they eventually settled the matter on the grounds that it would not be a zero-sum game and that flights would not be shifted from Narita to Haneda. The incidence revealed that the national government still maintains a crucial role in deciding such policy. At the same time, it is true that the policy initiated by the TMG and Ishihara eventually influenced the national government to change its approach.

According to the minutes of the capital region forum, the improvement of regional infrastructure, such as the expansion of airports and improvement of access, is widely supported among regional leaders.[10] They seem to share a common concern that something has to be done to improve the competitiveness of Tokyo for the benefit of the whole of Japan in a globalized economy. There is a popularly held perception that it is difficult to achieve a consensus among regional leaders because they are competing with each other. Though this may exist, they seem to be well aware of the advantage of uniting as one voice. After the regional conference in November 2009, they published some reports and asked the national government for more investment for regional infrastructure, including the ring roads.[11] The leaders have found that there is benefit in a united front. For instance, at the opening speech of CRF in November 2007, Ms. Doumoto, then governor of Chiba prefecture, remarked that "we are not happy with the level of infrastructure provision in the region. No matter how many times we lobby individually to the national government, however, the progress is very slow. I think CRF is a platform that can form our collective will and move the national government forward."

Regional leaders are also aware that they need to handle the matter carefully for it to succeed politically. Forming a united front and insisting on Tokyo's regional interest does not necessary win wider support from the national government and other regions; it may even be counterproductive because the move could be seen as simply protecting their own status. After all, although it is the wealthiest and most developed and region in Japan, three-quarters of the Japanese population live outside the Tokyo region. Nevertheless, regional officials often employ the rhetoric of national interest to serve their own ends and insist that the capital region is the one and only global city-region that can lead Japan in a globalized economy.

Conclusion

The whole system of governance in the Tokyo city-region has been challenged by globalization, and the role of the state has been under review as officials struggle to respond with effective policies. Efforts to mediate the new challenges faced by the GCR involve two key areas of response: regional policy coordination and changing intergovernmental relations.

There is now widespread recognition among both national and local government officials and business leaders that Japan is part of the globalized world and that cities and regions have become increasingly important units for national competitiveness. The global city or global city-region is highlighted as an economic motor to drive the national economy. In particular, the agglomeration of expert knowledge in finance and advanced producer services is seen as a key to winning intercity competition. As a result, the government has been concerned about the stagnation of Tokyo in the late 1990s and has turned to more aggressive promotional policies.

However, the scope of this promotional strategy is quite limited in terms of geographical scale and range of policy measures. It mainly focuses on the CBD and center core area of Tokyo, a mere 10-kilometer radius, and targets globally oriented service industries and high-class consumption. Other areas of the city-region have been included in the promotional strategy, but they are mainly cast in a supporting role.

At the same time, there are issues that Tokyo faces that are not addressed by urban policy, such as equity and immigration. It is clear that the gap between rich and poor is growing in terms of job status, income, location of housing, education, and quality of life. However, no effective policy measures have been put forward to tackle spatial inequality, and poverty is dealt with by weakening national measures, such as income support and educational allowances. Individuals increasingly are exposed to the market under the neoliberal rhetoric of individual responsibility (Yuasa 2009). As discussed in the last chapter, there are cities and towns located in the outer edge of the region that are losing population and jobs (Wakabayashi 2007), but their problems were not taken up in the regional conferences.

Regional development policies have been reorganized to enhance the advantage of the CBD and the center core of Tokyo. Regional transport infrastructure, such as the three ring roads, is planned in such a way as to maximize the efficiency and benefit of central Tokyo. Haneda airport has reemerged as an international gateway, but it has broken the long-established balance between Haneda and Narita and upset the municipal government around Narita where the local economy depends on the airport. The concern for maintaining balance and equity between different localities within the region is increasingly superseded by the desire for global competitiveness. The new, nationally driven wide-area regional plan still talks about the distribution of different social and economic functions within the region and seeks to coordinate them. In reality, however, in a global economy where incomes and job structures are polarized, it effectively brings a more hierarchical regional structure. The regional development priority is now firmly placed on upgrading the central part of Tokyo in preparation for global competition.

So how far is GCR government becoming regionalized? The national government has shown that it appreciates the importance of city-regions and is struggling to find a way of developing the governmental structure to match this. Meanwhile, though there is no formal government at the regional scale, regional political leaders have noticed that they have common interests and have started to build a loose consensus over a policy direction to realize them. They have become concerned in recent years that the region is losing its competitive edge and lagging behind Asian counterparts. Thus, they see it as common sense to do something to make the region a growth center for the Japanese economy. This kind of political pragmatism is supporting a common agenda that is evolving to recover regional competitiveness. These regional structures are informal, however, and it is inevitable that their policy capacity is limited. In our analysis, the most promising movement for increasing regional governance capacity might come from the capital region summit and the capital region forum. Though there are differences between members, they are united in thinking that Tokyo should be promoted on the national and global stage. They also agree that competitiveness is achieved not only from policies relating to economic development but also from other policies such as those on the environment, culture, and tourism and that these need to be mobilized into one package. It is still not clear to what extent they can influence the new Capital Region-Wide Area Plan, but it is difficult to ignore their voice once it is united.

How have these moves to regional awareness, and the greater acceptance of the need to respond to the global economy, affected intergovernmental relations? Until the 1980s, the national scale was privileged in the strategy of capital accumulation and state regulation for the whole nation under the developmental state. This approach was based on the belief that national economic growth would be achieved most effectively not by unrestricted market competition but by the coordinated actions of the national government (Johnson 1995; Murakami 1992). The spatial dimension of such coordination was found in regional planning policy, where the development priority, location of infrastructure projects, and allocation of the budget were centrally organized. The ideology of even development was mobilized to maintain regional balance, and it effectively sealed the privileged status of national government officials because they were seen as impartial guardians of the public interest. As a result, local initiatives were underdeveloped and local government officials tended to seek help from the national government rather than develop and mobilize local resources (Honma 1998; Igarashi and Ogawa 1993).

From the 1990s, however, this national coordinating function began to lose its coherence. Urban and regional policy was decentralized from the national scale, and individual cities and regions were expected to manage more by themselves (Itoh 1998). The national government has been rescaling its own territorial development strategy from the national level to the urban and region levels. The Tokyo region clearly benefited from this move and also from the increased emphasis on supporting winners in the global economic competition. If the global economy continues to privilege the agglomeration economy in finance and producer service, the position of political leaders in Tokyo, particularly the governor of TMG, gains strength no matter who is in office.

These changes raise the questions of whether the balance of power has shifted between the TMG and the national government and whether the tentative moves to regionalization have altered the relationship. There used to be clear leadership from the national government through the framework of the CNDP and regional planning, but this faded after the decentralization movement of the 1990s. In reading the records of the more recent regional conferences, there seems to be no dominant figure in their discussions. In terms of agenda setting, however, the TMG seems to be in the driving seat. Ishihara was first to claim that revitalizing the CBD and center core of Tokyo would be vital for Japan's future. It was Ishihara who identified the common regional agenda, such as the reintroduction of international flights at Haneda and installing the three ring roads. After initial suspicion, his agenda has now become the regional agenda. Though he is an experienced politician who knows how the national government works, it is doubtful that he gained leadership purely on the merits of his personality.[12] He was rather smart in seizing the economic and political opportunity to promote Tokyo within the context of globalization and decentralization. It is obvious, however, that the TMG cannot act alone, and the policy response of the city-region, in terms of an urban promotional strategy, is a joint project between the national government, the TMG, and other prefectures and designated cities. One might say that the governance of Tokyo has shifted from a position in which there was clear domination by the nation state within the developmental state framework to one of a political game involving many actors. However, there are two key players: the nation-state still draws on the legacy of its historical domination while the governor of the TMG is able to draw on the importance of Tokyo in the conditions of globalization. This sets the scene for interesting political debates to come.

PART V   *Pathways of Change*

10. Governance and Globalism

Political Responses of Four World City-Regions

ARE GLOBAL CITY-REGIONS (GCRs) FOLLOWING A common pathway? We assess this by comparing how local and global forces were played out in order to identify patterns of convergence and divergence in the governance process. In first looking at policy responses, the focus is on examining whether GCR policy agendas and public policies are leaning in any one direction. In particular, are progrowth biases and neoliberal public policies prevailing in the capitals of capitalism? We then turn to intergovernmental change, examining whether common patterns of governance emerges. Specifically, are processes of regionalization and political autonomization happening as GCRs experience economic restructuring? The answers will help assess how political mediation of global social and economic forces is changing.

Our general conclusion is that powerful globalizing tendencies mark the trajectory of governance, but the GCRs are hardly being pushed down a common pathway bringing diminishing choices for their governments. Global forces are not making the politics of place less important. Globalism and local governance are not mutually exclusive but are deeply intertwined. A complex and varied picture of changing governance is emerging. We detect increasing absorption with the matter of economic competitiveness among GCR governments, as some globalization critics fear, but the extent to which particular governments privilege this issue on a regional scale varies considerably. There are also some similar patterns of intergovernmental politics, but these developments are not suggestive of much political autonomization or regionalization. Most important, even when common political tendencies are evident, important differences remain in the ways particular world city-regions are mediating internationalizing forces.

Why are differences in policy and governance so prominent during a time when global pressures are profoundly remaking these city-regions in similar ways? It is because global economic restructuring does not render GCRs passive players in their own development. As chapter 1 showed, GCRs share many commonalities with respect to their economies, social development, and quality of life, but they do not always have to compete in the same ways to remain world city-regions. Indeed, they compete with different assets and liabilities. Some are more competitive in attracting international corporate headquarters, while others have remained lower-cost locations for other kinds of producer service businesses or, in the case of Tokyo, even manufacturing. Some provide more of an egalitarian social environment than others, backed up by intricate national safety nets. Some GCRs are more attractive places because they provide so many public amenities to enhance livability, while others draw more on what history and private culture can provide. GCRs do not prosper by always being the same.

This, in turn, enables local political choices to matter. Deeply embedded local, regional, and national institutional qualities, including the organization of regional political systems, and the role of higher-level governments, as well as public and private leadership traditions, strongly influence responses to similar social and economic challenges, making world city-regional governance quite variable. Even though economic globalization seems to be precipitating certain political commonalities atop the urban hierarchy, each city-region also asserts its own political logic and priorities. Let us look at how.

Changing Policy Agendas: Common Issues?

ECONOMIC COMPETITIVENESS

World city-regions all have forged global economic linkages in advanced producer services and finance and are competing internationally as entire regions, rather than just as core cities. Has this precipitated increasing attention to enhancing economic competitiveness? There are signs of this in all four city-regions. Nevertheless, the extent of this varies considerably, especially in how much it is given priority by particular governmental actors within the regions and the time period when economic competitiveness has become a priority. On this matter, Paris has shown a different pattern from those of London, New York, and Tokyo, with competitiveness being put on the political agenda much later.

Tokyo is highly absorbed with international competitiveness at all governmental levels, but this attention has been focused on central Tokyo, rather than on the larger metropolitan region. As noted earlier, Japan's booming period of export-oriented growth and prosperity in its relatively protected financial and service sectors started to crumble in the late 1970s. After overinvestment in property markets in the late 1980s, the bubble eventually burst, the whole economy contracted, and confidence in Tokyo shrank during the mid-1990s. During this "lost decade" and after, economic competitiveness emerged as a national policy agenda as well as a regional one. Successive national administrations under Hashimoto (1996–1998), Obuchi (1998–2000), and Koizumi (2001–2006) tried to revive the national economy by introducing more market discipline and efficiency. Deregulation of financial markets, streamlining the bureaucracy, decentralization, and shifting more responsibility to the local government became salient policies.

These changes in national policies enveloped Tokyo, making the issue of competitiveness a top priority for Governor Ishihara in his 1999 election campaign. He expressed concern over Tokyo losing world city status and lagging behind other Asian competitors, such as Shanghai and Singapore. He used the governorship to challenge the national government, claiming that Tokyo needed more than ever to lead the Japanese economy. He pressed the national government to continue to limit policies of spatial equalization in favor of concentrating more resources in the central part of Tokyo. This produced a series of measures for the central area to intensify land use, upgrade infrastructure, and improve mass transit, including connecting Narita airport with central Tokyo. This was further boosted by plans for facilities to host the Olympics in 2016.

These Tokyo-centered policies left the rest of the city-region as a secondary concern, particularly because so much of the region consists of scattered business and commercial centers, high-tech manufacturing clusters, suburban residential towns, and agricultural areas in the periphery. As a result, central Tokyo's competitiveness dominated regional discourse. Other than the circular megalopolis concept, the regional growth strategy put forward by Governor Ishihara, regional competitiveness issues have mostly been viewed in relation to central Tokyo.

London and New York rivaled each other in promoting greater regional competitiveness. As in Tokyo, however, the core cities also assumed increasing priority over the region. After World War II, the UK national government had a policy of decentralizing growth away from the congested core of London. These included policies to entice economic investment to the less developed regions of the country and, in the 1960s, had even included an office development ban in London. Within the southeast, this meant that considerable economic development took place in the favorable locations outside the Greater London boundary, such as the M4 corridor (Reading) and Milton Keynes new town. Many of the small towns in the region also saw substantial growth. Regional planners began to acknowledge the imbalance across the region and began encouraging investment in the less prosperous east—a policy that continues up to the present.

By the mid-1980s, the metropolitan area had lost most of its manufacturing industry and the Greater London Council (GLC) created an economic strategy that sought to encourage indigenous growth of small firms within London. However, the conservative national government during the 1980s favored a more laissez-faire economic approach, abolished the GLC in 1986, and supported minimal regional economic guidance. London's competitiveness in the rapidly growing business service and finance sectors focused attention on the impact of globalization and intercity competition. Led by the private sector and the national government, the 1990s saw policy shifts in ways that made London's competitive position in the world a key issue. Major developments to support this approach resulted—from Canary Wharf to Cross Rail.

Initially, the main competitors were seen to be Paris and Frankfurt, but as the decade progressed the concern was more to keep London's position as a world financial and business center alongside New York and Tokyo. The London Plan of 2004 gave priority to maintaining a world city objective, ensuring the metropolitan area grew economically and in population. Focus was on suitable land and offices for leading world companies. Although policies to enable this concentrated on the central area and docklands, there was also concern at the regional scale where the national government took the lead by the provision of major infrastructure, such as airports and ports. From the late 1990s, three regional development agencies set up in the region pursued a mandate to promote the competitiveness of their areas.

The New York region also become highly absorbed in the competitiveness of the core economy centered in Manhattan even as steady economic growth in the surrounding suburbs transformed many towns, villages, and cities in the tri-state area into virtual satellite economies, often in competition with Manhattan. During the 1980s, New York City was mired in recovering from the fiscal crisis of the 1970s and seeking ways of containing the flight of businesses and people to nearby and distant suburbs as well as to the Sunbelt. State government agencies, such as the port authority, together with the governors in New York, New Jersey, and Connecticut, and together with private groups, such as the regional plan association, sought to incorporate a regional perspective into many policy initiatives. Yet lack of any powerful regional governmental platform could hardly contain vigorous intraregional economic competition. The failure of the port authority's regional development planning efforts during the 1980s and strong emerging suburban economic centers further fragmented discourse over regional competitiveness.

Since the 1990s, New York City's resurgence as the prime economic engine of the tri-state area accompanied parallel growth in prime suburban areas. As competitiveness of the region became more and more closely identified with the fortunes of New York City, however, attention of policy makers throughout the region focused on finding ways of supporting the city's role as a surging world financial center. A leading part was played by the bistate Port Authority, which gave priority to modernizing and expanding the region's airports and seaport. Other state agencies in New York and New Jersey also began to collaborate more in seeking to upgrade mass transit services in order to address the problem of access to the region's core. By the turn of the century, Manhattan's virtual economic rebirth sent property prices soaring, business booming, and development quickening even after the tragedy of 2001. Key governmental players with a stake in the region forged a coalition to support a large program of megaprojects in regional transportation that were geared to promoting New York City's primacy as a world economic center.

Only in Paris did the local government significantly depart from promoting a regional competitiveness agenda, at least for the core area. During most of the period, economic competitiveness was not high on the agendas of the majority of local and regional actors, the city of Paris included. Although the regional council (Conseil

Régional d'Île de France [CRIF]) has always viewed the international rank of Île de France as important, this authority has rarely given it high priority compared with other issues. Local government traditions and partisan competition encourage most local government officials to pay heed to promoting issues of social well-being and equity, as discussed later. Yet in some respects, the Paris region actually moved in the direction of boosting economic growth almost as much as the other three world cities. This is because agencies of the national government—or state—took up a leading role in seeking ways of boosting the international economic position of Paris. This enabled local officials to concentrate on building their political base in other policy areas.

Although the national government's policy stance toward boosting the Paris regional economy has not been consistent, its presence has been continuous. Over time, state agencies have gradually shifted in favor of promoting programs to privilege Paris as the region's prime economic engine. Until the 2000s, the national government considered Paris too congested and believed its growth occurred to the detriment of other "provincial" regions. Its view as "Paris and the French desert" was hostile to continued growth in Paris and Île de France. Efforts were also undertaken to shift some public sector jobs and enterprises to the provinces and to deny access of firms to Paris. At the same time, this view of Paris's growth was very ambiguous. Many agencies engaged in planning and funding economic development actually supported the region's continued growth by supplying Paris with infrastructure, equipment, and facilities.

Since the 1990s, however, the national state's attitude significantly shifted in favor of Paris's growth and the economic primacy of Île de France. This has created conflicts and rivalries between the CRIF and local governments over the demand that Paris be more actively supported in its competition with other global cities. Particularly since 2007, with the election of Nicolas Sarkozy, central Paris and Île de France are considered to be spearheads for France's ability to meet international competition along with other world economic centers, especially the other three city-regions in our study.

SOCIAL EQUITY

As chapter 1 described, the economic success of GCRs brings ambivalent social consequences. On one hand, they enjoy a relatively high level of wealth and prosperity. This can facilitate attention to problems of social equity, such as unemployment, poverty, and ethnic and racial discrimination by making resources more available. Yet globalization has another edge. Our world cities all experience substantial social polarization and must manage growing wealth and inequality on a regional scale.

Yet what stands out most is how regional efforts attacking problems of social equity were relatively feeble and uncommon. Differences in attending to these social problems mostly are a function of higher governmental programs and national safety net resources, although particular urban regions sometimes attempted to give this added priority. In that respect, Paris and London have shown more engagement on social issues than have New York and Tokyo, each of them for different reasons.

In Paris and London, few new social programs of regional scope were attempted during the period. In both city-regions, national programs essentially dominated problems of social policy in employment and housing, leaving local and regional agencies with neither the financial means nor political authority to embark on many new ventures. Most attention to regional social issues was evident in Paris, where local officials and the dominant parties prided themselves on the priority they gave these problems. They were followed in the late 1990s by the socialist government, which enacted significant laws to fight social inequalities in urban areas (such as the 2000 Solidarity and Urban Regeneration Act, which imposed legal social housing thresholds on municipalities). Conflicts between the regional council, most county councils, and many municipalities on one side and the state on the other became harsh, particularly when national authorities prodded them to give more attention to commercial and business needs in their planning documents. Although local officials and the regional council voiced high priority for matters of social justice, in fact neither managed to actually launch or implement many new programs. At best, local and national officials supported increased national funding for housing and social initiatives since the mid-1980s. Nevertheless, socioterritorial disparities increased in the Paris region and the 2005 riots have shown that the social question persists.

London also experienced steady but moderate engagement in issues of social equity. This was a result of national, rather than local or regional, policies, however. As in France, policies related to overcoming personal or family poverty and their spatial character are mainly driven by national governments. Various welfare and educational programs are then administered by local government within the national policy framework. However, since there is a spatial dimension to the poverty issue, this social imbalance has been the focus of policy at the regional (via national government regional strategies) and the metropolitan levels. Some local authorities in the metropolitan area get more central government finance to deal with their special social needs, and for most of our period, the central government formulated area-based regeneration programs that focus on specific neighborhoods with social problems. During this time, there were dozens of different programs, but the common approach was for local authorities to bid for the finance as the central government decided how to distribute it. Overall, there was little regional coordination of these various programs. During the 1980s, the dominant approach to social need was to encourage trickle down and rely on these national safety net programs. The riots of the period partially undermined this view, however, leading to increases in the number of programs.

When the Labor government took over in 1997, there was a shift to more locally based programs. The regional development agencies, including the London Development Agency (LDA), were given responsibility to make distributional decisions over the resources for regeneration. Only when this happened was there some regional and local focus with a potential for spatial coordination. Otherwise, throughout the period the official spatial strategies at both regional and metropolitan levels acknowledged

imbalances between different areas. Efforts were made to encourage greater development in the more depressed areas but, as their powers of implementation were weak,
the impact has not been great.

Least attention to regional social disparities happened in tri-state New York and in
the Tokyo region. The New York GCR essentially lacks much capacity to mount social
programs of regional scope. The special state authorities that dominate urban development are rarely engaged in social planning of any kind due to their limited mandate
and/or their project-bound financing. The local governments seek to protect their
limited tax bases and usually avoid programs of social redistribution. Consequently,
regional attempts to challenge the region's large spatial disparities in income, access
to housing, unemployment, and family poverty were rare. This trend was reinforced
by cutbacks and changes in federal programs in housing, income maintenance, and
grants-in-aid since the 1980s, leaving states and localities more on their own in addressing most social ills. Aside from some uncommon cases of state and federal court
intervention involving racial discrimination in housing and employment in scattered
suburban governmental jurisdictions, regional intervention on issues of social equity
were mostly confined to studies by regional planning groups. Major attempts to address housing inequalities usually were confined to particular localities.

The Tokyo region was marked by the most regressive social agendas, even though
social equity was a foundation of postwar Japanese economic growth and the scale
of the problem has been less than in our other city-regions. Postwar national governments were keen to create stable middle-class families by various macroeconomic
policies, like progressive taxation, lifetime employment, a national health system, and
so on. Japan became one of the most equitable countries among those in the Organization for Economic Cooperation and Development (OECD) in the 1970s. This situation changed during the 1990s, however, particularly as the declining prosperity of the
Japanese economy enveloped Tokyo and discouraged traditional attention to social
intervention at any governmental level. As job stability was undermined, unemployment increased, poverty among the younger generation grew, and the gap between
rich and poor expanded. Further, spatial inequalities in employment, income, and
housing access emerged as so-called hot spots and cold spots within the Tokyo region,
reinforcing the historical division between middle-class areas in the south and west
and working-class areas in the north and east. New spatial inequalities are now found,
especially in the residential suburbs, which used to house quite homogeneous white-
collar commuters and their families.

During the last two decades, there have been few direct policy responses by the
national or local governments to address the issue. Although the Tokyo Metropolitan
Government (TMG) used to have quite progressive public housing policies that targeted ordinary working-class families, this has diminished since the mid-1990s, especially as the national government reoriented housing policy more in favor of market-
based provision. TMG followed this national policy. The target group for most new

programs shifted to special groups making specific claims, such as single mothers, unemployed elderly, and the disabled. Consequently, Tokyo has witnessed a growing number of homeless people since the middle of the 1990s, especially in big commercial centers like Shinjuku. TMG's policy has been to relocate them to hostels and limit their public presence but avoid addressing the fundamental problems creating homelessness.

ENVIRONMENT AND QUALITY-OF-LIFE POLICY

All four GCR regions gave increasing policy attention to environmental priorities and to the quality of life. The extent of this varied considerably among the GCRs, however—especially with respect to the local governmental response. In all of the city-regions, environmental policies are dominated by higher-level, especially national, governments. Local and regional policy agendas necessarily are secondary and are often driven by changes in national priorities, regulations, and funding.

For various reasons, we expected GCR politicians to favor enhancing the environmental quality of their cities. London, Paris, and New York no longer have large manufacturing-based industries (Tokyo also is becoming less reliant on manufacturing), past major sources of air and water pollutants. This economic change makes it easier to upgrade environmental standards. Further, all four GCR economies are dominated by white-collar job sectors and local governments must compete for this labor in part by supporting amenities and urban lifestyles requiring high environmental quality. GCRs have relatively prosperous electorates, known to be frequently supportive of promoting environmental issues. Thus, it is not surprising that significant new efforts to improve the local and regional environments were found in Tokyo, London, Paris, and New York.

Nevertheless, differences in regional and local engagement in environmental enhancement were considerable. London and Paris were leaders in this respect, in large part because local, regional, and national governmental policies were already highly integrated for regulating environmental standards. Strong environmental policies marked the Greater London region since the 1950s. These have been of two types: preventing the sprawl out from the metropolitan center and preserving good landscapes. Over the period, attempts to relax green belt preservation usually did not succeed even under conservative governments, whose voters and local politicians were the dominant voice of residents in the green belt. Even in the new millennium when relaxation was demanded because it was blamed for rising house prices, it has failed. On this occasion, the tension was between central government departments—the treasury focusing on the economy, and the departments responsible for the environment. But so far, the economic crisis starting in 2008 again put the idea of encroaching on the green belt on the back burner. Other landscape preservation policies in the greater southeast also were sometimes criticized for restricting the areas available to satisfy new housing demand. Yet these policies remained consistent throughout the period, as they have been developed in recent years by regional development agencies.

Within the metropolitan area, plans were put in place to protect the parks, open space, and Thames riverside, even though the last decade witnessed national and London policies to increase the house building within the built-up areas, putting considerable pressure on allowing development on incidental open space. The creation of the Greater London Authority (GLA) gave a further boost to environmental protection within London. The act required the new metropolitan government to formulate strategies on a number of new environmental topics, such as ecology, energy, and noise. Many new policies, such as the congestion charge, were adopted to seek reductions in the impact of car emissions, and in 2008 the London Plan formulated policies oriented to climate change, as the mayor sought to position the city as a world leader on this issue.

In Paris, there was increasing attention to the environment, but it varied significantly from one actor to the other. The case of transport planning is one such instance. During the last ten years or so, the regional authorities as well as the city of Paris approved mobility plans (*plans de déplacements urbains* or PDU). These plans focused on the development of public transport and soft modes, aiming at a significant reduction of car traffic in the metropolitan area. Since 2004, the regional council has considered the environmental question a top priority (this being due to the significant political presence of the Greens). This is expressed in the newly proposed regional master plan (Schéma Directeur de la Région Île de France or SDRIF), which made environmental issues a very high priority. In Paris itself, a similar attitude has not only prevailed but started earlier because the Greens became a major political force at the city level in 2001. As a consequence, several environmental policies have been implemented, including support for public transport, anticar policies (parking), and a compact city policy that stretches across many policy domains.

In contrast to governmental actors in the Paris region, the state was generally more ambiguous about supporting more aggressive environmental policies as it struggled to balance goals of sustainability and economic growth. For instance, it supported the extension of La Défense, even though the regional council complained that such extension would create more traffic jams and would worsen environmental conditions in the area. At the same time, however, in 2008 the state approved and implemented strict national legislation regarding auto emission pollution by means of the so-called bonus-malus tax system—that is, an additional tax on the more polluting vehicles.

The Tokyo region was less supportive in attending to a regional approach to environmental issues. Although the national government in Japan has a tradition of environmental consciousness, Tokyo lacks a clear environmental policy on a regional scale. As discussed earlier, Japan was known for pollution and environmental damage in the 1970s, but not any longer thanks to stricter regulations and technological advances in pollution control. Since the 1990s, a global perspective has been widely supported, particularly on such issues as greenhouse gas and carbon emissions. Yet Tokyo and its region remained relatively passive in seeking greater engagement on most environmental issues, preferring instead to rely on national officials to set its agendas.

Meanwhile, the TMG began to view environmental policies as having commercial as well as social importance because of growing recognition that environmental quality increased Tokyo's urban competitiveness. For example, the TMG made attempts to capitalize on its available assets to increase open space, even in central Tokyo. Even though the TMG lacks large open green spaces—indeed, it has the least amount of green open space among all four city-regions—it proposed increasing green space on its publicly owned land, such as in pedestrian districts and riverside walks. The TMG also undertook restoration of canals and launched projects to make the waterfront more accessible. Larger programs were also devised to utilize transportation policy in cooperation with national planners to diminish air pollution caused by automobile traffic and congestion. It proposed building three ring roads in Tokyo and the surrounding region to prevent traffic coming into the central part of Tokyo, and began to address the problem of the heat island.

In tri-state New York, attention to green issues also grew during the last three decades. This was due to new state and national regulations imposing these green policy objectives and because of occasional bottom-up efforts by environmental groups. Yet New York's regional efforts remained weakest compared to the other city-regions largely because its fragmented political system relies so extensively on go-it-alone efforts by individual local governments. Nevertheless, tightening federal and state environmental controls since the 1970s helped to precipitate a variety of measures to attack water and air pollution along with other forms of environmental hazards, particularly in New York City.

As for New York City itself, programs to upgrade the city's water supply, sewage, and solid waste disposal expanded. It also increased and upgraded acres of city-owned parkland and undertook quality-of-life campaigns to improve the city's streets and transit environments. But these were essentially local programs and they rarely assumed regional scope, except when made part of more extensive state government efforts. New York City's enormous size and largesse sometimes enabled it to act regionally, however. The city's remarkable program to purchase land in the upstate watershed hundreds of miles from its municipal borders was of this kind. Otherwise, regional cooperation for environmental quality remained scant in the New York metro area. The major exception to this was in cases where campaigns occasionally materialized to get governments within the region to seek preservation of undeveloped areas, wetlands, and watersheds.

Culture Competition in Quality of Life

Regarding quality-of-life amenities, all GCRs have become highly focused on promoting culture, tourism, and the arts as a form of economic development. This rapid commercialization of local artistic and cultural environments is being fueled by highly active governmental promotion of these job sectors.

There is considerable variation in how GCR governments seek to capitalize on local cultural assets, however. London exhibits modest strategic behavior. The importance of quality of life has been one of the stated aims of strategic policies since the creation of the GLA in 2000 and was in the first London Plan (2004). The improvement of mass transport and policies to promote ecodiversity and reduce pollution and noise have been part of this approach. There are specific policies that link quality of life to enhancing London's global competitiveness. One is the development of culture as an economic activity often oriented to boosting the tourist industry. Tourism, culture, and ethnic diversity are all seen as essential strengths in London's economy. The second dimension is the improvement of quality of life oriented to the international business sector. For instance, one of the major aims of all the London Plans has been to ensure a supply of high-quality office accommodation. These efforts sometimes have spilled over to upgrade some neighborhoods suffering from poor environmental quality of life. For example, the new mayor has argued that decaying neighborhoods contribute to the perception of London as a less attractive place than some of its competitors. His policies involve upgrading these areas, improving rundown parks, and planting 10,000 trees across the city.

The highly fragmented governmental structure in the tri-state New York region makes it difficult for any one government to assert leadership on quality of life and cultural amenity issues. Given this, New York City political leaders pay most of their attention to promoting quality-of-life improvements within the five boroughs, rather than seeking many regional innovations. Outside New York City, other local authorities do the same in their own jurisdiction. During and after the fiscal crisis of the 1970s, New York City's quality of life—understood in terms of safety and the quality of its public spaces—became a major issue. After the city's economy and revenue streams became more upbeat by the 1990s, every New York City mayor has given much greater attention to improving the city's environmental quality.

As the regional—and perhaps national—center of culture and the arts, New York City misses no opportunity for promoting this image as a tool for economic development. Nevertheless, the city lacks a coherent culture policy. The city government and business groups are able to launch numerous attractive media campaigns to call attention to New York's cultural assets, but there is little agreement about how cultural development can be stimulated through public policy. At best, strategic thinking about investing in art and culture is something that occasionally gets attended to in the course of boosting its commercial development.

In comparison with London and New York, Paris was a latecomer to the culture race. Perhaps this is because it has a long and well-established tradition as a city of beauty and culture. Indeed, culture and tourism have always been significant in the entire Île de France economy and have always been important to national and local political actors. The present period has not brought significant changes in this respect, but officials have become more conscious of the need to compete in order to capitalize on its cultural assets. The region as a whole has been in competition as the world capital of exhibitions, congresses, and leisure time with cities like Barcelona. For example, in 2009 some European newspapers suggested Paris was "*ringarde*" (old-fashioned) and, as a result, being abandoned by young people and tourists for Barcelona, Berlin, or London because those cities were alleged to have a more "modern" and "more fun" nightlife. This precipitated a decision by the mayor of Paris to appoint "Mr. Nightlife," a mediator between the neighborhoods' inhabitants and the entertainment community in order to maintain nightlife as an attractive aspect of the city. Nevertheless, compared to the other cities, Paris is most laid-back in promoting itself as a cultural center. There is no policy or regional strategy like London's that links culture, creativity, and global attractiveness. Only some scattered campaigns to promote arts and fashion in Paris or in its northern suburbs can be understood as new governmental efforts to cope with new competition in the globalization context.

In Tokyo, the governmental links between quality of life, culture, and tourism have been most recent but are growing tighter as local and national officials have come to acknowledge the advantages of cultural promotion. The national government and TMG place tourism and the visitor industry of leisure and entertainment as a leading sector in the twenty-first century. The central government established the Japan Tourism Agency in 2008 to devise a national strategy and coordinate projects. TMG also became more active in promoting Tokyo in international tourism, starting a "Yokoso (Welcome) Tokyo" campaign in recent years. The new emphasis on culture and tourism has had geographical implications. For example, the cultural promotion policy is not only about the usual cultural products and art forms; it also includes the natural environment and urban landscape itself, such as the canals and rivers that are now promoted as a cultural heritage and a component for supporting tourism.

SUMMING UP POLICY CHANGE: CONVERGENCE AND DIVERGENCE

In sum, all four world city-regions were highly absorbed in promoting their economic competitiveness no matter how fragmented their GCR political systems. Efforts to boost economic competitiveness easily permeated the policy agendas of nearly all major governments more than any other issue. Even in Paris, where local governments were least engaged in these issues, higher-level authorities asserted them, sometimes over the objections of local activists.

Nevertheless, there was only weak convergence among GCRs on regional policies to address specifically regional economic deficiencies. Further, we do not detect the emergence of new common regional agendas in any of the other issue areas in any of the city-regions. Even though regional economic competitiveness was a compelling issue among most actors in three of the regions, there is little relationship between other areas of public policy. In particular, GCRs that were most highly engaged in promoting economic growth were not necessarily more deficient in social equity or environmental policy attention. Differences in policy responses on these issues mainly reflected differences in national governmental programs and approaches and local political influences, especially with respect to environmental matters. Prominent signs of any common world city-region policy agenda did not emerge.

Changing Global City-Region Governance?

Are world city-regions experiencing similar changes in governance? As we discussed in the introduction, globalization could have two major impacts on the governance of city-regions. The first is increasing political regionalization as city-regions become a more relevant scale for policies for addressing metropolitan issues and challenges. The second concerns the relations between world city-regions and their national political hinterland, a process that we term "autonomization." Autonomization can happen when GCRs begin to assert new political power as they delink from nation-states in order to compete more effectively in global markets.

IS WORLD CITY GOVERNANCE REGIONALIZING?

Regionalization can take several forms. One is by means of new *dedicated governmental institutions* of regional scope that supplant extant local governments. A second way is by creating new *lateral governmental networks and authorities* at the local level that increase regional coordination. A third way is by the emergence of *regional leaders* in the public or private sectors asserting roles in setting regional governmental agendas. Finally, governmental regionalization may involve *higher governmental agencies* taking on new roles in managing regional issues. The latter effectively delegate regional intervention to bodies outside of the GCR but may involve substantial consultation with local officials. It is necessary to consider all of these potential avenues of change in order to evaluate how much or how little regionalization has taken place.

Overall, there were only scattered and limited signs of the first three forms of regionalization happening, with considerable variation in kind and intensity among the GCRs. The strongest trend was one of stepped-up regional management by higher-level governments. Ironically, all of these changes in the direction of a more organized regional politics must be viewed with reference to an important countertrend: increasing intergovernmental fragmentation and rivalry. The latter development diminished the impact of efforts to regionalize governance.

Dedicated, Lateral, and Centralizing Developments

London and Paris are the two cases where new regional agencies and increasing intervention by higher-level government combined to most boost regional approaches. At the beginning of the period, the strategic governance of the Greater London region consisted of the GLC at the core and the SERPLAN for the broader region. It was the central government that produced the strategic guidance policies for both areas, however. The GLC had to fit within this and SERPLAN was only an advisory body. In 1986, the GLC was abolished and the governance of the metropolitan area consisted of the weak hand of the central government, ad hoc bodies, and the lower tier of 32 boroughs and the City of London. There was very little of a strategic nature other than regional infrastructure decisions and setting up the London Dockland Development Corporation to attract investment to this area. However, with the Labour government in 1997 there was a move toward a more regional approach. Although Labour decentralized some central functions to assemblies in Scotland, Wales, and London, the new GLA in London established in 2000 had weaker powers than the old GLC and was a more streamlined body. Equally important, the central government maintained strong controls over GLA activities and finance. Review of its powers in 2007 gave it more say over large developments and housing strategy but no changes to the financial arrangements. However, since 2000 there has been strong political and strategic policy leadership for this metropolitan part of the region with the directly elected mayor, contrasting sharply with the previous period.

In terms of the broad city-region, there remains a distinct lack of regional governance. The establishment of the regional development agencies may seem a step in this direction but, as the region is split between three organizations, this leaves the central government in a pivotal coordinating role, all the more because the only collaborative planning body for the region, the SERPLAN, was abolished in 2001. Further, not only have there been frequent changes in how the RDAs operate, but also they were abolished by the national government in 2010.

The Paris region also experienced a simultaneous assertion of regional presence by the national government as well as new dedicated governmental authorities for the metropolitan area. A regional council was established in 1986 and since then has constantly gained power (more authority and increasing budget and staff). Today public transport is largely in the hands of the CRIF and so is the master plan, following reforms implemented in 2005. The regional council established a regional development agency in the early 2000s and a regional land corporation in 2006. However, as we have seen, the desire of the CRIF to play a stronger role in the governance of the region has been challenged by local governments and the state. The central government has become more involved in promoting the economy and development of Paris and its periphery. It has established new agencies and instruments for that purpose, such as the new ministry for the development of the capital region and the Operations of National Interest (located in the region). Most recently, a bill was put forward in the Parliament in 2009–10 to create a Société du Grand Paris controlled by the state.

The New York tri-state region remained the most disorganized. It not only lacked any superagencies for the entire region, but the hand of federal policy makers remained more distant than in the other nations with more integrated governmental systems. Yet the capacity of the tri-state area to act regionally increased somewhat, albeit in piecemeal and sometimes ad hoc ways. For one thing, the region's various advisory regional organizations, such as the regional plan association and the region's main transportation coordinating bodies were very active throughout the period. Although they lacked power to implement what they recommended, their plans often had the effect of pulling together the thinking of disparate government officials and state agencies involved in regional development affairs.

Most significant, however, was the enlarged presence of state agencies in regional coordination. With the backing of governors, especially in New York and New Jersey, state public benefit corporations played bigger roles than ever in promoting a variety of programs to boost the region's economy. This included massive new investments in transportation in recent years and efforts to put transit agencies with regional responsibilities on a firmer financial footing. The port authority also played an active role in modernizing and expanding the airports and seaport in the bistate part of the region while investing in a number of real estate projects to make the commercial and business infrastructure more competitive. Indeed, by the 1990s few major publicly assisted development projects happened without the powerful regulatory hand and financial support of state government agencies. After the devastation of 9/11, a plethora of city and state agencies mobilized in rebuilding the former World Trade Center site and challenging transportation bottlenecks in the Manhattan core.

Tokyo experienced the least lateral regionalization as the national government asserted its traditional view of Tokyo as the nation's prime economic engine. This was reinforced by the economic crisis beginning in the 1990s. The national government's efforts to boost Tokyo was not resisted by the TMG, which evinced little interest itself in expanding its own jurisdictional reach into its urban region. That left regional issues around Tokyo to be taken up mostly by national officials, particularly major ministries having regional offices. They played the dominant role in coordinating and implementing nationally designed policies in respective policy areas, such as infrastructure and health services.

Regional conferences, including the prefectures and municipal governments, were voluntarily organized since 1979 to discuss regional issues. However, this never led to regionalization in forms that linked the TMG and other local governments in the metropolitan area. The conferences submit policy recommendations to the national government but do not have legal status. Although they have supported the idea of devolving national government functions to lower tiers and creating regional government, this has yet to materialize. As a result of decentralization policy, the city-region has emerged as a desirable unit for national development, but there is still a long way to go before the creation of a regional government of any form. Thus, the TMG remains the leading influence in the region but in clear subordination to national ministries wary of giving up their positions of ascendancy.

Is a Regional Leadership Emerging?

In theory, scattered public officials can undertake regional advocacy roles when governmental management of whole metropolitan areas becomes more important. This may arise from prominent central city officials, such as mayors, who capitalize on the size and power of their governments to build a platform for establishing regional influence. Regional coalitions or multigovernmental forums may also attract those seeking to ensure suburban and small-town influence over the regional agenda. Alternatively, business leadership may become more regionalized and assertive. Unlike local governments with their entrenched jurisdictional stakes, business leaders have the potential to move more freely to organize forums to serve region-wide interests.

Neither development has happened on any major scale in any of our world city-regions, however. Central city officials often acted as if they represent regional interests, especially on economic and environmental issues. The mayors of Paris, London, and New York and the governor of Tokyo all voiced regional concerns and demonstrated sporadic engagement in issues of regional scope during the past three decades. They often played a key role in organizing some regional conferences. Yet this activism was never followed by the creation of new governmental organizations with power to coordinate, much less to implement policies. No mayor can be credited with the creation of regional governmental coalitions having lasting power. These officials all seemed to lack a sufficient power base for asserting regional leadership. None managed to offer any real incentives to entice other governments in the various regions to follow their lead on particular issues.

The few attempts by mayors to take on a regional leadership role were invariably regarded as threatening to other governments in the region. For example, although there is no actual regional leadership in Île de France, there was regular conflict over its possible emergence, especially among the regional council (its president), the mayor of Paris, and the state (ministers, prefects, or both). In recent years, this rivalry has actually produced competing metropolitan-wide initiatives, such as the Syndicat Paris-Métropole. The latter is viewed by the regional council as an attempt by the central government to seize a new coordinating role.

There was a complete lack of political leadership at the regional South East London. The central government was the only body to produce policies of any broad reach, focusing mainly on major infrastructure. Yet this has hardly helped coordination because it split the region into the three regional development authorities. Although these authorities held a few joint meetings mainly to produce promotional material for the whole of the greater southeast, they were answerable to the central government, not to governments in the region. GLA leadership is something of a proxy for wider regional leadership. The mayor is very visible and is constantly in the media as a London booster. Yet the mayor has not shown much interest in issues beyond his boundaries, except to comment on such things as airport expansion plans and other individual projects.

Similarly, the New York region also showed few signs of any emerging political center. The tri-state area is filled with governments that jealously guard their prerogatives and turf. There were sporadic efforts by New York City's mayor to speak for the region on some major transit, environmental, and economic issues, but these actions were never followed by programs that won a regional following. The bi-state port authority abandoned an attempt to formulate regional development plans during the early 1990s, and its role has not been picked up by others. It also does not represent local governments. Thus, New York's regional thinking is addressed mainly by voluntary associations, such as the Regional Plan Association and various professional conferences.

In Tokyo's case, the powerful presence of the national government has long discouraged regional leadership. In recent years, the governor of Tokyo has shown some political ambition to lead the region, voicing a megalopolis concept that regards the region as a single functional socioeconomic entity, and he has called for closer integration[1] in order to win global intercity competition. He also tried to extend his influence in the regional conference. The latter lacks legal status, however, and has earned only a cool reception from other governors and mayors. Indeed, a major regional dispute, the expansion of Haneda airport and its relation to Narita airport in Chiba prefecture, was never settled by the conference. Instead, it was resolved through the intervention of the national government.

Does Private Leadership Make Up for a Public Deficit?

Although the private business sector has the potential to assert regional leadership when the government fails to do so, business has yet to fulfill this role in any of the GCRs. Globalization is widely recognized as an important matter by business leaders, and they frequently express interest in specific projects of regional importance such as roads, transit, and environmental programs. In some cases, such as London, business leaders became more active in strategic matters, perhaps a sign of changing of business attitudes about regional coordination. Yet even in London this kind of advocacy rarely became transformed into active political leadership at the city-region scale.

In general, GCR business leaders remain weak advocates because they juggle crosscutting pressures and interests in regional governance. Some want to change the governance system in order to promote city-region-wide business interests. Yet most business leaders are inclined to preserve their own power by working within the governmental system they have rather than to expand new lateral networks that may or may not be as open to their influence. Further, many dominant corporate business players lack community roots; they are strongly oriented to the global economy of producer and financial services and prefer to spend their political capital on national regulatory and tax issues. As a result, the private sector has yet to assert itself significantly or consistently enough to make up for the lack of public sector cooperation in any of the city-regions.

There also are some obstacles to private sector leadership that are particular to each region. In Tokyo, business is quite disorganized despite the other centralized features of the regional political system. Business communities are organized locally, and their involvement is mostly limited to local property-based boosterism and revitalization by individual projects. A regional conference of business leaders started in 2006 but has yet to make any impact. In metropolitan Tokyo, business is represented by the Tokyo Chamber of Commerce and the Confederation of Japanese Industry (Keidanren). Both publish policy recommendations and they are frequently consulted by TMG officials in large-scale regeneration projects in central Tokyo, where leading businesses like developers, real estate, financial institutions, retailers, the tourism industry, and cultural industries all play a large role. Yet their political activities are usually targeted at national officialdom because this is where power is concentrated; there is little doubt that they place high priority on influencing specific projects, rather than attempting to play a role in setting strategic priorities.

New York business leaders also have shown little regional political activity, even though the tri-state area, unlike Tokyo, affords a highly decentralized governmental context that seems to beg for their participation. The organized business community plays a role in virtually all localities, but there has been no successful attempt to build a regional business organization. For its part, the highly visible Partnership for New York City remains dedicated to promoting business interests only in New York City, even though the partnership sometimes advocates a regional perspective on some issues, such as transportation planning, and it helps fund professional groups with a regional focus. As noted earlier, surveys of New York City business executives reveal their absorption with national governmental policies, such as immigration, taxes, and regulation, rather than with many regional issues.

Even without asserting organized regional leadership, New York business representatives already dominate the many boards of public corporations, local development commissions, and even nonprofit planning associations. The latter usually depend heavily on funding from corporate sponsors. Governors and state legislatures routinely parcel out the jobs running, reorganizing, and refinancing their public corporations to powerful business leaders. Consequently, private–public partnership relationships permeate almost every major project having regional impact. For example, during 2009 the New York governor organized a special commission to recommend ways of addressing the Metropolitan Transit Authority's (MTA) financial crisis arising from falling revenues and the need to modernize the authority's services. The commission was chaired by the very same prominent businessman who had previously run the MTA during the 1980s, when he also reorganized the authority's finances in order for it to embark on a vast capital investment program.

Compared with New York or Tokyo, Britain has a limited tradition of direct business participation in politics, even though traditional business organizations, such as the Confederation of British Industry (CBI) and chambers of commerce, have always lobbied the government, and the City of London Corporation has had influence beyond its narrow borders. Change took place in the 1990s when business saw a need for London to promote itself more aggressively in international competition. The globally oriented business sector—banks, the airport companies, British Airways, and large property and finance companies—organized London First to lobby for a change in London governance. The central government then supported London First in its approach. After the proposal for a metropolitan body was announced in 1997, London First switched its attention to the metropolitan level. They, along with the traditional business lobby organizations (CBI and chambers of commerce), prepared economic strategy documents to influence the new GLA and forged close relationships with the new mayor. As a result, they had a significant influence in ensuring that competitiveness and London's world city role were at the top of the mayor's strategic agenda. Meanwhile, at the regional scale, business was represented on the regional development boards but their involvement was less focused and influence weaker.

In Paris, business rarely had much influence on policies and strategies at the regional level, although some major firms appear to have easy access to national authorities. Yet there is no organization of business interests for the Paris region, and business groups within the region are highly fragmented and competing. Four chambers of commerce have been rivals over business's regional leadership, with the Paris chamber considering itself as the natural leader, at least of the core area. The chambers of commerce are in conflict with business associations (notably the Medef) regarding who should represent business, a deeply dividing issue in a corporatist-like state where chambers of commerce officially have the monopoly of business representation. National reform of chambers of commerce, implemented in 2010, aims at the regionalization of chambers of commerce. Although all chambers of commerce support this reform, it remains to be seen how it will be implemented in the Île de France case, considering the degree of conflict in the business sector. However fragmented and rivalry ridden, this does not seem to prevent business from involvement in regional strategic matters when their interests are at stake. For example, business's broad opposition materialized over the regional master plan and with the Grand Paris project.

Regional Fragmentation Continues

Relatively limited political regionalization is further diminished in significance by increasing rivalry and division among governments in at least three of the four GCRs. In Tokyo, there was least drift toward fragmented government. Here, contention among public officials in the ministries, prefectures, the TMG, and local governments was relatively contained by the almost continuously powerful role played by the national government in urban development, especially in recent years, as it battled with protracted economic woes at national and metropolitan scales. Elsewhere, however, regional political cooperation measurably decreased.

The New York region remained mired in economic competition among its various governments. Although New York and New Jersey state governmental players enlarged their intervention within the region, this was not usually very organized. The state agencies dominating urban development tended to proliferate and lack any

mechanism for pulling together in development planning except for their accountability to the state governors. Governors have been reluctant to challenge local prerogatives in the course of pursuing regional objectives even within their own states.
For example, in 2011 New York's governor Andrew M. Cuomo launched new regional
development councils all over New York State in order to stimulate regional economic
planning and development. Yet this initiative avoids treating the New York portion
of the tri-state region as a single region; it even provides New York City with its own
"regional" council (Applebome 2011). And of course very little cooperation on major
projects occurred among the three states. Even the Port Authority of New York and
New Jersey became bitterly divided for years by rivalries among board members seeking to defend the agenda preferences of the governors of the two states.

Governmental divisiveness and fragmentation also increased in Paris and in London despite the fact that national officials made efforts to promote regional perspectives. Ironically, these cases suggest that many forms of regional political fragmentation
actually can happen more easily when higher-level governments try to play a regional
coordinating role. This is because national intervention introduces a whole distinct
layer of intergovernmental and bureaucratic divisions into already fragmented metropolitan regions, unleashing added rivalry. Further, the willingness of national authorities to take on region-wide responsibilities relieves local governments of the need to
collaborate with each other to address issues that spill beyond their borders.

The Paris GCR precisely followed this pattern. The state is largely responsible for
the increasing political fragmentation within the capital region. In the last decade, for
instance, it constantly established new development corporations (such as Établissements Publics d'Aménagement [EPA]) on specific portions of Île de France, without
much consultation with local authorities. Although it could have sought local cooperation for its projects, its decisions and policies have rather contributed to new conflicts between local authorities. In this context, the main initiatives in favor of cooperation have been from the mayor of Paris. He organized the metropolitan conference
and then, in 2009, a new joint authority, Paris-Métropole, covering the largest part of
the urbanized region.

Fragmentation also increased by virtue of purely local political rivalries. The regional council, county councils, and the municipalities all vied for power and influence since France's decentralization in the 1980s. The reform of area-wide cooperation
between municipalities contributed to the multiplying of intermunicipal joint authorities with significant powers and resources. Although the regional CRIF has brought
some semblance of actual regional coordination, the CRIF remains weak in spite of its
increasing powers. Lacking the authority to implement its plans and organizing only
part of the economic region, it also suffers from a lack of clear and established leadership. It attempts to plan in a political and electoral system that favors municipalities
and departments. Recent assertion of leadership by state officials seeking to promote
Paris's economic competitiveness increased rivalry with the city of Paris and other

local governments favoring attention to social services and equity considerations in urban change.

London's political divisions were also reinforced by national governmental activism as it tried to remake the region's governance. After 1986, GLC powers were dispersed to the central government, ad hoc bodies, or the local government. At the same time, a multitude of central government regeneration initiatives, each with its own organization, further increased governmental divisions. Although the removal of the GLC was initially portrayed as a way of removing bureaucracy and simplifying governance, the central government added complexity. It orchestrated a strategic nonstatutory vision statement in the form of the London Pride Prospectus, bringing together local authorities and business organizations led by London First. The central government also set up a government office for London, a minister for London, and a cabinet committee for London. At the regional scale, the Thames Gateway Partnership was established as a way of bringing together the host of different agencies covering this area under one umbrella, but it lacked the statutory power to go any further. In sum, these various changes did little to enhance intergovernmental coordination within the region.

Only after the Labour government's arrival in 1997 was there a change in governmental coordination, albeit only for the central part of the region. The creation of the GLA enabled a coherent strategic approach coordinating all the various policies and providing a common framework for the policies of the lower-tier boroughs. Yet the GLA's limited financial capability, its reliance on central government funding, and its restricted jurisdiction essentially undermine its having a strategic regional influence. The latter is also undermined by the presence of three regional development agencies and by the departments of specific ministries. There was no overall authoritative means of coordinating these various bodies or conveying a regional picture except through the central government's major infrastructure decisions. Although the creation of the GLA improved coordination of the policy response in the metropolitan area, it also led to increased difficulties for intergovernmental relations. After 2000, there were significant tensions between the mayor and the central government and the power relationship between the GLA and the lower-tier authorities has been an ongoing struggle.

Delinking: Are World City-Regions Becoming More Autonomous?

Finally, does the economic primacy of being a world city-region bring new political power in relation to the nation-state? Although it is not possible to ascertain how much economic delinkage actually has occurred for the GCRs, our survey evaluates signs of political autonomization. As noted in the introduction, there are reasons to think that globalization enhances the ability of world city-regions to influence national policies. In order to succeed in international markets, national governments (and equally state and provincial governments) rely on the success of their most important economic engines, especially big regional ones. Over time, these regional systems may begin to delink or become more politically autonomous in driving their own development. But if this happens, it is unlikely that higher-level governments find virtue in allowing regional economic power houses to have the freedom and flexibility to shape their own economic destinies. What benefits a particular part of the national economy is not necessarily identical to what serves the whole. For example, the global finance sector, which plays a big role in world city economies is a much smaller presence in the national one. Higher-level governments are likely to resist delegating freedom of action to these subordinate giants, particularly when city-regions are also capitals of their nation-states. For this reason, greater intergovernmental conflict would be expected over new claims for greater political autonomy.

Given our limited time period and lack of any precise way of measuring autonomization, we look back at the broad patterns of GCR decision making for signs of the direction of change. The overall trend seems clear: Tightening national–local political linkages are occurring, rather than evidence of greater regional political autonomy.

The greatest tightening of national–local political linkage occurred in Tokyo. The Tokyo region dominates the Japanese economy to a degree not found elsewhere. Nevertheless, in Japan the relationship between national and local governments has long placed national authorities in charge of urban development, especially in its capital region. As globalization and industrial restructuring contributed to upgrading the economic status of Tokyo, the expectation grew even more that Tokyo, and particularly its central area, had to be reshaped and modernized to remain an engine to drive the whole national economy forward. At the same time, however, the national government had a duty to strike a balance between Tokyo and the rest of Japan.

Against the background of severe economic problems in the 1990s, the national government relied more than ever on Tokyo's global city function for reviving the national economy. For example, the national government had long maintained policies to redistribute wealth raised from Tokyo to other regions and cities. These programs were changed by national authorities after the 1990s as the economic situation, national budget deficit, and Tokyo's needs for reinvestment made it difficult to continue them. Reinvestment in Tokyo, particularly in its central core, was started by the close collaboration between Prime Minister Koizumi and Governor Ishihara. Prime examples include changing zoning regulations in the CBD, new megaprojects, reintroduction of international flights to Haneda airport, and giving financial backing to the failed Olympic bid for 2016. All of these decisions were crucial for regional and national economic recovery, but none of them were a reflection of new TMG power. Rather, all were made possible by the close collaboration between national and TMG officials pursuing similar objectives no matter which party was in power at the local or national levels of government. Even under the Democratic Party of Japan, which replaced the LDP in 2009, and despite drastic cutbacks in public spending, big infrastructure projects such as a new runway in Haneda airport remain on course without much contestation. However, in recent years decentralization and the need for a regional approach have been issues of increasing debate.

The Paris region also remained in the tight grip of the French state. There has been a movement toward greater decentralization since the early 1980s due to political reforms that affected all of France. The greater autonomy gained by local governments from these reforms has not significantly resulted in greater independence of action on the part of governments in Paris or Île de France despite their growing world city status. The competitiveness of Île de France now (especially during the last three years) is the focus of the national government. Signs of greater dependence of Île de France on the national government include a new minister for Paris and more direct and extensive intervention of national authorities in organizing regional affairs. Today many observers and local elected officials speak of a return of the state. A recent bill introduced into Parliament would give the state greater control over transport and urban development policy.

Whether a return of the state is happening remains to be seen. Nevertheless, the assertion of central governmental power in the capital region is meeting obstacles. The state does not have the same legitimacy as before because of the decentralization process that is now decades-old. Nor does it have the means to go its own way because it is unable to carry out its strategies and policies alone in a context where the involvement of local governments and other actors, such as the business sector, matter. A good illustration of this situation is the Grand Paris project, which would cost a rough estimate of between €21 to €35 billion over the next 15 years. The state can only put in a small part of the money and must turn to local governments and other actors for cooperation in the achievement of this project. Nevertheless, there is little sign that regional economic power is substantially changing political relations in favor of local actors.

The London region also has not been able to transform economic muscle into new political power. The southeast region not only lacked a regional voice throughout the survey period, but the central government has also controlled changes in regional policy. This region includes such a high proportion of the national GDP that it would become hugely powerful if it were to get its own regional government along the lines of Scotland or Wales. For that reason alone, Parliament continually made and remade London's governing institutions to serve their own interests, rather than substantially responding to regional political claims. When the GLC was challenging the central government led by Mrs. Thatcher in the 1980s, the GLC was abolished and the voice of metropolitan London disappeared for fourteen years. Pressure to reestablish a London government eventually led to the establishment of the GLA, but this was part of a governmental decentralization process that also included giving more political autonomy to Wales and Scotland. Devolution to London was highly circumscribed, particularly with respect to finance, governmental authority, and reach into the functional economic region. There is no doubt that the establishment of an elected mayor has given a stronger voice to London, but at the end of the day the central government's control of finances gives them ultimate control.

The New York region remained least coordinated by higher-level governments compared to the other three world cities. In large part, this is because of US federalism. The lack of a federal governmental tradition of regional planning and the importance of state government responsibility for so many economic and social policies invariably contain federal coordination, leaving the states as the key higher governmental players. Yet the state governors and legislative leaders have steadily tightened their control of regional development to a point where their approval is often necessary for specific development projects of any significance or for most big environmental initiatives. This has happened despite the fact that this intervention has tended to be sporadic, piecemeal, and relatively uncoordinated compared to patterns found in the GCRs with more integrated national governmental systems.

The New York region's relationship with the federal government grew more distant along with the increasing importance of the region's economy. In part, this was due to declining levels of grant assistance and the dismantling of many national urban programs since the 1980s. Although federal programs in transportation were subject to a small degree of regional oversight after federal legislation was passed requiring it as a condition of grant assistance, this never provided a strong platform for federal intervention.

Although federal governmental political coordination of the region has not grown much, the region has still become more reliant on federal governmental intervention. As the regional economy became increasingly dependent on financial services and international business, business and governmental leaders saw themselves having a big stake in a whole range of national regulatory and fiscal policies. But these issues rarely are significantly influenced by regional political pressures alone, rendering little opportunity for asserting local interests even on matters that are at the center of the region's development. This reality was underscored during the global financial crises starting in 2008. Wall Street and the other financial sectors that dominate the city and region were among the largest US recipients of federal monies, loans, and guarantees when Washington launched bailouts of the troubled industries. Even the massive economic stimulus passed by Congress provided a big spurt in federal grant assistance, but little more federal coordination of its wide-ranging programs. New York region governments were swept along in a tide of cash and regulations over which they had little influence.

Global City-Regions in Transition: Why Governance Matters

There are few signs of GCRs being pushed down a common pathway where local political choices are few or diminishing, making them ungovernable. Rather, divergence rivals commonalities in the ways these global power centers are managing the issues precipitated by their economic success. Indeed, local politics and policy choices matter a great deal, but in ways defying easy generalization or indicative of a single politics of world cities driven by global currents.

With respect to public policy, all of the GCRs are contending with essentially similar problems of economic modernization, addressing similar forms of social division and seeking to upgrade their environment and their quality of life to meet world standard expectations. The strongest area of regional policy convergence is in economic policy. There is a high degree of absorption by most city, suburban, and regional agencies with issues of economic competitiveness. Issues and programs for promoting regional growth and addressing local developmental obstacles were prominent almost everywhere. These issues easily percolated and diffused through even the most fragmented or organized regional political networks to appear on local, regional, and national agendas. By contrast, issues of social equity, the environment, and quality of life were treated in more isolated fashion unless tied to compelling matters of economic competitiveness.

This pattern of policy convergence, important as it is, does not suggest a single model of regional politics centered on growth, as some globalization theorists fear. First, progrowth issues were rarely characterized by much consensus among governments and agencies around specific programs for enhancing regional competitiveness. Diverse local visions of what programs of intervention could best stimulate the regional economy prevailed in every metropolitan area, often creating conflicts among local governments and higher governmental agencies. Though world city-regions are quite similar economic engines, each has considerable political slack for choosing ways of competing, drawing on many of their unique comparative advantages as places to live and work.

Second, the extent to which particular governments privilege the issue of economic competitiveness varies considerably. High priority characterizes Tokyo, London, and New York, but less in Paris, where national officials intervened to counter the limited involvement of some local governments in this area of public policy, but with only limited success.

Third, and perhaps most important, when governments were highly active in promoting business development, this did not necessarily diminish their policy efforts in the other program areas, promoting social equality and upgrading environmental standards. Regional political networks as a whole were less engaged in attending to the social fallout of their economic development. But policy contributions by higher-level governments commonly played a huge compensatory role where local and regional governmental agencies faltered or lacked resources for redistributive social programs or supporting green measures. Social and environmental policy responses are closely linked to national or (in the United States) state regulatory and welfare regimes rather than to local and regional systems. Differences in national safety net programs, not regional policies, mainly set prevailing political expectations and created or diminished local opportunities for social intervention.

Some political convergence is also evident in governance. But there is little sign that global pressures are fostering a common model organized around boosting economic competitiveness. Most important, there were only feeble signs of regionalization of local governance. Although there are reasons for expecting that lateral intergovernmental cooperation might grow as governments and communities within these metropolitan areas became more economically interdependent, only limited efforts in this direction were made anywhere. London witnessed the creation of a new strategic authority, but it has limited political boundaries that exclude much of the city-region. Paris saw the creation of some new regional planning bodies and conferences, but these lacked much power to implement their decisions and were in steady rivalry. Tokyo's big central area government remained as it had been for years. The New York tri-state area also failed to create any major political institutions to bridge its fragmented governmental networks.

None of the metropolitan areas experienced significant growth of new public or private regional leadership. Although mayors of the core cities within each metro area sometimes tried to assert a regional voice, there were few instances when this proved very successful or sustainable. In particular, stable regional coalitions failed to develop, even though governments sometimes came together to support particular projects when sponsored by higher-level governments. Finally, strong leadership by business groups also failed to materialize even in contexts where public sector regional leadership was in particularly big deficit, as in the New York metropolitan area. At best, corporate business players undertook to organize for brief periods in response to particular issues. In sum, the governance of the world city-regions has undergone substantial change, but a more cohesive and better organized politics has not yet materialized.

Perhaps the major form of political regionalization found in all four of the cases is the increasing role of national or other higher-level governments in managing issues having regional impact. Although there were fairly important differences in the ways and extent to which this was happening, there is little doubt displacement of problem solving to distant officials at higher levels was increasing in significance. Paralleling this trend, political autonomization was not much in evidence. Tokyo remained in tighter grip of national authorities after the nation's economic collapse in the 1990s. In Paris and London, economic development issues were actively managed by national authorities through the creation of new agencies, new programs, or even new metropolitan governments (as in London). Even in tri-state New York, state officials became more actively engaged in monitoring, approving, and funding economic development projects through state agencies with regional responsibilities or through direct action by governors and legislatures.

These efforts by higher-level governments did not seem to diminish the tendencies for division among governments within the various GCRs, however. Governmental fragmentation has grown almost everywhere. In Tokyo and London, large-scale metro governments failed to match the economic scale of the regions and left most issues of regional impact to local governments and national agencies to navigate and bargain over. In Paris and New York, weak regional leadership centers, continued fragmentation among governmental jurisdictions, and the failure of new or old regional forums to assume much power enabled disorganized politics to dominate most matters of regional scope.

In sum, world city-region politics remains highly variable because so much is influenced by the political logic flowing from each locality, multigovernmental networks, and particular national governmental contexts. Although internationalizing forces may be pulling four of the world's leading economic urban centers into common orbits, the political management of these capitals of capitalism are firmly bound up in local pathways, interests, and policy preferences. Their responses to global forces follow some common patterns, but they are as much a matter of governance as globalism.

Conclusion: Are Global City-Regions Governable?

Governability and Global City-Regions

LIFE AT THE TOP OF THE urban hierarchy entails a process of almost continuous social change and political transition at the bottom. Indeed, our survey has shown how the global economic success of global city-regions (GCRs) is contingent on their governments helping to make this so. It is difficult to separate the social and economic progress of a GCR from its governmental system. Both are linked in inextricable ways. For this reason, governability matters in GCRs. It matters in how land is developed, what gets developed, where new centers arise, how built environments are created, and who gains or loses. This pertains to areas as different as central business district (CBD) cores, university campuses, and industrial poles located along the urban peripheries. Without government intervention on a regional scale, business would languish and the social stresses accompanying urban regional development, such as access to affordable housing, would grow to unacceptable proportions. Governability especially matters for providing in timely fashion the critical infrastructure that integrates disparate parts of the GCR. This network of bridges, tunnels, highways, and mass-transit systems is invariably changing across entire regions and is constantly modernizing. Without successful regional transportation systems, the London, New York, Paris, and Tokyo GCRs would neither be *great* nor could they legitimately be called *city-regions*.

Although they may be successful as world economic giants, are they truly governable? How well do their governmental systems perform the critical functions necessary for GCRs to flourish as social and economic leaders? Even if they are presently governable, can these political systems remain governable in the future as GCRs change and develop during the twenty-first century?

Judging governability is difficult, if only because there is little consensus among academic experts or practitioners about the meaning of this term. The concept has been debated extensively and definitions often vary by national culture and governmental function.[1] Sometimes governability entails the issue of how well the democratic features of a political system enable government to serve its citizens. In the United States, this view is found among those who fear too much democracy undermines good government (Crozier, Huntington, and Watanuki 1975; Yates 1978). These critics believe excessive group conflict—or hyperpluralism—weakens government performance and even a common sense of citizenship. In Europe and Japan, the focus of the governability debate usually has been about preserving the role of the nation-state while encouraging governmental decentralization or legislative devolution. In Britain and in North America, the question of governability often addresses how much governmental authorities should rely on the private sector in carrying out public sector responsibilities (Savas 2005; Wolman and Goldsmith 1992).[2] Others look at governability as a matter of service delivery (Osborne and Gaebler 1992). Finally, governability is also viewed as governance—a process through which localities cooperate through voluntary interlocal agreements with the objective of sharing resources or undertaking mutually beneficial regulation (Ostrom, Tiebout, and Warren 1961; Parks and Oakerson 1989).

Concepts of Governability

Despite lack of agreement, it is still possible to consider whether our GCRs are governable or ungovernable without reconciling all perspectives. Understanding the different ways political institutions may bring about cooperation and develop policy responses within GCRs can do this. Such an approach seeks to evaluate governability from more than one perspective; it also employs different concepts or heuristic types to capture those perspectives (Weber 1947). By using this device, we are able to identify three different modes or capstone concepts for achieving governability: (1) integrated governance, (2) pragmatic adjustment, and (3) polycentric competition. Each concept values different organizational properties of governmental systems and different processes in performing public responsibilities.

Figure C.1 can better guide our discussion. The figure shows three concepts of governance along a continuum ranging from most to least organized by central decision makers. In this figure, the placement of our four GCRs along this continuum indicates that all of them fall under varying degrees of pragmatic adjustment. For illustrative purposes, however, we provide examples of other political entities to describe integrated governance and polycentric competition. The following discussion begins with two very opposite capstone concepts: integrated governance versus polycentric competition. It is followed by discussion of the prevailing form of governance in our GCRs, pragmatic adjustment.

INTEGRATED GOVERNANCE

Integrated governance looks at governability with respect to how well a political system is organized for the purpose of bringing together different centers of power in order to achieve collective goals. This implies an integrated system of governmental actors capable of imposing its authority and power on particularistic as well as

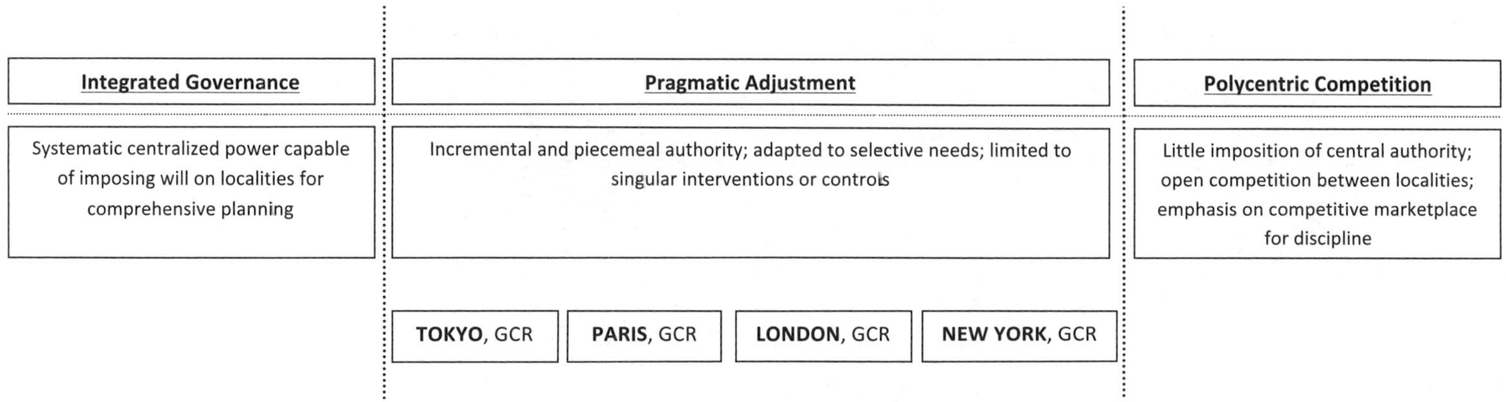

Integrated Governance	Pragmatic Adjustment	Polycentric Competition
Systematic centralized power capable of imposing will on localities for comprehensive planning	Incremental and piecemeal authority; adapted to selective needs; limited to singular interventions or controls	Little imposition of central authority; open competition between localities; emphasis on competitive marketplace for discipline
	TOKYO, GCR **PARIS**, GCR **LONDON**, GCR **NEW YORK**, GCR	

Figure C.1. Types of Governability: A Continuum

transsectoral interests by means of public policies and future visions espoused by leadership. Although integrated governance implies the need for considerable central-ization of power in order to function, it is not always necessary to rely on command-and-control functions. This kind of government can also occur if there is widespread political agreement among interests and decision makers. For example, such a con-sensus may be based on ideology, threat of an external enemy, economic crisis, or common shared political objectives. Integrated governance is also possible by invok-ing incentives or sanctions on particularistic interests. While this effort at governabil-ity has often emerged during wartime or by dictatorships, it has also been tried by de-mocracies in crisis (Putnam 1996). Phillip Selznick (1966) describes how, during the Great Depression, the head of the Tennessee Valley Authority (TVA) decisively gov-erned a large region in the United States by the cooptation of local leaders. The TVA carried out a centralized comprehensive plan for bringing electricity to southwestern portions of the country in dire need of modern energy. Similarly, Jim Bulpitt (1986) writes about central authorities in the United Kingdom during World War II being able to impose their will on local government authorities and agencies, either by coercion or by penetrating local institutions. The ministries at Whitehall were then able to mo-bilize local population within a specific framework of public action.

By these standards, it is doubtful that any of our four city-regions could qualify as integrated governance. In the preceding chapters, we have seen that power and au-thority are frequently divided in all our GCRs, although in very different ways. This often makes it impossible for many metropolitan-wide policies to routinely emerge as coherent planned programs. Some GCRs, such as the Tokyo region, have more integrated-style governance than others, and in France the state assumes a special presence not found in the London or New York regions. Yet even in Japan the central government has not been supportive of comprehensive planning by a single authority, and the Tokyo Metropolitan Government (TMG) is in rivalry with scatterings of other state agencies having specialized competencies in the central area as well as in the larger metropolitan region. In France, the central government, regional agencies, and local governments are in extensive rivalry despite the unitary character of the general governmental order. More often than not, policy challenges linked to global city devel-opment have not been met by integrated governmental action unless imposed upon local governments by higher-level governments. In particular, absence of integrated governance is most glaring on issues involving social inequalities, including income and housing disparities, access to jobs, environmental justice, and other matters of broad community concern. Even on most economic policies with regional implica-tions, there is remarkably little sustained planning supported by widespread intergov-ernmental collaboration. Indeed, the failure of extensive policy integration to emerge on these issues could threaten the sustainability of our GCRs over the long term, as discussed later in this chapter.

POLYCENTRIC COMPETITION

An alternative way of judging governability gives greater value to the virtues of government fragmentation. From this perspective, fragmented governments behave as if they were in a marketplace and compete with one another to attract residents. Polycentric competition enables citizens and businesses to "vote with their feet" by finding localities that offer optimal packages of services and tax burdens. Overall, the competition is supposed to produce more efficient services and ultimately provide a GCR with better governance. In this framework, political fragmentation and even rivalry are not necessarily viewed as debilitating for regional governance. Indeed, fragmentation is seen as functional because it provides choices to citizen-consumers and forces each locality to be more efficient. According to this reasoning, if localities are more efficient, a healthy region will emerge. Rather than a single government exercising control, a competitive public marketplace disciplines unworthy localities to perform better. Representing the "public choice" school, this notion of governability has a long tradition in the United States. Its advocates claim polycentric competition is more responsive to heterogeneous citizen preferences and therefore more democratic (Advisory Commission 1988; Ostrom, Tiebout, and Warren 1961).

Although this notion of governability has a convincing logic, the conditions it assumes are rarely achieved very often in the real world (Handler 1996; Keating 1995). For example, most citizens or businesses in city-regions are in fact not very mobile or lack many alternative service providers. Nevertheless, approximations of this model of governance are often considered to have profound implications for urban political systems everywhere, if only because size and scale matter in organizing and delivering efficient public services. Consequently, intergovernmental competitiveness, decentralization, and the idea of breaking up bureaucratic monopolies of power have gained traction among governmental reformers (Osborne and Gaebler 1992; Savas 1996; Schneider 1989).

From this perspective, our GCRs decidedly lack governability. In none of the city-regions is there extensive and fluid economic competition between governments across a broad range of services necessary to permit much choice for voter-consumers. In London, Paris, and Tokyo, the local and metropolitan governments can rely on outside sources for revenues, thereby diminishing fiscal pressures for them to engage in economic competition. Only in the New York region do local governments have enough fiscal autonomy to spur them to undertake aggressive competition. But even in this GCR, state governments interject themselves in local affairs by establishing policy mandates and tax restrictions that constrain competition. Besides, the ability of localities to engage in free-wheeling competition is also limited by access to transportation networks and other resources provided by agencies like the Port Authority of New York and New Jersey (PANYNJ). The autonomy that does exist allows localities to avoid shouldering social responsibilities and is a source of extensive social segregation, thus inefficiently concentrating the poor away from jobs and opportunities.

PRAGMATIC ADJUSTMENT

Another way of looking at governability is to view GCRs as engaging in incremental local cooperation. Using this lens, networks of localities can produce collective policies through interlocal agreements, coalition building on particular issues or programs, or delegating specialized functions to other public agencies. Various forms of political fragmentation characterize most democratic political systems; interest conflicts that get represented in them are often deeply rooted in history and are difficult to reconcile. Nevertheless, public officials sometimes find ways of pulling together despite these intergovernmental barriers and social divisions. Moreover, some policy responsibilities, such as environmental protection, cannot be efficiently provided by small-scale governments. This model assumes these services can be spun off to special regional governmental authorities, whose scale is more appropriate to the task. The result is a system capable of asserting some policy direction and collective responsibility. In this case, one can argue a case for governability—even if it is piecemeal and episodic (Kantor 2008; Savitch and Vogel 1996, 2000, 2009).

If this test is applied, all of our city-regions can be considered governable. Our review of thirty years is essentially a story of how fragmented, overlapping, and competing governmental actors constantly struggle to achieve limited, but significant, policy steering capability as they confront essentially similar issues of global city development. For example, in all of our cases, public transport is organized and successfully operated on somewhat of a regional scale. Horizontal or vertical cooperation among public authorities that compose the various GCRs is commonly difficult, especially in New York, London, and Paris, where power is most fragmented. Yet our analysis has shown how programs involving multiple governments have often emerged in all three metropolitan areas to stimulate economic modernization of local and regional economies.

By the same token, many social safety net programs that would strain the fiscal and administrative capacities of city-region governments are routinely handed off to national or other higher governmental authorities. Failures of metropolitan governments in the social realm or in environmental policy are often compensated by the actions of higher-level authorities running national programs. Despite their shortcomings, governments in all our GCRs managed to relieve many social and environmental hardships. They accomplished this in varying degrees and with mixed success. This relief could be seen in the publicly assisted housing and green space that allow modest-income classes some respite from the hardships of urban life. Without this intervention, our GCRs would be even more polarized than they are today and far less liveable as urban communities. To be sure, our GCRs have approached these issues differently. London relied on the central government with a metropolitan government to fill in vital functions; New York depended on public benefit corporations (PBCs) and bi-state authorities to patch together regional services; while Paris and Tokyo used the central government and bureaucratic discretion to bridge gaps in housing, universities, and economic development.

All of the four city-regions are governmental patchworks to a greater or lesser degree. None is organized to be coterminous with the actual interdependent metropolitan economy. Nevertheless, informal coordination among the various governmental parts of our city-regions permits them to realize certain common metropolitan-wide objectives. That is why each of the city-regions have increasingly turned to instruments such as PBCs, quangos, or special administrative agencies of one sort or another to carry out many intergovernmental functions, especially in infrastructure development, business development, and transportation. None of our city-regions are rudderless. In fits and starts, each has been able to mount enough sustained policy effort to measurably enhance economic competitiveness, social cohesion, and environmental quality during thirty years. Exactly how much effective governability each of the four city-regions has obtained in this way is difficult to assess. But their current levels have enabled them to obtain world economic and cultural leadership, while continuing to attract and sustain broad political support by their citizens and businesses.

Admittedly, achieving this kind of performance offers only a moderate threshold of political success. There are severe limitations to governability through pragmatic adjustment. One limitation is the inherent political bias in such fragmented government. Our analysis shows how all four GCRs are more capable of pulling together for promoting economic competitiveness than they are for addressing problems of social inequality or promoting better environmental quality. Those who govern GCRs tend to place a high priority on obtaining competitiveness in the global economic marketplace. Even in Paris, where many local and some regional officials gave exceptional attention to other regional objectives, their ability to shift policy away from concerns with economic development was limited. Their priorities have been challenged by pressures from the national government and weakened by lack of resources for changing policy direction.

Issues of regional scope, such as cases of airport locations, commercial land use development, and other projects considered strategic for attracting or retaining business investment receive sustained and diffuse attention from multiple governments because policy makers respond most easily to the threat of losing the game of global economic competition. Although they are not organized in accord with the competitive polyarchy model, fragmented governance and economic pressures at the local, regional, and international levels ensure rivalry for resources, power, and autonomy; this makes public decision makers at all governmental levels relatively responsive to pressures of economic competition. By contrast, the absence of equally compelling pressures to attend to the social miseries and costs of global city development makes collaboration among multiple groups, governments, and state agencies more difficult to sustain. This is true whether regional governance is the most decentralized (New York), segmented (London), or moderately decentralized in the hands of bureaucratic agencies (Paris and Tokyo). Social needs of citizens in our city-regions were addressed to varying degrees by national governments, state governments, and local-level authorities. But these issues usually did not appear prominently on regional or metropolitan agendas. This reality often generated conflicts or differences in priority between levels of government, whether national, regional, metropolitan, or local.

Pragmatic adjustment also presents problems for democracy and accountability. By relying extensively on informal governmental mechanisms to address region-wide problems or, in some cities, relying on actions of the national government, democratic participation in metropolitan areas becomes more difficult. When responsibility for many governmental activities is broken up and parcelled among multiple layers and kinds of public agencies, it is difficult for voters and organized interests to assign accountability for governmental performance. In particular, when issues spill over the borders of particular governmental jurisdictions in the metropolis, citizen efforts to inform policy makers or to seek changes in policy direction do not easily materialize. They easily fail because they are difficult to organize without an integrated and powerful political center at the metropolitan level.[3]

For example, without more integrated social and economic policies, the degradation of the living conditions of some inhabitants in terms of transport access, jobs, housing, and safety has the potential to increase social and political polarization. This can threaten mobilizing political support for policy innovation to address new conditions. As new global economic rivals emerge, the capability of our city-regions to engage in much forward metropolitan-wide planning could undermine their ability to adapt and remain competitive.

After everything else, informal and fragmented governance rewards short-term policy making while discouraging long-term planning. Global city governance has to address a wide range of policy issues having many different characteristics, some long-term, some short-term, some with local impact, some with regional impact, and each involving different interest considerations. The inability to draw all these dimensions together in order to establish priorities, evaluate worthwhile policy directions, and assess overall governmental performance discourages investing political capital into long-term planning around metropolitan-wide issues. The result is that some issues, such as climate change, social polarization, and quality of life, fall into policy voids, receiving less attention by the government at the metropolitan level. Only in Greater London since 2000 does the governmental system provide a well-organized metropolitan body with the ability to prepare long-term strategies, although limited to a particular set of functions. Nevertheless, the Greater London Authority's (GLA) weak resources and partial geographic reach limit its effectiveness. In London and elsewhere, local governments are absorbed with day to day chores, while strategic decisions are left to agencies with very limited power or are nobody's task.

Pragmatic adjustment may be an inherent characteristic of most GCRs. It may not be coincidental that all of our GCRs fall within the capstone concept of pragmatic adjustment governance. This may well be because advanced societies are by nature complex, and complexities breed pluralism and independence on the part of power brokers, private as well as public. As a consequence, coordination replaces command and second-best solutions are the only possibility (Kantor 2010; Savitch 2010) in organizing complex GCRs in pluralistic societies.

Where Are They Headed?

Where are GCRs headed as systems of governance? First, GCRs tend to succeed despite chronic governmental deficiencies. The continuous economic success of London, Paris, New York, and Tokyo is testament to the fact that the age of the GCR has arrived. The economic and governmental workings of city and metropolitan regions cannot be separated in practice even if they are fragmented politically. The historic urban centers and the peripheries of these global metropolises work as one as economies, as social communities, and as political orders despite their lack of highly integrated or efficient political systems. Although it is possible they would work better if they were more governable, we have no empirical basis for making such a projection. Given their ability to muddle through politically so far in so many ways, there is little reason to think they will not continue to remain leading GCRs for the short term. Nevertheless, their failure to pull more together for regional purposes, their short-term politics, and their uneven responsiveness to economic, social, and environmental issues may intensify their social problems as time goes on. Our analysis shows how each of these political orders has not yet demonstrated much capability for addressing serious social and economic problems that are unlikely to go away on their own. This is a profound political deficiency whose consequences may grow in time.

Second, improvements in governability are likely to remain difficult. It is possible that growing interdependence of city and suburban areas may bring about more governmental cohesion and political collaboration in the long run, as some urban scholars predict. In this case, more integrated or efficient governance may emerge. Nevertheless, our survey has not discovered many signs of this. To the contrary, there are powerful countervailing political forces discouraging this. One is the continuous weakness of territorial leadership in GCRs. Although the mayors of our central cities have intervened at the regional level and have tried to address city-region issues, they have not yet been able to build lasting regional coalitions or launch significant sustained programs of metropolitan governance. Fragmented city-region political systems do not offer many incentives that facilitate risk taking by even powerful and popular mayors, nor do they encourage the emergence of new political entrepreneurs devoted to this task.

Further, the promotion of sustained metropolitan political leadership is unlikely to come from the top. Divided power in the US federal system makes cross-state political collaboration on metropolitan governance issues uncommon and difficult. Even in unitary governmental orders, nation-states are wary of the political emancipation of city-regions. National officials see them as potential rivals whose economies profoundly affect national interests. The strategic importance of GCRs challenges the power and oversight of nation-state governments. Nevertheless, they remain very much in charge. If one considers the fragmentation and the rivalries in city-region governance systems on one hand, and the significant legal, political, financial, and economic resources of the nation-states on the other, it would not be surprising to think of them as potential masters of their major city-regions.

At the same time, however, national governmental authorities have little interest in taking direct charge of the governability of GCRs. In our survey, there is little sign of them asserting much political leadership in these territories except in unusual in-stances, such as in reorganizing government in London (most often to fulfil national partisan agendas) or prodding local governments in Paris to give more attention to economic issues. Nevertheless, national officials are generally reluctant to act as rou-tine policy mediators on metropolitan matters or in imposing their own visions of the future on these city-regions. Rather, even in the most unitary systems, such as Tokyo, they operate more subtle forms of control through setting frameworks, strategic pri-orities, legal limits, or financial constraints.

In sum, GCRs face difficult choices. On one hand, they are economic giants with a global reach and premier cultural status. On the other hand, they continually struggle to manage the social consequences of that success, calling into question their govern-ability. The crucible for our four city-regions is whether they can resolve this disequi-librium or continue to muddle along.

Notes

Introduction

1. Unless otherwise indicated, *global cities* and *global city-regions* are used interchangeably to mean the central areas and economic periphery, as elaborated later in this chapter.

2. For instance, the Globalization and World City Network Group or GaWC (GaWC 2000; see also Taylor 2004, 69) calculated the number of linkages in certain global business services for more than 300 cities. GaWC found London and New York occupying first and second place, followed by Paris in the fourth rank and Tokyo occupying the fiftieth rank. Other sources may yield different results. Nevertheless, as one prominent researcher put it, "there are only four cities all authorities agree upon: London, New York, Paris and Tokyo" (Taylor 2004, 39).

3. By governability, we mean the capacity of governmental institutions to function collectively in order to make authoritative decisions in order to solve common problems (Laswell 1936; Norris 2001; Chubb and Peterson 1989, 1–3). This also entails the control, regulation, or distribution values within the territorial parameters of a city-region. In using this definition, we also recognize that there are few absolutes in political life, and governability may be partial or apply to limited set of functions within a city-region. Thus, governability can also be viewed in relative terms or as a given point along a continuum of political capability.

4. Of course, governability is an important interest of all governments and citizens. This interest is likely to be pursued even if it has some economic costs. As Polanyi (1944) argued, economic revolutions are also political revolutions. Governmental activity is central to the success of economic innovation in capitalism. In his survey of the Industrial Revolution, Polanyi observed how the development of market capitalism necessitated widespread involvement of the state. He described why government at various levels was crucial for the development of industrial capitalism by organizing it, regulating its impact on business and labor alike, and by dealing with its social fallout. His conclusion was that free-wheeling markets are purely fictional; virtually all interests, including business, have a stake in using public means for managing the social consequences of market activities. If government's role were reduced to passive accommodation of economic change dictated by market pressures alone, it would undermine capitalism itself, not to mention the credibility and legitimacy of political institutions in general and even faith in democracy.

5. Political delinking occurs when national or higher-level governments shed governmental responsibilities, or lower-level government demands and receives more decisional autonomy.

6. According to these authors, such systems are frequently found in three major sectors: high technology, revitalized craft production, and as advanced producer and financial services. They are also becoming more important elsewhere.

7. Some theorists view so-called collective competition goods in local production systems as central elements in the regional enterprise; they believe public and private orchestration of planning, financing, and administration of these economic enclaves is central to their success (Crouch et al. 2001).

8. Consequently, geohistorical views of regionalization lack much precision about how much and where different or similar trends are emerging. It is ambiguous about the particular local policy responses or institutional mechanisms that are supposed to be fulfilling the need for growing "meso" or "regional" management of social and economic change (Brenner 2004, 22–23).

1. Four Global City-Regions: A Profile

1. As shown in the introduction, we employ four geographic subdivisions to examine our four city-regions. These are (1) the urban core or CBD, (2) the municipal area, (3) the region less the municipal area (rest of the region), and (4) the region or city-region. Two of these classifications—the municipal area (sometimes referred to as the metropolitan area and sometimes simply as the city) and the region—are most frequently used throughout this volume. When our subjects are not specified in either the text or a footnote, readers should understand that to mean the city-region.

2. Not shown in the table is rank number three, which is occupied by Hong Kong.

3. Figures are adjusted according to the household size.

4. Our data pertain to the municipality, not the region, unless otherwise stated.

5. Their primary purpose is to provide a tool for human resource managers and expatriate executives to compare cost of living and to calculate fair compensation policies for relocating employees, taking into consideration hardship based on living conditions. They collect and evaluate many kinds of information. For example, the Mercer Quality of Living Survey looks at thirty-nine quality-of-life variables from 235 cities grouped into ten categories, such as consumer goods, housing, medical and health care, recreation, and so forth. These variables are given different weights in leading to an overall conclusion about relative living standards in each city (but not metropolitan regions).

3. Strong Metropolitan Leadership

1. Although for comparative purposes in chapter 1 we described the Greater London Authority area as the "municipal area," in this chapter we will use the term "metropolitan area," as this is how it is described in all the London literature and policy documents.

4. Fragmented Metropolis, Decentralist Impulses

1. According to the latest publications of the US Bureau of the Census, the actual number of counties within the New York CSA is thirty-two. However, two counties (Middlesex, Connecticut, and Warren, New Jersey) lie only partially within this region and we have excluded them from this analysis, bringing our total to thirty. Note also that there is a Middlesex County in New Jersey and, as opposed to its namesake in Connecticut, is included in the CSA.

2. Reference to "the city" takes on peculiar meanings in New York. Residents of the Bronx, Brooklyn, Queens, and Staten Island often refer to Manhattan as "the city," while the use of this term in the distant and nearby suburbs can refer to either Manhattan or all five boroughs of New York City.

3. The notable exceptions are Staten Island and large parts of Westchester, Nassau, and Fairfield counties.

4. In addition to the port authority, there are three other very minor bi-state agencies that were also formed by interstate compact, the most prominent of which is the Palisades Interstate Park Commission, which maintains a stretch of parkland overlooking the Hudson River.

5. Parts of this discussion and factual information follow Kantor (forthcoming).

5. Managed Pluralism

1. Discussion of the Sterling Forest experience draws extensively on Botshon (2007).

6. A Fragmented and Conflicting Territory

1. A firm that wanted to settle in the Paris area had to receive the agreement of the state through a formal procedure.

7. Unregulated Competitive Decentralization

1. The Greens were already in the ruling political coalition at the regional level in 1998 but this coalition was more fragmented and unstable.

2. Paris-Plage, literally "Paris-Beach," is the transformation of the Seine riverbanks into beaches during the summer.

3. Vélib is an almost free rent-a-bike system all over the city of Paris and the first ring of the urban area. Auto-Lib will do the same with cars.

4. This is a significant pun, *pari* meaning "bet" in French.

8. New Challenges, Old Governance

1. There were also significant numbers of outgoing migrants from the region.

2. The TMR consists of Tokyo and three surrounding prefectures of Chiba, Saitama, and Kanagawa.

3. Those who left school and came into the labor market after the late 1990s are often referred to as a lost generation because of their plight.

4. For example, in 1979, the lowest (band 1) shared 3.5 percent of the total income and the highest (band 10) had 23.1 percent. This changed to 2.9 percent and 24.5 percent, respectively, in 1999.

5. They absorbed the increased population in the central part of Tokyo discussed in the last section.

6. Out-of-town shopping malls and roadside shops exist, but they are not close to the old residential area and not accessible for the elderly who do not drive.

7. "Municipality" means city, town, and village. They have equal legal status but are differentiated by population size.

8. Core cities and special case cities have smaller populations and less autonomy than designated cities.

9. This is sometimes claimed to be evidence of the central control thesis, but it has been revealed that other unitary states collected less than 20 percent (Reed 1986, 19).

10. In 2006, Yubari City in Hokkaido was declared bankrupt, and the responsibility for municipal administration was taken over by the national government.

11. There are four prefectures (TMG, Saitama, Chiba, Kanagawa) and five designated cities (Yoko-hama, Kawasaki, Chiba, Saitama, and Sagamihara). The cities are included due to their legal status, population size, and economic function, which make them major regional political leaders.

12. It is the largest popular vote for a single person in Japan, and can easily become a "beauty contest."

13. For instance, Governor Suzuki in the 1980s kept on good relations with the national administration at that time and followed the LDP.

14. For instance, those ex-bureaucrats who turned into elected politicians. They worked closely with political national leaders and were familiar with the policy-making process in their respective ministries.

15. Governor Ishihara of Tokyo was an MP and ex-minister of the LDP, but he was a maverick within the party.

16. He often made racist and antiforeigner statements in public.

17. In 1888, there were 71,314, and they were naturally created villages based on agricultural society, but they were reduced to 3,472 by 1961.

18. Core cities may undertake all the functions delegated to the designated cities with the exception of those that are more efficient if collectively handled by prefectures. The qualifications for a core city are a minimum population of 300,000 and land area of 100 square kilometers.

19. The administrative function of a special case city is the same as a core city, but the minimum population should be 200,000 to qualify.

9. World City Policies and the Erosion of the Developmental State

1. A similar plan was enacted for the Kansai Metropolitan Region in 1964.

2. The regions are divided into Hokkaido, Tohoku, Kanto, Chubu, Hokuriku, Kinki, Chugoku, Shikoku, and Kyushu.

3. The national administration also announced an intention to reduce CO_2 emissions by 25 percent compared to 1990 levels by 2020, which is a tougher measure.

4. The national capital region is bigger than TMR and includes Tochigi, Gunma, and Ibaragi prefectures located in the north of TMR.

5. The idea was first proposed in 1990 as a remedy against overconcentration of Tokyo and enacted in 1992. However, after the bubble collapse, the plan was suspended.

6. There was also a strong suspicion that he tried to use the region as a political platform to challenge the national political leadership.

7. This is now commonly called "circular megalopolis concept."

8. "Hub airport" means that passengers can be transferred between international and domestic flights at the same airport.

9. The construction of Narita airport cost so much money, time, and lives as a result of compulsory purchase and strong opposition from the landowners that the national government was morally obliged to maximize the capacity of the airport.

10. This can be accessed at http://www.9tokenshi-syunoukaigi.jp/pdf/forumu_kaisaigaiyou1.pdf.

11. The document can be accessed at http://www.9tokenshi-syunoukaigi.jp/pdf/forum_houkokusyo3.pdf.

12. His right-wing, ultranationalistic view is well known and he has many political enemies.

10. Governance and Globalism

1. For instance, the proposal envisioned three ring roads to link core business cities and reduce the traffic passing through central Tokyo.

Conclusion

1. With respect to local politics, see Yates (1978); Wood (1958); Ostrom, Tiebout, and Warren (1961); and Savitch and Vogel (1996).

2. In recent years, this debate has become blurred by the immense literature on urban governance, focusing more on processes than on substance, more on consensus building than on power, although this last concept is staging a comeback (Lefèvre and Weir forthcoming; LeGalès 2003; Travers 2005).

3. For this reason, current research tends to focus on the economic efficiency of the city-region while issues of democracy within the city-region receive less attention (Purcell 2007).

Bibliography

Abu-Lughod, J. 1999. *New York, Chicago, Los Angeles*. Minneapolis: University of Minnesota Press.

Advisory Commission on Intergovernmental Relations. 1988. *Metropolitan Organization: The St. Louis Case*. Washington, D.C.: Author.

Altshuler, A., and D. Luberoff. 2003. *Megaprojects*. Washington, D.C.: Brookings Institution.

Amin, A., ed. 1994. *Post-Fordism: A Reader*. Oxford: Blackwell.

———. 1999. "An Institutionalist Perspective on Regional Economic Development." *International Journal of Urban and Regional Research* 23: 365–78.

Amin, A., and N. Thrift. 1992. "Neo-Marshallian Nodes in Global Networks." *International Journal of Urban and Regional Research* 16: 571–87.

Andersen, H. T. 2002. "Globalization, Social Polarization and the Housing Market." *Danish Journal of Geography* 102.

Applebome, P. 2011. "In a Job-Creation Experiment, New York Regions Are Vying for Development Cash." *New York Times*, November 14: A23.

Asahi Shimbun. 2009. "Haneda Narita Ittai de Katsuyou [Integrated Operation of Haneda and Narita Airport]." *Asahi Shimbun*, October 15: 1.

Ascher, F. 2007. "Paris–Île de France, Comment Gouverner la Métropole Régionale?" Special issue, *Pouvoirs Locaux*, no. 73.

A. T. Kearney, Inc., and the Chicago Council on Global Affairs. 2008. "The 2008 Global Cities Index." *Foreign Policy*, October 15.

Bagli, C. V., and N. Confessore. 2010. "Take the No. 7 to Secaucus? That's a Plan." *New York Times*, November 17: A1, 31.

Barker, K. 2004. *Review of Housing Supply: Final Report Recommendations*. London: Her Majesty's Treasury.

———. 2006. *Review of Land Use Planning: Final Report*. London: Her Majesty's Treasury.

Barnes, R. A., and L. C. Ledebur. 1998. *The New Regional Economics*. Thousand Oaks, Calif.: Sage Publications.

Baxendall, R., and E. Ewen. 2010. "New Immigrants in Suburbia." In *American Urban Politics in a Global Age*, 5th ed., edited by P. Kantor and D. R. Judd, 177–84. New York: Longman.

Bell, D. 1973. *The Coming of Post-Industrial Society: A Venture in Social Forecasting*. New York: Basic Books.

Benjamin, G., and R. P. Nathan. 2001. *Regionalism and Realism: A Study of Governments in the New York Metropolitan Area*. Washington, D.C.: Brookings Institution.

Berg, B., and P. Kantor. 1996. "New York: The Politics of Conflict and Avoidance." In *Regional Politics*, edited by H. V. Savitch and R. K. Vogel, 25–50. Thousand Oaks, Calif.: Sage Publications.

Beveridge, A. 2003. "The Affluent of Manhattan." In *Gotham Gazette*. http://www.gothamgazette .com/article/demographics/20030611/5/421.

Blank, R. M., and R. Haskins, eds. 2001. *The New World of Welfare*. Washington, D.C.: Brookings Institution.

Bollens, S. 2003. "In Through the Back Door: Social Equity and Regional Governance." *Housing Policy Debate* 13, no. l: 631–57.

Botshon, A. 2007. *Saving Sterling Forest*. Albany: State University of New York Press.

Boudreau, J. A., and R. Keil. 2004. "In Search of a New Political Space? City-Regional Institution-Building and Social Activism in Toronto." Paper presented at the annual meeting of the Association of American Geographers, Philadelphia, March 15–19.

Brenner, E. 2009. "The Affordable Housing Holdouts." *New York Times,* August 23: WC RE 9.

Brenner, N. 2001. "World City Theory, Globalization, and the Comparative-Historical Method: Reflections on Janet Abu-Lughod's Interpretation of Contemporary Urban Restructuring." *Urban Affairs Review* 36, no. 6: 124–47.

———. 2003. "Metropolitan Institutional Reform and the Rescaling of State Space in Contemporary Western Europe." *European Urban and Regional Studies* 10, no. 4: 299–324.

———. 2004. *New State Spaces: Urban Governance and the Rescaling of Statehood*. New York: Oxford University Press.

———. 2009. "Open Questions on State Rescaling." *Cambridge Journal of Economies, Regions and Societies* 2, no. 1: 123–39.

Bruegmann, R. 2005. *Sprawl*. Chicago: University of Chicago Press.

Buck, N., I. Gordon, P. Hall, M. Harloe, and M. Kleinman. 2002. *Working Capital: Life and Labour in Contemporary London*. London: Routledge.

Bulpitt, J. 1986. *Territory and Power in the United Kingdom*. Manchester: University of Manchester Press.

———. 1989. "Walking Back to Happiness? Conservative Party Governments and Elected Local Authorities in the 1980s." In *The New Centralism*, edited by C. Crouch and D. Marquand. Oxford: Blackwell.

Burns, P., and M. O. Thomas. 2006. "Power, Politics, and the New Orleans Non-Regime." Paper presented to the American Political Science Association, Philadelphia, August 31.

Burroni, L., and C. Trigilia. 2001. "Italy: Economic Development through Local Economies." In *Local Production Systems in Europe: Rise or Demise?*, edited by C. Crouch, P. LeGalès, C. Trigilia, and H. Voelzkow, 46–78. Oxford: Oxford University Press.

Capital Region Summit. 2002. "Shuto Saisei ni Kansuru Apiiru [Call for the Capital Region Revitalization]." Tokyo, Tokyo Metropolitan Government, Headquarters of the Governor of Tokyo.

Caro, R. 1974. *The Power Broker*. New York: Vintage.

Castells, M. 1989. *The Information City*. Oxford: Basil Blackwell.

CCIP. 2007. "Paris-La Défense, Moteur d'attractivité internationale de l'Île de France." Paris: CCIP.

Central Intelligence Agency. 2004. *World Fact Book*. Washington, D.C.: GPO.

Center for an Urban Future. 2005. *Creative New York*. New York: City Futures.

Chandler, A. D. 1977. *The Visible Hand: The Managerial Revolution in American Business*. Cambridge, Mass.: Belknap Press.

Chase-Dunn, C. 1989. *Global Formation: Structures of the World Economy*. Oxford: Blackwell.

City of London. 2007. *Global Financial Centers Index*. London: City of London.

Clark, T. N., and V. Hoffmann-Martinot, eds. 1998. *The New Political Culture*. Boulder, Colo.: Westview.

Clarke, S. E., and G. L. Gaile. 1998. *The Work of Cities*. Minneapolis: University of Minnesota Press.

Collins, G. 2006. "Ending Years of Dispute, New York Buys the Final Piece of Sterling Forest." *New York Times*, November 28.

Confessore, N. 2008. "$8 Traffic Fee for Manhattan Fails in Albany." *New York Times*, April 8.

Cox, K. R., ed. 1997. *Spaces of Globalization*. London: Guilford Press.

CRIF. 2008. Report of the Commission. "Scenarii pour la métropole Paris-Île-de-France demain." Paris: CRIF.

———. 2008. "Schéma directeur de la région Île de France." Paris: CRIF.

Crouch, C., P. LeGalès, C. Trigilia, and H. Voelzkow, eds. 2001. *Local Production Systems in Europe: Rise or Demise?* Oxford: Oxford University Press.

———. 2004. *Changing Governance of Local Economies*. Oxford: Oxford University Press.

Crozier, M., S. P. Huntington, and J. Watanuki. 1975. *The Crisis of Democracy*. New York: New York University Press.

Currid, E. 2007. *The Warhol Economy*. Princeton, N.J.: Princeton University Press.

Cybriwsky, R. 1998. *Tokyo: The Shogun's City at the Twenty-First Century*. Chichester: John Wiley and Sons.

Dahl, R. E., and C. Lindblom. 1953. *Politics, Economics, and Welfare*. New York: Harper and Row.

Dallier, P. 2008. "Le grand Paris: un vrai projet pour un enjeu capital." *Information Report*, no. 262. Sénat.

Danielson, M. N. 1976. *The Politics of Exclusion*. New York: Columbia University Press.

Davezies, L. 2008. *Île de France: Croissance sans développement*. Report for the Caisse des Dépôts et Consignation, Paris.

Davies, J. C., and J. Mazurek. 1998. *Pollution Control in the United States*. Washington, D.C.: Resources for the Future.

Davis, J. 1988. *Reforming London: The London Government Problem 1855–1900*. Oxford: Oxford University Press.

Davis, M., 1990. *City of Quartz*. New York: Vintage.

———. 1998. *Ecology of Fear*. New York: Vintage.

Dear, M. 2000. *The Postmodern Urban Condition*. Oxford: Blackwell.

Department of Communities and Local Government. 2003. *The Sustainable Communities Plan*. London: HMSO.

Department for Transport. 2006. *Air Transport White Paper Progress Report*. London: HMSO.

———. 2007. *Ports Policy Review: Interim Report*. London: HMSO.

Dexia. 2008. *Sub-national Governments in the European Union: Organisation, Responsibilities, and Finance*. Paris: Dexia Editions.

Doig, J. W. 2001. *Empire on the Hudson*. New York: Columbia University Press.

Donzelot, J. 2004. "La ville à Trois Vitesses: Gentrification, Relégation, Périurbanisation." *Esprit* 303: 14–39.

Dore, R. 2000. *Stock Market Capitalism, Welfare Capitalism: Japan and Germany versus the Anglo-Saxons*. Oxford: Oxford University Press.

Douglass, M., and G. Roberts, eds. 2000. *Japan and Global Migration: Foreign Workers and the Advent of a Multicultural Society*. London: Routledge.

Dreier, P., J. Mollenkopf, and T. Swanstrom. 2001. *Place Matters*. Lawrence: University Press of Kansas.

Dunford, M., and G. Kafkalas. 1992. "The Global-Local Interplay: Corporate Geographies and Spatial Development Strategies in Europe." In *Cities and Regions in the New Europe*, edited by M. Dunford and G. Kafkalas, 155–81. London: Belhaven Press.

Economist. 2010. "New York's Recovery." 2010. *Economist*, November 20: 38.

Economist Intelligence Unit. 2005. *EIU Global Livability Rankings, 2005*. London: Economist Intelligence Unit.

———. 2006a. *Business Trip Index, 2006*. http://www.economist.com.

———. 2006b. *Index of Democracy, 2006*. http:// www.economist.com.

———. 2007a. *Livability Rankings: Sweet Spots*. http:// www.economist.com/markets/rankings.

———. 2007b. *Worldwide Cost of Living Survey*. http://www.economist.com/rankings.

———. 2008. *The World in 2008—Where Business is Pleasure*. http://www.economist.com/ theWorldIn/business.

Eisinger, P. K. 1988. *The Rise of the Entrepreneurial State: State and Local Economic Development Policies in the Unites States*. Madison: University of Wisconsin Press.

Empire State Development Corporation. 2007. "Delivering on the Promise of New York State." Report prepared by A. T. Kearney for ESDC.

Esping-Andersen, G. 1999. *Social Foundation of Postindustrial Economies*. Oxford: Oxford University Press.

Estèbe, P., and P. Le Galès. 2003. "La métropole Parisienne: à la recherche du pilote?" *Revue Française d'Administration Publique* 107: 345–57.

European Commission, Directorate-General Regional Policy. 2007. *Survey Perceptions of Quality of Life in 75 European Cities*. http://www. urbanaudit.org.

Evans, P. 1995. *Embedded Autonomy: States and Industrial Transformation*. Princeton, N.J.: Princeton University Press.

Fainstein, S. 1994. *The City Builders: Property, Politics, and Planning in London and New York*. Cambridge: Blackwell.

———. 2001. *The City Builders: Property, Politics, and Planning in London and New York*, 2nd ed. Lawrence: University of Kansas Press.

Feiock, R. C. 2007. "Rational Choice and Regional Governance." *Journal of Urban Affairs* 29, no. 1: 47–64.

Fernandez, M. 2009. "As the City Gains Low-Income Housing, the Market Takes It Away." *New York Times*, October 15: A27, 29.

Fiscal Policy Institute. 2009. *New York City: A Tale of Two Recessions*. New York: Fiscal Policy Institute.

Florida, R. 2004. *The Rise of the Creative Class*. New York: Basic Books.

Fessenden, F. 2006. "The Changing Face of the Suburbs." *New York Times*, December 31. http://www. nytimes.com/2006/12/31/nyregion/nyregionspecial2/31RCensus.html.

———. 2007. "Rich Get Richer While Poor Hold Their Own." *New York Times*, September 2. http:// www.nytimes.com/2007/09/02/nyregion/.../02censuswe.html.

Friedmann, J. 1986. "The World City Hypothesis." *Development and Change* 17, no. 1: 69–83.

———. 1995. "Where We Stand: A Decade of World City Research." In *World Cities in a World System*, edited by P. L. Knox and P. J. Taylor, 21–47. Cambridge: Cambridge University Press.

Frug, G. E. 1999. *City Making*. Princeton, N.J.: Princeton University Press.

Fuchs, G. 2003. "The Multimedia Industry." In *Globalization: Theory and Practice*, edited by E. Kofman and G. Young, 261–78. New York: Continuum.

Fujita, K. 1991. "A World City and Flexible Specialization: Restructuring the Tokyo Metropolis." *International Journal of Urban and Regional Research* 15: 269–84.

———. 2003. "Neo-Industrial Tokyo: Urban Development and Globalization in Japan's State-centered Developmental Capitalism." *Urban Studies* 40: 249–81.

Fujita, K., and R. C. Hill. 2007. "The Zero Waste City: Tokyo's Quest for Sustainable Development." *The Journal of Comparative Policy Analysis* 9, no. 4: 405–25.

———. 2011. "Industry Clusters and Transnational Networks: Japan's New Directions in Regional Policy." In *Locating Neoliberalism in East Asia: Neoliberalizing Spaces in Developmental States*, edited by R. C. Hill, B. G. Park, and A. Saito, 257–93. Oxford: Blackwell.

Fujiwara, K. 1998. "Nationalism, Reisen, Kaihatu [Nationalism, Cold War, Development]." In *20 Seiki*

System 4: Kaihatushugi [20th Century System: Developmentalism], edited by Institute of Social Science, 76–104. Tokyo: University of Tokyo Press.

Furman Center for Real Estate and Urban Policy. 2007. *State of New York City's Housing and Neighborhoods, 2007*. http://furmancenter.nyu.edu/SOC2007.html.

Gao, B. 1997. *Economic Ideology and Japanese Industrial Policy: Developmentalism from 1931 to 1965*. New York: Cambridge University Press.

Garreau, J. 1988. *Edge City: Life on the New Frontier*. New York: Knopf Doubleday.

Gelinas, N. 2008. "New York's Next Fiscal Crisis." *City Journal* 18, no. 3: 1–10.

Genda, Y. 2005. *A Nagging Sense of Job Insecurity*. Tokyo: International House of Japan.

Gilli, F., and J. M. Offner. 2008. *Paris, Métropole Hors Les Murs: Aménager et Gouverner un Grand Paris*. Paris: Sciences-Po.

GLA Economics. 2009. *London's Economic Outlook: Autumn 2009*. London: GLA.

Glaberson, W. 1992. "For Many in the New York Region, the City Is Ignored and Irrelevant." *New York Times*, January 2: A1, B4

Globalization and World Cities Research Network (GaWC). 2000. *Global Network Service Connectivities for 315 Cities in 2000*. http://www.lboro.ac.uk/gawc/datasets/da12.html.

Goldman, H. 2010. "New York City Budget Deficits May Be Larger Than Mayor Predicted." *Bloomberg News*, December 15.

Goodman, R., and I. Peng. 1996. "The East Asian Welfare State: Peripatetic Learning, Adaptive Change, and Nation-Building." In *Welfare State in Transition: National Adaptation in Global Economies*, edited by G. Esping-Andersen, 192–224. London: Sage Publications.

Goodman, R., G. White, and Huck-ju Kwon. 1998. *The East Asian Welfare Model: Welfare Orientalism and the State*. London: Routledge.

Gordon, I. R. 2003. "Capital Needs, Capital Growth and Global City Rhetoric in Mayor Livingstone's London Plan." Paper presented to Association of American Geographers Annual Meeting, New Orleans, March 7.

Gordon, I. R., T. Travers, C. M. E. Whitehead, and K. Scanlon. 2009. *London's Place in the UK Economy 2009–10*. London: City of London.

Gordon, P., and H. Richardson. 1997. "Are Compact Cities a Desirable Planning Goal?" *Journal of the American Planning Association* 63, no. 1: 95–107.

Graham, S., and S. Marvin. 2001. *Splintering Urbanism: Networked Infrastructures, Technological Mobilities, and the Urban Condition*. New York: Routledge.

Gravier, J. P. 1947. *Paris et le desert français*. Paris: Flammarion.

Grimes, W. 2001. *Unmaking the Japanese Miracle: Macroeconomic Politics 1985–2000*. Ithaca, N.Y.: Cornell University Press.

Gualini, E. 2001. *Planning and the Intelligence of Institutions*. Aldershot: Ashgate.

Gummer, J. 1996. "Celebrate London's Success—Don't Knock It." Paper presented to the Evening Standard/Architectural Foundation Debate on the Future of London, London, January.

Haar, C. M. 1996. *Suburbs Under Seige*. Princeton, N.J.: Princeton University Press.

Hacker, J. S. 2002. *The Divided Welfare State*. Cambridge: Cambridge University Press.

Hage, J., and C. Alter. 1997. "A Typology of Intergovernmental Relationships and Networks." In *Contemporary Capitalism: The Embeddedness of Institutions*, edited by J. R. Hollingsworth and R. Boyer, 94–126. Cambridge: Cambridge University Press.

Hall, P. 2002. "Blind Spots in Grand London Vision." *Regeneration and Renewal*, June 28: 12.

Hall, P., and K. Pain. 2006. *The Polycentric Metropolis: Learning from Mega-city Regions in Europe*. London: Earthscan.

Hall, P. A. 1999. "The Political Economy of Europe in an Era of Interdependence." In *Continuity and*

Change in Contemporary Capitalism, edited by H. Kitshelt, P. Lange, G. Marks, and J. D. Stephens, 135–64. Cambridge: Cambridge University Press.

Hall, P. A., and D. Soskice, eds. 2001. *Varieties of Capitalism*. New York: Oxford University Press.

Hamilton, D. K., and C. Stream. 2008. "Regional Environmental Policy." In *Urban and Regional Policies for Metropolitan Livability*, edited by D. K. Hamilton and P. S. Atkins, 324–45. Armonk, N.Y.: M. E. Sharpe.

Hamnett, C. 2003. *Unequal City: London in the Global Arena*. London: Routledge.

Handler, J. 1996. *Down from Bureaucracy*. Princeton, N.J.: Princeton University Press.

Harding, A. 2007. "Taking City Regions Seriously? Response to Debate on 'City Regions': New Geographies of Governance, Democracy and Social Reproduction." *International Journal of Urban and Regional Research* 31, no. 2: 443–58.

Hasan, L. 2008. "On Measuring the Complexity of Human Living." *PIDE* Working Paper no. 46. SSRN. http://ssm.com/abstract=1079902.

Hatch, W., and K. Yamamura. 1996. *Asia in Japan's Embrace: Building a Regional Production Alliance*. New York: Cambridge University Press.

Haughton, G., P. Allmendinger, D. Counsell, and G. Vigar. 2009. *The New Spatial Planning: Territorial Management with Soft Spaces and Fuzzy Boundaries*. London: Routledge.

Hebbert, M. 1992. "Governing the Capital." In *The Crisis of London*, edited by A. Thornley, 134–48. London: Routledge.

———. 1998. *London: More by Fortune than Design*. Chichester: Wiley.

Heinhelt, H., and D. Kubler. 2005. *Metropolitan Governance*. London: Routledge.

Hill, E. W., and I. Lendel. 2005. "Did 9/11 Change Manhattan and the New York Region as Places to Conduct Business?" In *Resilient City*, edited by H. Chernick, 23–61. New York: Russell Sage Foundation.

Hill, R. C., and J. W. Kim. 2000a. "Global Cities and Developmental States: New York, Tokyo and Seoul." *Urban Studies* 37, no. 12: 2165–2167.

Hill, R. C., and K. Fujita. 2000b. "State Restructuring and Local Power in Japan." *Urban Studies* 37: 637–90.

Hill, R. C., B. Park, and A. Saito, eds. 2011. *Locating Neoliberalism in East Asia: Neoliberalizing Spaces in Developmental States*. Oxford: Blackwell.

Hiramoto, K. 2000. *Rinkai Fuku Toshin Monogatari* [*A Story of the Tokyo Waterfront Subcenter*]. Tokyo: Chuou Kouron Sha.

Hirayama, Y. 2006. *Toukyou no Hateni* [*The Frontier of Tokyo*]. Tokyo: NTT Press.

Hirschman, A. O. 1970. *Exit, Voice, and Loyalty*. Cambridge, Mass.: Harvard University Press.

Hirst, P., and G. Thompson. 1996. *Globalization in Question*. Cambridge: Polity Press.

Hoffman, S. 1987. *Janus and Minerva: Essays in the Theory and Practice of International Politics*. Boulder, Colo.: Westview.

Holliday, I. 2000. "Productivist Welfare Capitalism: Social Policy in East Asia." *Political Studies* 48, no. 4: 706–23.

Hollingsworth, J. R., and R. Boyer. 1997. "Coordination of Economic Actors and Social Systems of Production." In *Contemporary Capitalism: The Embeddedness of Institutions*, edited by J. R. Hollingsworth and R. Boyer, 1–48. Cambridge: Cambridge University Press.

Honma, M. 1998. *Kokudo Keikaku wo Kangaeru* [*Thoughts about National Land Use Policy*]. Tokyo: Chuou Kourou Sha.

Horiuchi, M. 1992. "Ouka Seisaku no Yume no Ato [The Dream of Westernization Policy]." In *Mikan no Tokyo Keikaku* [*Unfinished Urban Planning in Tokyo*], edited by Y. Ishida, 10–34. Tokyo: Chikuma-Shobou.

HQs of Rejuvenation of Cities. 2001. *Toshi Saisei ni Torikumu Kihonteki Kangaekata* [*The Basic Ideas of Urban Regeneration*]. http://www.kantei.go.jp/jp/singi/tosisaisei/dai1/1siryou1.html.

Igarashi, T., and A. Ogawa. 1993. *Toshi Keikaku: Riken No Kouzu Wo Koete* [*Urban Planning: Beyond the Interest Group Politics*]. Tokyo: Iwanami Shoten.

Insight East. 2009. "Regional Jobs Lost in Recession Gaining Ground by 2015." *EEDA*, September 7.

Ingulsrud, J. E., and K. Allen. 2010. *Reading Japan Cool: Patterns of Manga Literacy and Discourse*. New York: Lexington Books.

Ishida, Y. 1992. *Nihon Kindai Toshikeikaku no Hyakunen* [*One Hundred Years of Japanese Modern Urban Planning*]. Tokyo: Jichitai Kenkyusha.

Itoh, S. 1998. "Kokudo Keikaku no Kangaekata [The Way We Think About Regional Planning]." *Chiiki Kaihatsu* [*Area Development*], no. 324.

Iwami, R. 2007. "Olympic Shouchi ni okeru Mokuteki to Shidan no Tentou [The Contradiction between Ends and Means in Tokyo's Bid for the Olympics]." In *Ishihara Tosei no Kenshou* [*Reviewing Ishihara Administration in the TMG*], edited by R. Iwami, H. Takei, and M. Komiya, 139–57. Tokyo: Aoki Shoten.

Jacobson, M. 2001. "From the Back to the Front: The Changing Character of Punishment in New York City." In *Rethinking the Urban Agenda*, edited by J. Mollenkopf and K. Emerson, 171–86. New York: The Century Foundation Press.

Jessop, B. 1998. "The Rise of Governance and the Risks of Failure: The Case of Economic Development." *International Social Science Journal* 50, no. 155: 29–45.

———. 2000. "The Crisis of the National Spatio-Temporal Fix and the Tendential Ecological Dominance of Globalizing Capitalism." *International Journal of Urban and Regional Research* 24, no. 2: 323–60.

———. 2002. *The Future of the Capitalist State*. London: Polity Press.

Jinno, N. 1995. "Toshi Keiei No Hatan Kara Saisei He [Transition of Urban Public Financial Management: From Collapse to Reconstruction]." In *Toshi Wo Keiei Suru* [*Planning the City*], edited by N. Jinno, 67–137. Tokyo: Toshi Shuppan.

Johnson, C. 1982. *MITI and the Japanese Miracle: The Growth of Industrial Policy 1925–1975*. Stanford, Calif.: Stanford University Press.

———. 1995. *Japan: Who Governs?* New York: W. W. Norton.

Joint Economic Committee, United States Congress. 2010. *State by State Snapshots*. http://jec.senate.gov/public/index.cfm?p=StateByStateReport.

Jonas, A. E. G., and K. Ward. 2007. "Introduction to a Debate on 'City Regions': New Geographies of Governance, Democracy and Social Reproduction." *International Journal of Urban and Regional Research* 31, no. 1: 169–78.

Jones, C. 2010. "Border Warfare: Can We Do It Differently This Time." *Spotlight on the Region*, 9, no. 2: 1–3.

Jouve, B., and C. Lefèvre. 2002. *Local Power, Territory, and Institutions in European Metropolitan Regions: In Search of Urban Gargantuas*. London: Frank Cass.

Judd, D. R., and S. Fainstein, eds. 1999. *The Tourist City*. New Haven, Conn.: Yale University Press.

Kamo, T. 2000. "An Aftermath of Globalization? East Asian Economic Turmoil and Japanese Cities Adrift." *Urban Studies* 37: 2145–65.

Kantor, P. 1995. *The Dependent City Revisited*. Boulder, Colo.: Westview Press.

———. 2002. "Terrorism and Governability in New York City." *Urban Affairs Review* 38, no. 1: 120–27.

———. 2006. "Regionalism and Reform: A Comparative Perspective on Dutch Urban Politics." *Urban Affairs Review* 41, no. 6: 800–829.

——. 2008. "Varieties of City Regionalism and the Quest for Political Cooperation: A Comparative Perspective." *Urban Research and Practice* 1, no. 2: 111–29.

——. 2010. "The Coherence of Disorder: A Realist Approach to the Politics of City Regions." *Polity* 42, no. 4: 434–60.

——. Forthcoming. "The United States: The Two Faces of American Urban Policy." In *The Politics of National Urban Policy: Europe, Britain and the United States in Comparative Perspective*, edited by E. D'Albergo. Wiesbaden, Germany: VS Verlag.

Kantor, P., and D. R. Judd, eds. 2007. *American Urban Politics in a Global Age.* New York: Longman.

Kantor, P., and H. V. Savitch. 2008. "New York's Regional Agenda." Paper delivered to the World Cities Research Group, London School of Economics, London, January 7.

Katz, B., ed. 2000. *Reflections on Regionalism.* Washington, D.C.: Brookings Institution.

Katz, B., and R. Puentes, eds. 2005. *Taking the High Road.* Washington, D.C.: Brookings Institution.

Katz, R. 2002. *Japanese Phoenix: The Long Road to Economic Revival.* Armonk, N.Y.: M. E. Sharp.

Katzenstein, P. J., R. O. Keohane, and S. Krasner. 1998. "International Organizations and the Study of World Politics." *International Organization* 52, no. 4: 645–86.

Kawakami, Y. 2008. *Kokudo Keikaku no Hensen: Kouritsu to Heikou no Keikakushisou* [*The Transition of Land Planning: Planning Ideas of Equity and Efficiency*]. Tokyo: Kajima Shuppan.

Keating, M. 1995. "Size, Efficiency and Democracy: Consolidation, Fragmentation and Public Choice." In *Theories of Urban Politics*, edited by D. Judge, G. Stoker, and H. Wolman, 117–35. London: Sage.

Keating, M., and J. Loughlin, eds. 1997. *The Political Economy of Regionalism.* London: Frank Cass.

King, A. 1990. *Global Cities: Post Imperialism and the Internationalization of London.* London: Routledge.

Kitshelt, H., P. Lange, G. Marks, and J. D. Stephens, eds. 1999. *Continuity and Change in Contemporary Capitalism.* Cambridge: Cambridge University Press.

Kleinman, M. 2001. "The Business Sector and the Governance of London." Paper presented at the European Urban Research Association Conference, Paris.

Kloosteerman, R. C., and S. Musterd. 2001. "The Polycentric Urban Region: Towards a Research Agenda." *Urban Studies* 38: 623–33.

Kofman, E., and G. Young, eds. 2003. *Globalization: Theory and Practice.* New York: Continuum.

Komiya, R., M. Okuno, and K. Suzuki, eds. 1984. *Nihon no Sangyo Seisaku* [*Japanese Industrial Policy*]. Tokyo: Tokyo University Press.

Koshizawa, A. 1991. *Tokyo no Toshi Keikaku* [*Urban Planning in Tokyo*]. Tokyo: Iwanami Shoten.

Kotkin, J. 2000. *The New Geography: How the Digital Landscape Is Reshaping the American Landscape.* New York: Random House.

——. 2002. "The Declustering of America." *Wall Street Journal*, August 12: 17.

Krasner, S. 1983. *International Regimes.* Ithaca, N.Y.: Cornell University Press.

Kyambi, S. 2005. *Beyond Black and White: Mapping New Immigrant Communities.* London: Institute for Public Policy Research.

IAURIF. 2001. *40 ans en Île-de-France: Rétrospective: 1960–2000.* Paris: Institut d'aménagement de la Région d'Île de France.

Laswell, H. 1936. *Politics: Who Gets What, When, and How.* New York: McGraw-Hill.

LDP. 1998a. *LDP Bulletin.* London: London Development Partnership.

——. 1998b. *Preparing for the Mayor and the London Development Agency.* London: London Development Partnership.

——. 2000. *Draft Economic Development Strategy.* London: London Development Partnership.

Ledebur, L. C., and W. R. Barnes. 1993. *All In It Together: Cities, Suburbs, and Economic Regions.* Washington, D.C.: National League of Cities.

Leemans, A. F. 1970. *Changing Patterns of Local Government*. The Hague: International Union of Local Authorities.

Lefèvre, C. 2003. "Paris–Île de France." In *Metropolitan Governance and Spatial Planning*, edited by W. Salet, A. Thornley, and A. Kreukels, 287–300. London: Spon Press.

———. 2009. "La Gouvernance de l'Île de France, Entre Décentralisation et Globalisation." Report for the Caisse des Dépôts et Consignations, Paris.

Lefèvre, C., and A. M. Romera. 2001. "The Economic Governance of Île de France." Gemaca, IAURIF, Paris.

Lefèvre, C., and M. Weir. Forthcoming. "Building Metropolitan Institutions." In *Oxford Handbook of Urban Politics*. Oxford: Oxford University Press

LeGalès, P. 2003. *European Cities, Social Conflicts, and Governance*. Oxford: Oxford University Press.

Lever, W. F. 1997. "Delinking Urban Economies: The European Experience." *Journal of Urban Affairs* 19, no. 2: 227–38.

Lindblom, C. E. 1977. *Politics and Markets*. New Haven, Conn.: Yale University Press.

———. 1988. *Democracy and the Market System*. Oslo: Norwegian University Press.

Lipset, S. M. 1981. *Political Man: The Social Bases of Politics*. Baltimore, Md.: The Johns Hopkins University Press.

Llewelyn-Davies. 1996. *Four World Cities: A Comparative Study of London, Paris, New York and Tokyo*. London: Llewelyn-Davies.

Logan, J., and H. Molotch. 1987. *Urban Fortunes*. Berkeley: University of California Press.

London Business Board. n.d. *The Business Manifesto for the Mayor and the Greater London Authority*. London: London Business Board.

Lowi, T. 1964. "American Business, Public Policy, Case Studies and Political Theory." *World Politics* 16: 677–715.

LTB and LFC. 2000. *Promoting the World City: Memorandum for the Mayor and the GLA*. London: London Tourist Board and London First Centre.

Machimura, T. 1992. "Urban Restructuring Process in Tokyo in the 1980s: Transforming Tokyo into a World City." *International Journal of Urban and Regional Research* 16: 114–28.

———. 2003. "Narrating A 'Global City' for 'New Tokyoites.'" In *Japan and Britain in the Contemporary World*, edited by H. Dobson and G. D. Hook, 196–212. London: Routledge.

MacLeod, Gordon. 2001. "New Regionalism Reconsidered: Globalization and the Remaking of Political Space." *International Journal of Urban and Regional Research* 25, no. 4: 804–29.

March, J. P., and J. Olsen. 1984. "The New Institutionalism: Organizational Factors in Political Life." *American Political Science Review* 7, no. 3: 734–49.

———. 1989. *Rediscovering Institutions*. New York: Free Press.

Matsushita, K. 1971. *Shibiru Minimamu no Shisou* [*The Philosophy of Civil Minimum*]. Tokyo: Iwanami Shoten.

———. 1995. *Sengo Seiji no Rekishi to Shisou* [*History and Thought of Postwar Politics*]. Tokyo: Chikuma Shobo.

Mayor of London. 2002. *The Draft London Plan*. London: Greater London Authority.

———. 2004. *The London Plan: Spatial Development Strategy for Greater London*. London: Greater London Authority.

———. 2008a. *The London Plan: Consolidated with Alterations Since 2004*. London: Greater London Authority.

———. 2008b. *Economic Recovery Plan*. London: Greater London Authority

———. 2009. *Rising to the Challenge: Proposals for the Mayor's Economic Development Strategy for Greater London*. London: Greater London Authority

McGeehan, P. 2008. "City and State Brace for Greater Demands on Diminishing Resources," *New York Times*, September 16. http://www.nytimes.com/2008/09/16/nyregion/16impact.html.

McKinsey Report. 2007. *Sustaining New York's and the U.S.'s Global Financial Services Leadership*. New York: Partnership for New York City.

Mearsheimer, J. J. 2001. *The Tragedy of Great Power Politics*. New York: Norton.

Mercer Human Resource Consulting. 2000. *Cost of Living Worldwide Ranking*. http://www.mercer.com.

———. 2007a. *Cost of Living Worldwide Ranking*. http://www.mercer.com. June 18.

———. 2007b. *Highlights from the 2007 Quality of Living Survey*, April 2, http://www.mercer.com.

Messina, P. 2001. *Regolazione Politica dello Sviluppo Locale*. Turin: UTET Libreria Sri.

Metropolitan Transportation Authority. 1978. *Access to the Core*. New York: MTA.

Mikuriya, T. 1990. *Shuto Wa Kokka Wo Koeruka?* [*Can Tokyo Take Over the State?*]. Tokyo: Yomiuri Shinbunsha.

Miller, D. 2002. *The Regional Governing of Metropolitan America*. Boulder, Colo.: Westview.

Milner, H. V. 1998. "Rationalizing Politics: The Emerging Synthesis of International, American and Comparative Politics." *International Organizations* 52, no. 4: 759–86.

Ministry of Land Infrastructure and Transport 2004. *Shutoken Haksho* [*White Paper on the Capital Region*]. Tokyo: MLIT.

———. 2006. *Shutoken Haksho* [*Whitepaper of Capital Region*]. Tokyo: MLIT.

Miyamoto, K. 1973. *Chiki Kaihatsu ha Koredeyoika?* [*Do We Have a Right Approach to Local Development?*]. Tokyo: Iwanami Shoten.

Mollenkopf, J. H., and M. Castells, eds. 1992. *Dual City*. New York: Russell Sage.

Moulaert, F., A. Rodriguez, and E. Swyngedouw. 2005. *The Globalized City: Economic Restructuring and Social Polarization in European Cities*. Oxford: Oxford University Press.

Moynihan, D. P. 1970. *Maximum Feasible Misunderstanding*. New York: Free Press.

Mullins, J., ed. 2006. "Employment in the Construction Industry." *Monthly Labor Review* 129, no. 10.

Murakami, Y. 1992. *Han Koten no Seijikeizaigaku* [*Anti-Classical Political Economy*]. Tokyo: Chuou Kouronsha.

Muramatsu, M. 1997. *Local Power in the Japanese State*. Berkeley: University of California Press.

National Academy of Sciences. 1999. "New York City's Plan to Protect Drinking Water Should Focus More on Controlling Dangerous Pathogens." http://www.8.nationalacademies.org/onpinews/newsitem.aspx?RecordID=9677.

Navarro, M. 2009. "Bloomberg Drops an Effort to Cut Building Energy Use." *New York Times*, December 5. http://www.nytimes.com/2009/12/05/science/earth/05bloomberg.html.

New York City, Department of Housing Preservation and Development. 2009. "Mayor Bloomberg's Affordable Housing Plan." May: 1–4. http://www.nyc.gov/hpd.

New York Foundation for the Arts. 2001. *Culture Counts: Cultural Life for New York City*. New York: Foundation for the Arts.

Newman, M., and A. Hull. 2009. "The Futures of the City Region." *Regional Studies* 43, no. 6: 777–87.

Newman, P. 2000. "Changing Patterns of Regional Governance in the EU." *Urban Studies* 37, nos. 5–6: 895–908.

Newman, P., and A. Thornley. 1997. "Fragmentation and Centralization in the Governance of London: Influencing the Urban Policy and Planning Agenda" *Urban Studies* 34, no. 7: 967–88.

———. 2005. *Planning World Cities: Globalization and Urban Politics*. New York: Palgrave Macmillan.

Newton, K. 1982. "Is Small Really So Beautiful? Is Big Really So Ugly? Size, Effectiveness and Democracy in Local Government." *Political Studies* 30, no. 2: 190–206.

Norris, D. F. 2001. "Prospects for Regional Governance under the New Regionalism: Economic Imperatives vs. Political Impediments." *Urban Affairs Review* 23, no. 5: 557–71.

Nye, J. S., Jr. 1988. "Neorealism and Neoliberalism." *World Politics* 40, no. 2: 235–51.

Obama, B. 2008. "Organizing for America: Urban Policy." http://origin.barachobama.com/issues/urban_policy.

Office of the Deputy Prime Minister. 2003. *Sustainable Communities: Building for the Future*. London: ODPM.

Ohmae, K. 1999. *The Borderless World: Power and Strategy in the Interlinked Economy*, revised ed. New York: HarperCollins Publishers.

Ohnishi, T. 2005. "Kouiki Chihou Keikaku no Tenkai to Kadai [The Development and Problem of Regional Planning]." *Toshi Mondai* [*Urban Problem*] 96, no. 710–15.

Oliver, J. E. 2001. *Democracy in Suburbia*. Princeton, N.J.: Princeton University Press.

Olson, M. 1965. *The Logic of Collective Action*. Cambridge, Mass.: Harvard University Press.

Orfield, G. 1998. *MetroPolitics*. Washington, D.C.: Brookings Institution.

Organization for Economic Cooperation and Development Data. 2004. *Local Government Budgeting in Russia*. Paris: OECD.

Osborne, D., and T. Gaebler. 1992. *Reinventing Government*. New York: Addison-Wesley.

Ostrom, V., C. M. Tiebout, and R. Warren. 1961. "The Organization of Government in Metropolitan Areas: A Theoretical Inquiry." *The American Political Science Review* 55, no. 4: 831–42.

Ostrum, V., R. Bish, and E. Ostrum. 1988. *Local Government in the United States*. San Francisco: Institute for Contemporary Studies.

Ozaki, M. 2007. "Orinpik, spoutsu ibent to toshi [The Olympics: Sports Event and City]." In *Tokyo Mondai* [*Tokyo and Its Challenges*], edited by T. Shibata, 61–82. Kyoto: Creates Kamogawa.

Pain, K. 2008. "Examining 'Core-Periphery' Relationships in a Global City-Region: The Case of London and South East England." *Regional Studies* 42, no. 8: 1161–72.

Partnership for New York City. 2006a. *Growth or Gridlock? The Economic Case for Traffic Relief and Transit Improvement for a Greater New York*. New York: Partnership for New York City.

———. 2006b. *Cities of Opportunity*. New York: Partnership for New York City.

Parks, R. B., and R. J. Oakerson. 1988. "Local Government Constitutions: A Different View of Metropolitan Governance." Presented at the annual meeting of the American Political Science Association, Washington, D.C., September.

———. 1989. "Metropolitan Organization and Governance: A Local Public Economy Approach." *Urban Affairs Quarterly* 25, no. 1: 18–29.

Pastore, M., T. W. Lester, and J. Scoggins. 2009. "Why Regions? Why Now? Who Cares?" *Journal of Urban Affairs* 32, no. 3: 269–96.

Pecorella, R., and J. M. Stonecash, *Governing New York State*. Albany, N.Y.: State University of New York Press.

Perben Commission 2008. *Imaginer les métropoles d'avenir*. Paris: National Assembly.

Peterson, P. E., and M. Rom. 1990. *Welfare Magnets*. Washington, D.C.: Brookings Institution.

Pierce, N. 1993. *Citistates*. Washington, D.C.: Seven Locks Press.

Pierson, P. 2000. "Increasing Returns, Path Dependency, and the Study of Politics." *American Political Science Review* 94, no. 2: 251–68.

Pimlott, B., and N. Rao. 2002. *Governing London*. Oxford: Oxford University Press.

Polanyi, K. 1944. *The Great Transformation*. New York: Beacon.

Pouvoirs, L. 2007. "Comment Gouverner la Métropole Regionale?" Special issue, *Paris–Île de France*, no. 73.

Pred, A. 1977. *City Systems in Advanced Economies*. London: Hutchinson.

Premier Ministre. 1991. *Livre blanc sur l'Île de France*. Paris: Premier Ministre.

Pressman, J., and A. Wildavsky. 1973. *Implementation*. Berkeley: University of California Press.

Puentes, R., and L. Bailey. 2005. "Increasing Funding and Accountability for Metropolitan Transport Decisions." In *Taking the High Road*, edited by B. Katz and R. Puentes, 139–68. Washington, D.C.: Brookings Institution.

Purcell, M. 2007. "City-Regions, Neoliberal Globalization, and Democracy: A Research Agenda." *International Journal of Urban and Regional Research* 31, no. 1: 197–206.

Putnam, R. 1993. *Making Democracy Work*. Princeton, N.J.: Princeton University Press.

Rabe, B. G. 2000. "Power to the States: The Promise and Pitfalls of Decentralization." In *Environmental Policy*, edited by N. J. Vig and M. E. Kraft, 32–54. Washington, D.C.: CQ Press.

Reed, S. R. 1986. *Japanese Prefecture and Policymaking*. Pittsburgh, Pa.: University of Pittsburgh Press.

Regional Plan Association. 1996. *Region at Risk*. New York: Regional Plan Association.

———. 2004. *An Assessment of the 2005–2009 Capital Needs of the Metropolitan Transportation Authority*. New York: Regional Plan Association.

———. n.d. *MTA Capital Assessment Report*. New York: Regional Plan Association.

Regional Plan Association and Citizens Housing and Planning Council. 2004. *Out of Balance: The Housing Crisis from a Regional Perspective*. New York: Regional Plan Association.

Reich, R. B. 1992. *The Work of Nations*. New York: Vintage Books.

Reichl, A. 1999. *Reconstructing Times Square*. Lawrence: University Press of Kansas.

Rhodes, G. 1970. *The Government of London: The Struggle for Reform*. London: Weidenfeld and Nicolson.

Roberts, S. 2007. "New York's Gap between Rich and Poor Is Nation's Widest, Census Says." *New York Times*, August 29, http://www.nytimes.com/2007/08/29/nyregion.

———. 2009. "Westchester Adds Housing to Desgregation Pact." *New York Times*, August 11, http://www.nytimes.com/2009/08/11/nyregion/11settle.html?=westchester and housing.

———. 2010. "Federal Monitor Rejects Westchester's Plan to Address Segregation with Fair Housing." *New York Times*, February 12: A27.

Pogrebin, R. 2007. "Arts Groups Seek Plums in a New Budget Pie." *New York Times*, February 1, http://www.nytimes.com/2007/02/01/arts/01cult.

Robson, W. 1948. *The Government and Misgovernment of London*. London: Allen and Unwin.

Roch, M. 2000. *Mega-Events and Modernity*. London: Routledge.

Rose, M. 1979. *Interstate*. Knoxville: University of Tennessee Press.

Rusk, D. 1999. *Inside Game, Outside Game*. Washington, D.C.: Brookings Institution.

Sabel, C. F. 1997. "Constitutional Orders: Trust Building and Response to Change." In *Contemporary Capitalism: The Embeddedness of Institutions*, edited by J. R. Hollingsworth and R. Boyer, 129–41. Cambridge: Cambridge University Press.

Saito, A. 2003. "Urban Development in a Global City: Waterfront Sub-Centre Development in Tokyo." *Urban Studies* 40: 283–308.

———. 2011. "State-Space Relations in Transition: Urban and Regional Planning Policy in Japan." In *Locating Neoliberalism in East Asia: Neoliberalizing Spaces in Developmental States*, edited by R. C. Hill, B.-G. Park, and A. Saito, 59–85. Oxford: Blackwell.

Saito, A., and A. Thornley. 2003. "Shifts in Tokyo's World City Status and the Urban Planning Response." *Urban Studies* 40: 665–85.

Salamore, B. G., and A. Stephan. 1998. *New Jersey Politics and Government*, 2nd ed. Lincoln: University of Nebraska Press.

Salet, W. 2003. "Amsterdam and the North Wing of the Randstad." In *Metropolitan Governance and Spatial Planning*, edited by W. Salet, A. Thornley, and A. Kreukels., 175–88. London: Spon Press.

Salet, W., and A. Faudi, eds. 2000. *The Revival of Strategic Spatial Planning.* Amsterdam: KNAW Edita.

Salet, W., A. Thornley, and A. Kreukels. 2003. *Metropolitan Governance and Spatial Planning.* London: Spon Press.

Sassen, S. 1991. *The Global City.* Princeton, N.J.: Princeton University Press.

———. 1994. *Cities in a Global Economy.* Thousand Oaks, Calif.: Pine Forge Press.

———. 1998. *Globalization and Its Discontents.* New York: New Press.

———. 1999. *Remaking New York.* Minneapolis: University of Minnesota Press.

———. 2001. *The Global Cities, 2nd Edition: New York, London, Tokyo.* Princeton, N.J.: Princeton University Press.

———. 2006. *Territory, Authority, Rights.* Princeton, N.J.: Princeton University Press.

———, ed. 2002. *Global Networks, Linked Cities.* New York: Routledge.

Sato, T. 2000. *Fubyodou Shakai Nippon* [*Japan's Unequal Socie*ty]. Tokyo: Chukou Shisho.

Savas, E. S. 2005. *Privatization in the City.* Washington, D.C.: CQ Press.

Savitch, H. V. 1988. *Post-Industrial Cities: Politics and Planning in New York, Paris and London.* Princeton, N.J.: Princeton University Press.

———. 2010. "Rescaling for a Global World." *Progress in Planning* 73: 11–16.

Savitch, H. V., and R. K. Vogel, eds. 1996. *Regional Politics: America in a Post-City Age.* Thousand Oaks, Calif.: Sage Publications.

———. 2009. "Regionalism and Urban Politics." In *Theories of Urban Politics*, 2nd ed., edited by J. S. Davies and D. L. Imbroscio. Los Angeles: Sage.

Savitch, H. V., and P. Kantor. 2002. *Cities in the International Marketplace.* Princeton, N.J.: Princeton University Press.

Savitch, H. V., P. Kantor, and S. V. Haddock. 1997. "The Political Economy of Urban Regimes." *Urban Affairs Review* 32, no. 3: 348–77.

Savitch, H. V., and P. Kantor. 2003. "Urban Strategies for a Global Era." *American Behavioral Scientist* 46: 1002–33.

Saxenian, A. L. 1994. *Regional Advantage.* Cambridge, Mass.: Harvard University Press.

Schaede, U., and W. Grimes. 2003. *Japan's Managed Globalization: Adapting to the Twenty-First Century.* New York: E. M. Sharp.

Schattschneider, E. E. 1960. *The Semi-Sovereign People: A Realists View of American Democracy.* New York: Holt, Rinehart and Winston.

Schill, M. H., ed. 1999. *Housing and Community Development in New York City.* Albany: State University of New York Press.

Schneider, B. R. 1999. "The *Desarrollista* State in Brazil and Mexico." In *The Developmental State*, edited by M. Woo-Cumings. Ithaca, N.Y.: Cornell University Press.

Schneider, M. 1989. *The Competitive City.* Pittsburgh, Pa.: University of Pittsburgh Press.

Schwartz, A. 1999. "New York City and Subsidized Housing: Impacts and Lessons of the City's $5 Billion Capital Budget Housing Plan." *Housing Policy Debate* 10, no. 4: 839–77.

Schwieger, A. 2010. "All's Fair in Westchester?" *Next American City*, May 24: 1–2. http://americancity.org/buzz/entry/2153.

Scott, A. J. 1996. "Regional Motors of the Global Economy." *Futures* 28, no. 5: 391–411.

———, ed. 2001. *Global City-Regions: Trends, Theory, Policy.* Oxford: Oxford University Press.

———. 2003. "Regions, Globalization, Development." *Regional Studies* 37, no. 6: 579–93.

———. 2008. "Resurgent Metropolis: Economy, Society and Urbanization in an Interconnected World." *International Journal of Urban and Regional Research* 32, no. 3: 548–64.

Scott, A. J., and M. Storper. 1992. "Industrialization and Regional Development." In *Pathways to Industrialization and Regional Development*, edited by M. Storper and A. J. Scott. New York: Routledge.

————. 1998. *Regions and the World Economy.* London: Oxford University Press.

Sellers, J. M. 2002. *Governing from Below.* Cambridge: Cambridge University Press.

Selznick, P. 1966. *TVA at the Grass Roots.* New York: Harper and Row

Shibata, T., ed. 2008. *Tokyo Mondai [Tokyo and Its Challenges].* Kyoto: Creates Kamogawa.

Short, J. R. 2004. *Global Metropolitan: Globalizing Cities in a Capitalist World.* London: Routledge.

Sites, W. 2003. *Remaking New York.* Minneapolis: University of Minnesota Press.

Slater, E. 2004. "The Flickering Global City." *Journal of World Systems Research* 10, no. 3: 591–608.

Smith, N. 2004. "Scale Bending and the Fate of the National." In *Scale and Geographic Inquiry*, edited by E. Sheppard and R. McMaster. Oxford: Blackwell.

Smothers, R. 2000. "Feud Over How Port Authority Spends Money Creates and Impasse." *New York Times*, February 24, http://www.nytimes.com/2000/02/24/nyregion/feud-over-how-port -authority-spends-money-creates-an-impasse.html.

————. 2000. "Port Authority Rift Revealed States' Competitive Instincts." *New York Times*, June 6, http://www.nytimes.com/2000/06/06/nyregion/port-authority-rift-revealed-states-competitive -instincts.html.

Soja, E. 1989. *Postmodern Geographies.* London: Verso.

————. 1991. "Poles Apart: Urban Restructuring in New York and Los Angeles." In *Dual City: Restructuring New York,* edited by J. H. Mollenkopf and M. Castells, 361–76. New York: Russell Sage.

Sonobe, M. 2001. *Gendai Daitoshi Shakairon: Bunkyokuka suru Toshi? [Contemporary Metropolitan Society: Dual City?].* Tokyo: Toshindo.

Sorensen, A. 2002. *The Making of Urban Japan: Cities and Planning from Edo to the Twenty-First Century.* London: Routledge.

Soskice, D. 1999. "Divergent Production Regimes: Coordinated and Uncoordinated Market Economies in the 1980s and 1990s." In *Continuity and Change in Contemporary Capitalism*, edited by H. Kitshelt, P. Lange, G. Marks, and J. D. Stephens, 101–34. Cambridge: Cambridge University Press.

Standard and Poor's. 2010. "Housing Indices." S&P/Case-Shiller *Home Price Indices*, November 30, http://www.standardandpoors.com/indices/sp-case-shiller-home-price-indices/en/us/ ?indexId=spusa-cashpidff--p-us----.

Statistic Bureau of Japan. 2004. *Statistical Handbook of Japan.* http://www.stat.go.jp/english/data/ handbook/c17cont.htm.

Steiner, K. 1965. *Local Government in Japan.* Stanford, Calif.: Stanford University Press.

Stoker, G. 1991. *The Politics of Local Government.* London: Macmillan.

————. 1995. "Regime Theory and Urban Politics." In *Theories of Urban Politics*, edited by D. Judge, G. Stoker, and H. Wolman, 54–71. London: Sage Publications.

————. 1998. "Governance as Theory: Five Propositions." *International Social Science Journal* 155: 17–28.

Stone, C. N. 1989. *Regime Politics: Governing Atlanta, 1946–1988.* Lawrence: University Press of Kansas.

Stone, C. N., and H. Sanders, eds. 1987. *The Politics of Urban Development.* Lawrence: University Press of Kansas.

Stonecash, J. M., and A. Widestrom. 2006. "Political Parties and Elections." In *Governing New York State*, edited by R. F. Pecorella and J. M. Stonecash, 49–72. Albany: State University of New York Press.

Stonecash, J. M., and M. H. Paley. 2006. "The Politics of Transportation." In *Governing New York State*, edited by R. F. Pecorella and J. M. Stonecash, 371–90. Albany: State University of New York Press.

Storper, M. 1997. *The Regional World: Territorial Development in a Global Economy.* New York: Guildford Press.

Storper, M., and A. Scott. 1995. "The Wealth of Regions: Market Forces and Policy Imperatives in Local and Global Growth." *Futures* 27: 505–26.

Swanstrom, T., P. Dreier, C. Casey, and R. Flack. 2006. "Pulling Apart: Economic Segregation in Suburbs and Central Cities in Major Metropolitan Areas, 1980–2000." In *Redefining Urban and Suburban America*, edited by A. Berube, B. Katz, and R. E. Lang, 143–66. Washington, D.C.: Brookings

Sze, J. 2007. *Noxious New York*. Cambridge, Mass.: MIT Press.

Tachibanaki, T. 2009. *Confronting Income Inequality in Japan: A Comparative Analysis of Causes, Consequences, and Reform*. Cambridge, Mass.: MIT Press.

Taira, N. 2001. "Kanjyou Megaroporisu ni kansuru ichikousatsu [A Thought about Circular Megalopolis Structure]." Paper presented at Policy Messe, Hosei University, Tokyo, December 14–16.

Tajima, J. 2003. "Chinese Newcomers in the Global City Tokyo: Social Networks and Settlement Tendencies." *International Journal of Japanese Sociology* 12: 68–78.

Takei, H. 2007. "Ishihara Tosei no Rekishiteki Ichi to Sekaitoshi Kousou [Ishihara Administration in Historical Perspective and Global City Strategy]." In *Ishihara Tosei no Kenshou [Reviewing Ishihara Administration in TMG]*, edited by R. Iwami, H. Takei, and M. Komiya, 13–44. Tokyo: Aoki Shoten.

Taylor, P. 2004. *World City Network: A Global Analysis*. London: Routledge.

Taylor, P. D., R. F. Walker, and J. V. Beaverstock. 2002. "Firms and Their Global Services Networks." In *Global Networks, Linked Cities*, edited by S. Sassen, 93–116. New York: Routledge.

Thornley, A. 1993. *Urban Planning under Thatcherism: The Challenge of the Market*. London: Routledge.

Thornley, A., Y. Rydin, K. Scanlon, and K. West. 2005. "Business Privilege and the Strategic Planning Agenda of the Greater London Authority." *Urban Studies* 42, no. 11: 1947–68.

Tiebout, C. 1964. "A Pure Theory of Local Expenditures." *Journal of Political Economy* 64: 416–24.

Togo, H. 1993. *Tokyo Kaizou Keikaku no Kiseki [The History of the Reconstruction Plan for Tokyo]*. Tokyo: The Tokyo Institute for Municipal Research.

Toki, H. 2003. *Tokyo Mondai no Seijigaku [Politics of Tokyo's Problems]*. Tokyo: Nihon Hyoronsha.

Tokyo Chamber of Commerce and Industry (TCCI). 2008. *Doushusei to Daitoshi Seido no Arikata [Regional Government and Metropolitan Institution]*. Tokyo: TCCI.

Tokyo Metropolitan Government. 2000. *Tokyo To Toshi Hakusho 2000: Kokusai Toshi Tokyo no Miryoku wo Takameru [Urban White Paper of Tokyo 2000: Increase the Attractiveness of International City Tokyo]*. Tokyo: TMG.

———. 2001a. *Tokyo Megalopolis Concept*. Tokyo: TMG.

———. 2001b. *Kankou Sangou Shinkou Plan [Tourist Industry Promotion Plan]*. Tokyo: TMG.

———. 2006a. *Juunenngo no Tokyo [Tokyo in Ten Years]*. Tokyo: TMG.

———. 2006b. *The Games of the XXXI Olympiad Proposal to the Japanese Olympic Committee*. Tokyo: TMG.

———. 2008. *Juunenngo no Tokyo, Jikkou Puroguramu [Tokyo in Ten Years, Implementation Plan]*. Tokyo: TMG.

Torrance, M. 2008. "Forging Global Governance? Urban Infrastructures as Networked Financial Products." *International Journal of Urban and Regional Research* 32, no. 1: 1–21.

Toyoda, T. 2007. "Social Polarization and Socio-Spatial Structure of Metropolitan Areas: A Comparative Analysis of Income Inequality in Tokyo, Osaka and Nagoya." *The Annals of Japanese Association for Urban Sociology* 25: 5–21.

Travers, T. 2004. *The Politics of London: Governing an Ungovernable City*. Basingstoke: Palgrave Macmillan.

Trigilia, C. 2001. "Social Capital and Local Development." *European Journal of Social Theory* 4, no. 4: 427–42.

Trust for Public Land. 2008. "Sterling Forest Capstone Protected." http://www.tpl.org/tier3_print. cfm?folder_id630&content_itemid=21043&mod_type=1.

Turner, M. A., S. J. Popkin, and L. Rawlings. 2009. *Public Housing and the Legacy of Segregation.* Washington, D.C.: Urban Institute Press.

US Census Office. 2008. *American Community Survey.* Washington, D.C.: US Census Office.

US Census Office. 2006. *Crime in Select Cities, 2006.* Washington, D.C.: US Census Office.

US Government, General Accounting Office. 1998. *Welfare Reform: States Are Restructuring Programs to Reduce Welfare Dependency.* Washington, D.C.: US General Accounting Office.

Urban Task Force. 1999. *Towards an Urban Renaissance.* London: Routledge.

US Agency for International Development. n.d. *Watershed Management for Urban Water Supply: The New York City Experience.* Washington, D.C.: USAID.

US Office of Management and Budget. 2009. *Budget of the United States Government, Historical Tables, Annual, Table 414.* Washington, D.C.: US Government Printing Office.

Veltz, P. 1996. *Mondialisation, villes, territoires, l'économie d'archipel.* Paris: Presses Universitaires de France.

———. 1997. "The Dynamics of Production Systems, Territories, and Cities." In *Cities, Enterprises, and Society on the Eve of the 21st Century*, edited by F. Moulaert and S. J. Scott, 78–96. London: Pinter.

Vig, N. J., and M. E. Kraft. 2000. *Environmental Policy.* Washington, D.C.: CQ Press.

Vitale, A. S. 2008. *City of Disorder.* New York: New York University Press.

Wakabayashi, M. 2007. *Kougai no Shakaigaku* [*Sociology of Suburbs*]. Tokyo: Chikuma Shinsho.

Waley, P. 2007. "Tokyo-as-World-City: Reassessing the Role of Capital and the State in Urban Restructuring." *Urban Studies* 44: 1465–90.

Wallin, B. A. 2005. *Budgeting for Basics: The Changing Landscape of City Finances.* Washington, D.C.: Brookings Institution.

Waltz, K. N. 1979. *Theory of International Politics.* New York: McGraw Hill.

———. 1997. "Evaluating Theories." *American Political Science Review* 91: 913–17.

White, J. B. 1998. "Old Wine, Cracked Bottles: Paris, Tokyo and the Global City Thesis." *Urban Affairs Review* 33, no. 4: 451–77.

Wilson, J. Q. 1973. *Political Organizations.* New York: Basic Books.

Wolman, H., and M. Goldsmith. 1992. *Urban Politics and Policy: A Comparative Approach.* Oxford: Basil Blackwell.

Wood, R. 1958. "Metropolitan Government 1975: An Extrapolation of Trends: The New Metropolis: Greenbelt, Grassroots or Gargantua?" *American Political Science Review* 52: 108–22.

Wood, R. C. 1961. *1400 Governments.* Cambridge, Mass.: Harvard University Press.

Yamazaki, A. 1998. *Nihon no Kokudo Keikaku to Chikiki Kaihatu* [*Land Planning and Territorial Development in Japan*]. Tokyo: Toyo Keizai Shinposha.

Yates, D. 1978. *The Ungovernable City: The Politics of Urban Problems and Policy Making.* Cambridge, Mass.: MIT Press.

Yuasa, M. 2009. *Han Hinkon: "Suberidai Shakai" karano dasshutu* [*Antipoverty: Escaping from "Sliding Society"*]. Tokyo: Iwanami Shoten.

Zukin, S. 1995. *The Cultures of Cities.* Oxford: Blackwell.

Index

Paul Kantor is professor emeritus of political science at Fordham University. His teaching and research interests include American and comparative politics and public policy, urban politics in the United States and Western Europe, and urban political economy. A past president of the Urban Politics Section of the American Political Science Association, he is author of several books including, with H. V. Savitch, *Cities in the International Marketplace: The Political Economy of Urban Development in North America and Western Europe* (2002).

Christian Lefèvre is a professor at University Paris Est, director of the French Institute of Urban Affairs (IFU), and a research fellow at the Laboratoire Techniques, Territoires et Societes (LATTS). His major interests concern the issues of metropolitan public policies and politics, development strategies, and the international relations of cities. He is a member of the executive committee of the European Urban Research Association (EURA) and chief editor of the online academic journal *Metropoles*.

Asato Saito is an independent scholar working in Tokyo. He formerly taught at the University of Singapore. His research has focused on the impact of globalization and state restructuring upon urban and regional development policy of Japan. His recent publication includes *Locating Neoliberalism in East Asia: Neoliberalizing Spaces in Developmental States* (2011) coedited with Bae-Gyoon Park and Richard C. Hill.

H. V. Savitch is the Brown and Williamson Distinguished Research Professor in the School of Urban and Public Affairs at the University of Louisville. A past president of the Urban Politics Section of the American Political Science Association, he has published twelve books on various aspects of urban development, public policy, and regional governance including, most recently *Cities in a Time of Terror: Space, Territory, and Local Resilience* (2008). Savitch has been a Fulbright Fellow and held research appointments in France, Great Britain, Israel, and Chile.

Andy Thornley is professor emeritus of urban planning at the London School of Economics. His research explores the relationship between urban planning and politics at the level of planning systems and political ideology, strategic planning and city governance, and the power of different interests in development projects. He is the author of several books, including most recently *Planning World Cities: Globalization and Urban Politics* (second edition, 2011).

(continued from page ii)